SOUTH
ASIAN
PHRASEBOOK

9 LANGUAGES
BURMESE CHINESE
FILIPINO INDONESIAN
KHMER LAO MALAY
THAI VIETNAMESE

Published by Thomas Cook Publishing
A division of Thomas Cook Tour Operations Limited
PO Box 227
Unit 18 Coningsby Road
Peterborough PE3 8SB
United Kingdom

E-mail: books@thomascook.com
www.thomascookpublishing.com

ISBN 13: 978-1-84157-502-5
ISBN 10: 1-84157-502-X

Production/DTP Editor: Steven Collins
Original translation by Tongue-Tied, Sussex/Hertfordshire, UK
Original Editor: Wendy M Wood
New translations for this edition by Pioneer Typesetting Services, Singapore
Original text design by 183 Books, Peterborough
Text layout by Pioneer Typesetting Services, Singapore
Cover design: Liz Lyons Design, Oxford
Cover picture: David Crausby/Alamy
Printed and bound in Spain by: Grafo Industrias Graficas, Basauri

CONTENTS

CONTENTS

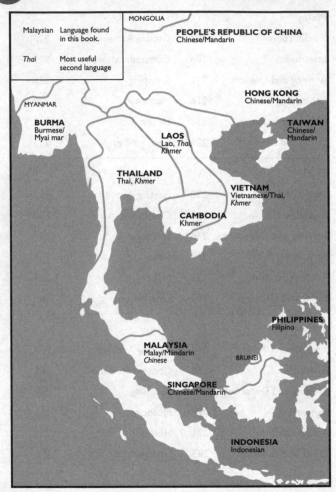

| Malaysian | Language found in this book. |
| *Thai* | Most useful second language |

MONGOLIA

PEOPLE'S REPUBLIC OF CHINA
Chinese/Mandarin

HONG KONG
Chinese/Mandarin

MYANMAR

TAIWAN
Chinese/Mandarin

BURMA
Burmese/
Myai mar

LAOS
Lao, *Thai,
Khmer*

THAILAND
Thai, *Khmer*

VIETNAM
Vietnamese/Thai,
Khmer

CAMBODIA
Khmer

PHILIPPINES
Filipino

MALAYSIA
Malay/Mandarin
Chinese

BRUNEI

SINGAPORE
Chinese/Mandarin

INDONESIA
Indonesian

This newly updated phrasebook from Thomas Cook Publishing contains a selection of essential and helpful vocabulary in nine of the languages most commonly spoken in South-East Asia. Each phrase is shown first in English, followed by the foreign-language translation and then a simple phonetic transcription, which will prove the most useful guide when trying to speak words and phrases if you are not familiar with the language. In cases where the phrase is most likely to be seen on a notice or sign, or spoken by a native language speaker to you, the foreign-language version is shown first, followed by its phonetic transcription and then the English meaning.

Where there is both a formal and informal way of speech, the formal one will be indicated so that no offence could inadvertently be caused.

Each chapter has been divided into themed sections with subheadings for quick reference. You will find shaded boxes containing essential words that will help you at the station or airport, and while dining out, shopping and driving. Chapters begin with an introduction to the language and some practical details about the language's mother country or countries, and sometimes a few technical pointers on grammar and pronunciation.

Any attempt to speak a few words in the native tongue of these countries is always greatly appreciated by locals, and this phrasebook aims to enrich your travelling experience as well as help with day-to-day essentials.

Good luck!

This newly updated phrasebook from Thomas Cook Publishing contains a selection of essential words, a helpful vocabulary, of the languages most commonly spoken in South-East Asia. Each phrase is shown first in English followed by the foreign language translation and then a simple phonetic transcription which will give the user useful phrases when arriving at basic words and phrases if you are not familiar with the language. In cases where the phrase is most likely to be spoken to you (rather or sign) or spoken by a native (please alert so to you), the foreign-language version is shown first, followed by the phonetic transcription and then the English meaning.

Where there is a formal and informal way of speaking the formal one will be indicated so that no offence could inadvertently be caused.

Each chapter has been divided into themed sections with subheadings for quick reference. You will find shaded boxes containing essential words that will help you at the station, restaurant and when dining out, shopping and driving. Chapters begin with an introduction and a few phrases and some dialogue alerts about the language, themed boxes of food etc, and sometimes a few cultural pointers on grammar and pronunciation.

Any attempt to speak a few words in the native tongue of these countries is always greatly appreciated by locals and this phrasebook aims to enrich your travelling experience as well as help with day-to-day essentials.

Good luck!

BURMESE

မြန်မာစကား

B U R M E S E

INTRODUCTION

Officially known as Myanmar since 1989, referring to both the language and the country, Burma, Burmese belongs to a family called the Sino-Tibetan languages. Other dialects, like Karen, Chin, Shan and Kachin are spoken, along with some English in the main cities. Like Chinese and Tibetan, Burmese is "tonal" – where different words that sound rather similar are differentiated by pitch (sharp high, normal high tone, and a low tone).

NB: In recognition of the undemocratic military regime governing Burma, tourists have been asked by popular leader Aung San Suu Kyi not to visit the country. For further information on Burma, please visit: www.fco.gov.uk and www.amnesty.org

Addresses for Travel and Tourist Information

Australia: Burmese Embassy, 22 Arkana Street, Yarralumla, Canberra ACT 2600
Tel: 02 6273 3811; Fax: 02 6273 3181

Canada: Burmese Embassy, 85 Range Road, apartment No. 902-903, The Sandringham, Ottawa, Ontario K1N 8J6
Tel: 613 232 6434; Fax: 613 232 6435

Burma Facts

CAPITAL: Pyinmana (New site 200 miles north of former site Yangon)

CURRENCY: Kyat (MMK). I Kyat = 100 Pyas.

OPENING HOURS: Banks: Mon-Fri, 1000-1400.

TELEPHONES: To dial in, Tel: International Access Code + 95. Outgoing, Tel: 00 + Country Code.

EMERGENCY NUMBERS: Police, Tel:199; Fire, Tel:191; Ambulance, Tel: 192.

PUBLIC HOLIDAYS: Jan 4 – Independence Day; Feb 12 – Union Day; May 1 – May Day; June 16 – Martyrs' Day; Dec 5 – National Day; Dec 25 – Christmas Day.

Technical Language Hints

- Try to pick up the Burmese number writing system, as this will be very helpful.

- There are different grammatical endings to say depending on whether you are male or female, and whether you are speaking to a male or female. These have been indicated in the text with the signs (M) and (F). Note also that the gender of the speaker(s) also determines which pronoun is used for "I/we" and "you" – this is also noted in the text.

- Lastly, the reader should substitute his / her own name in place of the "_____" sign, where used in the text, as it is more polite.

B
U
R
M
E
S
E

Basic Words and Phrases

Yes
ဟုတ်တယ်
Hote Tae

No
မဟုတ်ဘူး
Ma Hote Buu

Please
ကျေးဇူးပြု၍
Kyayzu Pyu Ywayt

Thank you
ကျေးဇူးတင်ပါတယ်
Kyayzu Tin Pa Dae

Hello
မင်္ဂလာပါ
Mingala Pa

Goodbye
နှုတ်ဆက်ပါတယ်
Hnote Set Pa Dae

Excuse me
ခွင့်ပြုပါ
Khwint Pyu Pa

Sorry
ဝမ်းနည်းပါတယ်
Wun Ne Pa Dae

How
ဘယ်လိုလဲ
Bai Lo Le

When
ဘယ်တော့လဲ
Bai Dawt Le

Why
ဘာကြောင့်လဲ
Ba Gyaunt Le

What
ဘာလဲ
Ba Le

Who
ဘယ်သူလဲ
Bai Thu Le

That's O.K.
အဆင်ပြေပါတယ်
Ahsinpyay Pa Dae

Perhaps
ဖြစ်နိုင်ပါတယ်
Phyit Nai Pa Dae

To
သို့
Thoe

From
မှ
Hma

Here
ဒီမှာ
De Hmar

There
ဟိုမှာ
Ho Hmar

I don't understand
ကျွန်တော် နားမလည်ဘူး
Kyundaw Nar Ma Le Bu

I don't speak Burmese
ကျွန်တော်ဗမာစကားမပြောတတ်ဘူး။
Kyino Burma Ziga Ma Pyaw Ta Buu

Do you speak English?
ခင်ဗျား အင်္ဂလိပ်လို ပြောလား
Khinbyar Ingalate Lo Pyaw Lar

Can you please write it down?
ကျေးဇူးပြု၍ ရေးချပြပါ
Kyayzu Pyu Ywayt Yaycha Pya Pa

Please can you speak more slowly?
ကျေးဇူးပြု၍ နေးနေး ပြောပါ
Kyayzu Pyu Ywayt Hnay Hnay Pyaw Pa

Greetings

**Good morning /
Good afternoon /
Good evening / Goodnight**
ကောင်းသော မနက်ခင်း / ကောင်းသော
နေ့လည်ခင်း / ကောင်းသော ညနေခင်း /
ကောင်းသောည
Kaungthaw Manetkhin / Kaungthaw Naylekhin / Kaungthaw Nyanaykhin / Kaungthaw Nya

Pleased to meet you
တွေ့ရတာ ဝမ်းသာပါတယ်
Twayt Ya Dar Wunthar Pa Dae

How are you?
နေကောင်းလား
Nay Kaung Lar

Well, thank you. And you?
နေကောင်းတယ်၊ ကျေးဖူးတင်ပါတယ်၊ ခင်ဗျားကော
Nay Kaung Dae, Kyayzu Tin Pa Dae, Khinbyar Kaw

My name is ...
ကျွန်တော့်နာမည် ... ပါ
Kyunote Narmae ... Pa

This is my friend / boyfriend / girlfriend / husband / wife / brother / sister
ကျွန်တော့် (ကျွန်မ) သူငယ်ချင်း / ရည်းစား / ယောင်မလေး / ယောက်ျား / မိန်းမ အကို / အမ ဖြစ်ပါတယ်
Dar Kyundawt ("Kyunma" For Female) Thungechin / Yeezar / Kaungmalay / Yaukyar / Meinma / Ahko / Ahma Phyit Pa Dae

Where are you travelling to?
ဘယ်ကို ခရီးသွား မလိုလဲ
Bae Ko Khayee Thwar Malo Le

I am / we are going to ...
ကျွန်ုပ် / ကျွန်တော်တို့... ကို သွားမလို့ပါ
Kyunnote / Kyunote Toe ... Ko Thwar Malo Pa

How long are you travelling for?
ခင်ဗျား ခရီးသွားတာ ဘယ်လောက်ကြာပြီလဲ
Khinbyar Khayee Thwar Dar Bae Laut Kyar Be Le

Where do you come from?
ခင်ဗျား ဘယ်က လာတာလဲ
Khinbyar Bae Ka Lar Dar Le

I am / we are from Australia / Britain / Canada / America
ကျွန်တော် / ကျွန်တော်တို့ ဩစတေးလျ / ဗြိတိန် / ကနေဒါ / အမေရိက ကပါ
Kyundaw / Kyundaw Toe Oustralear / Byeetain / Kanaydar / Ahmayrikar Ka Pa

We are on holiday
ကျွန်တော်တို့ အားလပ်ရက် ခရီးထွက်ကြတာပါ
Kyundaw Toe Arr Lut Yet Khayee Htwet Kya Da Pa

This is our first visit here
ဒါ ကျွန်တော်တို့ ရဲ့ ပထမဆုံး ခရီးပါ
Dar Kyundaw Toe Yei Pahtamasone Khayee Pa

How old are you?
ခင်ဗျား အသက် ဘယ်လောက်လဲ
Khinbyar Ahthet Be Laut Le

I am ... years old
ကျွန်တော့် အသက် ... နှစ်ပါ
Kyundaw Ahthet ... Hnit Pa

I am a businessman / business woman / doctor / journalist / manual worker / administrator / scientist / student / teacher
ကျွန်တော် (ကျွန်မ) စီးပွားရေး လုပ်ငန်းရှင် / စီးပွားရေးလုပ်ငန်းရှင်အမျိုးသမီး / ဆရာဝန် / စာနယ်ဇင်း ဆရာ / ကျရာ လုပ်သား / အုပ်ချုပ်ရေးမှူး / သိပ္ပံပညာရှင် / ကျောင်းသား / ဆရာ တစ်ယောက်ပါ
Kyundaw ("Kyunma" For Female) See Pwar Yay Loatngunshin / See Pwar Yay Loatngunshin Ahmyoethamee / Sayarwun / Sar Nae Zine Sayar / Karya Louthar / Oatchoteyayhmu / Thait Pan Pinnyashin / Kyaung Thar / Sayar Ta Yauk Pa

Would you like / may I have a cigarette?
စီးကရက် တစ်လိပ် လောက် သောက်ပါလား / ပါရစေ
See Karet Talaik Laut Thaut Pa Lar / Pa Yasae

Do you mind if I smoke?
ကျွန်တော် ဆေးလိပ် သောက်လို့ ရပါသလား
Kyundaw Saylait Thaut Lo Ya Pa Thalar

B U R M E S E

Do you have a light?
မီးတစ်တို့ လောက်ပါ
Mee Tatoe Laut Pa

**I am waiting for my husband /
wife / boyfriend / girlfriend**
ကျွန်တော် (ကျွန်မ) ယောက်ျား / မိန်းမ /
ရည်းစား / ကောင်မလေး ကို စောင့်နေတာပါ
*Kyundaw ("Kyunma" For Female)
Yaukyar / Meinma / Yeezar /
Kaungmalay Ko Saunt Nay Dar Pa*

Days

Monday
တနင်္လာနေ့
Taninlar Nay

Tuesday
အင်္ဂါနေ့
Ingar Nay

Wednesday
ဗုဒ္ဓဟူးနေ့
Boadahhu Nay

Thursday
ကြာသပတေးနေ့
Kyarthapatay Nay

Friday
သောကြာနေ့
Thautkyar Nay

Saturday
စနေနေ့
Sanay Nay

Sunday
တနင်္ဂနွေနေ့
Taninganway Nay

Morning
မနက်ခင်း
Manet Khinn

Afternoon
နေ့လည်ခင်း
Nayle Khinn

Evening
ညနေခင်း
Nyanay Khinn

Night
ည
Nya

Yesterday / Today / Tomorrow
မနေ့က / ဒီနေ့ / မနက်ဖြန်
Manayka / Deenay / Manet Phyun

Numbers

Zero
သုံည
Thonya

One
၁
Tit

Two
၂
Hnit

Three
၃
Thone

Four
၄
Lay

Five
၅
Ngar

Six
၆
Chauk

Seven
၇
Khunit

Eight
၈
Shit

Nine
၉
Koe

Ten
၁၀
Tasae

Eleven
၁၁
Satit

Twelve
၁၂
Tasehnit

Thirteen
၁၃
Tasethone

Fourteen
၁၄
Taselay

Fifteen
၁၅
Tasengar

Sixteen
၁၆
Tasechauk

Seventeen
၁၇
Tasekhun

Eighteen
၁၈
Taseshit

Nineteen
၁၉
Tasekoe

Twenty
၂၀
Hnasae

Twenty-one
၂၁
Hnasetit

Twenty-two ၂၂ *Hnasehnit*	**Thirty** ၃၀ *Thonesae*
Forty ၄၀ *Laysae*	**Fifty** ၅၀ *Ngarsae*
Sixty ၆၀ *Chauksae*	**Seventy** ၇၀ *Khunasae*
Eighty ၈၀ *Shitsae*	**Ninety** ၉၀ *Koesae*
One hundred ၁၀၀ *Tayar*	**Five hundred** ၅၀၀ *Ngaryar*
One thousand ၁၀၀၀ *Tahtaung*	**One million** ၁၀ ၀၀၀၀၀ *Tathann*

Time

What time is it?
ဘယ်နှစ်နာရီလဲ
Baena Naryee Le

It is ...
အခု ... ရှိပါပြီ
Ahkhu ...Shee Pa Pyee

9.00
ကိုးနာရီ
Koe Naryee

9.05
ကိုးနာရီ ငါးမိနစ်
Koe Naryee Ngar Meenit

9.15
ကိုးနာရီ ဆယ့်ငါး
Koe Naryee Sengar

9.20
ကိုးနာရီ နှစ်ဆယ်
Koe Naryee Hnasae

9.30
ကိုးနာရီ ခွဲ
Koe Naryee Khwe

9.35
ကိုးနာရီ သုံးဆယ့်ငါး
Koe Naryee Thonesengar

9.40
ကိုးနာရီ လေးဆယ်
Koe Naryee Laysae

9.45
ကိုးနာရီ လေးဆယ့်ငါး
Koe Naryee Laysengar

9.50
ကိုးနာရီ ငါးဆယ်
Koe Naryee Ngarsae

9.55
ကိုးနာရီ ငါးဆယ့်ငါး
Koe Naryee Ngarsengar

12.00 / Midday / Midnight
ဆယ့်နှစ်နာရီ / ညလည် / သန်းခေါင်
Sahnit Naryee / Nay Le / Thankhaung

Money

I would like to change these traveller's cheques / this currency
ကျွန်တော် ဒီ ချပ်လက်မှတ် / ပိုက်ဆံ ကို လဲချင်လို့ပါ
Kyundaw Dee Chet Lethmut / Paiksan Ko Le Chin Lo Pa

**B
U
R
M
E
S
E**

How much commission do you charge? (What is the service charge?)

ကော်မရှင် ဘယ်လောက် ရသလဲ
(ဝန်ဆောင်ခ ဘယ်လောက်လဲ)

*Kawmashin Belaut Yu Thale
(Wunsaung Kha Belaut Le)*

Can I obtain money with my MasterCard?

ကျွန်တော် မာစတာ ကဒ်နဲ့ ပိုက်ဆံ ထုတ်လို့
ရသလား

Kyundaw Master Kut Ne Paiksan Htoat Lo Ya Thalar

Where is the nearest ATM?

အနီးဆုံး အေတီအမ် ဘယ်မှာလဲ

Ahneesone ATM Bae Hmar Le

My name is ... Some money has been wired to here for me to collect

ကျွန်တော်နာမည် ... ပါ ကျွန်တော်ဆီ
ငွေလွှဲလိုက်လို့ လာထုတ်တာပါ

Kyundaw Narmae ... Pa Kundaw Si Ngwe Lwae Lait Lo Lar Htoat Dar Pa

ARRIVING AND DEPARTING

Airport

Excuse me, where is the check-in desk for ... airline?

... လေကြောင်းရဲ့
ချက်ကင် ကောင်တာ ကိုသိပါရစေ။

... Laygyaung Yae Chet Kin Kaungtar KoThi Payasei

What is the boarding gate / time for my flight?

ကျွန်တော် လေယာဉ်ပျံရဲ့ ဂိတ်က /
ထွက်ချိန်က ဘာပါလဲ

Kyundaw Layyinpyun Yae Gate Ka / Htwet Chein Ka Ba Pa Le

How long is the delay likely to be?

ဘယ်လောက်ကြာကြာ နောက်ကျမှာပါလဲ

Bae Laut Kyar Kyar Naut Kya Hmar Pa Le

Where is the duty-free shop?

အခွန်လွတ်ဆိုင် က ဘယ်မှာပါလဲ

Ahkhun Lwut Saing Ka Bae Hmar Pa Le

Which way is the baggage reclaim?

တန်ဆာအိတ်တွေ ဘယ်မှာ သွားယူရမှာလဲ

Tansar Eit Tway Be Hmar Thwar Yu Ya Hmar Pa Le

I have lost my luggage. Please can you help?

ကျွန်တော့်ခရီးဆောင်ဝန်စည်စလယ်ပျောက်သွားပြီ။
ကျွန်တော့်ကိုကူညီပေးပါအုံး

Kyundaw KharYiHsaunWanSiSarLet Pyauk Thwar Pi Kyundaw Ko Ku Nyee Pe Pa Ohn

I am flying to ...

ကျွန်တော် ... ကို လေကြောင်းခရီးသွားမလို့

Kyundaw ...Ko Laygyaung Khayee Thwar Ma Lo

Where can I get the bus to the city centre?

မြို့ထဲကို သွားတဲ့ ဘတ်စ်ကား က
ဘယ်မှာပါလဲ

Myo Hte Ko Thwar Te Buskar Ka Bae Hmar Pa Le

Trains and Boats

Where is the ticket office / information desk?

လက်မှတ်ရုံ /
စုံစမ်းရေး ဌာန က ဘယ်မှာပါလဲ

Let Hmut Yone / Sonesannyay Htarna Ka Bae Hmar Pa Le

B U R M E S E

Which platform does the train / speedboat / ferry to ... depart from?
ဘယ်ပလက်ဖောင်းကနေ
... ကို သွားတဲ့ ရထား / ပချိတ် / ကတိုဆိပ်
Bae Plat Faung Ka Nay
... Ko Thwar Te Yahtar / Pechate / Kadoe Saik Hmar Le

Where is platform ...?
... ပလက်ဖောင်းဘယ်မှာလဲ
... Plat Faung Bae Hmar Le

When is the next train / boat to ...?
... ကို သွားတဲ့ပ ရထား / လှေ ဘယ်ကော့ ထွက်မှာလဲ
...Ko Thwar Te Yahtar / Hlay Bae Tawt Htwet Hmar Le

Is there a later train / boat to ...?
... ကို သွားတဲ့ နောက်ရထား /
လှေ ရှိဂါသေးလား
... Ko Thwar Te Naut Yahtar / Hlay Shee Pa Thay Lar

Notices and Signs

စားသောက်တွဲ
Sar Thaut Twe
Buffet (Dining) car

ဘတ်စ်ကား
Buskar
Bus

သောက်ရေ / သုံးရေ
Thaut Yay / Thone Yay
Drinking / Non-drinking Water

အဝင်
Ah-Win
Entrance

အထွက်
Ah-Htwet
Exit

ဆေးရုံ
Sayon
Hospital

ပြန်ကြားရေး
Pyun Kyar Yay
Information

အိတ် အပ်ဌာန (အိတ်ထားရာ နေရာ)
Eit Ut Htarna (Eit Htar Yar Nayar)
Left luggage (Baggage claim)

အိတ်ထားတဲ့ လော့ကားတွေ
Eit Htar Te Locker Tway
Luggage lockers

စာတိုက်
Sar Taik
Post office

ပလက်ဖောင်း
Plat Faung
Platform

ရထား (သံလမ်း) ဘူတာ
Yahtar (Than Lun) Buutar
Railway (Railroad) station

လေဆိပ်
Laysate
Airport

ရဲဌာန
Ye Htarna
Police station

17

B U R M E S E

ဆိပ်ကမ်း
Sate Kann
Port

စားသောက်ဆိုင်
Sar Thaut Saing
Restaurant

ဆေးလိပ် သောက်ရ / မသောက်ရ
Saylate Thaut Ya / Mathaut Ya
Smoking / Non-smoking

တယ်လီဖုန်း
Telee Fone
Telephone

လက်မှတ်ရုံ
Let Hmut Yone
Ticket office

ချက်ကင်ကောင်တာ
Chet Kin Kaungtar (Check-in Counter)
Check-in desk

အချိန်ဇယား (ဝင်ချိန် ထွက်ချိန် စာရင်း)
Ahchain Zayarr (Winchain Htwetchain Sayinn)
Timetables (Schedules)

အိမ်သာ (သန့်စင်ခန်း)
Ein Thar (Thantsin Khann)
Toilets (Restrooms)

မ / ကျား
Ma / Kyar
Ladies / Gentlemen

မြေအောက်လမ်း (မြေအောက်ရထား)
Myay Oaut Lun (Myay Oaut Yahtar)
Underground (Subway)

စောင့်ဆိုင်းနားနေခန်း
Saunt Sine Nar Nay Khann
Waiting room

Buying a Ticket

I would like a first-class / second-class single (oneway) / return (round-trip) ticket to ...
ကျွန်တော် ... ကို သွားတဲ့ ပထမတန်း / ဒုတိယတန်း တစ်ကြောင်း (အသွား) / အပြန် (အသွား–အပြန်) လက်မှတ် ရရှင်လိုပါ
Kyundaw ... Ko Thwar Te Pahtama Tann / Duteya Tann Ta Gyaung (Ahthwar) / Ahpyun (Ahthwar-Ahpyun) Let Hmut Ya Chin Lo Pa

Is it an express (fast) train / bus?
ဒီဟာ အထူး (အမြန်) ရထား / ဘတ်စ်ကားပါလဲ
Dee Har Ahhtoo (Ahmyun) Yahtar / Buskar Pa Le

Is my rail pass valid on this train / ferry / bus?
ဒီလက်မှတ်နဲ့ ဒီရထား / ကတို / ဘတ်စ်ကား စီးလို့ ရပါသလား
Dee Let Hmut Ne Dee Yahtar / Kadoe / Buskar Si Lo Ya Pa Thalar

I would like an aisle / window seat
ကျွန်တော် အလယ်လမ်း / ပြတင်းပေါက် ထိုင်ခုံကြိုက်ပါတယ်
Kyundaw Ahlaelun / Padinepauk Htinekhone Kyaik Pa Dae

No smoking / smoking, please
ကျေးဇူးပြု၍ ဆေးလိပ် မသောက်ရ / သောက်ရတဲ့ နေရာ ပြပါ
Kyayzu Pyu Ywayt Saylate Mathaut Ya / Thaut Ya De Nayyar Pay Pa

We would like to sit together
ကျွန်တော်တို့ အတူတူ ထိုင်ချင်ပါတယ်
Kyundaw Toe Ahtutu Htine Chin Pa Dae

ARRIVING AND DEPARTING

I would like to make a seat reservation
ကျွန်တော် ထိုင်ခုံနေရာ ကြိုတင်
စီစဉ်ထားချင်ပါတယ်
Kyundaw Htinekhone Nayyar Kyotin Sisin Htar Chin Pa Dae

I would like to reserve a couchette / sleeper for one person / two people / my family
ကျွန်တော် ဆိုဖါ ထိုင်ခ / အိပ်စင် ကို
တစ်ယောက်စာ / နှစ်ယောက်စာ /
မိသားစု တစ်ခုစာ ကြိုတင်စီစဉ်ချင်ပါတယ်
Kyundaw Sofa Htinekhone / Eitsin Ko Tayauksar / Hnayauksar / Mitharsu Takhusar Kyotin Sisin Chin Pa Dae

I would like to reserve a cabin
ကျွန်တော် အခန်းငယ် တစ်ခု
ကြိုတင်စီစဉ်ချင်ပါတယ်
Kyundaw Ahkhann Nge Takhu Kyotin Sisin Chin Pa Dae

Timetables (Schedules)

ရောက်သည်
Yauk Thee
Arrive

... မှာ ဆင်းပါမယ်
... Hmar Hsinn Pa Mae
Calls (Stops) at ...

အစားအသောက် ဝန်ဆောင်မှု
Ahsar Ahthaut Wun Saung Hmu
Catering service

... မှာပြောင်းစီးမယ်
... Hmar Pyaung Si Mae
Change at ...

တစ်ဆက်ထဲ / တစ်ဆင့်
Taset Htae / Tasint
Connection / Via

နေ့စဉ်
Nay Sin
Daily

မိနစ် လေးဆယ်တိုင်း
Meenit Laysae Tine
Every 40 minutes

ပထမတန်း
Pahtama Tann
First class

တစ်နာရီခြား
Ta Naryee Char
Hourly

ထိုင်ခုံ နေရာ စီစဉ်ချင်းကို
အားပေးပါကယ်
Htinekhone Nayyar Sisin Chin Ko Arr Pay Pa Dae
Seat reservations are recommended

ဒုတိယတန်း
Duteya Tann
Second class

အပိုကြေး ပေးရန်
Ahpokyay Pay Yan
Supplement payable

BURMESE

19

Luggage

How much will it cost to send (ship) my luggage in advance?
ကျွန်တော်အိတ်ကို အရင် ပို့နှင့်မယ်ဆိုရင် ဘယ်လောက်ကျပါသလဲ
Kyundaw Eit Ko Ahyin Poe Nint Mae So Yin Bae Laut Kya Pa Thale

Where is the left luggage (baggage claim) office?
အိတ်အပ်ဌာန (အိတ်ထားရာ နေရာ) ရုံးခန်းက ဘယ်မှာပါလဲ
Eit Ut Htarna (Eit Htar Yar Nayar) Yone Khann Ka Bae Hmar Pa Le

What time do you open / close?
ဘယ်အချိန်မှာ ဖွင့် / ပိတ်ပါသလဲ
Bae Ahchain Hmar Phwint / Pate Pa Thale

Where are the luggage trolleys (carts)?
အိတ်သယ်ဖို့လှည်း (ထော်လီ) တွေ ဘယ်မှာပါလဲ
Eit Thae Phoe Hle (Htawlee) Tway Bae Hmar Pa Le

Where are the lockers?
လော့ကာတွေ ဘယ်မှာပါလဲ
Locker Tway Be Hmar Pa Le

I have lost my locker key
ကျွန်တော် လော့ကာသော့ပျောက်သွားလို့
Kyundaw Locker Thuot Pyaut Thwar Lo

On Board

Is this seat free?
ဒီထိုင်ခုံ အားပါသလား
Dee Htine Khone Arr Pa Thalar

Excuse me, you are sitting in my reserved seat
ခွင့်ပြုပါ၊ ခင်ဗျား ထိုင်နေတာ ကျွန်တော် ထိုင်ခုံပါ
Khwint Pyu Pa, Khinbyar Htine Nay Tar Kyundaw Htine Khone Pa

Which station is this?
ဒီဘူတာ ဘယ်ဘူတာလဲ
Dee Buutar Ba Buutar Le

What time is this train / bus / ferry / flight due to arrive / depart?
ဒီရထား / ဘတ်စ်ကား / ကတို့ / လေယာဉ် ဘယ်အချိန် ဆိုက် / ထွက်မှာလဲ
Dee Yahtar / Buskar / Kado / Layyin Bae Ahchain Site / Htwet Hmar Le

Travelling with Children

Do you have a high chair / babysitting service / cot?
ခင်ဗျားတို့မှာ ထိုင်ခုံရှည် / ကလေးထိုင် / ကလေးပုခက် ရှိပါသလား
Khinbyar Toe Hmar Htine Khone Shay / Kalay Htane / Kalay Pakhet Shee Pa Thalar

Where is the nursery / playroom?
ကလေး ထိန်းဌာန / ကစားကွင်း ဘယ်မှာပါလဲ
Kalay Htane Htarna / Kasar Kwinn Bae Hmar Pa Le

Where can I warm the baby's bottle?
ကျွန်တော့ကလေး နို့ဘူး ဘယ်မှာ နွေးရမလဲ
Kyundaw Kalay Noebuu Bae Hmar Hnway Ya Ma Le

Customs and Passports

Passports, please!
နိုင်ငံကူးလက်မှတ် ပြပါ၊ ကျေးဇူးပြု၍
Naingan Kuu Let Hmut Pya Pa! Kyayzu Pyu Ywayt

I have nothing / wine / spirits (alcohol) / tobacco to declare
ကျွန်တော့်မှာ ကြေညာဖို့ ဘာမှ မပါဘူး / ဝိုင် / အရက် / ဆေးလိပ် ပါ ပါတယ်
Kyundaw Hmar Kyaynya Phoe Barhma Ma Pa Buu / Wine / Ahyet / Saylate Pa Ba Dae

I will be staying for ... days / weeks / months
ကျွန်တော် ...ရက် / ပတ် / လ နေမှာပါ
Kyundaw ...Yet / Part / La Nay Hmar Pa

SIGHTSEEING

Asking the Way

Excuse me, do you speak English?
တဆိတ်လောက် ပြောပြပဘာလား၊ ခင်ဗျား အင်္ဂလိပ်လို ပြောတတ်လား
Tasate Laut Phyay Pay Pa Lar, Khinbyar Inngalate Lo Pyaw Tut Lar

Excuse me, can you help me please?
တစ်ဆိတ်လောက် ကျွန်တော်ကို ကူညီ ပါလား
Tasate Laut Kyundaw Ko Kuu Nyee Pa Lar

Where is the Tourist Information Office?
တိုးရစ်စ် ပြန်ကြားရေး ဌာန ဘယ်မှာပါလဲ
Tourist Pyun Kyar Yay Htana Bae Hmar Pa Le

Excuse me, is this the right way to ...?
တဆိတ်လောက်ပြောပြပါလား၊ ဒီလမ်းက ... ကို သွားတဲ့ လမ်းပါလား
Tasate Laut Phyay Pay Pa Lar, Dee Lun Ka ... Ko Thwar Te Lun Pa Lar

... the cathedral / the tourist information office / the castle / the old town
ဘုရားကျောင်း / တိုးရစ်စ် ပြန်ကြားရေး ဌာန / ရဲတိုက် / မြို့ဟောင်း
Phayar Kyaung / Tourist Pyun Kyar Yay Htana / Yetite / Myo Haung

Can you tell me the way to the railway (rallroad) station / bus station / taxi rank (stand) / city centre (downtown) / beach?
ကျွန်တော်ကို ဘူတာရုံ (သံလမ်း) ဘတ်စ်ကားမှတ်တိုင် / တက်ကစီကားဂိတ် / မြို့လယ် (မြို့ထဲ) / ကမ်းခြေ သွားတဲ့ လမ်းပြပေးပါ
Kyundaw Ko Buutar Yone (Than Lun) Buskar Hmutine / Taxi Kar Gate / Myo Le (Myo Hte) / Kannchay Thwar Te Lun Pya Pay Pa

First / second / left / right / straight ahead
ပထမ / ဒုတိယ / ဘယ်ဘက် / ညာဘက် / ရှေ့တည့်တည့်
Pahtama / Dytiya / Bae Bat / Nyar Bat / Shay Te Te

At the corner / at the traffic lights
ဒေါင့်ချိုးမှာ / မီးပွိုင့်မှာ
Daunt Choe Hmar / Mee Point Hmar

Where is the nearest police station / post office?
အနီးဆုံး ရဲစခန်း / စာတိုက် ဘယ်မှာ ပါလဲ
Ahneesone Yesakhann / Sartite Bae Hmar Pa Le

Is it near / far?
နီးသလား / ဝေးသလား
Nee Thalar / Way Thalar

BURMESE

Do I need to take a taxi / catch a bus?
ကျွန်တော် တက်ကစီနဲ့ / ဘတ်စ်ကားနဲ့ သွားရမှာလား
Kyundaw Taxi Ne / Buskar Ne Thaw Ya Hmar Lar

Do you have a map?
ခင်ဗျားမှာ မြေပုံ ရှိလား
Khinbyar Hmar Myaypone Shee Lar

Can you point to it on my map?
ကျွန်တော့် မြေပုံမှာ ထောက်ပြပါ
Kyundaw Myaypone Hmar Htaut Pya Pa

Thank you for your help
ကူညီတာ ကျေးဇူးတင်ပါတယ်
Kuu Nyee Tar Kyayzu Tin Pa Dae

How do I reach the motorway / main road?
ကျွန်တော် ကားလမ်းမ / မိန်းလမ်းကို ဘယ်လို သွားရမလဲ
Kyundaw Karlun Ma / Main Lun Ko Bae Lo Thwar Ya Ma Le

I think I have taken the wrong turning
ကျွန်တော် လမ်းကွေ့တာ မှားပြီ ထင်တယ်
Kyundaw Lun Kwayt Tar Hmar Pe Htin Dae

I am looking for this address
ကျွန်တော် ဒီလိပ်စာကို ရှာနေတာပါ
Kyundaw Dee Latesar Ko Shar Nay Tar Pa

I am looking for the ... hotel
ကျွန်တော် ... ဟိုတယ်ကို ရှာနေတာပါ
Kyundaw ... Hotel Ko Shar Nay Tar Pa

How far is it to ... from here?
ဒီနေရာကနေ ... ကို ဘယ်လောက်ဝေးလဲ
Dee Nay Yar Ka Nay ... Ko Bae Laut Way Le

Carry straight on for ... Kilometres
... ကီလိုမီတာလောက် ဆက်သွားပါ
... Kilo Meter Laut Set Thwar Pa

Take the next turning on the right / left
ညာဘက်က / ဘယ်ဘက်က အကွေ့ကို ချိုးလိုက်ပါ
Nya Bat Ka / Bae Bat Ka Ahkwayt Ko Choe Lite Pa

Turn right / left at the next crossroads / traffic lights
နောက်လမ်းဆုံ / မီးပွိုင့် မှာ ညာ / ဘယ် ချိုးပါ
Naut Lunsone / Mee Point Hmar Nya / Bae Choe Pa

You are going in the wrong direction
ခင်ဗျားလမ်းမှားနေပြီ
Khinbyar Lun Hmar Nay Pee

Where is the cathedral / church / museum / pharmacy?
ဘုန်းတော်ကြီးကျောင်း / ဘုရားကျောင်း / ပြတိုက် / ဆေးဆိုင် ဘယ်မှာပါလဲ
Phonetawgyi Kyaung / Phayar Kyaung / Pyatite / Saysaing Bae Hmar Pa Le

How much is the admission / entrance charge?
ဝင်ကြေး / ဝင်ခ ဘယ်လောက် ပေးရပါလဲ
Win Gyay / Win Kha Bae Laut Pay Ya Pa Le

Is there a discount for children / students / senior citizens?

ကလေးခ / ကျောင်းသားခ / နိုင်ငံခြားသားခ လျော့ချပါသလား

Kalay Kha / Kyaungthar Kha / Naingan Gyithar Kha Short Kaut Pa Thalar

What time does the next guided tour (in English) start?

နောက်ခရီးသွားလမ်းညွှန် (အင်္ဂလိပ်လို) ကယ်တော့စမှာပါလဲ

Naut Khayee Thwar Lun Nyun (Ingalate Lo) Bae Tawt Sa Hmar Pa Le

One / two adults / children, Please

ကလေး / လူကြီး တစ်ယောက် / နှစ်ယောက် ထွက်ပြပါ

Kalay / Lugyi Ta Yauk / Hna Yauk Ahtwet Pay Pa

May I take photographs here?

ဒီနေရာ ဓါတ်ပုံရိုက်လို့ရလား

Dee Nay Yar Dut Pone Yite Lo Ya Lar

At the Tourist Office

Do you have a map of the town / area?

ခင်များမှာ မြို့တွင်း / ဒေသတွင်း မြေပုံရှိပါသလား

Khinbyar Hmar Myo Twin / Daethu Twin Myaypone Shee Pa Thalar

Do you have a list of accommodation?

ခင်များမှာ နေရာ ထိုင်ခင်း စာရင်းရှိပါသလား

Khinbyar Hmar Nay Yar Htine Khin Saryinn Shee Pa Thalar

Can I reserve accommodation?

ကျွန်တော် နေရာထိုင်ခင်း တစ်ခု စီစဉ်ချင်ပါတယ်

Kyundaw Nay Yar Htine Khin Ta Khu Sisin Chin Pa Dae

ACCOMMODATION

Hotels

I have a reservation in the name of ...

ကျွန်တော် ... နာမည်နဲ့ ကြိုတင် စီစဉ် ထားပါတယ်

Kyundaw ... Narmae Ne Kyotin Sisin Htar Pa Dae

i wrote to / faxed / telephoned you last month / last week

ကျွန်တော် ခင်များဆီကို အရင်လ / အရင်အပတ်ကစာရေး / ဖက်စ်ပို့ / တယ်လီဖုန်း ဆက်ခဲ့တယ်လေ

Kyundaw Khinbyar Si Ko Ahyin La / Ahyin Ahpart Ka Saryay / Fax Poe / Telefone Set Khe Tae Lay

Do you have any rooms free?

ခင်များမှာ အခန်းလွတ် ရှိပါသလား

Khinbyar Hmar Ahkhann Luot Shee Pa Thalar

I would like to reserve a single / double room with / without bath / shower

ကျွန်တော်ရေချိုးကန် ရေလုံးကက်ရေချိုးခန်းပါ / ပပါသော တစ်ယောက် / နှစ်ယောက်ကိုအိပ်ခန်းဟစ်ခန်း ကြိုစီစီတုတ်စ်ပေးထားချင်ပါတယ်

Kyundaw YaychoeKan / Yaypann Tat Yaychoekhann Pa / Ma Pa Thaw Tyayauk / Hnayank Eithkann Takhann Kyotin Sayinn Pay Htar Chin Pa Dae

I would like bed and breakfast / (room and) full board

ကျွန်တော် အိပ်ခန်းနဲ့ မနက်စာပါတာ / အကုန်ပြည့်စုံတာ ရေရပါ့ငပ်ပါတယ်

Kyundaw Eitkhan Ne Manetsar Par Tar / Ahkone Pyaytsone Tar Ya Chin Pa Dae

How much is it per night?

တစ်ညကို ဘယ်လောက်လဲ

Tanya Ko Bae Laut Le

B
U
R
M
E
S
E

**B
U
R
M
E
S
E**

Is breakfast included?
မနက်စာ ပါပါသလား
Manetsar Pa Par Thalar

Do you have any cheaper rooms?
ဒီထက်ဈေးချိုတဲ့ အခန်း ရှိပါသေးလား
Dee Htet Zay Cho Te Ahkhan Shee Pa Thay Lar

I would like to see / take the room
ကျွန်တော် အခန်း ကြည့် / ယူချင်ပါတယ်
Kyundaw Ahkann Kyee / Yu Chin Pa Dae

I would like to stay for ... nights
ကျွန်တော် ... ညနေချင်ပါတယ်
Kyundaw ... Nya Nay Chin Pa Dae

The shower / light / tap / hot water doesn't work
ရေပန်း / မီး / ရေဖက်ငုတ် / ရေပူ က ပျက်နေပါတယ်
Yaypun / Mee / Yaysat Ngote / Yaypu Ka Pyet Nay Pa Dae

At what time / where is breakfast served?
ဘယ်အချိန် / ဘယ်နေရာ မှာ မနက်စာ ကျွေးတာလဲ
Bae Ahchin / Bae Nayyar Hmar Manetsar Kyway Tar Le

What time do I have to check out?
ဘယ်အချိန်မှာ ရှင်းပေး (ချက်ကောက်လုပ်) ရပါမလဲ
Bae Ahchain Hmar Shinn Pay (Check-Out Loat) Ya Pa Ma Le

Can I have the key to room number ... ?
အခန်းနံပါတ် ... ရေး သော့ ရချင်ပါတယ်
Ahkhann Nanbut ... Yae Thauot Ya Chin Pa Dae

My room number is ...
ကျွန်တော် အခန်းနံပါတ်က ... ပါ
Kyundaw Ahkhann Nanbut Ka ... Pa

My room is not satisfactory / not clean enough / too noisy
ကျွန်တော် အခန်းက သိပ်မကောင်းဘူး / သိပ်မသန့်စင်ဘူး / အလွန်ဆူညံပါတယ်
Kyundaw Ahkhann Ka Thate Ma Kaung Buu / Thate Mathantshinn Buu / Ahlune Sunyan Pa Dae

Please can I change rooms?
ကျေးဇူးပြု၍ အခန်းပြောင်းလို့ရမလား
Kyazu Pyu Ywayt Ahkhann Pyaung Lo Ya Ma Lar

Where is the bathroom?
ရေချိုးခန်း ဘယ်မှာပါလဲ
Yay Choe Khann Bae Hmar Pa Le

Do you have a safe for valuables?
ခင်များတို့မှာ အဖိုးတန်ပစ္စည်းတွေအတွက် မခန်တက်တာ ရှိသလား
Khinbyar Toe Hmar Ahphoe Tan Pyitsee Tway Ahtwet Meekhan Titar Shee Thalar

Is there a laundry / do you wash clothes?
အဝတ်လျှော်ဆိုင် ရှိသလား / ခင်များတို့ အဝတ်လျှော်ပေးပါသလား
Ahwut Shaw Saing Shee Thalar / Khinbyar Toe Ahwut Shaw Pay Pa Thalar

I would like an air-conditioned room
လေအေးစက်ပါတဲ့ အခန်း ကြိုက်ပါတယ်
Layaye Set Pa Tat Ahkhann Kyaik Pa Dae

Do you accept traveller's cheques / credit cards?
ခရီးသွားချက်လက်မှတ် / အကြွေးကဒ်တွေ လက်ခံပါသလား
Khayee Thwar Check Let Hmut / Ahkyway Card Tway Let Khan Pa Thalar

24

May I have the bill please?
စာရင်းရှင်းဖို့ ဘောက်ချာ ယူခဲ့ပါ။ ကျေးဇူးပြု၍
Sayinn Shinn Phoe Bautchar Yuu Khe Pa Kyayzu Pyu Ywayt

Excuse me, I think there may be a mistake in this bill
ခွင့်ပြုပါ၊ ဒီစာရင်းမှားနေတယ်လို့
ကျွန်တော်ထင်ပါတယ်
Khwint Pyu Pa, Dee Sayinn Hmar Nay Te Lo Kyundaw Htin Pa Dae

Youth Hostels

How much is a dormitory bed per night?
အဆောင်အိပ်စင်ခ ကစ်ညဘယ်လောက်လဲ
Ahsaung Eitsin Ka Tanya Bae Laut Le

I am / am not an HI member
ကျွန်တော်လူငယ်အဆောင်ရဲ့ အိတ်ချ် အိုင် အဖွဲ့ဝင်
တစ်ယောက်ပါ / မဟုတ်ပါ
Kyundaw Lu Nge Ahsaung Yae HI Ahphweyt Win Tayaut Pa / Ma Hote Pa

May I use my own sleeping bag?
ကျွန်တော် ကိုယ်ပိုင် အိပ်ယာလိပ်ကို
သုံးလို့ရပါသလား
Kyundaw Kopaing Eit Yarlate Ko Thone Lo Ya Pa Thalar

What time do you lock the doors at night?
ည ဘယ်အချိန်မှာ တံခါးပိတ်ပါသလဲ
Nya Bae Ahchain Hmar Tagar Pate Pa Tha Le

Camping

May I camp for the night / two nights?
ဒီည / နှစ်ညလောက် စခန်းချပါရစေ
Dee Nya / Hnanya Laut Sakhann Cha Pa Ya Sae

Where can I pitch my tent?
ကျွန်တော်တဲကို ဘယ်မှာထိုးရမလဲ
Kyundaw Te Ko Bae Hmar Htoe Ya Ma Le

How much does it cost for one night / week?
တစ်ည / တစ်ပတ် ဘယ်လောက် ကျပါသလဲ
Tanya / Tapart Bae Laut Kya Pa Tha Le

Where are the washing facilities?
ဆေးကြောဘို့ နေရာ ဘယ်မှာပါလဲ
Say Kyaw Phoe Nayyar Bae Hmar Pa Le

Is there a restaurant / supermarket / swimming pool on site / nearby?
စားသောက်ဆိုင် / ကုန်တိုက်ကြီး /
ရေကူးကန် ရှိပါသလား / နီးပါသလား
Sar Thaut Saing / Konetite Kyee / Yaykuu Kan Shee Pa Thalar / Nee Pa Thalar

Do you have a safety deposit box?
ခင်ဗျားမှာ လုံခြုံရေး အာမခံသေတ္တာ ရှိပါသလား
Khinbyar Hmar Lonechone Yay Armakhan Titar Shee Pa Thalar

B U R M E S E

EATING AND DRIKING

Cafés and Bars

I would like a cup of / two cups of / another coffee / tea
ကျွန်တော် ကော်ဖီ / လက်ဖက်ရေ တစ်ခွက် / နှစ်ခွက် / နောက်ထပ်လိုချင်ပါတယ်
Kyundaw Kawfee / Lafet Yay Takhwet / Hnakhwet / Naut Htut Lo Chin Pa Dae

With / without milk / sugar
နို့ / သကြား ပါ / မပါ
Noe / Thagyar Pa / Ma Pa

I would like a bottle / glass / two glasses of mineral water / red wine / white wine, please
ကျွန်တော့်ကိုစမ်းရေ / ဝိုင်းနီ / ဝိုင်းဖြူ တစ်ပုလင်း / ခွက် / နှစ်ခွက်ကိုပေးပါ။
Kyundaw Ko Sanye / WaingNi / WaingPhuu TaPuling / Khwet / HnaKhwet Ko Pay Pa

I would like a beer / two beers, Please
ကျွန်တော့်ကိုဘီယာတစ်ခွက် / နှစ်ခွက် ကိုပေးပါ။
Kyundaw Ko Piya TaKhwet / HnaKhwet Ko Pay Pa

Please may I have some ice?
ကျေးဇူးပြု၍ ရေခဲ နည်းနည်းပေးပါလား
Kyayzu Pyu Ywayt Yaykhe Ne Ne Pay Pa Lar

Do you have any matches / cigarettes / cigars?
မီးခြစ် / စီးကရက် / ဆေးလိပ် ရှိပါသလား
Meechit / Sigarat / Saylate Shee Pa Thalar

Restaurants

Can you recommend a good / cheap restaurant in this area?
ဒီနေရာမှာ ဈေးချိုတဲ့ စားသောက်ဆိုင် ညွှန်ပြပေးပါလား
Dee Nayyar Hmar Zaycho Te Sarthaut Saing Nyun Pya Pay Pa Lar

I would like a table for ... people
ကျွန်တော် လူ ... ယောက်အတွက် စားပွဲတစ်လုံးလိုချင်ပါတယ်
Kyundaw Lu ...Yaut Ahtwet Sapwe Talone Lo Chin Pa Dae

Do you have a non-smoking area?
ဆေးလိပ် မသောက်ရတဲ့ နေရာ ရှိပါသလား
Saylate Mathaut Ya Te Nayyar Shee Pa Thalar

Waiter / Waitress!
စားပွဲထိုး / ညီ့ကြို
Sapwe Htoe / Aetgyo

Excuse me, please may we order?
ကျေးဇူးပြု၍မှာကြားပါရစေ
Kyayzu Pyu Ywayt Hmar Kyar Pa Ya Sae

Do you have a set menu / children's menu / wine list?
ခင်ဗျားတို့မှာ အသင့်တွဲပြီး ဟင်းလျာ / ကလေးဟင်း / ဝိုင်စာရင်း ရှိပါသလား
Khinbyar Toe Hmar Ahthint Twe Pyee Hinlyar / Kalay Hinn / Wine Sayinn Shee Pa Thalar

Do you have any vegetarian dishes?
သတ်သတ်လွတ်ဟင်း ဘာများရှိပါသလဲ
Thut Thut Luot Hinn Ba Myar Shee Pa Tha Le

Do you have any local specialities?
ခင်ဗျားတို့မှာ ဒေသထွက် အထူးအမယ်တွေ ရှိပါသလား
Khinbyar Toe Hmar Daetha Htwet Ahtoo Amae Tway Shee Pa Thalar

Are vegetables included?
ဟင်းသီးဟင်းရွက်ပါပါသလား
Hinthee Hinywet Par Pa Thalar

Could i have it well-cooked / medium / rare please?
ကျက်နပ်အောင် / ကျက်ရုံအောင် / အသင့်ကျက်ရုံဖျဖျ ချက်လျှင်ရလား။
Kyat Nat Anug / Kyat Yon Aung / Apawyan Kyat Yonl Imyu Chet Hlyin Ya Lar

What does this dish consist of?
ဒီဟင်းကိုဘာများနဲ့ချက်သလဲ။
Dee Hin Ko Ba Myar Ne Chet Tha Le

I am a vegetarian. Does this contain meat?
ကျွန်တော် သက်သတ်လွတ်စားပါတယ် ဒီထဲမှာ အသားပါပါသလား
Kyundaw Thet Thut Luot Sar Pa Dae Dee Hte Hmar Ahthar Par Pa Thalar

I do not eat nuts / dairy products / meat / fish
ကျေးဇူးပြု၍ကျွန်တော် အဆန် / နို့ယွက်ပစ္စည်း / အသား / ငါး မစားပါ
Kyazu Pyu Ywayt Kyundaw Ahsun / Noehtwet Pitsee / Ahthar / Ngar Masar Pa

Not (very) spicy, please
အစပ်(သိပ်)မထည့်ပါနဲ့
Ahsut (Thate) Ma Hte Pa Ne

I would like the set menu, please
ကျေးဇူးပြု၍ ကျွန်တော်ကို မိတ်ဖက်ဟင်းတွဲ စာရင်းပေးပါ
Kyayzu Pyu Ywayt Kyundaw Ko Matephet Hinn Twe Sayin Pay Pa

We are still waiting to be served
ကျွန်တော်တို့ စားဖို့စောင့်နေကြပါတယ်
Kyundaw Toe Sar Phoe Saunt Nay Kya Pa Dae

Please bring a plate / knife / fork
ကျေးဇူးပြု၍ပန်းကန်တစ်ချပ် / ဓား / ခရင်း တစ်ချောင်းယူခွဲပါ
Kyazu Pyu Ywayt Pakan Tachut / Dar Tachaung / Khayinn Tachaung Yu Khe Pa

Excuse me, this is not what I ordered
ခွင့်ပြုပါ၊ ဒါကျွန်တော်မှာထားတာမဟုတ်ပါဘူး
Khwint Pyu Pa, Dar Kyundaw Hmar Htar Tar Ma Hote Pa Buu

May I have some / some more bread / water / coffee / tea?
ကျွန်တော်ကိုပေါင်မုန့် / ရေ / ကော်ဖီ / လက်ဖက်ရေပေး / ထပ်ပေးပါအုံး
Kynudaw Ko Paung Mont / Yay / Kawfee / Lafetyay Pay / Htut Pay Pa Ohn

May I have the bill, please?
ကျေးဇူးပြု၍ စာရင်းရှင်းပါရစေ
Kyayzu Pyu Ywayt Sayinn Shin Pa Ya Sae

Does this bill include service?
စာရင်းထဲမှာ ဝန်ဆောင်မှု ပါပါသလား
Sayinn Hte Hmar Wunsaung Hmu Par Pa Thalar

Do you accept traveller's cheques / MasterCard / US dollars?
ခရီးသွားချက်လက်မှတ် / မာစတာကဒ် / အမေရိကန်ဒေါ်လာ လက်ခံပါသလား
Khayee Thwar Check Let Hmut / MasterCard / Ahmayrikan Dollar Let Khan Pa Thalar

B U R M E S E

Can I have a receipt, please?
ကျေးဇူးပြု၍ ငွေလက်ခံဖြတ်ပိုင်း ပေးပါလား
Kyayzu Pyu Ywayt Ngwe Let Khan Phyut Pine Pay Pa Lar

Where is the toilet (restroom), please?
အိမ်သာ (သန့်စင်ခန်း) ဘယ်မှာပါလဲ
Einthar (Thantsin Khann) Bae Hmar Pa Le

On the Menu

မနက်စာ / ညနေစာ / ညစာ
Manetsar / Naylesar / Nyasar
Breakfast / Lunch / Dinner

ပထမဦးဆုံးဟင်း
Pa Hta Ma Wu Hson Hin
First courses

ဟင်းရည်
Hin Yei
Soups

အဓိကဟင်းလျာ
Ahdika Hinnlyar
Main courses

ငါးဟင်း	အသားဟင်း
NgarHin	*A Thar Hin*
Fish dishes	**Meat dishes**
အမဲသား	အသားလွှာ
A Mee Thar	*A Thar Hlwar*
Beef	**Steak**
ဝက်သား	နွားကလေးသား
Wat Thar	*Nwar Kalei Thar*
Pork	**Veal**

ကြက်သား	သိုးသား
Kyet Thar	*Thoe Thar*
Chicken	**Lamb**

ဝက်ပေါင်
Wet Paung
Ham

သက်သတ်လွတ်ဟင်းများ
Thet Thut Luot Hinn Myar
Vegetarian dishes

ဟင်းသီးဟင်းရွက်များ
Hinnthee Hinnywet Myar
Vegetables

အာလူးကြော်
Arloo Gyaw
Chips (french fries)

အာလူးပြုတ် / ကြော် / ထောင်း
Ar Luu Pyout / Kyaw / Htaung
Boiled / sauté / mashed potatoes

ထမင်း	ချိစ်
Htamin	*Cheese*
Rice	**Cheese**

အချိုပွဲ
Ahcho Pwe
Desserts

ရေခဲမုန့်	ကိတ်မုန့်များ
Yaykhe Mont	*Cake Mont Myar*
Ice cream	**Cakes**
တို့စရာ	သစ်သီး
Toesayar	*Thitthee*
Pastries	**Fruit**

ပေါင်မုန့်
Paung Mont
Bread

အသေးစားပေါင်မုန့်
A T Heiizar PaungMont
Rolls

ပေါင်မုန့်ကင်
Paung Mont Kin
Toast

ထောပတ်
Htawpart
Butter

ဆား / ငရုတ်ကောင်း
Hsar / Ngayote Kaung
Salt / pepper

သကြား
Thagyar
Sugar

အထူးစားဖွယ်
Ahtoo Sarphwe
Specialities

ဒေသထွက်အထူး
Daetha Htwet Ahtoo
Local specialities

အသင့်တွဲဟင်း
Ahthint Twe Hinn
Set Menu

ဝိုင်စာရင်း
Waing Saryinn
Wine list

ဝိုင်းနီ
WaingNi
Red wines

ဝိုင်းဖြူ
WaingPhu
White wines

ပန်နုရောင်ဝိုင်း
PanNuYaung Waing
Rosé wines

စပါကလင် ဝိုင်
Sparkling Wine
Sparkling wines

ဘီယာ
Beer
Beer

ပုလင်းဘီယာ / စည်ဘီယာ ဘီယာကြမ်း
Palin Beer / Si Beer Beer (Gyun)
Bottled beer /
Draught (draft) beer

အရက်မပါအချိုရည်
Ahyet Mapar Ahcho Yee
Non-alcoholic drinks

သောက်ရေသန့်
Thaut Yay Thant
Mineral water

သစ်သီးဖျော်ရည်
Thitthee Phyawyee
Fruit juices

လိမ္မော်ရေ
Lainmaw Yay
Orange juice

လင်မနစ်ရည်   ရေခဲ
LinMaNit Yei   *YeiKhee*
Lemonade   **Ice**

ကော်ဖီမစ် / ကော်ဖီခါး / ပေါင်းဖံကော်ဖီ
KawPhiMit / KawPhiKhar /
PaungKhun KawPhi
White coffee / black coffee /
espresso coffee

နို့ပါလက်ဖက်ရည် / သံပုရိုထည့်ဂ္ဂက်ဖက်ရည်
Noe Par Laphet Yei / Thanparoo Thei
Laphet Yei
Tea with milk / with lemon

ချောကလက် (ဖျော်ရေ)
Chawkalet (Phyawyay)
Chocolate (drink)

B
U
R
M
E
S
E

နို့
Noe
Milk

သရေစာ / အစာပေါ့
Thayaysar / Ahsarpyay
Snacks / Light meals

အသုပ်
Ahthote
Salads

အသားညှုပ်ပေါင်မုန့်
Ahthar Hnyut Paung Mont
Sandwiches

ဥများ
Oo Myar
Eggs

ဝက်အူချောင်း
Wet Oo Chaung
Sausage

ကြက်ဥပြုတ် / ကျော် / အကြေ
Kyet Oo Pyote / Kyaw / Ahkyay
Boiled / fried / scrambled eggs

Typical local dishes

ထမင်းသုပ်
Htaminn Thoat
Rice salad

ကြက်သား အုန်းနို့ ကြက်ဥ ခေါက်ဆွဲ
Kyetthar Ohnoe Kyet Oo Kaukswae
Egg-noodle in chicken coconut gravy

ငါးဟင်းရည် နဲ့ မုန့်ဟင်းခါး
Ngarr Hinyay Ne Moat Hinn Khar
Rice noodle in fish soup

ကြက်သား ဟင်းရည်နဲ့ မုန့်ဟင်းခါး
Kyetthar Hinyay Ne Moat Hinn Khar
Rice noodles with chicken curry

ကြက်သားကြာဆန် ပူပူလေး
Kyettharr Kyarzan Pu Pu Lay
Vermicelli in hot chicken soup

GETTING AROUND

Public Transport

Where is the bus stop / coach stop / nearest metro (subway) station?
ဘတ်စ်ကားမှတ်တိုင် / ဘူတာရုံ / အနီးဆုံးမြေအောက်ဘူတာဘယမှာလဲ။
Batskar Hmattine / BuutarYon / Ahneesone Myeiaunt Buutar Bae Hmar Le

When is the next / last bus to ...?
... ကို သွားမယ့်နောက် / နောက်ဆုံး ဘတ်စ်ကား ဘယ်တော့လဲ
... Ko Thwar Mae Naut / Nautsone Buskar Bae Tawt Le

How much is the fare to the city centre (downtown) / railway station / airport?
မြို့ထဲ (မြို့လည်) / ဘူတာကြီး / လေဆိပ် ကို သွားရင် ဘယ်လောက် ကျပါသလဲ
Myo Hte (Myo Le) / Buutar Gyi / Laysate Ko Thwar Yin Bae Laut Kya Pa Tha Le

Will you tell me when to get off?
ဘယ်တော့ဆင်းရမယ်ဆိုတာ ပြောပြပါလား
Bae Tawt Hsinn Ya Mae Sodar Pyaw Pya Pa Lar

Does this bus go to ... ?
ဒီဘတ်စ်ကားက ... ကိုသွားပါသလား
Dee Buskar Ka ... Ko Thwar Pa Thalar

Which number bus goes to ... ?
... ကို ဘယ်ဘတ်စ်ကား နံပါတ် ရောက်ပါသလဲ
... Ko Bae Buskar Nunbut Yaut Pa Tha Le

May I have a single (oneway) / return (round-trip) / day ticket / book of tickets?
ကျွန်တော် တစ်ကြောင်း(အသွား) /
အပြန်(အသွား–အပြန်) /
နေ့ချင်းစီးလက်မှတ် / လက်မှတ်စာအုပ်
လိုချင်လို့ပါ
Kyundaw Tagyaung (Ahthwar) / Ahpyun (Ahthwar-Ahpyun) / Naychinsii Let Hmut / Let Hmut Sar Oat Lo Chin Lo Pa

Taxis and Rickshaws

I would like to go to ...
ကျွန်တော် ... ကို သွားချင်လို့ပါ
Kyundaw ... Ko Thwar Chin Lo Pa

How much will it cost?
ဘယ်လောက်ကျပါသလဲ
Bae Laut Kya Pa Tha Le

Please may I stop here?
ကျေးဇူးပြု၍ ဒီနားမှာ ရပ်ပါရစေ
Kyayzu Pyu Ywayt Dee Nayyar Hmar Yut Pa Ya Sae

I would like to order a taxi today / tomorrow / at 2pm to go from ... to ...
ကျွန်တော် ဒီနေ့ / မနက်ဖြန် / နှစ်နာရီမှာ
... ကနေ ... ကို သွားဖို့ တက်ကစီ တစ်စင်း
ခေါ်ချင်လို့ပါ
Kyundaw Dee Nay / Manet Phyun / Hna Naryee Hmar ... Ka Nay ... Ko Thwar Phoe Taxi Tazine Khaw Chin Lo Pa

Entertainment

Can you recommend a good bar / nightclub?
ဘားဆိုင်ကောင်းကောင်း /
နိုက်ကလပ်ကောင်းကောင်း ညွှန်ပြပေးပါလား
Barsaing Kaung Kaung / Nitekalut Kaung Kaung Hnyon Pya Pay Pa Lar

Do you know what is on at the cinema (playing at the movies) / theatre at the moment?
ရုပ်ရှင်ရုံမှာ / ကပွဲရုံမှာ အခု ဘာပွဲပြနေပါသလဲ
Yoteshin Yone Hmar / Kapwe Yone Hmar Ahkhu Ba Pwe Pya Nay Pa Tha Le

I would like to book (purchase) ... tickets for the matinee / evening performance on Monday
ကျွန်တော်တနင်္လာနေ့နေ့ပွဲ / ညပွဲ
လက်မှတ်...စောင်မှာ (ဝယ်)ချင်ထယ်။
Kyundaw Taninlar Nay Nay Pwe / Nya Pwe Let Hmut ... Saung Hmar (Wae) Chin Dae

What time does the film / performance start?
ဘယ်အချိန်မှာရုပ်ရှင် / ဇါတ်ပွဲပြမလဲ။
Be Akhyein My Yout Hyin / Za Pwe Pya Ma Le

COMMUNICATIONS

Post

How much will it cost to send a letter / postcard / this package to Britain / Ireland / America / Canada / Australia / New Zealand?
စာ / ပို့စ်ကဒ် / ဒီအထုပ်ကို ဗြိတိန် /
အိုင်ယာလန် / အမေရိက / ကနေဒါ /
ဩစတေးလျ / နယူးဇီလန်သို့ ပို့ချင်ပါတယ်
ဘယ်လောက်ကျမှာပါလဲ

BURMESE

BURMESE

Sar / Post Kart / Dee Ahaut Ko Byeetain / Irrland / Ahmayrikar / Kanadar / Oustralear / Nayuziland Thot Pot Chin Par Dae Bae Laut Kya Hmar Par Le

I would like one stamp / two stamps
ကျွန်တော် တံဆိပ်ခေါင်း၊ တစ်ခု / နှစ်ခု လိုချင်ပါတယ်
Kyandaw Tasait Chaung Titkhut / Hnitkhut Lo Chin Par Tae

I'd like ... stamps for postcards to send abroad, please
ကျေးဇူးပြု၍ ကျွန်တော် နိုင်ငံခြားတိုင်းပြည်သို့ ကဒ်ပို့ရန် ... တံဆိပ်ခေါင်း လိုချင်ပါတယ်
Kyayzu Pyu Ywayt Kyundaw Naing Ngai Char Taing Pye Thot Kat Pot Yan ... Tasait Chaung Lo Chin Par Tae

Phones

I would like to make a telephone call / reverse the charges to (make a collect call to) ...
ကျွန်တော် တယ်လီဖုန်း ခေါ် / ကြိုတင် နေရာယူချင်လို့ပါ (ခေါ်ချင်တဲ့နေရာ) ...
Kyandaw Tele Phone Khaw / Kyotin Nayyar Yu Chin Lo Par (Khaw Chin Dae Nayyar) ...

Which coins do I need for the telephone?
ကျွန်တော် တယ်လီဖုန်းခေါ်ရန် ဘယ်အကြွေစေ့ လိုလဲ
Kyandaw Tele Phone Khaw Yan Bae Ahkyawy Sae Lo Le

The line is engaged (busy)
လိုင်းမအားပါ
Line Ma Arr Pa

The number is ...
နံပါတ် ... ဖြစ်တယ်
Nanbut ... Phyt Tae

Hello, this is ...
မင်္ဂလာပါ၊ ဒီဟာ ... ဖြစ်တယ်။
Minglar Par, Dee Har ... Phyt Tae

Please may I speak to ...?
ကျွန်တော် ... နဲ့ စကားပြောချင်တယ်။
Kyundaw ... Ne Sakar Pyaw Chin Dae

He / she is not in at the moment. Can you call back?
အခုသူ / သူမ မရှိဘူး။
နောင်မှာဖုန်းဆက်ပေးပါ။
Ahkhu Thu / Thuma Ma Shee Pa. Naung Hmar Phan Hsat Pey Par

SHOPPING

Shops

စာအုပ်ဆိုင် / စာရေးကရိယာဆိုင်
Sar Ooat Saing / Sar Yae KaYai Yar Saing
Bookshop / Stationery

ကျောက်မျက်ရတနာ / လက်ဆောင်
Kyauk Myat Ya Ta Nar / Lack Saung
Jeweller / Gifts

ရှူးဖိနပ်များ
Shoe Phae Nut Myar
Shoes

ကုန်မာများ
Kong Mar Myar
Hardware

ဆံပင်ညှပ်သူ
Sapyin Hnyut Thu
Hairdresser

ယောက်ကျားများ၏ / မိန်းမများ၏
(Yauk Kyar Myar Ei) /
(Mainn Ma Myar Ei)
(men's) / (women's)

ပေါင်မုန့်ဖုတ်သူ
Paung Moint Phote Thu
Baker

ဖုန်းများ
Phone Myar
Phones

ကုန်တိုက်ကြီး
Kaung Taik Kyi
Supermarket

ဓါတ်ပုံဆိုင်
Dutt Pone Saing
Photo-Shop

ခရီးသွား ကိုယ်စားလှယ်
Khayee Thwar Ko Sar Hteal
Travel agent

ဆေးဝါး
Say War
Pharmacy

In the Shops

What time do the shops open / close?
ဆိုင်ဘယ်အချိန် ဖွင့် / ပိတ်ပါသလဲ
Saing Be Ahchang Phunt /
Pait Par Tha Le

Where is the nearest market?
အနီးဆုံးဈေးက ဘယ်နားမှာလဲ
Ahnee Sone Zay Ka Be Nar Hmar Le

Can you show me the one in the window / this one?
ခင်ဗျား ကျွန်တော်ကို ပြတင်းပေါက်ပြပေး
နိုင်မလား / ဒါလား
Kyinbyar Kyunduw Ko Pyadin Pauk
Pya Pay Naing Ma Lar / Dar Lar

Can I try this on?
ကျွန်တော် ဝတ်ကြည့်လို့ ရလား
Kyandaw Wait Kyee Lot Ya Lar

What size is this?
ဒီဟာ ဘာဆိုဒ်လဲ
Dee Har Bar Size Lae

This is too large / too small / too expensive
ဒီဟာက သိပ်ကြီး / သိပ်သေး / သိပ်ဈေးကြီးတယ်
Dee Har Ka Thait Kyee / Thait Thae /
Thait Zay Kyee Tae

Do you have any others?
ခင်ဗျားမှာ တစ်ခြားဟာ ရှိသေးလား
Khinbyar Hmar Tachar Har Shee Thae
Lar

My size is ...
ကျွန်တော့်အရွယ် ... ဖြစ်ကာယ်
Kyanduw Ayuwl ... Phyt lae

Where is the changing room / children's / cosmetic / ladieswear / menswear / food department?
အဝတ်လဲခန်း / ကလေး / အလှပြင်ပစ္စည်း /
အမျိုးသမီးဝတ် / အမျိုးသားဝတ် /
အစားအသောက် ရောင်းတဲ့နေရာ ဘယ်မှာလဲ
Ahwuit Laee Khann / Kalay /
Ahla Pyin Pyitsee / Ahmyothamee /
Ahmyothar / Asar Athaut Yaung Teat
Nayyar Bae Hmar Le

BURMESE

BURMESE

I would like ... a quarter of a kilo / half a kilo / a kilo of bread / butter / cheese / ham / this fruit

ကျွန်တော် ကီလိုတစ်စိတ် / ကီလိုတစ်ဝက် / တစ်ကီလို ပေါင်မုန့် / ထောပတ် / ချိစ် / ဝက်ပေါင် / ဒီအသီး လိုချင်ပါတယ်

Kyundaw Kilo Titsait / Kilo Tiwaik / Titkilo Paung Moint / Htaw Patt / Cheese / Wet Paung Chaut / Dee Ahthee Lo Chin Par Dae

How much is this?

ဒီဟာဘယ်လောက်လဲ

Dee Har Bae Laut Le

I'll take this one, thank you

ကျွန်တော် ဒီဟာကို ယူမယ်၊ ကျေးဇူးတင်ပါတယ်

Kyundaw Dee Har Ko Yu Mae, Kyae Zu Tin Par Dae

Do you have a carrier (shopping) bag?

ခင်ဗျားမှာ သယ်တဲ့အိတ် (ဈေးဝယ်) အိတ် ရှိလား

Khinbyar Hmar Thae Dae Eit (Zay Wail) Eit Shee Lar

Do you have anything cheaper / larger / smaller / of better quality?

ခင်ဗျားဆီမှာဈေးပေါ / ပိုကြီး / ပိုယ် / ပိုကောင်း တာရှိရဲ့လား။

Khinbyar His Hmar Zay Poo / Poe Kyii / Poe Nge / Poe Kaung Tar Hyi Ye Lar

I would like a film / to develop this film for this camera

ကျွန်တော်ဖလင်တစ်လိပ်လို / ဒီကင်မရာရဲ့ ဖလင်ဆေးချင်တယ်။

Kyundaw Pha Ling Ta Leit Loo / Dee Kin Ma Yar Ye Phaling Hseii Chin Dae

I would like some batteries, the same size as this old one

ကျွန်တော် ဘက်ထရီအချို့၊ နဂိုအရွယ် အတိုင်း လိုချင်ပါတယ်

Kyundaw Batters Achot, Nago Ahyawl Ahtaing Lo Chin Par Dae

Would you mind wrapping this for me, please?

ကျေးဇူးပြု၍ ကျွန်တော် အတွက် ဒီဟာလေး ထုတ်ပေးပါ

Kyayzu Pyu Ywayt Kyundaw Ahtwet Dee Har Lay Htaut Pay Par

Sorry, but you seem to have given me the wrong change

ဝမ်းနည်းပါယ် ခင်ဗျားမှားပြီ ထင်တယ်

Wun Nee Par Dae, Khinbyar Hmar Pye Htin Dae

MOTORING

Car Hire (Rental)

I have ordered (rented) a car in the name of ...

ကျွန်တော် ... နာမည်နှင့် ကားမှာ (ငှါး) ချင်လို့ပါ

Kyundaw ... Nar Mae Hnit Car Hmar (Hnar) Chin Lot Par

How much does it cost to hire (rent) a car for one day / two days / a week?

တစ်ရက် / နှစ်ရက် / တစ်ပတ် အတွက် ကားငှါး ဘယ်လောက်ကျပါသလဲ

Tityet / Hnityey / Titpat Ahtwet Car Hnar Kha Bae Laut Kya Par Thale

Is the tank already full of petrol (gas)?

တိုင်ကီမှာ ဓါတ်ဆီ (ဓါတ်ငွေ့)
အပြည့်ရှိလား
*Tike Hmar Dutsi (Dut Ahnwae)
Ahpyae Shee Lar*

**Is insurance and tax included?
How much is the deposit?**

အာမခံ နှင့် အခွန်ငွေ
ပါသလား၊ စရံ ဘယ်လောက်လဲ
*Ahmakhan Hnint Ahchun Ngwe
Par Thalar. Sayan Bae Laut Le*

By what time must I return the car?

ကျွန်တော်တယ်အချိန်မှာ ကားပြန်ပေးရမှာလဲ
*Kyundaw Bae Ahchang Hmar Car Pyan
Pay Ya Hmar Le*

I would like a small / large / family / sports car with a radio / cassette player

ကျွန်တော် ရေဒီယို / ကက်ဆက်နှင့် အသေး /
အကြီး / မိသားစု / ကစားစရာ ကားလိုချင်ပါတယ်
*Kyundaw Yaediro / Ketset Hnint
Ahthaee / Ahkyee / Mitharsu /
Kasar Sayar Car Lo Chin Par Dae*

Do you have a road map?

ဇင်ဗျားမှာ လမ်းပြမြေပုံရှိလား
*Khinbyar Hmar Lan Pya Myaypon Shee
Lar*

Parking

How long can I park here?

ကျွန်တော် ဒီမှာ ဘယ်လောက်ကြာအောင်
ရပ်လို့ ရပါသလဲ
*Kyandaw Dee Hmar Bae Laut Kyar
Aung Yat Lot Ya Pa Tha Le*

Is there a car park near here?

ဒီနားမှာ ကားရပ်ရန် နေရာ ရှိပါသလား
*Dee Nar Hmar Car Yat Yan Nayyar
Shee Pa Tha Lar*

At what time does this car park close?

ဘယ်အခိန်မှာ ကားရပ်ရန်နေရာ ပိတ်ပါသလဲ
*Bae Ahchain Hmar Car Yut Yan Nayyar
Pait Par Tha Le*

Signs and Notices

တစ်လမ်းသွား
TitLan Thwar
One way

မဝင်ရ
Ma Win Ya
No entry

မရပ်ရ
Ma Yat Ya
No parking

ကွေ့ပတ်သွားရသောလမ်း
Kwe Part Thwar Ya Thaw Lan
Detour (diversion)

ရပ်
Yat
Stop

ပေး (အလျှော့ပေး) သည်
Pay (Ahshort Pay) Thee
Give way (yield)

ကုန်းလျှောလမ်း
Kone Shaew Lan
Slippery road

BURMESE

35

MOTORING

ပိုပြီး မယူပါနှင့်
Poe Ma Yu Par Hnint
No overtaking

အန္တရာယ် ရှိတယ်
Antayal Shee Tae
Danger!

BURMESE

At the Filling Station

Unleaded (lead-free) / standard / premium / diesel
ခဲမင်းဆောင်မှု မရှိ / အတန်းအစား / အာမခံကြေး / ဒီဇယ်
Chaung Saung Hmu Ma Shee / Atan Asar / Armakhan Kyee / Disel

Fill the tank please
ကျေးဇူးပြု၍ အပြည့်ဖြည့်ပါ
Kyayzu Pyu Ywayt Ahpyae Phye Par

Do you have a road map?
ခင်ဗျားမှာ လမ်းပြမြေပုံ ရှိသလား
Khinbyar Hmar Lan May Pon Shee Tha Lar

How much is the car wash?
ကားရေဆေးခ ဘယ်လောက်လဲ
Car Yae Say Kha Bae Laut Le

Breakdowns

I've had a breakdown at ...
ကျွန်တော် ... ကျိုးသွားပြီ
Kyundaw ...Kyo Thwar Pyee

I am a member of the [motoring organisation]
ကျွန်တော် အဖွဲ့ဝင် ... [အဖွဲ့အစည်း]
Kyundaw Ahphuit Win [Ahphuit Ahsie]

I am on the road from ... to ...
ကျွန်တော် ... လမ်းမှ ... သို့ သွားလမ်းမှာပါ
Kyundaw ...Lan Hma ...Thot Thwar Lan Hmar Par

I can't move the car. Can you send a tow-truck?
ကျွန်တော်ကားသွားလို့ မရတော့ဘူး ခင်ဗျား ကြိုးနဲ့ဆွဲပေးနိုင်မလား
Kyundaw Car Thwar Lot Ma Ya Tat Bu. Khinbyar Kyo Net Swee Pay Naing Ma Lar

I have a flat tyre
ကျွန်တော်မှာ ပြားသော တာယာတစ်ခု ရှိတယ်
Kyundaw Hmar Pyar Thaw Tayar Tichu Shee Dae

The windscreen (windshield) has smashed / cracked
ကားမှန် အစိတ်ကွဲ / ကွဲအက်သွားပြီ
Car Hman Ahsait Sait Kwe / Kwe Eitt Thwar Pye

There is something wrong with the engine / brakes / lights / steering / gearbox / clutch / exhaust
အင်ဂျင် / ဘရိတ် / မီး / စီရာတိုင် / ဂီယာဘောက် / ကလပ် / အိတ်ဇော တစ်ခုခု ပျက်ပြီ
Ingine / Bayake / Mee / Siyartaing / Giyar Box / Kalut / Eitzaw Tichu Khu Pyat Pyi

It's overheating
ထိုဟာ အပူလွန်နေတယ်
Htoo Har AhpuLwin Nay Tae

It won't start
ထိုဟာ မစနိုင်တော့ဘူး
Htoo Har Ma Sa Naing Tat Bu

Where can I get it repaired?
ကျွန်တော် ဘယ်မှာ ပြင်လို့ ရနိုင်ပါသလဲ
Kyandaw Be Hmar Pyin Lot Ya Naing Pa Tha Le

Can you take me there?
အဲဒီနေရာသို့ ခင်များကျွန်တော့်ကို ခေါ် သွားနိုင်မလား
Ere Dee Nayyar Thot Khinbyar Kyunday Ko Khaw Thwar Naing Ma Lar

Will it take long to fix?
တည့်မြဲဖို့ အချိန်ယူရမယ်
Tee Myal Pho Achain Yu Ya Mae

How much will it cost?
ဒါဘယ်လောက်ကျမယ်လဲ
Dar Bae Loat Kya Thale

Please can you pick me up / give me a lift?
ကျေးဇူးပြု၍ ကျွန်တော့်ကို ဓါတ်လှေခါးဆီ ပို့ပေးပါ
Kyayzu Pyu Ywayt Kyundaw Ko Dut Hlay Khar Si Pot Pay Pa

Accidents and Traffic Offences

Can you help me? There has been an accident
ကူညီပါ။ မယောဂ်ကနေ့ ထိခိုက်မှု ဖြစ်နေပါတယ်
Kuu Nyi Par. Ma Taw Tasa Hti Chait Hmu Phyt Nay Par Dae

Please call the police / an ambulance
ကျေးဇူးပြု၍ ရဲ / အရေးပေါ်ကားခေါ်ပါ
Kyayzu Pyu Ywayt Ye / Ahyaypaw Khaw Par

Is anyone hurt?
တစ်ယောက်ယောက်နာသွားလား
Tayauk Yauk Nar Thwar Lar

I'm sorry, I didn't see the sign
ကျွန်တော့်ဝမ်းနည်းပါတယ်၊ ကျွန်တော် ဆိုင်းဘုတ်ကို မမြင်လို့ပါ
Kyundaw Wun Nee Par Dae. Kyundaw Sing Boat Ko Ma Myin Lot Par

Must I pay a fine? How much?
ကျွန်တော် နောက်ကျကြေး ဘယ်လောက်ပေးရမှာလဲ၊ ဘယ်လောက်လဲ
Kyandaw Naut Kya Kyee Bae Laut Pay Ya Hmar Le, Bae Laut Le

Show me your documents
မင်းရဲ့ အထောက်အထားများကို ပြပါ
Khinbyar Yet Ahaut Ahtar Myar Ko Pya Pa

Pharmacy

Do you have anything for a stomach ache / headache / sore throat / toothache?
ခင်များ မှာ ဗိုက်နာ / ခေါင်းကိုက် / လည်ချောင်းနာ / သွားနာ ပျောက်ဆေး ရှိလား
Khinbyar Hmar Bit Nar / Gaung Kite / Le Chaung Nar / Thwar Nar Pyaut Say Shee Lar

I need something for diarrhoea / constipation / a cold / a cough / insect bites / sunburn / travel (motion) sickness (car) (plane) (boat)
ကျွန်တော် ဝမ်းလျော / ဝမ်းချုပ် / အအေးမိ / ချောင်းဆိုး / အကောင်ကိုက် / နေလောင် / ကားမူး (လေယာဉ်မူး) (လှေမူး) (ဖြစ်နေလို့) (တစ်ခုခု ပေးပါ)
Kyundaw Wunshaw / Wunchote / Ah Ayemi / Chaung Hsoe / Ahkaung Kite / Nay Laung / Kar Muu (Layyin Muu) (Hlay Muu) Phyit Nay Lo Ta Khu Khu Pay Pa

37

HEALTH

B U R M E S E

How much / how many do I take?
ဘယ်လောက် / ဘယ်လောက်များများ
သောက်ရမလဲ
*Bae Laut / Bae Laut Myar Myar
Thaut Ya Ma Le*

How often do I take it / them?
ဘယ်နှစ်ခါ သောက်ရမလဲ
Bae Nakhar Thaut Ya Ma Le

I am / he is / she is taking this medication
ကျွန်တော် / သူ / သူမ ဒီဆေးသောက်နေရတယ်
*Kyundaw / Thu / Thuma Dee Say Thaut
Nay Ya Da*

How much does it cost?
ဘယ်လောက်ကြာပြီလဲ
Bae Laut Kya Pa Le

Can you recommend a good doctor / dentist?
ဆရာဝန်ကောင်းကောင်း /
သွားဆရာဝန်ကောင်းကောင်းနှင့် ပြပေးပါလား
*Sayawun Kaung Kaung / Thwar
Sayawun Kaung Kaung Hnyon Pya Pay
Pa Lar*

Is it suitable for children?
ကလေးတွေနဲ့ တည့်ပါသလား
Kalay Tway Ne Te Pa Thalar

Doctor

I have a pain here / in my arm / leg / chest / stomach
ကျွန်တော် ဒီနေရာ / လက်မောင်းမှာ /
ခြေထောက် / ရင်ဘတ် / ဗိုက်မှာနာနေလို့ပါ
*Kyundaw Dee Nayyar / Let Maung
Hmar / Chaydauk / Yinbut / Bite Hmar
Nar Nay Lo Pa*

Please call a doctor, this is an emergency
ဆရာဝန် ခေါ်ပါ၊ ဒါ အရေးပေါ်ကပါ
Sayawun Khaw Pa, Dar Ahyaypaw Pa

I would like to make an appointment to see the doctor
ကျွန်တော် ဆရာဝန်နဲ့ တွေ့ဖို့
ချိန်းဆိုချင်ပါတယ်
*Kyundaw Sayawun Ne Twayt Phoe
Chain So Chin Pa Dae*

I am diabetic / pregnant
ကျွန်တော် (ကျွန်မ) ဆီးချိုရောဂါသည် /
ကိုယ်ဝန်သည်ပါ
*Kyundaw ("Kyunma" For Female)
Seecho Yawga Thae / Kowun Thae Pa*

I need a prescription for ...
ကျွန်တော် ... ရဲ့ထွက်လိုပါတယ်
Kyundaw ... Ahnyune Ahtwet Lo Pa Dae

Can you give me something to ease the pain?
ကျွန်တော် ကို အနာသက်သာအောင်
တစ်ခု ခု ပေးပါ
*Kyundaw Ko Ahnar Thet Thar Aung
Takhu Khu Pay Pa*

I am / he is / she is allergic to penicillin
ကျွန်တော် / သူ / သူမ ပနီစီလင် မတဲ့ဘူး
*Kyundaw / Thu / Thu Ma Penicillin Ma
Tae Buu*

Does this hurt?
နာလား
Nar Lar

You must / he must / she must go to hospital
ခင်ဗျား / သူ / သူမ ဆေးရုံတက်ရမယ်
*Khinbyar / Thu / Thu Ma Sayyon Tet Ya
Mae*

B
U
R
M
E
S
E

Take these once / twice / three times a day

ဒီဟာတွေ ကို တစ်နေ့ တစ်ကြိမ် / နှစ်ကြိမ် / သုံးကြိမ် သောက်ပါ

Dee Har Tway Ko Tanay Tagyain / Hnagyain / Thonegyain Thaut Pa

I am / he is / she is taking this medication

ကျွန်တော် / သူ / သူမ ဒီဆေး သောက်နေရတာယ်

Kyundaw / Thu / Thuma Dee Say Thaut Nay Ya Da

I have medical insurance

ကျွန်တော့်မှာ ဆေး အာမခံ ရှိတယ်

Kyundaw Hmar Say Armakhan Shee Dae

Dentist

I have toothache

ကျွန်တော် သွားကိုက်နေတယ်

Kyundaw Thwar Kite Nay Dae

My filling has come out

ကျွန်တော် ဆေးထည့်ထားတာ ထွက်ကုန်ပြီ

Kyundaw Say Hte Htartar Htwet Kone Pyee

I do / do not want to have an injection first

ကျွန်တော် ဆေး အရင် ကိုးချင်ပါယ် / မလိုချင်ပါဘူး

Kyundaw Say Ahyin Htoe Chin Dae / Ma Htoe Chin Buu

EMERGENCIES

Help!

ကူကြပါ

Kae Kya Pa

Fire!

မီးရှို့

Mee Byoe

Stop!

ရပ်

Yut

Call an ambulance / a doctor / the police / the fire brigade!

သူနာတင်ကား / ဆရာဝန် / ရဲ / မီးသတ်အဖွဲ့ ကိုအကြောင်းကြားလိုက်ပါ။

ThuNarTinKur / Sayawun / Ye / Mee Thut Ahpwet Ko Agyaung Kyar Lite Pa

Please may I use a telephone?

တယ်လီဖုန်းကိုသုံးပါရစေ။

Telee Fone Ko Thone Par Ya Sae

I have had my traveller's cheques / credit cards / handbag / rucksack / (knapsack) / luggage / wallet / passport / mobile phone stolen

ကျွန်တော့်မှာ ခရီးသွား ချက်လက်မှတ် / အကြွေးဝယ်ကဒ် / ခရီးဆောင်အိတ် / ကျောပိုးအိတ် / (နောက်ပိုးလွယ်အိတ်) / တန်ဆာအိတ် / ပိုက်ဆံအိတ် / နိုင်ငံကူးလက်မှတ် / လက်ကိုင်ဖုန်း အခိုးခံရလို့

Kyundaw Hmar Khayee Thwar Chet Let Hmut / Ahkyway Wae Card / Khayee Saung Eit / Kyaw Poe Eit / (Naut Poe Lwae Eit) / Tansar Eit / Paiksan Eit / Naingan Kuu I et Hmut / Let Kaing Phone Ah Khoe Khun Ya Lo

May I please have a copy of the report for my insurance claim?

ကျေးဇူးပြု၍ ကျွန်တော့် အာမခံဗာတမ်းကို မိတ္တူကူး ပါရစေ

Kyayzy Pyu Ywayt Kyundaw Armakhan Sartan Ko Mate Tu Kuu Pa Ya Sae

BURMESE

Can you help me? I have lost my daughter / my son / my companion(s)
ကူညီပါအုံး ။ ကျွန်တော့ သမီး /
သား / အဖော် (တွေ) ပျောက်သွားလို့
Ku Nyee Pa Ohn? Kyundaw Thamee / Thar / Ahphaw (Tway) Pyauk Thwar Lo

Please go away / leave me alone
သွားပါ / ထားခဲ့ပါ
Thwar Pa / Htar Khe Pa

I'm sorry
ကျွန်တော်ဝမ်းနည်းပါတယ်
Kyundaw Wun Ne Pa Dae

I want to contact the British / American / Canadian / Irish / Australian / New Zealand / South African consulate
ကျွန်တော် ဗြိတိသျှ / အမေရိကန် /
ကနေဒါနိုင်ငံ / အိုင်ယာလန် /
သြစတေးလျား / နယူးဇီလန် /
တောင်အာဖရိက သံရုံးနဲ့ဆက်သွယ်ချင်ပါတယ်
Kyundaw Byee Ti Sha / Ahmayrikan / Kanayda Naingan / Ireland / Oustaylear / New Zealand / Taung Africa Thanyone Ne Set Thwe Chin Pa Dae

I'm / we're / he is / she is ill / lost / injured
ကျွန်တော် / ကျွန်တော်တို့ / သူ / သူမ
ဖျား / လမ်းမှား / ဒဏ်ရာရ နေတယ်။
Kyundaw / Kyundaw Toe/ Thu / Thu Ma Toe Phyar / Lun Hmar / Danyar Ya Nei Dae

They are ill / lost / injured
သူတို့ ဖျား / လမ်းမှား / ဒဏ်ရာရ နေတယ်။
Thu Toe Phyar / Lun Hmar / Danyar Ya Nei Dae

CHINESE
中文

C
H
I
N
E
S
E

INTRODUCTION

More people speak Mandarin (the spoken language of Chinese) than any other language in the world. It is the official language of the People's Republic of China, and is widely spoken throughout East Asia, particularly in Taiwan and Singapore.

Chinese belongs to a linguistic family called the Sino-Tibetan languages. Compared to western languages, they seem quite different: they are monosyllabic and there is noticeably less inflection. They are known as "tonal": words with different meanings that sound rather similar are differentiated by pitch (high, medium, low, falling or rising).

Modern Chinese assigns a single symbol or character to each word. Since 1892, Chinese words other than personal and place-names, have been transliterated phonetically in the English-speaking world (known as hanyu pinyin), to ease western comprehension. In this phrasebook we will be using the most widely-used method of transliteration.

Addresses for Travel and Tourist Information

Australia: Chinese Embassy; 15 Coronation Drive, Yarralumla ACT 2600. Tel: 02 6273 4780; Fax: 02 6273 4878; Web: http://au.china-embassy.org/eng

Canada: Chinese Embassy; 515 St Patrick St, Ottawa, Ontario K1N 5H3. Tel: 613 789 3434; Fax: 613 789 1911; Web: www.chinaembassycanada.org/eng

UK: Chinese Embassy; 49-51 Portland Place London W1B 1JL. Tel: 020 7299 4049; Web: www.chinese-embassy.org.uk/eng

USA: Chinese Embassy; 2300 Connecticut Ave NW, Washington DC 20008. Tel: 202 338 6688 or 202 328 2517

People's Republic of China Facts

CAPITAL: Beijing

CURRENCY: Yuan (¥); 1 Yuan =10 mao/jiao=100 fen.

OPENING HOURS: Banks: Most banks are open Mon-Fri 0900-1200 and 1400-1700; in the major cities some will be open at the weekend. Shops: nearly all open daily, keeping late hours. Museums usually have one closing day each week (Mon or Tues), and will close for lunch.

TELEPHONES: To dial mainland China, Tel: International Access Code + 86 + Area Code minus first zero + number. Outgoing, Tel: 00+ Country Code + Area Code minus first zero + number.

EMERGENCY NUMBERS: Police, Tel: 110; Fire, Tel: 119; Ambulance, Tel: 120; (In Hong Kong and Macau, dial 999 for any emergency service.)

PUBLIC HOLIDAYS: **Mainland China**: Jan 1-3 – New Year's Day; Jan/Feb (7 Days) – Chinese New Year; May 1-7 – Labour Day; Oct 1-7 – National Day of the People's Republic of China.
Hong Kong: Jan 1 – New Year's Day; Jan/Feb – Chinese New Year; Apr 5 – Ching Ming (Tomb-Sweeping) Festival; Good Friday; Easter; May 1 – Labour Day; the second Sunday of May – Feast of Buddha (Feast of the bathing of Lord Buddha); June/July (the 5th day of the 5th lunar month) – Dragon Boat Festival (Tuen Ng); July 1 – Hong Kong Special Administrative Region Establishment Day; Sept/Oct (the 15th Day of the 8th lunar month) – Mid-Autumn Festival; Oct 1 – National Day of the People's Republic of China; Chung Yeung Festival; Dec 24-25 – Christmas Day;
Macau: Jan 1 – New Year's Day; Jan/Feb – Chinese New Year; Apr 5 – Ching Ming (Tomb-Sweeping) Festival; Good Friday; Easter; May 1 – Labour Day; the second Sunday of May – Feast of Buddha (Feast of the bathing of Lord Buddha); June/July (the 5th day of the 5th lunar month) – Dragon Boat Festival (Tuen Ng); Sept/Oct (the 15th Day of the 8th lunar month) – Mid-Autumn Festival; Oct 1 – National Day of the People's Republic of China; Chung Yeung Festival; Nov 2 – All Souls' Day; Dec 8 – Feast of the Immaculate Conception; Dec 20 – Macau Special Administrative Region Establishment Day; Dec 21 – Winter Solstice; Dec 24-25 – Christmas Day.

Technical Language Hints

- Try to keep your tone as bland as possible – this will help difficulties over meaning varying over tone – the word you mean will usually be evident by context. After that, you can start copying the speech patterns of native speakers and you will soon be much more at ease with the different tones.

- Concentrate on getting word order right. It is very important, as Chinese can otherwise be grammatically vague: verb tense is not expressed and there is no indication that verbs, nouns and adjectives agree with each other in number or case.

- When listening to spoken Chinese, ease translation by trying to break up each string of words into single syllables. Many words that sound complex will in fact be compounds – formed by chaining syllables together.

C H I N E S E

Basic Words and Phrases

Yes 是 *Sh*	**No** 不是 *Boo-Sh*
Please 请 *Ching*	**Thank you** 谢谢 *Shie-Shie*
Hello 你好 *Nee-How*	**Goodbye** 再见 *Dsai-Jian*
Excuse me 请问 *Ching-When*	**Sorry** 对不起 *Dway-Boo-Chee*
How 怎么 *Dsen-Mo*	**When** 几时 *Jee-Sh*
Why 为什么 *Way-Shen-Mo*	**What** 什么 *Shen-Mo*
Who 谁 *Shwee*	
That's O.K. 没关系 *May-Gwan-Shee*	**Perhaps** 可能 *Ke-Nung*
To 去 *Chew*	**From** 来自 *Lie-Ds*
Here 这里 *Jer-Lee*	**There** 那里 *Na-Lee*

I don't understand
我不懂
Wo-Boo-Dong

I don't speak Mandarin
我不会说中文
Wo Boo-Hway Sho Jong-When

Do you speak English?
你会说英语吗?
Nee Hway Sho Ying-Yu Ma

Can you please write it down?
能请你写下来吗?
Nung Ching-Nee Shie-Shia-Lie Ma

Please can you speak more slowly?
能请你说慢点吗?
Nung Ching Nee Sho-Man-Dian Ma

Greetings

**Good morning /
Good afternoon /
Good evening / Goodnight**
早上好 / 下午好 / 晚上好 / 晚安
*Dsao-Shang-How / Shia-Woo-How /
Wan-Shang-How / Wan-An*

Pleased to meet you
很高兴认识你
Hen-Gao-Shing Ren-Sh-Nee

How are you?
你好吗?
Nee How Ma

Well, thank you. And you?
我很好。 谢谢。 你呢?
Wo Hen-Hao. Shie-Shie. Nee Ne

My name is ...
我的名字叫…
Wo De Mean-Ds Jiao ...

This is my friend / boyfriend / girlfriend / husband / wife / brother / sister
这是我的朋友 /男朋友 /女朋友 /
丈夫 /妻子 /兄弟 /姐妹
Jer-Sh Wo De Peng-Yoh / Nan-Peng-Yoh /
Nue-Peng-Yoh / Jang-Foo / Chee-Ds /
Shiong-Dee / Jie-May

Where are you travelling to?
你 /你们要去哪里旅行?
Nee / Nee-Men Yao Chew Na-Lee
Lue-Shing

I am / we are going to ...
我 /我们要去…
Wo / Wo-Men Yao Chew ...

How long are you travelling for?
你 /你们要旅行多久?
Nee / Nee-Men Yao Lue-Shing
Duo-Jiou

Where do you come from?
你 /你们是哪里人?
Nee / Nee-Men Sh Na-Lee Ren

I am / we are from Australia / Britain / Canada / America
我 /我们是澳大利亚人 /
英国人 /加拿大人 /美国人
Wo / Wo-Men Sh Ao-Da-Lee-Ya Ren /
Ying-Guo Ren / Jia Na-Da Ren /
May-Guo Ren

We are on holiday
我们在度假
Wo-Men Dsai Do-Jia

This is our first visit here
我们是第一次来这里
Wo-Men Sh Dee-Yee-Ch Lie Jer-Lee

How old are you?
你几岁了?
Nee Jee-Shway-Le

I am ... years old
我…岁了
Wo ... Shway Le

I am a businessman / business woman / doctor / journalist / manual worker / administrator / scientist / student / teacher
我是商人 /商人 /医生 /记者 /
劳动者 /管理人员 /科学家 /
学生 /老师
Wo Sh Shang-Ren / Shang-Ren /
Yee-Sheng / Jee-Jer / Lao-Dong-Jer /
Gwan-Lee-Ren-Yuan / Ke-Shue-Jia /
Shue-Sheng / Lao-Sh

Would you like / may I have a cigarette?
你要吸烟吗? /我可以吸烟吗?
Nee Yao Shee-Yan Ma / Wo Ke-Yee
Shee-Yan Ma

Do you mind if I smoke?
你介意我吸烟吗?
Nee Jie-Yee Wo Shee-Yan Ma

Do you have a light?
你有打火机吗?
Nee Yoh Da-Huo-Jee Ma

I am waiting for my husband / wife / boyfriend / girlfriend
我在等我的丈夫 /妻子 /
男朋友 /女朋友
Wo Dsai Deng Wo De Jang-Foo /
Chee-Ds / Nan-Peng-Yoh /
Neu-Peng-Yoh

C
H
I
N
E
S
E

45

ESSENTIALS

CHINESE

Days

Monday
星期一
Shing-Chee-Yee

Tuesday
星期二
Shing-Chee-Er

Wednesday
星期三
Shing-Chee-San

Thursday
星期四
Shing-Chee-S

Friday
星期五
Shing-Chee-Woo

Saturday
星期六
Shing-Chee-Leo

Sunday
星期天
Shing-Chee-Tian

Morning
早上
Dsao-Shang

Afternoon
下午
Shia-Woo

Evening
晚上
Wan-Shang

Night
夜晚
Yeh-Wan

Yesterday / Today / Tomorrow
昨天/今天/明天
Dsuo-Tian / Jin-Tian / Mean-Tian

Numbers

Zero
零
Ling

One
一
Yee

Two
二
Er

Three
三
San

Four
四
S

Five
五
Woo

Six
六
Leo

Seven
七
Chee

Eight
八
Ba

Nine
九
Jiou

Ten
十
Sh

Eleven
十一
Sh-Yee

Twelve
十二
Sh-Er

Thirteen
十三
Sh-San

Fourteen
十四
Sh-S

Fifteen
十五
Sh-Woo

Sixteen
十六
Sh-Leo

Seventeen
十七
Sh-Chee

Eighteen
十八
Sh-Ba

Nineteen
十九
Sh-Jiou

Twenty
二十
Er-Sh

Twenty-one
二十一
Er-Sh-Yee

Twenty-two
二十二
Er-Sh-Er

Thirty
三十
San-Sh

Forty
四十
S-Sh

Fifty
五十
Woo-Sh

Sixty
六十
Leo-Sh

Seventy
七十
Chee-Sh

Eighty
八十
Ba-Sh

Ninety
九十
Jiou-Sh

One hundred
一百
Yee-Bye

Five hundred
五百
Woo-Bye

One thousand
一千
Yee-Chain

One million
一百万
Yee-Bye-Wan

Time

What time is it?
现在几点了?
Shian-Dsai Jee-Dian Le

It is ...
现在…
Shian Dsai ...

9.00
九点
Jiou-Dian

9.05
九点零五分
Jiou-Dian-Ling-Woo-Fen

9.15
九点十五分
Jiou-Dian-Sh-Woo-Fen

9.20
九点二十分
Jiou-Dian-Er-Sh-Fen

9.30
九点半
Jiou-Dian-Ban

9.35
九点三十五分
Jiou-Dian-San-Sh-Woo-Fen

9.40
九点四十分
Jiou-Dian-S-Sh-Fen

9.45
九点四十五分
Jiou-Dian-S-Sh-Woo-Fen

9.50
九点五十分
Jiou-Dian-Woo-Sh-Fen

9.55
九点五十五分
Jiou-Dian-Woo-Sh-Woo-Fen

12.00 / Midday / Midnight
十二点/正午/半夜
Sh-Er-Dian / Jeng-Woo / Bann-Yeh

Money

I would like to change these traveller's cheques / this currency
我想兑换这些旅行支票/现金
Wo Shiang Dway-Hwan Jer-Shie Lue-Shing Ds-Piao / Shian-Jean

How much commission do you charge? (What is the service charge?)
你收取多少佣金?
(服务费是多少?)
Nee Shou-Chew Duo-Shao Yong-Jean (Foo-Woo-Fay Sh Duo-Shao)

Can I obtain money with my MasterCard?
我能用万事达卡取现金吗?
Wo Nung Yong Wan-Sh-Da-Ka Chew Shian-Jean Ma

CHINESE

Where is the nearest ATM?
最近的自动取款机在哪里?
Dsway-Jean De Ds-Dong-Chew-Kwan-Jee Dsai Na-Lee

My name is ... Some money has been wired to here for me to collect
我的名字叫…我来领取一笔电汇款
Wo De Mean-Ds Jiao... Wo Lie Ling-Chew Yee-Bee Dian-Hway-Kwan

ARRIVING AND DEPARTING

Airport

Excuse me, where is the check-in desk for ... airline?
请问, …航班的登机手续在哪里办理?
Ching When, ... Hang-Bann De Deng-Jee Sho-Shu Dsai Na-Lee Bann Lee

What is the boarding gate / time for my flight?
我的航班的登记口在哪里? /
几点登机?
Wo De Hang-Ban De Deng-Jee-Ko Dsai Na-Lee / Jee Dian Deng-Jee

How long is the delay likely to be?
大约会延误多长时间?
Da Yue Hway Yan-Woo Duo Chang Sh-Jian

Where is the duty-free shop?
免税商店在哪里?
Mian-Shway Shang-Dian Dsai Na-Lee

Which way is the baggage reclaim?
怎样去行李认领处?
Dsen-Yang Chew Shing-Lee-Ren-Ling-Choo

I have lost my luggage. Please can you help?
我的行李丢了。你能帮忙吗?
Wo De Shing-Lee Dew Le. Nee Nung Bang-Mang Ma

I am flying to...
我要飞往…
Wo Yao Fay-Wang...

Where can I get the bus to the city centre?
我到哪里乘坐开往市中心的公共汽车?
Wo Dao Na-Lee Cheng-Dsuo Kai Wang Sh-Jong-Shin De Gong-Gong-Chee-Che

Trains and Boats

Where is the ticket office / information desk?
售票处 /问询台在哪里?
Shou-Piao-Choo / When-Shun-Tie Dsai Na-Lee

Which platform does the train / speedboat / ferry to ... depart from?
这辆火车 /这艘快艇 /这艘渡轮是停在哪一个站台的?
Jer Liang Huo-Che / Jer So Kwai-Ting / Jer So Do-Loon Sh Ting Dsai Na Yee Ge Jan-Tie De

Where is platform ...?
…站台在哪里?
... Jan-Tie Dsai Na-Lee

48

When is the next train / boat to ...?

下一班去… 的火车/轮船什么时候开?

Shia Yee Bann Chew... De Huo-Che / Loon-Chwan Shen-Mo-Sh-Hou Kai

Is there a later train / boat to ...?

还有下一班去… 的火车/轮船吗?

Hi Yoh Shia-Yee-Bann Chew... De Huo Che / Loon-Chwan Ma

Notices and Signs

餐车
Tsan-Che
Buffet (Dining) car

公共汽车
Gong-Gong-Chee-Che
Bus

饮用/非饮用水
Yin-Yong / Fay-Yin-Yong Shway
Drinking / Non-drinking water

入口
Roo-Ko
Entrance

出口
Choo-Ko
Exit

医院
Yee-Yuan
Hospital

问询处
When-Shun-Choo
Information

行李寄存处 (行李认领处)
Shing-Lee-Jee-Tswun-Choo (Shing-Lee-Ren-Ling-Choo)
Left luggage (Baggage claim)

行李存放箱
Shing-Lee-Tswun-Fang-Shiang
Luggage lockers

邮局
Yoh-Joo
Post office

站台
Jan-Tie
Platform

火车站
Huo-Che Jan
Railway (Railroad) station

机场
Jee-Chang
Airport

警察局
Jing Cha-Joo
Police station

海港
Hi-Gang
Port

餐馆
Tsan-Gwan
Restaurant

吸烟区/非吸烟区
Shee-Yan-Choo / Fay Shee-Yan-Choo
Smoking / Non-smoking

C
H
I
N
E
S
E

C H I N E S E

电话
Dian-Hwa
Telephone

售票处
Sho-Piao-Choo
Ticket office

登记处
Deng-Jee-Choo
Check-in desk

时间表(车次表)
Sh-Jian Biao (Che-Ts Biao)
Timetables (Schedules)

厕所(洗手间)
Tse-Suo (Shee-Shou Jian)
Toilets (Restrooms)

女洗手间/男洗手间
Nue Shee-Shou-Jian /
Nan Shee-Shou-Jian
Ladies / Gentlemen

地铁
Dee-Tyeh
Underground (Subway)

候车室
Hou-Che-Sh
Waiting room

Buying a ticket

I would like a first-class / second-class single (oneway) / return (round-trip) ticket to ...
我要买一张去…的头等舱单程/
往返票
Wo Yao Mai Yee-jang Chew...
De Tou-Deng-Tsang Dan-Cheng /
Wang-Fan Piao

Is it an express (fast) train / bus?
这是特快火车/公共汽车吗?
Jer-sh Te-Kwai Huo-Che /
Gong-Gong-Chee-Che Ma

Is my rail pass valid on this train / ferry / bus?
我的通票能乘坐这辆火车/
这艘渡轮/这辆公共汽车吗?
Wo De Tong-Piao Nung Cheng-Dsuo
Jer Liang Huo-Che / Jer So Do-Chuan /
Jer Liang Gong-Gong-Chee-Che Ma

I would like an aisle / window seat
我想要靠走道/窗的座位
Wo Shiang Yao Kao Dsou-Dao /
Chuang De Dsuo-Way

No smoking / smoking, please
请不要吸烟/请吸烟
Ching Boo-Yao Shee-Yan /
Ching Shee-Yan

We would like to sit together
我们想坐在一起
Wo-Men Shiang Dsuo Dsai Yee-Chee

I would like to make a seat reservation
我想预订一个座位
Wo Shiang Yu-Ding Yee-Ge Dsuo-Way

I would like to reserve a couchette / sleeper for one person / two people / my family
我想预订一个/两个/家人的
卧铺/床位。
Wo Shiang Yu-Ding Yee-Ge /
Liang-Ge / Jia-Ren De Woo-Poo /
Chwang-Way

C
H
I
N
E
S
E

I would like to reserve a cabin
我想预订一个软卧包厢
*Wo Shiang Yu-Ding Yee-Ge Rwan-Woo
Bao-Shiang*

Timetables (Schedules)

到达
Dao-Da
Arrive

经停…站
Jing Ting... Dsan
Calls (Stops) at ...

送餐服务
Song-Tsan Foo-Woo
Catering service

在…换车
Dsai... Hwan-Che
Change at ...

连接/经过
Lian-Jie / Jing-Guo
Connection / Via

每日
May-Ri
Daily

每隔四十分钟
May Ge S-Sh Fen-Jong
Every 40 minutes

头等舱
Tou-Deng-Tsang
First class

每小时
May-Shiao-Sh
Hourly

建议预订座位
Jian-Yee Yu-Ding Dsuo-Way
**Seat reservations are
recommended**

二等舱
Er-Deng-Tsang
Second class

应付补票费
Ying Foo Boo-Piao-Fay
Supplement payable

Luggage

**How much will it cost to send
(ship) my luggage in advance?**
请问提前寄送(船运)我的行李要
多少钱?
*Ching When Tea-Chain Jee-Song
(Chwan-Yun) Wo De Shing-Lee Yao
Duo-Shao-Chain*

**Where is the left luggage
(baggage claim) office?**
请问行李寄存处(行李认领处)
在哪里?
*Ching When Shing-Lee Jee-Tswun-Choo
(Shing-Lee Ren Ling-Choo) Dsai Na Lee*

What time do you open / close?
你们什么时候开门/关门?
*Nee-Men Shen-Mo Sh-Hou Kai-Men /
Gwan-Men*

**Where are the luggage trolleys
(carts)?**
请问行李推车在哪里?
*Ching When Shing-Lee Tway-Che Dsai
Na Lee*

Where are the lockers?
请问行李存放箱在哪里?
Ching When Shing-Lee
Tswun-Fang-Shiang Dsai Na Lee

I have lost my locker key
我的行李存放箱的钥匙丢了
Wo De Shing-Lee-Tswun-Fang-Shiang
De Yao-Sh Dew Le

On Board

Is this seat free?
这个座位有人吗?
Jer-Ge Dsuo-Way Yoh Ren Ma

Excuse me, you are sitting in my reserved seat
很抱歉,你坐在我预订的
位置上了
Hen Bao-Chain, Nee Dsuo Dsai Wo
Yu-Ding De Way-Ds Shang Le

Which station is this?
这是哪一站?
Jer Sh Na-Yee-Jan

What time is this train / bus / ferry / flight due to arrive / depart?
这班火车 /公共汽车 /渡轮 /航班
什么时候到达 /出发?
Jer Bann Huo-Che / Gong-Gong-Chee-
Che / Do-Loon / Hang-Bann Shen-Mo
Sh-Hou Dao-Da / Choo-Fa

Travelling with Children

Do you have a high chair / babysitting service / cot?
请问有高脚椅 /婴儿托管服务 /
婴儿床吗?

Ching When Yoh Gao-Jiao-Yee /
Ying-Er Tuo-Gwan Foo-Woo /
Ying-Er-Chwang Ma

Where is the nursery / playroom?
请问育幼室 /儿童游乐室在哪里?
Ching When Yu-Yoh-Sh /
Er-Tong Yoh-Le-Sh Dsai Na-Lee

Where can I warm the baby's bottle?
请问我在哪里可以加热孩子的
奶瓶?
Ching When Wo Dsai Na-Lee Ke Yee
Jia-Re Hi-Ds De Nai-Pin

Customs and Passports

Passports, please!
请出示你的护照!
Ching Choo-Sh Nee De Hoo-Jao

I have nothing / wine / spirits (alcohol) / tobacco to declare
我没有物品报关。 /我有酒 /
烈酒 /烟草报关
Wo May Yoh Woo-Pin Bao-Gwan. /
Wo Yoh Jiou / Lyeh-Jiou /
Yan-Tsao Bao-Gwan

I will be staying for ... days / weeks / months
我要逗留…天 /星期 /月
Wo Yao Dou-Lio... Tian /
Shing-Chee / Yue

SIGHTSEEING

Asking the Way

Excuse me, do you speak English?
请问,你会说英语吗?

Ching When, Nee Hway Shuo Ying-Yu Ma

Excuse me, can you help me please?
请问，你能帮我吗？
Ching When, Nee Nung Bang Wo Ma

Where is the Tourist Information Office?
游客服务中心在哪里？
Yoh-Ke Foo-Woo Jong-Shin Dsai Na-Lee

Excuse me, is this the right way to ...?
请问，这是去…的路吗？
Ching When, Jer-Sh Chew... De Loo Ma

... the cathedral / the tourist information office / the castle / the old town
…教堂 /游客服务中心 /城堡 /古城
... Jiao-Tang / Yoh-Ke Foo-Woo-Jong-Shin / Cheng-Bao / Goo-Cheng

Can you tell me the way to the railway (railroad) station / bus station / taxi rank (stand) / city centre (downtown) / beach?
请问怎么去火车站 /公共汽车站 / 出租车站 /市中心 /海滩？
Ching When Dsen-Mo Chew Hue Che Jan / Gung-Gong-Chee-Che Jan / Choo-Dsoo-Che Jan / Sh-Jong-Shin / Hi-Tan

First / second / left / right / straight ahead
第一 /第二 /左转 /右转 /直走
Dee-Yee / Dee-Er / Dsuo-Jwan / Yoh-Jwan / J-Dsou

At the corner / at the traffic lights
转角处 /交通灯处
Jwan-Jiuo Choo / Jiao-Tong-Dung Choo

Where is the nearest police station / post office?
请问最近的警察局 /邮局在哪里？
Ching When Dsway-Jean De Jean-Cha-Ju / Yoh-Ju Dsai Na-Lee

Is it near / far?
近 /远吗？
Jean / Yuan Ma

Do I need to take a taxi / catch a bus?
我需要搭出租车 /公共汽车吗？
Wo Shu Yao Da Choo-Dsoo-Che / Gong-Gong-Chee-Che Ma

Do you have a map?
你有地图吗？
Nee Yoh Dee-Too Ma

Can you point to it on my map?
你能帮我在地图上指出来吗？
Nee Nung Bang Wo Dsai Dee-Too Shang Ds-Chew-Lie Ma

Thank you for your help
谢谢你的帮助
Shie-Shie Nee De Bang-Joo

How do I reach the motorway / main road?
请问我要怎么上快速公路 /主干道？
Ching When Wo Yao Dsen-Mo Shang Kwai-Sue-Gong-Loo / Joo-Gan-Dao

I think I have taken the wrong turning
我想我转错方向了
Wo Shiang Wo Jwan Tsuo Fang-Shiang Le

I am looking for this address
我在找这个地方
Wo Dsai Jao Jer-Ge Dee Fang

**C
H
I
N
E
S
E**

I am looking for the ... hotel
我在找…酒店
Wo Dsai Jao... Jiou-Dian

How far is it to ... from here?
从这里去…有多远?
Tsong Jer-Lee Chew... Yoh Duo Yuan

**Carry straight on for ...
kilometres**
直走…公里
J-Jiou ... Gong-Lee

**Take the next turning on the
right / left**
下一个转弯处转右/左
*Shia-Yee-ge Jwan-Wan-Choo
Jwan Yoh / Dsuo*

**Turn right / left at the next
crossroads / traffic lights**
下一个十字路口/交通灯处转右/左
*Shia-Yee-Ge Sh-Ds Loo-Ko /
Jiao-Tong-Dung Choo Jwan Yoh / Dsuo*

**You are going in the wrong
direction**
你走错方向了
Nee Dsou Tsuo Fang-Shiang Le

**Where is the cathedral /
church / museum / pharmacy?**
请问大教堂/教堂/博物馆/
药店在哪里?
*Ching When Da-Jiao-Tang /
Jiao-Tang / Bo-Woo-Gwan /
Yao-Dian Dsai Na Lee*

**How much is the admission /
entrance charge?**
门票/入场费是多少钱?
*Men-Piao / Roo-Chang-Fay Sh
Duo-Shao-Chain*

**Is there a discount for children /
students / senior citizens?**
儿童/学生/老年人有折扣吗?
*Er-Tong / Shue-Sheng / Lao-Nian-Ren
Yoh Jer-Ko Ma*

**What time does the next
guided tour (in English) start?**
下一次导游游览(英语)什么时候
开始?
*Shia-Yee-Ts Dao-Yoh Yoh-Lan (Ying-Yu)
Shen-Mo Sh-Hou Kai-Sh*

**One / two adults / children,
please**
一个/两个成人/儿童
Yee-Ge / Liang-Ge Cheng-Ren / Er-Tong

May I take photographs here?
我可以在这里拍照吗?
Wo Ke-Yee Dsai Jer-Lee Pie-Jao Ma

At the Tourist Office

**Do you have a map of the
town / area?**
你有这个城镇/地区的地图吗?
*Nee Yoh Jer-Ge Cheng-Jeng / Dee-Chew
De Dee-Too Ma*

**Do you have a list of
accommodation?**
你有本地的住宿手册吗?
*Nee Yoh Ben-Dee De Dsoo-Soo
Shou-Che Ma*

Can I reserve accommodation?
我可以预订住宿吗?
Wo Ke-Yee Yu-Ding Dsoo-Soo Ma

54

ACCOMMODATION

Hotels

I have a reservation in the name of ...
我用…的名字预订了房间
Wo Yong ... De Mean-Ds Yu-Ding
Le Fang-Jian

I wrote to / faxed / telephoned you last month / last week
我上个月/上周写信/发传真/打电话来确认过
Wo Shang-Ge-Yue / Shang-Jiou
Shie-Shin / Fa-Chwan-Jien /
Da-Dian Hwa Lie Chue-Ren Guo

Do you have any rooms free?
你这里有空房间吗?
Nee Jer-Lee Yuh Kong-Fang-Jian Ma

I would like to reserve a single / double room with / without bath / shower
我想要预订一间带/不带浴室/淋浴的单人间/双人间
Wo Shiang Yao Yu-Ding Yee-Jian Die /
Boo-Die Yu-Sh / Lin-Yu De
Dan-Ren-Jian / Shwang-Ren-Jian

I would like bed and breakfast / (room and) full board
我要订含早餐的住宿/全天包餐的住宿
Wo Yao Ding Han Dsao-Tsan De
Dsoo-Soo / Chwan-Tian-Bao-Tsan De
Dsoo-Soo

How much is it per night?
多少钱一晚?
Duo-Shao-Chain Yee Wan

Is breakfast included?
包括早餐吗?
Bao-Ko Dsao-Tsan Ma

Do you have any cheaper rooms?
有没有便宜一点的房间?
Yoh-May-Yoh Pian-Yee Yee-Dian De
Fang-Jian

I would like to see / take the room
我想看看/要这个房间
Wo Shiang Kan-Kan / Yao Jer-Ge
Fang-Jian

I would like to stay for ... nights
我要住…晚
Wo Yao Joo ... Wan

The shower / light / tap / hot water doesn't work
淋浴/灯/水龙头/热水坏了
Lin-Yu / Deng / Shway-Long-Tou /
Re-Shway Hwai Le

At what time / where is breakfast served?
早餐几点供应? / 早餐在什么地方?
Dsao-Tsan Jee-Dian Gong-Ying /
Dsao-Tsan Dsai Shen-Mo Dee-Fang

What time do I have to check out?
几点退房?
Jee Dian Tway-Fang

Can I have the key to room number ... ?
请给我…号房间的钥匙
Ching Gay Wo... How Fang-Jian De
Yao-Sh

My room number is ...
我的房间号是…
Wo De Fang-Jian-How Sh ...

C H I N E S E

My room is not satisfactory / not clean enough / too noisy
我的房间不好/不够干净/太吵了
Wo De Fang-Jian Boo-How / Boo-Gou Gan-Jing / Tie-Chao-Le

Please can I change rooms?
我可以换个房间吗?
Wo Ke-Yee Hwan Ge Fang-Jian Ma

Where is the bathroom?
浴室在哪里?
Yu-Sh Dsai Na Lee

Do you have a safe for valuables?
请问有没有保险柜寄存贵重物品?
Ching When Yoh-May-Yoh Bao-Shian-Gway Jee-Tswun Gway-Jong-Woo-Pin

Is there a laundry / do you wash clothes?
有洗衣店吗? /你们提供洗衣服务吗?
Yoh Shee-Yee-Dian Ma / Nee-Men Tea-Gong Shee-Yee-Foo-Woo Ma

I would like an air-conditioned room
我要一间有空调的房间
Wo Yao Yee-Jian Yoh Kong-Tiao De Fang-Jian

Do you accept traveller's cheques / credit cards?
你们接受旅行支票/信用卡吗?
Nee-Men Jie-So Lue-Shing Ds-Piao / Shing-Yong-Ka Ma

May I have the bill please?
请结账?
Ching-Jie-Jang

Excuse me, I think there may be a mistake in this bill
对不起,账单好像不对
Dway-Boo-Chee, Jang-Dan How Shiang Boo-Dway

Youth Hostels

How much is a dormitory bed per night?
请问,每个床位多少钱一晚?
Ching When, May-Ge Chwang-Way Duo-Shao-Chain Yee-Wan

I am / am not an HI member
我是/我不是HI会员
Wo-Sh / Wo-Boo-Sh Hi Hway-Yuan

May I use my own sleeping bag?
我可以用自己的睡袋吗?
Wo Ke-Yee Yong Ds-Jee De Shway-Die Ma

What time do you lock the doors at night?
你们晚上几点锁门?
Nee-Men Wan-Shang Jee-Dian Suo-Men

Camping

May I camp for the night / two nights?
我可以露营一/两晚吗?
Wo Ke-Yee Loo-Ying Yee-Wan / Liang-Wan Ma

Where can I pitch my tent?
哪里可以搭帐篷?
Na-Lee Ke-Yee Da-Jang-Pung

How much does it cost for one night / week?
露营一晚/周多少钱?
Loo-Ying Yee-Wan /
Jiou Duo-Shao-Chain

Where are the washing facilities?
请问洗手间在哪里?
Ching When Shee-So-Jian Dsai Na Lee

Is there a restaurant / supermarket / swimming pool on site / nearby?
这里/附近有餐馆/超市/
游泳池吗?
Jer-Lee / Foo-Jean Yoh Tsan-Gwan /
Tsao-Sh / Yoh-Yong-Ch Ma

Do you have a safety deposit box?
请问有没有保险箱寄存贵重物品?
Ching When Yoh-May-Yoh
Bao-Shian-Shiang Jee-Tswun
Gway-Jong-Woo-Pin De

EATING AND DRINKING

Cafés and Bars

I would like a cup of / two cups of / another coffee / tea
我想要一杯/两杯/再来一杯
咖啡/茶
Wo Shiang Yao Yee-Bay / Liang-Bay /
Dsai Lie Yee-Bay Ka-Fay / Cha

With / without milk / sugar
加/不加奶/糖
Jia / Boo-Jia Nai / Tang

I would like a bottle / glass / two glasses of mineral water / red wine / white wine, please
请来瓶/杯/两杯矿泉水/红葡萄酒/
白葡萄酒
Ching Lie Ping / Bay /
Liang-Bay Kwang-Chwan-Shway /
Hong-Poo-Tao-Jiou / Bye-Poo-Tao-Jiou

I would like a beer / two beers, please
请来杯/两杯啤酒
Ching Lie Bay / Liang-Bay Pee-Jiou

Please may I have some ice?
请加一些冰
Ching Jia Yee-Shie Bing

Do you have any matches / cigarettes / cigars?
请问你有火柴/香烟/雪茄吗?
Ching When, Nee Yoh Huo-Tsai /
Shiang-Yan / Shue-Jiu Ma

Restaurants

Can you recommend a good / cheap restaurant in this area?
能推荐一下这个地区好的/便宜的
餐馆吗?
Nung Tway-Jian Yee-Shia Jer-Ge
Dee-Chew How De / Pian-Yee De
Tsan-Gwan Ma

I would like a table for ... people
我想预订一个…人的餐桌
Wo Shiang Yu-Ding Yee-Ge ...
Ren De Tsan-Dsuo

Do you have a non-smoking area?
你们有非吸烟区吗?
Nee-Men Yoh Fay-Shee-Yan-Chew Ma

Waiter / Waitress!
服务员/服务小姐
Foo-Woo-Yuan / Foo-Woo-Shiao-Jie

CHINESE

57

C
H
I
N
E
S
E

Excuse me, please may we order?
请问，我们可以点菜吗?
Ching-When, Wo-Men Ke-Yee Dian-Tsai Ma

Do you have a set menu / children's menu / wine list?
你们有套餐 / 儿童餐 / 酒水单吗?
Nee-Men Yoh Tao-Tsan / Er-Tong-Tsan / Jiou-Shway-Dan Ma

Do you have any vegetarian dishes?
你们有素食吗?
Nee-Men Yoh Sue-Sh Ma

Do you have any local specialities?
你们有本地特色菜吗?
Nee-Men Yoh Ben-Dee-Te-Se-Tsai Ma

Are vegetables included?
包括蔬菜吗?
Bao-Kuo Shoo-Tsai Ma

Could I have it well-cooked / medium / rare please?
请做成全熟 / 半熟 / 生的
Ching Dsuo Cheng Chwan-Shoo / Bann-Shoo / Sheng De

What does this dish consist of?
这道菜是什么做的?
Jer-Dao-Tsai Sh Shen-Mo Dsuo De

I am a vegetarian. Does this contain meat?
我是素食者。这道菜有肉吗?
Wo-Sh Sue-Sh-Jer. Jer Dao Tsai Yoh Ro Ma

I do not eat nuts / dairy products / meat / fish
我不吃坚果 / 乳制品 / 肉 / 鱼
Wo Boo-Ch Jian-Guo / Roo-Ds-Pin / Ro / Yu

Not (very) spicy, please
请不要放(太多)辣椒
Ching Boo-Yao Fang (Tie-Duo) La-Jiao

I would like the set menu, please
我想点套餐
Wo Shiang Dian Tao-Tsan

We are still waiting to be served
我们还在等服务员来点菜
Wo-Men Hi Dsai Deng Foo-Woo-Yuan Lie Dian-Msai

Please bring a plate / knife / fork
请给我一个盘 / 一付刀 / 叉
Ching Gay-Wo Yee-Ge Pan / Yee-Foo Dao / Cha

Excuse me, this is not what I ordered
对不起，我没有点这道菜
Dway-Boo-Chee, Wo May-Yoh Dian Jer-Dao-Tsai

May I have some / some more bread / water / coffee / tea?
请给我来 / 加一些面包 / 水 / 咖啡 / 茶。
Ching Gay Wo Lie / Jia Yee-Shie Mian-Bao / Shway / Ka-Fay / Cha

May I have the bill, please?
请结账
Ching-Jie-Jang

Does this bill include service?
这份账单包括服务费吗?
Jer-Fen Jang-Dan Bao-Ko Foo-Woo-Fay Ma

C
H
I
N
E
S
E

Do you accept traveller's cheques / MasterCard / US dollars?
你们接受旅行支票/万事达卡/
美元吗?
Nee-Men Jie-So Lue-Shing Ds-Piao / Wan-Sh-Da-Ka / May-Yuan Ma

Can I have a receipt, please?
请给我发票
Ching Gay-Wo Fa-Piao

Where is the toilet (restroom), please?
请问厕所(洗手间)在哪里?
Ching When, Tse-Suo (Shee-Shou-Jian) Dsai Na Lee

On the Menu

早餐/午餐/晚餐
Dsao-Tsan / Wou-Tsan / Wan-Tsan
Breakfast / Lunch / Dinner

前菜	汤
Chain-Tsai	*Tang*
First courses	**Soups**

主菜	鱼
Joo-Tsai	*Yu*
Main courses	**Fish dishes**

肉类	牛肉
Ro-Lay	*New- Ro*
Meat dishes	**Beef**

牛排	猪肉
New-Pie	*Joo-Ro*
Steak	**Pork**

小牛肉	鸡肉
Shiao-New-Ro	*Jee-Ro*
Veal	**Chicken**

羊肉	火腿
Yang-Ro	*Huo-Tway*
Lamb	**Ham**

素餐
Sue-Tsan
Vegetarian dishes

蔬菜
Shoo-Tsai
Vegetables

薯条
Shoo-Tiao
Chips (french fries)

水煮/煎/马铃薯泥
Shway-Joo / Jian / Ma-Ling-Shwoo-Nee
Boiled / sauté / mashed potatoes

米饭	奶酪
Mee-Fan	*Nai-Lao*
Rice	**Cheese**

甜点	冰淇淋
Tian-Dian	*Bing-Chee-Lin*
Desserts	**Ice cream**

蛋糕	糕点
Dan-Gao	*Gao-Dian*
Cakes	**Pastries**

水果	面包
Shway-Guo	*Mian-Bao*
Fruit	**Bread**

C H I N E S E

面包卷
Mian-Bao-Juan
Rolls

烤面包
Kao-Mian-Bao
Toast

黄油
Hwang-Yoh
Butter

盐/胡椒
Yan / Hoo-Jiao
Salt / pepper

糖
Tang
Sugar

特色菜
Te-Se-Tsai
Specialities

本地特色菜
Ben-Dee-Te-Se-Tsai
Local specialities

套餐
Tao-Tsan
Set Menu

酒水单
Jiou-Shway-Dan
Wine list

红葡萄酒
Hong-Poo-Tao-Jiou
Red wines

白葡萄酒
Bye-Poo-Tao-Jiou
White wines

桃红葡萄酒
Tao-Hong Poo-Tao-Jiou
Rosé wines

汽酒
Chee-Jiou
Sparkling wines

啤酒
Pee-Jiou
Beer

瓶装啤酒/散装啤酒
Ping-Juang Pee-Jiou /
San-Juang Pee-Jiou
**Bottled beer /
Draught (draft) beer**

不含酒精的饮料
Boo Han Jiou-Jing De Yin-Liao
Non-alcoholic drinks

矿泉水
Kwang-Chuan-Shway
Mineral water

果汁
Guo-Ds
Fruit juices

橙汁
Cheng-Ds
Orange juice

柠檬汁
Ning-Meng-Ds
Lemonade

冰
Bing
Ice

牛奶咖啡/黑咖啡/
意大利香浓咖啡
New-Nai Ka-Fay / Hey-Ka-Fay /
Yee-Da-Lee Shiang-Nong Ka-Fay
**White coffee / black coffee /
espresso coffee**

茶加牛奶/加柠檬
Cha Jia New-Nai / Jia Ning-Meng
Tea with milk / with lemon

热巧克力
Re Chiao-Ke-Lee
Chocolate (drink)

牛奶
New-Nai
Milk

小吃/便餐
Shiao-Ch / Bian-Tsan
Snacks / Light meals

沙拉
Sha-La
Salads

三明治
San-Mean-Ds
Sandwiches

蛋
Dan
Eggs

香肠
Shiang-Chang
Sausage

水煮/煎/炒蛋
Shway-Joo / Jian / Tsao-Dan
Boiled / fried / scrambled eggs

Typical Local Dishes

北京鸭
Bay-Jing-Yah
Peking duck

梅菜扣肉
May-Tsai-Kou-Ro
Pork with salted vegetables

佛跳墙
Foo-Tiao-Chiang
**"Buddha jump over the wall"
– a mixture of herbs and
seafood**

鱼翅
Yu-Ch
Sharks fin

宫保鸡丁
Gong-Bao-Jee-Ding
Diced chicken with dried chilli

GETTING AROUND

Public Transport

**Where is the bus stop /
coach stop / nearest metro
(subway) station?**
请问公共汽车站/游览车站/
最近的地铁站在哪里?
*Ching When, Gong-Gong-Chee-Che Jan /
Yoh-Lan-Che Jan / Dsway-Jean De
Dee-Tyeh-Dsan Dsai Na Lee*

When is the next / last bus to ...?
下一班/末班去…的公共汽车是
几时?
*Shia-Yee-Bann / Mo-Bann Chew...
De Gong-Gong-Chee-Che Sh Jee-Sh*

**How much is the fare to the
city centre (downtown) / railway
station / airport?**
去市中心/火车站/机场多少钱?
*Chew Sh-Jong-Shing / Huo-Che-Jan /
Jee-Chang Duo-Shao-Chain*

**Will you tell me when to get
off?**
请问几点开车?
Ching When, Jee-Dian Kai-Che

Does this bus go to ... ?
这辆公共汽车是去…的吗?
*Jer-Liang Gong-Gong-Chee-Che Sh Chew
... De Ma*

Which number bus goes to ...?
请问几号公共汽车是去…的?
*Ching When, Jee-How
Gong-Gong-Chee-Che Sh Chew... De*

C
H
I
N
E
S
E

May I have a single (oneway) / return (round-trip) / day ticket / book of tickets?

我要买一张单程票/往返票/日票/套票
Wo Yao Mai Yee-Jang Dan-Cheng-Piao / Wang-Fan-Piao / R-Piao / Tao-Piao

Taxis and Rickshaws

I would like to go to ...

我想去…
Wo Shiang Chew ...

How much will it cost?

多少钱?
Duo-Shao-Chain

Please may I stop here?

可以在这里停车吗?
Ke-Yee Dsai Jer-Lee Ting Che Ma

I would like to order a taxi today / tomorrow / at 2pm to go from ... to ...

今天/明天/下午两点,我想订一辆出租车去/从…去…
Jean-Tian / Mean-Tian / Shia-Woo-Liang-Dian,Wo Shiang Ding Yee-Liang Choo-Dsoo-Che Chew / Cong… Chew…

Entertainment

Can you recommend a good bar / nightclub?

能推荐一家好的酒吧/夜总会吗?
Nung Tway-jian Yee-jia How De Jiou-Ba / Yeh-Jong-Hway Ma

Do you know what is on at the cinema (playing at the movies) / theatre at the moment?

你知道电影院/剧院现在在上映什么电影吗?
Nee-J-Dao Dian-Ying-Yuan / Ju-Yuan Shian-Dsai Dsai Shang-Ying Shen-Mo Dian-Ying Ma

I would like to book (purchase) ... tickets for the matinee / evening performance on Monday

我想订(买)…星期一早场/晚场表演的票
Wo Shiang Ding (Mai) ... Shing-Chee-Yee Dsao-Chang / Wan-Chang Biao-Yan De Piao

What time does the film / performance start?

电影/表演什么时候开始?
Dian-Ying / Biao-Yan Shen-Mo Sh-Hou Kai-Sh

COMMUNICATIONS

Post

How much will it cost to send a letter / postcard / this package to Britain / Ireland / America / Canada / Australia / New Zealand?

寄封信/寄张明信片/寄个包裹去英国/爱尔兰/美国/加拿大/澳大利亚/新西兰要多少钱?
Jee Feng Shin / Jee Jang Mean-Shin-Pian / Jee Ge Bao-Guo Chew Ying-Guo / Ai-Er-Lan / May-Guo / Jia-Na-Da / Ao-Da-Lee-Ya / Shin-Shee-Lan Yao Duo-Shao-Chain

I would like one stamp / two stamps

我想买一张/两张邮票
Wo Shiang Mai Yee-Jang / Liang-Jang Yoh-Piao

I'd like ... stamps for postcards to send abroad, please
我想买…张邮票寄明信片去国外
Wo Shiang Mai ... Jang Yoh-Piao Jee
Mean-Shin-Pian Chew Guo-Why

Phones

I would like to make a telephone call / reverse the charges to (make a collect call to) ...
我想打电话给… /我想打对方付费
电话给…
Wo Shiang Da-Dian-Hwa Gay... /
Wo Shiang Da Dway-Fang-Foo-Fay
Dian-Hwa Gay ...

Which coins do I need for the telephone?
打电话需要用哪种硬币?
Da Dian-Hwa Shoo-Yao Yong Na-Jong
Ying-Bee

The line is engaged (busy)
占线(线路忙)
Jan-Shian (Shian-Loo-Mang)

The number is ...
电话号码是…
Dian-Hwa-How-Ma Sh...

Hello, this is ...
你好, 我是…
Nee-How, Wo-Sh ...

Please may I speak to ...?
请找…
Ching-Jao ...

He / she is not in at the moment. Can you call back?
他 /她现在不在。你可以一会再打
来吗?
Ta / Ta Shian-Dsai Boo-Dsai. Nee
Ke Yee Yee-Hway Dsai Da Lie Ma

Shops

书店/文具店
Shoo-Dian / When-Ju-Dian
Bookshop / Stationery

珠宝行/礼品店
Joo-Bao-Hang / Lee-Pin-Dian
Jeweller / Gifts

鞋店
Shie-Dian
Shoes

五金店
Woo-Jean-Dian
Hardware

发廊
Fa-Lang
Hairdresser

男式/女式
Nan-Sh / Nue-Sh
(men's) / (women's)

烤面包店
Kao-Mian-Bao Dian
Baker

手机店
So-Jee Dian
Phones

超市
Tsao-Sh
Supermarket

照相馆
Dsao-Shiang-Gwan
Photo-Shop

CHINESE

63

CHINESE

旅行社
Lue-Shing-Sher
Travel agent

药店
Yao-Dian
Pharmacy

In the Shops

What time do the shops open / close?
这家商店几时开门/关门?
Jer-Jia Shang-Dian Jee-Sh Kai-Men / Gwan-Men

Where is the nearest market?
最近的市场在哪里?
Dsway-Jean De Sh-Chang Dsai Na Lee

Can you show me the one in the window / this one?
可以给我看看橱窗里的那个/这个吗?
Ke-Yee Gay Wo Kan-Kan Choo-Chwang-Lee De Na-Ge / Jer-Ge Ma

Can I try this on?
可以试穿吗?
Ke Yee Sh-Chwan Ma

What size is this?
尺码多大?
Ts-Ma Duo Da

This is too large / too small / too expensive.
这件太大/太小/太贵了
Jer-Jian Tie-Da / Tie-Shiao / Tie-Gway Le

Do you have any others?
还有其他的吗?
Hi-Yoh Chee-Ta De Ma

My size is ...
我的尺码是…
Wo-De Ts-Ma Sh ...

Where is the changing room / children's / cosmetic / ladieswear / menswear / food department?
更衣室/童装/化妆品/女装/
男装/食品柜台在哪里?
Geng-Yee-Sh / Tong-Dswang / Hwa-Dswang-Pin / Nue-Dswang / Nan-Dswang / Sh-Pin-Gway-Tie Dsai Na Lee

I would like ...a quarter of a kilo / half a kilo / a kilo of bread / butter / cheese / ham / this fruit
我想买…两斤半/半公斤/一公斤
面包/黄油/奶酪/火腿/这种水果
Wo Shiang Mai ... Liang-Jean-Bann / Bann-Gong-Jean / Yee-Gong-Jean Mian-Bao / Hwang-Yoh / Nai-Lao / Hwoo-Tway / Jer-Jong Shway-Guo

How much is this?
这个多少钱?
Jer-Ge Duo-Shao-Chain

I'll take this one, thank you
我要买这个，谢谢
Wo Yao Mai Jer-Ge, Shie-Shie

Do you have a carrier (shopping) bag?
有购物袋吗?
Yoh Gou-Woo-Die Ma

Do you have anything cheaper / larger / smaller / of better quality?
有更便宜/大/小/质量更好的吗?
Yoh Geng Pian-Yee / Da / Shiao / J-Liang Geng-How De Ma

I would like a film / to develop this film for this camera
我想买一卷胶卷。/我想冲洗这部相机里的胶卷
Wo Shiang Mai Yee-Juan Jiao-Juan. / Wo Shiang Chong-Shee Jer-Boo Shiang-Jee Lee De Jiao-Juan

I would like some batteries, the same size as this old one
我想买一些和旧的型号相同的电池
Wo Shiang Mai Yee-Shie Hee Jiou-De Shing How Shiang-Tong De Dian-Ts

Would you mind wrapping this for me, please?
能不能请你帮我包装一下
Nung-Boo-Nung Ching Nee Bang-Wo Bao-Juang Yee Shia

Sorry, but you seem to have given me the wrong change
对不起，你可能找错钱了
Dway-Boo-Chee, Nee Ke-Nung Jan Cuo-Chain Le

MOTORING

Car Hire (Rental)

I have ordered (rented) a car in the name of ...
我用…的名字订(租)了一辆车
Wo Yong... De Mean-Ds Ding (Dsoo) Le Yee-Liang-Che

How much does it cost to hire (rent) a car for one day / two days / a week?
一天/两天/一周的租金是多少钱?
Yee-Tian / Liang-Tian / Yee-Jou De Dsoo-Jean Sh Duo-Shao-Chain

Is the tank already full of petrol (gas)?
油箱已经加满汽油(气)了吗?
Yoh-Shiang Yee-Jing Jia Man Chee-Yoh (Chee) Le Ma

Is insurance and tax included? How much is the deposit?
包括保险和税款吗? 需要多少押金?
Bao-Ko Bao-Shian Hee Shway-Kwan Ma? Shu Yao Duo-Shao Ya-Jean

By what time must I return the car?
我应该什么时候还车?
Wo Ying-Gai Shen-Mo Sh-Hou Hwan-Che

I would like a small / large / family / sports car with a radio / cassette player
我想买一辆有收音机/磁带播放器的小/大/家用/运动型车
Wo Shiang Mai Yee-Liang Yoh Shou-Yin-Jee / Ts-Die Bo-Fang-Chee De Shiao / Da / Jia-Yong / Yun-Dong-Shing Che

Do you have a road map?
你有道路图吗?
Nee Yoh Dao-Loo-Too Ma

Parking

How long can I park here?
我可以在这里停多久?
Wo Ke-Yee Dsai Jer-Lee Ting Duo-Jiou

C H I N E S E

Is there a car park near here?
这附近有停车场吗?
Jer Foo-Jean Yoh Ting-Che-Chang Ma

At what time does this car park close?
这个停车场几点关?
Jer-Ge Ting-Che-Chang Jee-Dian Gwan

Signs and Notices

单行
Dan-Shing
One way

禁止通行
Jean-J-Tong-Shing
No entry

禁止停车
Jean-J-Ting-Che
No parking

绕行 (改道)
Rao-Shing (Gai-Dao)
Detour (diversion)

停
Ting
Stop

让路
Rang-Loo
Give way (yield)

路滑
Loo-Hwa
Slippery road

禁止超载
Jean-J-Tsao-Dsai
No overtaking

危险
Way-Shian
Danger!

At the Filling Station

Unleaded (lead-free) / standard / premium / diesel
无铅 (不含铅) /标准/顶级/柴油
Woo-Chain (Boo-Han-Chain) / Biao-Jun / Ding-Jee / Chai-Yoh

Fill the tank please
请加满油
Ching Jia Man Yoh

Do you have a road map?
你有道路图吗?
Nee Yoh Dao-Loo-Too Ma

How much is the car wash?
洗车多少钱?
Shee-Che Duo-Shao-Chain

Breakdowns

I've had a breakdown at ...
我的车在…出了故障
Wo-De-Che Dsai ... Choo Le Goo-Jang

I am a member of the [motoring organisation]
我是[车友会]的会员
Wo-Sh [Che-Yoh-Hway] De Hway-Yuan

I am on the road from ... to ...
我在从…到…的路上
Wo Dsai Cong ... Dao ... De Loo-Shang

I can't move the car. Can you send a tow-truck?
我的车不能发动了。你们可以派辆拖车来吗？
Wo-De-Che Boo Nung Fa-Dong Le. Nee-Men Ke-Yee Pie Liang Tuo-Che Lie Ma

I have a flat tyre
我的车胎扁了
Wo De Che-Tie Bian Le

The windscreen (windshield) has smashed / cracked
挡风玻璃碎了 / 裂了
Dang-Feng-Bo-Lee Sway Le / Lyeh Le

There is something wrong with the engine / brakes / lights / steering / gearbox / clutch / exhaust
引擎 / 刹车 / 车灯 / 方向盘 / 变速箱 / 离合器 / 排气管出了问题
Yin-Ching / Sa-Che / Che-Dung / Fang-Shiang-Pan / Bian-Shoo-Shiang / Lee-Hee-Chee / Pie-Chee-Gwan Choo Le When-Tea

It's overheating
过热
Guo-Re

It won't start
不能发动
Boo Nung Fa-Dong

Where can I get it repaired?
到哪里可以修理？
Dao Na-Lee Ke-Yee Shio-Lee

Can you take me there?
你可以带我去那吗？
Nee Ke-Yee Die-Wo Chew Na Ma

Will it take long to fix?
修理需要多长时间？
Shio-Lee Shoo-Yao Duo-Chang Sh-Jian

How much will it cost?
多少钱？
Duo-Shao-Chain

Please can you pick me up / give me a lift?
可以顺路载我 / 让我搭顺风车吗？
Ke Yee Shun-Loo Dsai Wo / Rang Wo Da Shun-Feng-Che Ma

Accidents and Traffic Offences

Can you help me? There has been an accident.
可以帮忙吗？这里发生了车祸
Ke Yee Bang-Mang Ma? Jer-Lee Fa Sheng Le Che-Huo

Please call the police / an ambulance
请打电话叫警察 / 救护车
Ching Da-Dian-Hwa Jiao Jing-Cha / Jiou-Hoo-Che

Is anyone hurt?
有人受伤吗？
Yoh Ren Shou-Shang Ma

I'm sorry, I didn't see the sign
对不起，我没有看见路标
Dway-Boo-Chee, Wo May-Yoh Kan-Jian Loo-Biao

Must I pay a fine? How much?
必须交罚款吗？ 多少钱？
Bee-Shu Jiao Fa-Kwan Ma? Duo-Shao-Chain

C
H
I
N
E
S
E

**C
H
I
N
E
S
E**

Show me your documents
请出示你的证件
Ching Chew-Sh Nee De Jeng-Jian

HEALTH

Pharmacy

Do you have anything for a stomach ache / headache / sore throat / toothache?
有治胃痛/头痛/喉咙痛/牙痛的药吗?
Yoh J Way-Tong / Tou-Tong / Hou-Long-Tong / Ya-Tong De Yao Ma

I need something for diarrhoea / constipation / a cold / a cough / insect bites / sunburn / travel (motion) sickness (car) (plane) (boat)
我想买治疗腹泻/便秘/感冒/咳嗽/蚊虫叮咬/晒伤/晕(车)(飞机)(船)的药
Wo-Shiang-Mai J-Liao Foo-Shie / Bian-Me / Gan-Mao / Ke-Shou / When-Cong-Ding-Yao / Shai-Shang / Yun (Che) (Fay Jee) (Chuan) De Yao

How much / how many do I take?
我应该服用多少?
Wo Ying-Gai Foo-Yong Duo-Shao

How often do I take it / them?
多长时间服用一次?
Duo-Chang Sh-Jian Foo-Yong Yee-Ch

I am / he is / she is taking this medication
我/他/她在吃这种药
Wo / Ta / Ta Dsai Ch Jer-Jong Yao

How much does it cost?
多少钱?
Duo-Shao-Chain

Can you recommend a good doctor / dentist?
能推荐一位好医生/牙医吗?
Nung Tway-Jian Yee-Way How-Yee-Sheng / Ya-yee Ma

Is it suitable for children?
儿童适用吗?
Er-Tong Sh-Yong Ma

Doctor

I have a pain here / in my arm / leg / chest / stomach
我这里/手臂/腿/胸/胃痛
Wo Jer-Lee / Shou-Bee / Tway / Shiong / Way-Tong

Please call a doctor, this is an emergency
请叫医生, 有紧急情况
Ching Jiao Yee-Sheng, Yoh Jean-Jee-Ching-Kwang

I would like to make an appointment to see the doctor
我想预约医生看病
Wo Shiang Yu-Yue Yee-Sheng Kan-Bing

I am diabetic / pregnant
我有糖尿病/怀孕了
Wo Yoh Tang-Niao-Bing / Hwai-Yun Le

I need a prescription for ...
我需要治疗…的处方
Wo Shoo-Yao J-Liao... De Choo-Fang

Can you give me something to ease the pain?
可以给我开些止痛药吗?
Ke-Yee Gay-Wo Kai Shie J-Tong-Yao Ma

I am / he is / she is allergic to penicillin
我/他/她对青霉素过敏?
Wo / Ta / Ta Dway Ching-May-Sue Guo-Mean

Does this hurt?
痛吗?
Tong Ma

You must / he must / she must go to hospital
你/他/她必须去医院
Nee / Ta / Ta Bee-Shoo Chew Yee-Yuan

Take these once / twice / three times a day
每天服用一/两/三次
May-Tian Foo-Yong Yee / Liang / San-Ch

I am / he is / she is taking this medication
我/他/她在吃这种药
Wo / Ta / Ta Dsai Ch Jer-Jong Yao

I have medical insurance
我有医疗保险
Wo Yoh Yee-Liao-Bao-Shian

Dentist

I have toothache
我牙痛
Wo Ya-Tong

My filling has come out
我补的牙齿掉出来了
Wo Boo De Ya-Ch Diao-Chew-Lie Le

I do / do not want to have an injection first
我要/不要先打针
Wo Yao / Boo-Yao Shian Da-Jen

EMERGENCIES

Help!
救命
Jiou-Mean

Fire!
救火
Jiou-Hwoo

Stop!
停下
Ting-Shia

Call an ambulance / a doctor / the police / the fire brigade!
打电话叫救护车/医生/警察/消防车
Da-Dian-Hwa Jiao Jiou-Hoo Che / Yee-Sheng / Jing-Cha / Shiao-Fang-Che

Please may I use a telephone?
可以借用一下电话吗?
Ke Yee Jie-Yong Yee-Shia Dian-Hwa Ma

I have had my traveller's cheques / credit cards / handbag / rucksack / (knapsack) / luggage / wallet / passport / mobile phone stolen
我的旅行支票/信用卡/手提包/背包/行李/钱包/护照/手机被偷了
Wo De Lue-Shing J-Piao / Shing-Yong-Ka / Shou-Tea-Bao / Bay-Bao / Shing-Lee / Chain-Bao / Hoo-Jao / Shou-Jee Bay Tou Le

May I please have a copy of the report for my insurance claim?
我需要一份我的保险索赔的复印件
Wo Shoo Yao Yee-Fen Wo De Bao-Shian Suo-Pei De Foo-Yin-Jian

CHINESE

C H I N E S E

Can you help me? I have lost my daughter / my son / my companion(s)
我的女儿/儿子/同伴走丢了,
你可以帮我吗?
Wo De Nue-Er / Er-Ds / Tong-Bann Dsou Dew Le, Nee Ke-Yee Bang Wo Ma

Please go away / leave me alone
请走开/不要打扰我
Ching Dsou-Kai / Boo-Yao Da-Rao-Wo

I'm sorry
对不起
Dway-Boo-Chee

I want to contact the British / American / Canadian / Irish / Australian / New Zealand / South African consulate
我想和英国/美国/加拿大/爱尔兰/
澳大利亚/新西兰/南非领事馆
联络
Wo Shiang Hee Ying-Guo / May-Guo / Jia-Na-Da / Ai-Er-Lan / Ao-Da-Lee-Ya / Shin-Shee-Lan / Nan-Fay Ling-Sh-Gwan Lian Luo

I'm / we're / he is / she is ill / lost / injured
我/我们/他/她生病/迷路/
受伤了。
Wo / Wo-Men / Ta / Ta Sheng-Bing / Me-Loo / Sho-Shang Le

They are ill / lost / injured
他们生病/迷路/受伤了
Ta-men Sheng-Bing / Mee-Loo / Sho-Shang Le

FILIPINO

F
I
L
I
P
I
N
O

INTRODUCTION

Backed up by English, Filipino is the national language of the Philippines, and is said by many to be a combination of all the different Philippines' indigenous languages. Borrowed words aside, its spots are essentially Tagalog, the traditional mother tongue of the area. Filipino is the most widely known language of the Philippines, and is also the predominant language of Manila and Luzon. English is widely spoken in the Philippines, particularly for commerce, government and international relations; and most signs are displayed in English, but in the more remote areas it is a good idea to have Filipino phrases to hand.

Addresses for Travel and Tourist Information

Australia: Philippine Embassy; 1 Moonah Place, Yarralumla, Canberra, ACT 2600. Tel: 02 6273 2535; Fax: 02 6273 3984; Email: cbrpe@philembassy.au.com; Web: www.philembassy.au.com/cnt-home.htm
Philippine Department of Tourism, Level 1, Philippine Centre, 27-33 Wentworth Avenue, Sydney NSW 2000. Tel: 02 9283 0711; Fax: 02 9283 0755; Web: www.tourism.gov.ph

Canada: Philippine Consulate General, 161 Eglinton Avenue East, Suite 800, Toronto, Ontario M4P 1J5. Tel: 416 922 7181; Fax: 416 922 2638; Email: torontopc@philcongen-toronto.com; Web: www.philcongen-toronto.com

UK: Philippine Department of Tourism, 146 Cromwell Rd, London SW7 4EF. Tel: 020 7835 1100; Email: infotourism@wowphilippines.co.uk

USA: Embassy of the Philippines 1600 Massachusetts Avenue NW, Washington DC 20036. Tel: 202 467 9300; Fax: 202 467 9417; Web: www.philippineembassy.com
Philippine Consulate General, 556 Fifth Avenue, New York. Tel: 212 764 1330/575 4774; Fax: 212 382 1146; Email: newyork@pcgny.net; Web: www.pcgny.net

Philippines Facts

CAPITAL: Manila

CURRENCY: Philippine Peso (₱); (1 Peso + 100 centavos)

OPENING HOURS: Banks are open 0900-1500 Mon-Fri and are closed on public holidays. Most shopping centres, department stores and supermarkets are open from 1000-2000 daily.

TELEPHONES: To dial in, Tel: International Access Code + 63 + Area Code minus the first zero. Outgoing, Tel: 00 and the Country Code.

EMERGENCY NUMBERS: Police, Tel: 166; Fire, Tel: 7575; Ambulance, Tel: 7575.

PUBLIC HOLIDAYS: Jan 1 – New Year's Day; Maundy Thursday; Good Friday; April 9 – Day of Valour; May 1 – Labor Day; June 12 – Independence Day; June 23 – Manila Day; Nov 1 – All Saint's Day; Nov 30 – Bonifacio Day, Dec 25 – Christmas Day; Dec 30 – Rizal Day.

Technical Language Hints

- Each vowel in a sequence of vowels is pronounced individually.

- The word "ng" indicates possssion (eg. "This is the child's bag" (Ito ang bag ng bata) and is pronounced "nang". However, the same word "ng" is often used as suffixes to indicate possession [eg. "This is my book" (Ito ang aking libro).]. A similar theme runs for "mga"- indicating plural possession (ours, theirs), which is pronounced "mah-nga", with emphasis falling on the last "a".

73

FILIPINO

Alphabet

a	b
ah	*b*
c	d
c	*d*
e	f
e	*f*
g	h
g	*h*
i	j
ee	*j*
k	l
k	*l*
m	n
m	*n*
ñ	ng
nya	*ng*
o	p
o	*p*
q	r
q	*r*
s	t
s	*t*
u	v
oo	*v*
w	x
w	*x*
y	z
y	*z*

Basic Words and Phrases

Yes
Oo
O-o

No
Hindi
Heen-Dee

Please
Paki
Pah-Kee

Thank you
Salamat
Sah-Lah-Maht

Hello
Hello
Hello

Goodbye
Paalam
Pah-A-Lam

Excuse me
Ipagpaumanhin ninyo
I-Pahg-Pah-Oo-Man-Hin Nin-Yo

Sorry
Pasensiya na
Pah-Sen-See-Yah Na

How
Paano
Pah-A-No

When
Kailan
Kah-Ee-Lahn

Why
Bakit
Bah-Keet

What
Ano
Ah-No

Who
Sino
See-No

That's O.K.
OK lang
OK Lang

Perhaps
Siguro
See-Goo-Ro

To
Sa
Sa

From
Mula
Moo-Lah

Here
Dito
Dee-To

There
Diyan
Jahn

I don't understand
Hindi ko maintindihan
Heen-Dee Ko Mah-Een-Teen-Dee-Han

I don't speak Filipino
Hindi ako nakakakapagsalita ng
Filipino
*Heen-Dee Ah-Ko Nah-Kah-Kah-Pahg-
Sah-Lee-Tah Nang Filipino*

Do you speak English?
Nakakapagsalita ka ba ng Ingles?
*Nah-Kah-Kah-Pahg-Sah-Lee-Tah Ka Ba
Nang Eengles*

Can you please write it down?
Puwede bang pakisulat mo?
*Poo-We-De Bahng Pah-Kee-Soo-Laht
Mo*

**Please can you speak more
slowly?**
Puwede bang magsalita ka nang
dahan-dahan?
*Poo-We-De Bahng Mahg-Sah-LeeTah
Kah Nahng Dah-Hahn-Dah-Hahn*

Greetings

**Good morning /
Good afternoon /
Good evening / Goodnight**
Magandang umaga / Magandang
hapon / Magandang gabi / Goodnight
*Mah-Gahn-Dahng Oo-Mah-Gah /
Mah-Gahn-Dang Hah-Pon /
Mah-Gahn-Dahng Gah-Bi / Goodnight*

Pleased to meet you
Ikinagagalak kong makilala ka
*Ee-Kee-Nah-Gah-Gah-Lahk Kong
Mah-Kee-Lah-Lah Kah*

How are you?
Kumusta ka?
Koo-Moos-Tah Kah

Well, thank you. And you?
Mabuti naman. Ikaw?
Mah-Boo-Tee Nah-Mahn. E-Kahw

My name is ...
Ang pangalan ko ay ...
Ahng Pah-Ngah-Lahn Ko Ahy...

**This is my friend / boyfriend /
girlfriend / spouse / brother /
sister**
Ito ang aking kaibigan / boyfriend /
girlfriend / asawa / kapatid (sibling)
*Ee-To Ahng A-Keeng Kah-Ee-Bee-Gahn /
Boyfiend / Girlfiend / Ah-Sah-Wah
(Spouse) / Kah-Pah-Teed (Sibling)*

Where are you travelling to?
Saan ka magbibiyahe?
Sah-An Kah Mahg-Bee-Bee-Yah-He

I am / we are going to ...
Pupunta ako / kami sa ...
Poo-Poon-Tah Ah-Ko / Kah-Mee Sah ...

How long are you travelling for?
Gaano ka katagal magbibiyahe?
*Gah-Ah-No Kah Kah-Tah-Gahl-Mahg-
Bee-Bee-Yah-He*

Where do you come from?
Taga saan ka?
Tah-Gah Sah-An Kah

**I am / we are from Australia /
Britain / Canada / America**
Ako / kami ay taga Australia /
Britania / Canada / Amerika
*Ah-Ko / Kah-Mee Ahy Tah-Gah
Australia / Britania / Canada / Amerika*

We are on holiday
Nagbabakasyon kami
Nahg-Bah-Bah-Kahs-Yon Kah-Mee

F
I
L
I
P
I
N
O

F I L I P I N O

This is our first visit here
Ito ang unang bisita naming dito
*Ee-To Ahng Oo-Nahng Beesee-Tah
Nah-Meen Dee-To*

How old are you?
Ilang taon ka na?
Ee-Lahng Tah-On Kah Nah

I am ... years old
Ako ay ... taon na
Ah-Ko Ahy ... Tah-On Nah

**I am a businessman /
businesswoman / doctor /
journalist / manual worker /
administrator / scientist /
student / teacher**
Ako ay isang negosyante / doctor /
peryodista / manggagawa /
administrador / siyentista /
estudyanye / guro
*Ah-Ko Ahy Ee-Sahng Ne-Gos-Yahn-Te /
Dok-Tor / Per-Yo-Dees-Tah /
Mahng-Gah-Gah-Wah/ Ahd-Mee-Nees-
Trah-Dor / See-Yen-Tees-Tah /
Es-Tood-Yahn-Te / Goo-Ro*

**Would you like / may I have a
cigarette?**
Gusto mo ba ng sigarilyo? / puedeng
humingi ng sigarilyo
*Goos-To Mo Bah Nahng
See-Gah-Ril-Yo / Poo-We-Deng
Hoo-Mee-Ngee Nahng See-Gah-Ril-Yo*

Do you mind if I smoke?
Maaari bang manigarilyo?
*Mah-Ah-Ah-Ri Bahng
Mah-Nee-Gah-Reel-Yo*

Do you have a light?
May posporo ka ba?
Mahy Pos-Po-Ro Kah Bah

**I am waiting for my spouse /
boyfriend / girlfriend**
Hinihintay ko ang aking asawa /
boyfriend / girlfriend
*Hee-Nee-Heen-Tahy Ko Ahng A-Keeng
Ah-Sah-Wah / Boyfriend / Girlfriend*

Days

Monday Lunes *Loo-Nes*	**Tuesday** Martes *Mahr-Tes*
Wednesday Miyerkoles *Mee-Yer-Ko-Les*	**Thursday** Huwebes *Hoo-We-Bes*
Friday Biyernes *Bee-Yer-Nes*	**Saturday** Sabado *Sah-Bah-Do*
Sunday Linggo *Leeng-Go*	
Morning Umaga *Oo-Mah-Gah*	**Afternoon** Hapon *Hah-Pon*
Evening Gabi *Gah-Bee*	**Night** Gabi *Gah-Bee*

Yesterday / Today / Tomorrow
Kahapon / Ngayon / Bukas
Kah-Hah-Pon / Ngah-Yon / Boo-Kahs

Numbers

Zero Sero *Se-Ro*	**One** Isa *Ee-Sah*

Two
Dalawa
Dah-Lah-Wah

Three
Tatlo
Taht-Lo

Four
Apat
Ah-Paht

Five
Lima
Lee-Mah

Six
Anim
A-Neem

Seven
Pito
Pee-To

Eight
Walo
Wah-Lo

Nine
Siyam
See-Yahm

Ten
Sampu
Sahm-Poo

Eleven
Labing-isa
Lah-Beeng-Ee-Sah

Twelve
Labindalawa
Lah-Been-Dah-Lah-Wah

Thirteen
Labintatlo
Lah-Been-Taht-Lo

Fourteen
Labing-apat
Lah-Beeng-Ah-Paht

Fifteen
Labinlima
Lah-Been-Lee-Mah

Sixteen
Labing-anim
La-Beeng-A-Neem

Seventeen
Labimpito
La-Beem-Pee-To

Eighteen
Labingwalo
Lah-Beeng-Wah-Lo

Nineteen
Labinsiyam
Lah-Been-See-Yahm

Twenty
Dalawampu
Dah-Lah-Wahm-Poo

Twenty-one
Dalawampu't-isa
Dah-Lah-Wahm-Poot Ee-sah

Twenty-two
Dalawampu't dalawa
Dah-Lah-Wahm-Poot Dah-Lah-Wah

Thirty
Tatlumpu
Taht-Loom-Poo

Forty
Apatnapu
Ah-Paht-Nah-Poo

Fifty
Limampu
Lee-Mahm-Poo

Sixty
Animnapu
Ah-Neem-Nah-Poo

Seventy
Pitumpu
Pee-Toom-Poo

Eighty
Walampu
Wah-Loom-Poo

Ninety
Siyamnapu
See-Yahm-Na-Poo

One hundred
Isang daan
Ee-Sahng Dah-An

Five hundred
Limang daan
Lee-Mahng-Dah-Ahn

One thousand
Isang libo
Ee-Sahng Lee-Bo

One million
Isang milyon
Ee-Sahng Meel-Yon

Time

What time is it?
Anong oras na?
Ah-Nong O-Rahs Nah

F
I
L
I
P
I
N
O

**F
I
L
I
P
I
N
O**

It is...
... na
... Na

9.00
Alas nuwebe
A-Lahs Nu-We-Be

9.05
Alas nuwebe singko
A-Lahs Nu-We-Be Seeng-Ko

9.15
Alas nuwebe kinse
A-Lahs Nu-We-Be Keen-Se

9.20
Alas nuwebe beinte
A-Lahs Nu-We-Be Beyn-Te

9.30
Alas nuwebe trenta
A-Lahs Nu-We-Be Tren-Ta

9.35
Alas nuwebe trentay singko
A-Lahs Nu-We-Be Trenta Seeng-Ko

9.40
Alas nuwebe kuwarenta
A-Lahs Nu-We-Be Ku-Wa-Ren-Ta

9.45
Alas nuwebe kuwarentay singko
A-Lahs Nu-We-Be Ku-Wa-Ren-Tai Seeng-Ko

9.50
Alas nuwebe singkuwenta
A-Lahs Nu-We-Be Sing-Ku-Wen-Ta

9.55
Alas nuwebe singkuwentay singko
A-Lahs Nu-We-Be Sing-Ku-Wen-Ti Seeng-Ko

12.00 / Midday / Midnight
Alas dose / tanghali / hatinggabi
A-Lahs Do-Se/ Tang-Ha-Lee / Hah-Ting-Gah-Bi

Money

I would like to change these traveller's cheques / this currency
Gusto kong ipagpalit itong traveler's cheque / itong pera
Goos-To Kong Ee-Pahg-Pah-Lit Ee-Tong Traveller's Cheques / Ee-Tong Pe-Rah

How much commission do you charge? (What is the service charge?)
Magkano ang komisyong sinisingil ninyo? (Ano ang service charge?)
Mahg-Kah-No Ahng Ko-Mees-Yong See-Nee-See-Ngeel Neen-Yo? (Ah-No Ahng Service Charge)

Can I obtain money with my MasterCard?
Maaari ba akong kumuha na pera sa pamamagitan ng MasterCard ko?
Mah-Ah-Ah-Ri Bah Ah-Kong Koo-Moo-Hah Nahng Pe-Rah Sah Pah-Mah-Mah-Gee-Tahn Nahng Mastercard Ko

Where is the nearest ATM?
Saan ang pinakamalapit na ATM?
Sah-An Ahng Pee-Nah-Kah-Mah-Lah-Peet Nah ATM

My name is ...Some money has been wired to here for me to collect
Ako si ...May pera akong kukunin na ipinadala sa akin dito
Ah-Ko See ...Mahy Pe-Rah Ah-Kong Koo-Koo-Neen Nah Ee-Pee-Nah-Dah-Lah Sah A-Keen Dee-To

ARRIVING AND DEPARTING

Airport

Excuse me, where is the check-in desk for ...airline?
Ipagpaumanhin ninyo, nasaan ang check-in desk para sa airline na ...?
Ee-pahg-Pah-Oo-Mahn-Heen Neen-Yo, Nah-Sah-An Ahng Check-In Desk Pah-Rah Sah Airline Na...

What is the boarding gate / time for my flight?
Anong boarding gate / oras ng flight ko?
Ah-Nong Boarding Gate / O-Rahs Nahng Flight Ko

How long is the delay likely to be?
Mga gaano katagal ng pagka-antala?
Mah-Ngah Gah-Ah-No Kah-Tah-Gahl Ahng Pahg-Kah-Ahn-Tah-Lah

Where is the duty-free shop?
Nasaan ang duty-free shop?
Nah-Sah-An Ahng Duty-Free Shop

Which way is the baggage reclaim?
Saan ang daan papunta sa baggage reclaim?
Sah-Ahn Ahng Dah-Ahn Pah-Poon-Tah Sah Baggage Reclaim

I have lost my luggage. Please can you help?
Nawala ang aking bagahe. Tulungan naman ninyo ako?
Nah-Wah-Lah Ahng A-Keeng Bah-Gah-He. Too-Loo-Ngahn Nah-Mahn Neen-Yo Ah-Ko

I am flying to ...
Lilipad ako patungo sa...
Lee-Lee-Pahd Ah-Ko Pah-Too-Ngo Sah...

Where can I get the bus to the city centre?
Saan ang sasakyan na bus papunta sa sentro ng siyudad?
Sah-An Ahng Sah-Sahk-Yahn Nah Bus Pah-Poon-Tah Sah Sen-Tro Nahng See-Yoo-Dahd

Trains and Boats

Where is the ticket office / information desk?
Nasaan ang ticket office / information desk?
Nah-Sah-An Ahng Ticket Office / Information Desk

Which platform does the train / speedboat / ferry to ...depart from?
Aling sakayan ang panggagalingan ng tren / speedboat / ferry patungong ...
A-Leeng Sah-Kah-Yahn Ahng Pahng-Gah-Gah-Lee-Ngahn Nahng Tren / Speedboat / Ferry Pah-Too-Ngong ...

Where is platform...?
Saan ang sakayang...?
Nah-Sah-An Ahng Sah-Kah-Yahng ...

When is the next train / boat to ...?
Kailan ang susunod na tren / barko papuntang...?
Kah-Ee-Lahn Ahng Soo-Soo-Nod Nah Tren / Bahr-Ko Pah-Poon-Tahng ...

Is there a later train / boat to ...?
May mas huli pa bang tren / barko papuntang...?

F I L I P I N O

Mahy Mahs Hoo-Lee Pah Bahng
Tren / Bahr-Ko Pah-Poon-Tahng...

Notices and Signs

Buffet (Dining) car
Buffet (Dining) Car
Buffet (Dining) car

Bus
Bus
Bus

Naiinom / Hindi naiinom na tubig
Nah-Ee-Ee-Nom / Heen-Dee
Nah-Ee-Ee-Nom Nah Too-Beeg
**Drinking / Non-drinking
Water**

Pasukan
Pah-Soo-Kahn
Entrance

Labasan
Lah-Bah-Sahn
Exit

Ospital
Os-Pee-Tahl
Hospital

Impormasyon
Eem-Por-Mahs-Yon
Information

Naiwanang Bagahe
(Pagkuha ng Bagahe)
Nah-Ee-Wah-Nahng Bah-Gah-He
(Pahg-Koo-Hah Nahng Bah-Gah-He)
Left luggage (Baggage claim)

Mga locker ng bagahe
*Mah-Ngah Locker Nahng
Bah-Gah-He*
Luggage lockers

Post office
Post Office
Post office

Sakayan
Sah-Kah-Yahn
Platform

Estasyon ng tren
Es-Tahs-Yon Nahng Tren
Railway (Railroad) station

Paliparan
Pah-Lee-Pah-Rahn
Airport

Estasyon ng pulisya
Es-Tahs-Yon Nahng Poo-Lees-Yah
Police station

Daungan
Dah-Oo-Ngahn
Port

Restoran
Res-To-Rahn
Restaurant

Smoking / Non-smoking
Smoking / Non-Smoking
Smoking / Non-smoking

Telepono
Te-Le-Po-No
Telephone

Bilihan ng tiket
Bee-Lee-Hahn Nahng Tee-Ket
Ticket office

Check-in Desk
Check-in Desk
Check-in desk

Listahan ng oras (Mga Skedyul)
*Lis-Tah-Hahn Nahng O-Rahs
(Mah-Ngah Sked Yool)*
Timetables (Schedules)

Mga Palikuran (Mga CR)
*Mah-Ngah Pah-Lee-Koo-Rahn
(Mah-Ngah C-R)*
Toilets (Restrooms)

Babae / Lalaki
Bah-Bah-E / Lah-Lah-Kee
Ladies / Gentlemen

Underground (Subway)
Underground (Subway)
Underground (Subway)

Hintayan
Heen-Tah-Yahn
Waiting room

Buying a Ticket

I would like a first-class / second-class single (oneway) / return (round-trip) ticket to ...
Gusto ko ng isang first-class /
second-class single (one way) /
pabalik (balikan) na tiket papuntang...
*Goos-To Ko Nahng I-Sahng First-Class /
Second-Class Single (One Way) /
Pah-Bah-Leek (Bah-Li-Kahn) Nah
Tee-Ket Pah-Poon-Tahng...*

Is it an express (fast) train / bus?
Ekspres (mabilis) ba itong tren / bus?
*Eks-Pres (Mah-Bee-Lees) Bah
Ee-Tong Tren / Bus*

Is my rail pass valid on this train / ferry / bus?
Tama ba ang boarding pass ko sa
tren / ferry / bus na ito?
*Tah-Mah Bah Ahng Boarding Pass Ko
Sah Tren / Ferry / Bus Nah Ee-To*

I would like an aisle / window seat
Gusto ko ng upuang nasa may
pasilyo / bintana
*Gus-To Ko Nahng Oo-Poo-Ang Nah-Sah
Mahy Pah-Seel-Yo / Bin-Tah-Nah*

No smoking / smoking, please
Sa no smoking / smoking nga
Sah No Smoking / Smoking Ngah

We would like to sit together
Gusto naming magkatabi
*Goos-To Nah-Meeng
Mahg-Kah-Tah-Bee*

I would like to make a seat reservation
Gusto kong mapareserba ng upuan
*Goos-To Kong Mahg-Pah-Re-Ser-Bah
Nahng Oo-Poo-An*

I would like to reserve a couchette / sleeper for one person / two people / my family
Gusto kong magpareserba ng isang
kuwarto para sa isang tao / dalawang
tao / pamilya ko
*Goos-To Kong Mahg-Pah-Re-Ser-Bah
Nahng Ee-Sang Koo-Wahr-To Pah-Rah
Sah Ee-Sahng Tah-O / Dah-Lah-Wahng
Tah-O/ Pah-Meel-Yah Ko*

I would like to reserve a cabin
Gusto kong magpareserba ng isang
kabin
*Goos-To Kong Mahg-Pah-Re-Ser-Bah
Nahng Ee-sahng Kah-Been*

FILIPINO

81

FILIPINO

Timetables (Schedules)

Darating
Dah-Ra-Ting
Arrive

Tumatawag (Humihinto) sa
*Too-Mah-Tah-Wahg
(Hoo-Mee-Heen-To) Sah …*
Calls (Stops) at...

Catering service
Catering Service
Catering service

Mag-pa-leet sa...
Mahg-Pah-Leet Sah…
Change at...

Koneksiyon / Dadaan sa
Ko-Nek-SeeYon/ Dah-Dah-Ahn Sah
Connection / Via

Araw-araw
Ah-Rahw – Ah-Rahw
Daily

Bawat 40 minutos
Bah-Waht 40 Mee-Noo-Tos
Every 40 minutes

First class
First Class
First class

Oras-oras
O-Rahs-O-Rahs
Hourly

Inirerekomenda ang
pagpapareserba ng upuan
*Ee-Nee-Re-Re-Ko-Men-Dah Ahng
Pahg-Pah-Pah-Re-Ser-Bah Nahng
Oo-Poo-Ahn*

Seat reservations are recommended

Second class
Second Class
Second class

Mabayaran ang karagdagan
*Mah-Bah-Yah-Rahn Ahng
Kah-Rahg-Dah-Gahn*
Supplement payable

Luggage

How much will it cost to send (ship) my luggage in advance?
Magkano ang bayad para unahing ipadala ang aking bagahe?
*Mahg-Kah-No Ahng Bah-Yahd
Pah-Rah Oo-Nah-Heeng Ee-Pah-Dah-Lah Ahng A-Keeng Bah-Gah-He*

Where is the left luggage (baggage claim) office?
Nasaan ang opisina ng naiwanang bagahe (Baggage Claim)?
*Nah-Sah-An Ahng O-Pee-See-Nah
Nahng Nah-Ee-Wah-Nahng
Bah-Gah-He (Baggage Claim)*

What time do you open / close?
Anong oras kayo bukas / sara?
*Ah-Nong O-Rahs Kah-Yo Boo-Kahs /
Sah-Rah*

Where are the luggage trolleys (carts)?
Nasaan ang mga trolleys (carts) ng mga bagahe?
*Nah-Sah-An Ahng Mah-Ngah Trolis
(Carts) Nahng Mah-Ngah
Bah-Gah-He*

Where are the lockers?
Nasaan ang mga lockers?
Nah-Sah-An Ahng Mah-Ngah Lockers

I have lost my locker key
Nawala ko ang suis ng aking locker
Nah-Wah-Lah Ko Ahng Soo-See Nahng A-Keeng Locker

On Board

Is this seat free?
May nakaupo dito?
Mahy Nah-Kah-Oo-Po Dee-To

Excuse me, you are sitting in my reserved seat
Pasensiya na, nakaupo ka sa ipanareserba kong upuan
Pah-Sen-See-Yah Nah, Nah-Kah-Oo-Po Kah Sah Ee-Pee-Nah-Re-Ser-Bah Kong Oo-Poo-Ahn

Which station is this?
Anong istasyon ito?
Ah-Nong Ees-Tahs-Yon Ee-To

What time is this train / bus / ferry / flight due to arrive / depart?
Anong oras darating / aalis ang tren / bus / ferry / eroplanong ito?
Ah-Nong O-Rahs Dah-Rah-Ting / Ah-Ah-Lees Ahng Tren / Bus / Ferry / E-Ro-Plah-Nong Ee-To

Travelling with Children

Do you have a high chair / babysitting service / cot?
Meron ba kayong mataas na upuan / tagapag-alaga ng bata / kama kayo?

Me-Ron Bah Kah-Yong Mah-Tah-As Nah Oo-Poo-Ahn / Tah-Gah-Pahg-Ah-Lah-Gah Nahng Bah-Tah / Kah-Mah Bah Kah-Yo

Where is the nursery / playroom?
Nasaan ang nursery / palaruan
Nah-Sah-An Ahng Nursery / Pah-Lah-Roo-Ahn

Where can I warm the baby's bottle?
Saan ako puwedeng mapainit ng bote ng bata?
Sah-An Ah-Ko Poo-We-Deng Mahg-Pah-I-Neet Nahng Bo-Te Nahng Bah-Tah

Customs and Passports

Passports, please!
Passport po!
Pahs-Port Po

I have nothing / wine / spirits (alcohol) / tobacco to declare
Wala akong idedeklara na alak / mga alak (alcohol) / sigarilyo
Wah-Lah Ah-Kong I-De-Dek-Lah-Ruh Nah A-Lahk / Muh-Ngah A-Lakh / See-Gah-Reel-Yo

I will be staying for...days / weeks / months
Titira ako dito ng mga ... araw / lingo / buwan
Tee-Tee-Rah Ah-Ko Dee-To Nahng Mah-Ngah ...A-Rahw / Leeng-Go / Bu-Wahn

F
I
L
I
P
I
N
O

83

F
I
L
I
P
I
N
O

SIGHTSEEING

Asking the Way

Excuse me, do you speak English?
Ipagpaumanhin ninyo, nakakapagsalita ba kayo ng Ingles?
Ee-Pahg-Pah-Oo-Mahn-Heen Neen-Yo, Nah-Kah-Kah-Pahg-Sah-Lee-Tah Bah Kah-Yo Nahng Eeng-Les

Excuse me, can you help me please?
Ipagpaumanhin ninyo, puwede ba ninyo akong tulungan?
Ee-Pahg-Pah-Oo-Mahn-Heen Neen-Yo, Poo-We-De Bah Neen-Yo Ah-Kong Too-Loo-Ngahn

Where is the Tourist Information Office?
Nasaan ang Tourist Information Office?
Nah-Sah-An Ahng Tourist Information Office

Excuse me, is this the right way to ...?
Ipagpaumanhin ninyo, ito ba ang tamang daan papuntang…?
Ee-Pahg-Pah-Oo-Mahn-Heen Neen-Yo, Ee-To Bah Ahng Tah-Mahng Dah-An Pah-Poon-Tahng ...

... the cathedral / the tourist information office / the castle / the old town
... sa simbahan / tourist information office / sa palasyo / sa lumang bayan
...Sah Seem-Bah-Hahn / Sah Tourist Information Office / Sah Pah-Lahs-Yo / Sah Loo-Mahng Bah-Yahn...

Can you tell me the way to the railway (railroad) station / bus station / taxi rank (stand) / city centre (downtown) / beach?
Maaari ba ninyong ituro sa akin ang daan papuntang estasyon ng tren / estasyon ng bus / hintayan ng taksi / sa bayan / sa tabing-dagat?
Mah-Ah-Ah-Ri Bah Nin-Yong I-Too-Ro Sah A-King Ahng Dah-An Pah-Poon-Tahng Es-Tahs-Yon Nahng Tren / Es-Tahs-Yon Nahng Bus / Hin-Tah-Yahn Nahng Tahk-Si / Sah Bah-Yahn / Sah Tah-Beeng-Dah-Gaht

First / second / left / right / straight ahead
Una / ikalawa / kaliwa / kanan / diretso
Oo-Nah / Ee-Kah-Lah-Wah / Kah-Lee-Wah / Kah-Nahn / Dee-Ret-So

At the corner / at the traffic lights
Sa kanto / sa may traffic lights
Sah Kahn-To / Sah Mahy Traffic Lights

Where is the nearest police station / post office?
Nasaan ang pinakamalapit na estasyon ng pulisya / post opis?
Nah-Sah-An Ahng Pee-Nah-Kah-Mah-Lah-Peet Nah Es-Tahs-Yon Nahng Poo-Lees-Yah / Post O-Pees

Is it near / far?
Malapit ba / malayo ba?
Mah-Lah-Peet Bah / Mah-Lah-Yo Bah

Do I need to take a taxi / catch a bus?
Kailangan ko bang sumakay sa taksi / sumasakay sa bus?
Kah-Ee-Lah-Ngahn Ko Bahng Soo-Mah-Kahy Sah Tahk-See / Soo-Mah-Kahy Sah Bus

Do you have a map?
May mapa ba kayo?
Mahy Mah-Pah Bah Kah-Yo

Can you point to it on my map?
Maaari ba ninyong ituro sa akin sa mapa?
Mah-Ah-Ah-Ree Bah Neen-Yong Ee-Too-Ro Sah A-Keen Sah Mah-Pah

Thank you for your help
Maraming salamat sa tulong ninyo
Mah-Rah-Meeng Sah-Lah-Maht Sah Too-Long Neen-Yo

How do I reach the motorway / main road?
Paano ako makakarating sa highway?
Pah-A-No Ah-Ko Mah-Kah-Kah-Rah-Teeng Sah Highway

I think I have taken the wrong turning
Nagkamali yata ako ng linikuan
Nahg-Kah-Mah-LiYah-Tah Ah-ko Nahng Lee-Nee-Koo-Ahn

I am looking for this address
Hinahanap ko ang address na ito
Hee-Nah-Hah-Nahp Ko Ahng Ahd-Dres Nah Ee-To

I am looking for the ...hotel
Hinahanap ko ang ...na hotel
Hee-Na-Ha-Nahp Ko Ang ... Na Ho-Tel

How far is it to ...from here?
Gaano ito kalayo ang ... Mula rito?
Gah-Ah-No Ee-To Kah-Lah-Yo Ahng ... Moo-Lah Ree-To

Carry straight on for ... kilometres
Dumiretso ka ng mga ... kilometro

Du-Mee-Ret-So Kah Nahng Mah-Ngah ...Kee-Lo-Met-Ro

Take the next turning on the right / left
Lumiko ka sa sususnod na kanto sa kanan / kaliwa
Loo-Mee-Ko Kah Sah Soo-Soo-Nod Nah Kahn-To Sah Kah-Nahn / Kah-Lee-Wah

Turn right / left at the next crossroads / traffic lights
Kumanan / kumaliwa ka sa susunod na kanto / traffic light
Koo-Mah-Nahn / Koo-Mah-LeeWah Kah Sah Soo-Soo-Nod Nah Kahn-To / Traffic Light

You are going in the wrong direction
Papunta ka sa maling direksiyon
Pah-Poon-Tah Kah Sah Mah-Leeng Dee-Rek-SeeYon

Where is the cathedral / church / museum / pharmacy?
Nasaan ang katedral / simbaan / museyo / botika?
Nah-Sah-An Ahng Kah-Ted-Rahl / Seem-Bah-Hahn / Moo-Se-O / Bo-Tee-Kah

How much is the admission / entrance charge?
Magkano ang bayad / bayad para makapasok?
Mahg-Kah-No Ahng Bah-Yahd / Bah-Yahd Pah-Rah Mah-Kah-Pah-Sok

Is there a discount for children / students / senior citizens?
May diskuwento ba para sa mga bata / mga estudyante / mga matatanda?
Mahy Dees-Koo-Wen-To Bah Pah-Rah Sah Mah-Ngah Bah-Tah / Mah-Ngah Es-Tood-Yahn-Te / Mah-Ngah Mah-Tah-Tahn-Dah

F I L I P I N O

What time does the next guided tour (in English) start?
Anong oras mag-uumpisa ang susunod na guided tour (sa Ingles)?
Ah-Nong O-Rahs Mahg-Oo-Oom-Pee-Sah Ahng Soo-Soo-Nod Nah Guided Tour (Sah Ingles)

One / two adults / children, please
Isa / dalawang pangmatanda / bata nga
Ee-Sah / Dah-Lah-Wahng Pahng-Mah-Tahn-Dah / Bah-Tah Ngah

May I take photographs here?
Puwede ba akong kumuha ng litrato ditto?
Poo-We-De Bah Ah-Kong Koo-Moo-Hah Nahng Leet-Rah-To Dee-To

Do you have a map of the town / area?
Meron ba kayong mapa ng bayan / lugar?
Me-Ron Bah Kah-Yong Mah-Pah Nahng Bah-Yahn / Loo-Gahr

Do you have a list of accommodation?
Meron ba kayong listahan ng tirahan?
Me-Ron Bah Kah-Yong Lees-Tah-Hahn Nahng Tee-Rah-Hahn

Can I reserve accommodation?
Maaari ba akong magpareserba ng tirahan?
Mah-Ah-Ah-Ri Bah Ah-Kong Mahg-Pah-Re-Ser-Bah Nahng Tee-Rah-Hahn

I have a reservation in the name of ...
May ipinareserba ako sa pangalan ni ...
Mahy Pee-Nah-Re-Ser-Bah Ah-Ko Sah Pah-Ngah-Lahn Nee...

I wrote to / faxed / telephoned you last month / last week
Sumulat / nag-fax / tumawag ako sa inyo noong isang buwan / nakaraang linggo
Soo-Moo-Laht / Nahg-Fax / Too-Mah-Wahg Ah-Ko Sah Een-Yo No-Ong Ee-Sahng Boo-Wahn / Nah-Kah-Rah-Ang Leeng-Go

Do you have any rooms free?
May bakante ba kayong kuwarto?
Mahy Bah-Kahn-Te Bah Kah-Yong Koo-Wahr-To

I would like to reserve a single / double room with / without bath / shower
Gusto kong mapareserba ng isang pang-isahang / pangdalawahang kuwarto na may / walang cr / banyo
Goos-To Kong Mahg-Re-Ser-Bah Nah Ee-Sahng Pahng-Ee-Sah-Hahng / Pahng-Dah-Lah-Wah-Hahng Koo-Wahr-To Nah Mahy / Wah-Lahng C-R / Bahn-Yo

I would like bed and breakfast / (room and) full board
Gusto ko ng tulugan at almusal / (kuwarto) full board
Goos-To Ko Nahng Too-Loo-Gahn Aht Ahl-Moo-Sahl / (Koo-Wahr-To) full board

How much is it per night?
Magkano ang isang gabi?
Mahg-Kah-No Ahng Ee-Sahng Gah-Bee

Is breakfast included?
Kasama ba ang almusal?
Kah-Sah-Mah Bah Ahng Ahl-Moo-Sahl

Do you have any cheaper rooms?
May mas mura bang kuwarto?
Mahy Mahs Moo-Rah Bahng Koo-Wahr-To

I would like to see / take the room
Gusto kong makita / kunin ang kuwarto
Goos-To Kong Mah-Kee-Tah / Koo-Neen Ahng Koo-Wahr-To

I would like to stay for ...nights
Gusto kong tumigil dito ng ... gabi
Goos-To Kong Too-Mee-Geel Dee-To Nahng ...Gah-Bee

The shower / light / tap / hot water doesn't work
Hindi gumagana ang shower / ilaw / gripo / mainit na tubig
Hin-Dee Goo-Mah-Gah-Nah Ahng Shower / Ee-Lahw / Gree-Po / Muh-Ee-Neet Nah Too-Beeg

At what time / where is breakfast served?
Anong oras / saan iaahin ang almusal?
Ah-Nong O-Rahs / Sah-An I-Ah-A-Heen Ahng Ahl-Moo-Sahl

What time do I have to check out?
Anong oras akong kinakailangang mag-check out?
Ah-Nong O-Rahs Ah-Kong Kee-Nah-Kah-Ee-Lah-Ngahng Mahg-Check Out

Can I have the key to room number ... ?
Puwede ko bang makuha ang susi ng kuwartong ...?
Poo-We-De Ko Bahng Mah-Koo-Hah Ahng Soo-See Nahng Koo-Wahr-Tong...

My room number is ...
Ang numero ko ay...
Ang Nu-Me-Ro Ko Ay ...

My room is not satisfactory / not clean enough / too noisy
Ang aking kuwarto ay hindi kasiya-siya / hindi malinis / masyadong maingay
Ahng A-Keeng Koo-Wahr-To Ahy / Heen-Dee Kah-See-Yah-Sec-Yah / Heen-Dee Mah-Lee-Nees / Mahs-Yah-Dong Mah-Ee-Ngahy

Please can I change rooms?
Maaari ba akong magpalit ng kuwarto?
Mah-Ah-Ah-Ri Bah Ah-Kong Mahg-Pah-Leet Nahng Ku-Wahr-To

Where is the bathroom?
Nasaan ang cr?
Nah-Sah-An Ahng C-R

Do you have a safe for valuables?
Meron ba kayong safe para sa mga bagay na mahahalaga?
Me-Ron Bah Kah-Yong Safe Pah-Rah Sah Mah-Ngah Bah-Gahy Nah Mah-Hah-Hah-Lah-Gah

Is there a laundry / do you wash clothes?
Puwede bang magpalaba / tumatanggap ba kayo ng mga labahin?
Poo-We-De Bahng Mahg-Pah-Lah-Bah / Too-Mah-Tahng-Gahp Bah Kah-Yo Nahng Mah-Ngah Lah-Bah-Heen

I would like an air-conditioned room
Gusto ko ng isang air-con na kuwarto
Goos-To Ko Nahng Ee-Sahng Air-Con Nah Koo-Wahr-To

Do you accept traveller's cheques / credit cards?
Tumatanggap ba kayo ng traveler's cheques / mga credit card?
Too-Mah-Tahng-Gahp Bah Kah-Yo Nahng Traveler's Cheques / Ma-Ngah Credit Card

May I have the bill please?
Ang tsit nga?
Ahng TSeet Ngah

Excuse me, I think there may be a mistake in this bill
Ipagpaumanhin ninyo, may mali yata dito sa tsit
Ee-Pahg-Pah-Oo-Mahn-Heen Neen-Yo, Mahy Mah-Li Yah-Tah Dee-To Sah TSeet

Youth Hostels

How much is a dormitory bed per night?
Magkano ang isang kama sa dormitory sa isang gabi?
Mahg-Kah-No Ahng Ee-sahng Kah-Mah Sah Dormitory Sah Ee-Sahng Gah-Bee

I am / am not an HI member
Ako ay / hindi miyembro ng HI
Ah-Ko Ahy / Heen-Dee Mee-Yem-Bro Nahng Hee

May I use my own sleeping bag?
Puwede ko bang gamitin ang sarili kong sleeping bag?
Poo-We-De Ko Bahng Gah-Mee-Teen Ahng Sah-Ree-Lee Kong Sleeping Bag

What time do you lock the doors at night?
Anong oras kayo nagsasara ng pinto sa gabi?
Ah-Nong O-Rahs Kah-Yo Nahg-Sah-Sah-Rah Nahng Peen-To Sah Gah-Bee

Camping

May I camp for the night / two nights?
Puwede ba akong mag-camp ngayong gabi / dalawang gabi?
Poo-We-De Bah Ah-Kong Mahg-Camp Ngah-Yon Gah-Bee / Dah-Lah-Wahng Gah-Bee

Where can I pitch my tent?
Saan ako puwedeng magtayo ng aking tent?
Sah-An Ah-Ko Poo-We-Deng Mahg-Tah-Yo Nahng A-Keeng Tent

How much does it cost for one night / week?
Magkano ang isang gabi / linggo?
Mahg-Kah-No Ahng Ee-Sahng Gah-Bee / Leeng-Go

Where are the washing facilities?
Nasaan ang labahan?
Nah-Sah-An Ahng Lah-Bah-Hahn

Is there a restaurant / supermarket / swimming pool on site / nearby?
May kainan / supermarket / swimming pool ditto / na malapit dito?
Mahy Kah-Ee-Nahn / Supermarket / Swimming Pool Dee-To / Nah Mah-Lah-Peet Dee-To

Do you have a safety deposit box?
Meron ba kayong safety deposit box?
Me-Ron Bah Kah-Yong Safety Deposit Box

Do you have any matches / cigarettes / cigars?
May posporo / sigarilyo / tabako ka ba?
Mahy Pos-Po-Ro / See-Gah-Reel-Yo / Tah-Bah-Ko Kah Bah

Cafés and Bars

I would like a cup of / two cups of / another coffee / tea
Gusto ko ng isa / dalawang tasa / isa pang kape / tsa
Goos-To Ko Nahng Ee-Sah / Dah-Lah-Wahng Tuh-Sah / Ee-Sah Pahng Kah-Pe / Chah-A

With / without milk / sugar
May / walang gatas / asukal
Mahy / Wah-Lahng Gah-Tahs / Ahsoo-Kahl

I would like a bottle /glass / two glasses of mineral water / red wine / white wine, please
Gusto ko ng isang bote / baso / dalawang baso ng mineral water / red wine / white wine nga
Goos-To Ko Nahng Ee-sahng Bo-Te / Bah-So / Dah-Lah-Wahng Bah-So Nahng Mineral Water / Red Wine / White Wine Ngah

I would like a beer / two beers, please
Gusto ko ng isang serbesa / dalawang serbesa nga
Goos-To Ko Nahng Ee-sahng Ser-Be-Sah / Dah-Lah-Wahng Ser-Be-Sah Ngah

Please may I have some ice?
Puwedeng humingi ng yelo?
Poo-We-Deng Hoo-Mee-Ngi Nahng Ye-Lo

Restaurants

Can you recommend a good / cheap restaurant in this area?
May mairerekomenda ka bang isang magandang / murang kainan sa lugar na ito?
Mahy Mah-Ee-Re-Re-Ko-Men-Dah Kah Bahng Ee-Sahng Mah-Gahn-Dahng / Moo-Rahng Kah-Ee-Nahn Sah Loo-Gahr Nah Ee-To

I would like a table for ...people
Gusto ko ng isang mesa para sa ...tao
Goos-To Ko Nahng Ee-Sahng Me-Sah Pah-Rah Sah ... Tah-O

Do you have a non-smoking area?
Meron ba kayong lugar para sa hindi naninigarilyo?
Me-Ron Bah Kah-Yong Loo-Gahr Pah-Rah Sah Heen-Dee Nah-Nee-Nee-Gah-Reel-Yo

Waiter / Waitress!
Boss / Miss!
Boss / Miss

Excuse me, please may we order?
Puwede na ba kaming mag-order?
Poo-We-De Nah Bah Kah-Meeng Mahg-Or-Der

Do you have a set menu / children's menu / wine list?
Meron ba kayong menu / menu para sa mga bata / listahan ng alak?

FILIPINO

Me-Ron Bah Kah-Yong Me-Nu / Me-Nu Pah-Rah Sah Mah-Ngah Bah-Tah / Lees-Tah-Hahn Nahng A-Lahk

Do you have any vegetarian dishes?
Meron ba kayong mga ulam na pang-vegetarian?
Me-Ron Bah Kah-Yong Mah-Ngah Oo-Lahm Nah Pahng-Vegetarian

Do you have any local specialities?
Meron ba kayong lokal na espesiyalidad?
Me-Ron Bah Kah-Yong Lo-Kahl Nah Es-Pe-See-Yah-Lee-Dahd

Are vegetables included?
Kasama ba ang mga gulay?
Kah-Sah-Mah Bah Ahng Mah-Ngah Goo-Lahy

Could I have it well-cooked / medium / rare please?
Puwede bang bigyan ninyo ako ng lutong-luto / half-cooked / medyo luto?
Poo-We-De Bahng Beeg-Yahn Neen-Yo Ah-Ko Nahng Loo-Tong-Loo-To / Half-Cooked / Med-Yo Loo-To

What does this dish consist of?
Ano ang mga sangkap ng ulam na ito?
Ah-No Ahng Mah-Ngah Sahng-Kahp Nahng Oo-Lahm Nah Ee-To

I am a vegetarian. Does this contain meat?
Vegetarian ako. May karne ba ditto?
Vegetarian Ah-Ko. Mahy Kahr-Ne Bah Dee-To

I do not eat nuts / dairy products / meat / fish
Hindi ako kumakain ng mga produktong may mani / gatas / karne / isda
Heen-Dee Ah-Ko Koo-Mah-Kah-Een Nahng Mah-Ngah Pro-Dook-Tong Mahy / Mah-NeeGah-Tahs / Kahr-Ne / Ees-Dah

Not (very) spicy, please
Huwag nga (masyadong) maanghang
Hu-Wahg Ngah (Mahs-Yah-Dong) Mah-Ahng-Hahng

I would like the set menu, please
Puwede ko bang makita ang menu
Poo-We-De Ko Bahng Mah-Kee-Tah Ahng Me-Nu

We are still waiting to be served
Naghihintay pa lang kaming masilbihan
Nahg-Hee-Heen-Tahy Pah Lahng Kah-Meeng Mah-Seel-Bee-Hahn

Please bring a plate / knife / fork
Puwede bang bigyan mo kami ng plato / kutsilyo / tinidor
Poo-We-De Bahng Beeg-Yahn Mo Kah-Mee Nahng Plah-To / Koot-Seel-Yo / Tee-Nee-Dor

Excuse me, this is not what I ordered
Ipagpaumanhin mo, hindi ito ang inorder ko
Ee-Pahg-Pah-Oo-Mahn-Heen Mo, Heen-Dee Ee-To Ahng Ee-Nor-Der Ko

May I have some / some more bread / water / coffee / tea?
Bigyan mo nga ako ng / konti pang tinapay / tubig / kape / tsaa?
Beeg-Yahn Mo Ngah Ah-Ko Nahng / Kon-Tee Pahng Tee-Nah-Pahy / Too-Beeg / Kah-Pe / Chah-A

May I have the bill, please?
Ang tsit nga?
Ahng T-Seet Ngah

Does this bill include service?
Kasama na ba sa tsit ang service charge?
Kah-Sah-Mah Nah Bah Sah Tseet Ahng Service Charge

Do you accept traveller's cheques / MasterCard / US dollars?
Tumatanggap ba kayo ng mga traveler's cheques / MasterCard / US dollar?
Too-Mah-Tahng-Gahp Bah Kah-Yo Nahng Mah-Ngah Traveler's Cheques/ Mastercard / US Dollar

Can I have a receipt, please?
Puwede bang bigyan mo ako ng resibo?
Poo-We-De Bahng Beeg-Yahn Mo Ah-Ko Nahng Re-See-Bo

Where is the toilet (restroom), please?
Nasaan ang cr?
Nah-Sah-An Ahng C.R

On the Menu

Almusal / Tanghalian / Hapunan
Ahl-Moo-Sahl / Tahng-Hah-Lee-Ahn / Hah-Poo-Nahn
Breakfast / Lunch / Dinner

Mga unang iaahin
Mah-Ngah Oo-Nahng I-Aha-Heen
First courses

Mga Sopas
Mah-Ngah So-Pahs
Soups

Mga Ulam
Mah-Ngah Oo-Lahm
Main courses

Mga Isdang Ulam
Mah-Ngah Ees-Dahng Oo-Lahm
Fish dishes

Mga Karneng Ulam
Mah-Ngah Kahr-Neng Oo-Lahm
Meat dishes

Beef	Steak
Beef	*Steak*
Beef	**Steak**

Karne ng Baboy
Kahr-Ne Nahng Bah-Boy
Pork

Karne ng Guya
Kahr-Ne Nahng Goo-Yah
Veal

Manok
Mah-Nok
Chicken

Karne ng Tupa
Kahr-Ne Nahng Too-Pah
Lamb

Hamon
Hah-Mon
Ham

Mga Ulam na Gulay
Mah-Ngah Oo-Lahm Nah Goo-Lahy
Vegetarian dishes

F
I
L
I
P
I
N
O

F
I
L
I
P
I
N
O

Mga Gulay
Mah-Ngah Goo-Lahy
Vegetables

Chips (french fries)
Chips (French Fries)
Chips (French fries)

Nilaga / iginisa / mashed na patatas
Nee-Lah-Gah / Ee-Gee-Nee-Sah /
Mashed Nah Pah-Tah-Tahs
**Boiled / sauté /
mashed potatoes**

Kanin
Kah-Neen
Rice

Keso
Keh-So
Cheese

Panghimagas
Pahng-Hee-Mah-Gahs
Desserts

Sorbesa
Sor-Be-Tes
Ice cream

Cakes
Cakes
Cakes

Pastries
Pastries
Pastries

Prutas
Proo-Tahs
Fruit

Mga Tinapay
Mah-Ngah Tee-Nah-Pahy
Bread

(Non-existent in Tagalog)
Rolls

Toast
Toast
Toast

Mantekilya
Mahn-Tee-Keel-Yah
Butter

Asin / paminta
Ah-Seen / Pah-Meen-Tah
Salt / pepper

Asukal
Ah-Soo-Kahl
Sugar

Mga Espesiyalidad
Mah-Ngah Es-Pe-See-Yah-Lee-Dahd
Specialities

Mga lokal na espesiyalidad
Mah-Ngah Lo-Kahl Nah
Es-Pe-See-Yah-Lee-Dahd
Local specialities

Set Menu
Set Menu
Set Menu

Listahan ng alak
Lees-Tah-Hahn Nahng A-Lahk
Wine list

Mga Red Wine
Mah-Ngah Red Wine
Red wines

Mga White wine
Mah-Ngah White Wine
White wines

Mga Rose wine
Mah-Ngah Rose Wine
Rosé wines

Mga sparkling wine
Mah-Ngah Sparkling Wine
Sparkling wines

Serbesa
Ser-Be-Sah
Beer

Nakaboteng serbesa / draught
(draft) na serbesa
Nah-Kah-Bo-Teng Ser-Be-Sah /
Draught (Draft) Nah Ser-Be-Sah
Bottled beer /
draught (draft) beer

Mga inuming walang alkohol
Mah-Ngah Ee-Noo-Meeng
Wah-Lahng Ahl-Ko-Hol
Non-alcoholic drinks

Mineral water
Mineral water
Mineral water

Mga fruit juice
Muh-Ngah Fruit Juice
Fruit juices

Orange juice
Orange Juice
Orange juice

Lemonade   Ice
Lemonade   *Ice*
Lemonade   **Ice**

May gatas / walang gatas na kape /
espressong kape
Mahy Gah-Tas / Wa-lahng Gah-Tas
Nah Kah-Pe / Es-Pres-Song Kah-Pe
White coffee / black coffee /
espresso coffee

Tsaang may gatas / may kalamansi
Tsah-Ang Mahy Gah-Tahs /
Mahy Kah-Lah-Mahn-Si
Tea with milk / with lemon

Tsokolate (inumin)
Tso-Ko-Lah-Te (Ee-Noo-Meen)
Chocolate (drink)

Gatas
Gah-Tahs
Milk

Mga Snack / Magagaang Pagkain
Mah-Ngah Snack /
Mah-Gah-Gah-Ang Pahg-Kah-Een
Snacks / Light meals

Mga Salad
Mah-Ngah Salad
Salads

Mga Sandwich
Mah-Ngah Sundwich
Sandwiches

Mga Itlog
Mah-Ngah Eet-Log
Eggs

Sausage
Sausage
Sausage

Nilaga / prito / scrambled na itlog
Nee-La-Gah / Pree-To / Scrambled
Na Eet-Log
Boiled / fried / scrambled eggs

Typical local dishes

Adobong Manok
Ah-Do Bong Mah-Nok
Stewed chicken in dark, tangy
sauce

Escabecheng Isda
Es-Ka-Bet-Cheng Ees-Da
Sweet and sour fish

F
I
L
I
P
I
N
O

Lechon
Let-Son
Whole pig roasted over live coals

Sinigang
See-Nee-Gang
Soup of meats & seafoods boiled with tamafind

Halo-halo
Hah-Lo-Hah-Lo
Dessert of various preserved sweets with shaved ice

GETTING AROUND

Public Transport

Where is the bus stop / coach stop / nearest metro (subway) station?
Nasaan ang hintuan ng bus / coach / pinakamalapit na estasyon ng MRT?
Na-Sa-Ahn Ang Hin-Tu-Ahn Nang Bus / Coach / Pee-Nah-Kah-Mah-Lah-Peet Nah Es-Tahs-Yon Nahng MRT

When is the next / last bus to ...?
Kailan ang susunod / huling bus papuntang..?
Kah-Ee-Lahn Ahng Soo-Soo-Nod / Hoo-Leeng Bus Pah-Poon-Tahng...

How much is the fare to the city centre (downtown) / railway station / airport?
Magkano ang pamasahe papunta sa sentro (bayan) / estasyon ng railway / paliparan

Mahg-Kah-No Ahng Pah-Mah-Sah-He Pah-Poon-Tah Sah Sen-Tro (Bah-Yahn) / Es-Tahs-Yon Nahng Railway / Pah-LeePah-Rahn

Will you tell me when to get off?
Puwedeng sabihin mo ako kung kailan bababa?
Poo-We-Deng Sah-Bee-Hahn Mo Ah-Ko Koong Kah-Ee-Lahn Bah-Bah-Bah

Does this bus go to ...?
Pumupunta ba ang bus sa...?
Poo-Moo-Poon-Tah Bah Ahng Bus Sah...

Which number bus goes to...?
Anong numero ang bus papuntang...?
Ah-Nong Noo-Me-Ro Ahng Bus Pah-Poon-Tahng...

May I have a single (oneway) / return (round-trip) / day ticket / book of tickets?
Bigyan mo nga ako ng papunta / pabalik (balikan) / araw na tiket / mga tiket
Beeg-Yahn Mo Ngah Ah-Ko Nahng Pah-Poon-Tah / Pah-Bah-Leek (Bah-Lee-Kahn) / A-Rahw Nah Tee-Ket / Mah-Ngah Tee-Ket

Taxis and Rickshaws

I would like to go to ...
Gusto kong pumunta sa ...
Goos-To Kong Poo-Moon-Tah Sah ...

How much will it cost?
Magkano ang bayad?
Mahg-Kah-No Ahng Bah-Yahd

Please may I stop here?
Puwede ba akong bumaba dito?
Poo-We-De Bah Ah-Kong Boo-Mah-Bah Dee-To

I would like to order a taxi today / tomorrow / at 2pm to go from ... to...
Gusto kong magpakuha ng taksi ngayon / bukas / sa alas 2 ng hapon mula... papuntang ...
Goos-To Kong Mahg-Pah-Koo-Hah Nahng Tahk-See Ngah-Yon / Boo-Kahs / Sah Ah-lahs 2 Nahng Hah-Pon Moo-Lah... Pah-Poon-Tahng ...

Entertainment

Can you recommend a good bar / nightclub?
May mairerekomenda ka bang magandang bar / nightclub?
Mahy Mah-I-Re-Re-Ko-Men-Dah Kah Bahng Mah-Gahn-Dahng Bar / Nightclub

Do you know what is on at the cinema (playing at the movies) / theatre at the moment?
Alam mo ba kung ano ang palabas sa sinehan (mapapanood sa sinehan) / teatro ngayon?
Ah-Iahm Mo Bah Koong Ah-No Ahng Pah-Lah-Bahs Sah See-ne-Hahn (Mah-Pah-Pah-No-Od Sah See-Ne-Hahn) / Te-Aht-Ro Ngah-Yon

I would like to book (purchase) ... tickets for the matinee / evening performance on Monday
Gusto kong bumili ng ... na tiket para sa matinee / palabas sa gabi sa Lunes

Goos-To Kong Boo-Mee-Li Nahng ... Nah Tee-Ket Pah-Rah Sah Matinee / Pah-Lah-Bahs Sah Gah-Bee Sah Loo-Nes

What time does the film / performance start?
Anong oras mag-uumpisa ang sine / palabas?
Ah-Nong O-Rahs Mahg-Oo-Oom-Pee-Sah Ahng See-Ne / Pah-Lah-Bahs

COMMUNICATIONS

Post

How much will it cost to send a letter / postcard / this package to Britain / Ireland / America / Canada / Australia / New Zealand?
Magkano ang bayad kung magpapadala ng isang sulat / postcard / ng paketeng ito papuntang Britain / Ireland / Amerika / Canada / Australia / New Zealand?
Mahg-Kah-No Ahng Bah-Yahd Koong Mahg-Pah-Pah-Dah-Lah Nahng Ee-Sahng Soo-Laht / Postcard / Nahng Pah-Ke-Teng Ee-To Puh-Poon-Tahng Britain / Ireland / Amerika / Canada / Australia / New Zealand

I would like one stamp / two stamps
Gusto ko ng isang selyo / mga dalawang selyo
Goos-To Ko Nahng Ee-Sahng Sel-Yo / Mah-Ngah Dah-Lah-Wahng Sel-Yo

I'd like ... stamps for postcards to send abroad, please
Gusto ko ng mga... na selyo para sa mga postcard na ipapadala sa ibang bansa

F
I
L
I
P
I
N
O

Goos-To Ko Nahng Mah-Ngah ... Nah Sel-Yo Pah-Rah Sah Mah-Ngah Postcard Nah I-Pah-Pah-Dah-Lah Sah I-Bahng Bahn-Sah

Phones

I would like to make a telephone call / reverse the charges to (make a collect call to) ...
Gusto kong tumawag / mag-collect call sa ...
Goos-To Kong Too-Mah-Wahg / Mahg-Collect Call Sa ...

Which coins do I need for the telephone?
Aling barya ang kailangan ko para sa telepono?
A-Leeng Bahr-Yah Ahng Kah-Ee-Lah-Ngahn Ko Pah-Rah Sa Te-Le-Po-No

The line is engaged (busy)
Bisi ang linya
Bee-See Ahng Leen-Yah

The number is ...
Ang numero ay ...
Ahng Noo-Me-Ro Ahy ...

Hello, this is ...
Hello, si ...ito
Hello, See ...Ee-To

Please may I speak to...?
Puwede bang makausap si ...?
Poo-We-De Bahng Mah-Kah-Oo-Sahp See...

He / she is not in at the moment. Can you call back?
Wala siya dito ngayon. Puwede bang tumawag ka ulit?
Wah-Lah See-Yah Dee-To Ngah-Yon. Poo-We-De Bahng Too-Mah-Wahg Kah Oo-Lit

Shops

Tindahan ng mga libro / Stationery
Teen-Dah-Hahn Nahng Mah-Ngah Leeb-Ro / Stationery
Bookshop / Stationery

Tindahan ng alahas / mga Regalo
Teen-Dah-Hahn Nahng Ah-Lah-Hahs / Mah-Ngah Re-Gah-Lo
Jeweller / Gifts

Mga sapatos
Mah-Ngah Sah-Pah-Tos
Shoes

Hardware
Hardware
Hardware

Tagapag-ayos ng buhok
Tah-Gah-Pahg-Ah-Yos Nahng Boo-Hok
Hairdresser

(barbero) / (tagapag-ayos ng buhok ng babae)
Bahr-Be-Ro / Tah-Gah-Pahg – Ah-Yos Nahng Boo-Hok Nahng Bah-Bah-E
(men's) / (women's)

Panadero
Pah-Nah-De-Ro
Baker

Mga Telepono
Mah-Ngah Te-Le-Po-No
Phones

Supermarket
Supermarket
Supermarket

Photo-Shop
Photo-Shop
Photo-Shop

Travel agent
Travel Agent
Travel agent

Botika
Bo-Tee-Kah
Pharmacy

In the Shops

What time do the shops open / close?
Anong oras nagbubukas / nagsasara ang mga shop?
Ah-Nong O-Rahs Nahg-Boo-Boo-Kahs / Nahg-Sah-Sah-Rah Ahng Mah-Ngah Shop

Where is the nearest market?
Nasaan ang pinakamalapit ng palengke?
Nah-Sah-An Ahng Pee-Nah-Kah-Mah-Lah-Peet Nah Pah-Leng-Ke

Can you show me the one in the window / this one?
Puwede bang makita ko iyong nasa iskaparate / ito?
Pu-We-De Bahng Mah-Kee-Tah Ko Ee-Yong Nah-Sah Ees-Kah-Pah-Rah-Te / Ee-To

Can I try this on?
Puwede bang isukat?
Pu-We-Deng Bahng Ee-Soo-Kaht

What size is this?
Anong size ito?
Ah-Nong Size Ee-To

This is too large / too small / too expensive.
Masyadong malaki / masyadong maliit / masyadong mahal.
Mahs-Yah-Dong Mah-Lah-Kee / Mahs-Yah-Dong Mah-Lee-Eet / Mahs-Yah-Dong Mah-Hahl

Do you have any others?
Meron pa ba kayong iba?
Me-Ron Pah Bah Kah-Yong Eebah

My size is ...
... ang size ko
... Ahng Size Koh

Where is the changing room / children's / cosmetic / ladieswear / menswear / food department?
Nasaan ang palitan / pambata / cosmetic / gamit pambabae / gamit panlalaki / food department?
Nah-Sah-An Ahng Pah-Lee-Tan / Pahm-Bah-Tah / Cosmetic / Gah-Meet Pahm-Bah-Bah-E / Gah-Meet Pahn-Lah-Lah-Kee / Food Department

I would like ...a quarter of a kilo / half a kilo / a kilo of bread / butter / cheese / ham / this fruit
Gusto ko ng... quarter na kilo / kalahating kilo / isang kilo ng tinapay / butter / keso / hamon / ng prutas na ito
Goos-To Ko Nahng ... Quarter Nah Kee-Lo / Kah-Luh-Hah-Teeng Kee-Lo / Ee-sahng Kee-Lo Nahng Tee-Nah-Pahy / Butter / Ke-So / Hah-Mon / Nahng Proo-Tahs Nah Ee-To

How much is this?
Magkano ba ito?
Mahg-Kah-No Bah Ee-To

97

FILIPINO

I'll take this one, thank you
Bibilhin ko ito, salamat
Bee-Beel-Heen Ko Ee-To, Sah-Lah-Maht

Do you have a carrier (shopping) bag?
Meron ba kayong lalagyang (shopping) bag?
Me-Ron Bah Kah-Yong Lah-Lahg-Yahng (Shopping) Bag

Do you have anything cheaper / larger / smaller / of better quality?
Meron ba kayong mas mura / mas malaki / mas maliit / may maas magandang kalidad?
Me-Ron Bah Kah-Yong Mahs Moo-Rah / Mahs Mah-Lah-Kee / Mahs Mah-Lee-Eet / Mahy Mahs Mah-Gahn-Dahng Kah-Lee-Dahd

I would like a film / to develop this film for this camera
Gusto ko ng isang film / ipadevelop itong film para sa kamerang ito
Goos-To Ko Nahng Ee-Sahng Fillm / Ee-Pah-Develop Ee-Tong Film Pah-Rah Sah Kah-Me-Rahng Ee-To

I would like some batteries, the same size as this old one
Gusto ko ng mga baterya, kapareho ng size ng lumang ito
Goos-To Ko Nahng Mah-Ngah Bah-Ter-Yah, Kah-Pah-Re-Ho Nahng Size Nahng Loo-Mahng I-To

Would you mind wrapping this for me, please?
Puwede bang pakibalot ito para sa akin?
Poo-We-De Bahng Pah-Kee-Bah-Lot Ee-To Pah-Rah Sah A-Keen

Sorry, but you seem to have given me the wrong change
Sori, ngunit nagkamali ka yata ng naibigay na sukli
So-Ri, Ngoo-Nit Nahg-Kah-Mah-Li Kah Yah-Tah Nahng Nah-Ee-Bi-Gahy Nah Sook-Li

MOTORING

Car Hire (Rental)

I have ordered (rented) a car in the name of ...
Nagpakuha (nagparenta) ako ng kotse sa pangalan ni...
Nahg-Pah-Koo-Hah (Nahg-Pah-Ren-Tah) Ah-Ko Nahng Kot-Se Sah Pah-Ngah-Lahn Nee ...

How much does it cost to hire (rent) a car for one day / two days / a week?
Magkano ang upa (renta) ng isang kotse para sa isang araw / dalwang araw / isang linggo?
Mahg-Kah-No Ahng Oo-Pah (Rentah) Nahng I-Sahng Kot-Se Pah-Rah Sah I-Sahng A-Rahw / Dah-Lah-Wahng A-Rahw / I-Sahng Ling-Go

Is the tank already full of petrol (gas)?
Puno ba ng gas ang tangke?
Poo-No Bah Nahng Gahs Ahng Tahng-Ke

Is insurance and tax included? How much is the deposit?
Kasama ba ang insurance at tax? Magkano ang deposit?
Kah-Sah-Mah Bah Ahng Insurance Aht Tax? Mahg-Kah-No Ahng De-Po-Sit

By what time must I return the car?

Anong oras ko dapat ibalik ang kotse?
Ah-Nong O-Rahs Ko Dah-Paht Ee-Bah-Leek Ahng Kot-Se

I would like a small / large / family / sports car with a radio / cassette player

Gusto ko ng isang maliit / malaki / pampamilya / sports na kotse na may radyo / cassette player
Gus-To Ko Nahng Ee-Sahng Mah-Lee-Eet / Mah-Lah-Kee / Pahm-Pah-Meel-Yah / Sports Nah Kot-Se Nah Mahy Rahd-Yo / Cassette Player

Do you have a road map?

Meron ka bang isang mapa?
Me-Ron Kah Bahng Ee-Sahng Mah-Pah

Parking

How long can I park here?

Gaano katagal akong puwedeng magparada dito?
Gah-Ah-No Kah-Tah-Gahl Ah-Kong Poo-We-Deng Mahg-Pah-Rah-Dah Dee-To

Is there a car park near here?

May malapit bang paradahan dito?
Mahy Mah-Lah-Peet Bahng Pah-Rah-Dah-Hahn Dee-To

At what time does this car park close?

Anong oras nagsasara ang paradahang ito?
Ah-Nong O-Rahs Nahg-Sah-Sah-Rah Ahng Pah-Rah-Dah-Hahng Ee-To

Sign and Notices

One Way
One Way
One way

No Entry
No Entry
No entry

No Parking
No Parking
No parking

Detour
Detour
Detour (diversion)

Stop
Stop
Stop

Give way
Give Way
Give way (yield)

Slippery road
Slippery Road
Slippery road

No overtaking
No Overtaking
No overtaking

Danger!
Danger
Danger!

F
I
L
I
P
I
N
O

F I L I P I N O

At the Filling Station

Unleaded (lead-free) / standard / premium / diesel
Unleaded (walang lead) / Standard / premium / diesel
Unleaded (Wa-Lahng Lead) / Standard / Premium / Diesel

Fill the tank please
Pakipuno ang tangke
Pah-Kee-Poo-No Ahng Tahng-Ke

Do you have a road map?
Meron ba kayong mapa?
Me-Ron Bah Kah-Yong Mah-Pah

How much is the car wash?
Magkano ang magpalinis ng kotse?
Mahg-Kah-No Ahng Mahg-Pah-Pah-Lee-Nees Nahng Kot-Se

Breakdowns

I've had a breakdown at ...
Nasiraan ako sa ...
Nah-See-Rah-Ahn Ah-Ko Sah ...

I am a member of the [motoring organisation]
Ako ay isang miyembro ng [motoring organisation]
Ah-Ko Ahy Ee-Sahng Mi-Yem-Bro Nahng [Motoring Organization]

I am on the road from ...to ...
Nasa daan ako mula ... hanggang ...
Nah-Sah Dah-An Ah-ko Moo-Lah ... Hahng-Gahng ...

I can't move the car. Can you send a tow-truck?
Hindi ko mapatakbo ang kotse. Puwedeng magpadala kayo ng hihila?

Heen-Dee Ko Mah-Pah-Tahk-Bo Ahng Kot-Se. Poo-We-Deng Mahg-Pah-Dah-Lah Kah-Yo Nahng Hee-Hee-Lah

I have a flat tyre
May flat tire ako
Mahy Flat Tire Ah-Ko

The windscreen (windshield) has smashed / cracked
May basag / lamat ang windscreen (windshield)
Mahy Bah-Sahg / Lah-Maht Ahng Windscreen (Windshield)

There is something wrong with the engine / brakes / lights / steering / gearbox / clutch / exhaust
May sira ang makina / brake / mga ilaw / manibela / gearbox / clutch / exhaust
Mahy See-Rah Ahng Mah-Kee-Nah / Brake / Mah-Ngah Ee-Lahw / Mah-Ni-Be-Lah / Gearbox / Clutch / Exhaust

It's overheating
Nag-o-overheat
Nahg-O-Overheat

It won't start
Ayaw umandar
Ah-Yahw Oo-Mahn-Dahr

Where can I get it repaired?
Saan ko maaaring maipagawa?
Sah-An Ko Mah-Ah-Ah-Reeng Mah-Ee-Pah-Gah-Wah

Can you take me there?
Puwede ba ninyo akong dalhin doon?
Poo-We-De Bah Neen-Yo Ah-Kong Dahl-Heen Do-On

Will it take long to fix?
Matatagalan bang ayusin

Mah-Tah-Tah-Gah-Lahn Bahng
Ah-Yu-Seen

How much will it cost?
Magkano ang gastos?
Mahg-Kah-No Ahng Gahs-Tos

Please can you pick me up / give me a lift?
Puwedang sunduin ako / makisakay?
Poo-We-Deng Soon-Doo-Een Ah-Ko /
Mah-Kee-Sah-Kahy

Accidents and Traffic Offences

Can you help me? There has been an accident
Puwede bang pakitulungan ako?
Nagkaroon ng isang aksidente
Poo-We-De Bahng Pah-Kee-Too-Loo-
Ngahn Ah-Ko? Nahg-Kah-Ro-On Nahng
Ee-Sahng Ahk-See-Den-Te

Please call the police / an ambulance
Pakitawagan ang pulis / ambulansiya
Pah-Kee-Tah-Wah-Gahn Ahng
Poo-Lees / Ahm-Boo-Lahn-See Yah

Is anyone hurt?
May nasaktan ba?
Mahy Nah-Sahk-Tahn Bah

I'm sorry, I didn't see the sign
Pasensiya, hindi ko nakita ang sign
Pah-Sen-See-Yah, Heen-Dee Ko
Nah-Kee-Tah Ahng Sign

Must I pay a fine? How much?
Dapat ba akong magbayad ng multa?
Magkano?
Dah-Paht Bah Ah-Kong Mahg-Bah-Yahd
Nahng Mool-Tah? Mahg-Kah-No

Show me your documents
Ipakita mo sa akin ang mga dokumento mo
Ee-Pah-Kee-Tah Mo Sah A-Keen Ahng
Mah-Ngah Do-Koo-Men-To Mo

HEALTH

Pharmacy

Do you have anything for a stomach ache / headache / sore throat / toothache?
May gamot ka ba para sa sakit ng tiyan / sakit sa ulo / minamalat / sakit sa ngipin
Mahy Gah-Mot Kah Bah Pah-Rah Sah
Sah-Keet Nang Tee-Yahn / Sah-Keet
Sah Oo-Lo / Mee-Nah-Mah-Laht /
Sah-Keet Sah Ngee-Peen

I need something for diarrhoea / constipation / a cold / a cough / insect bites / sunburn / travel (motion) sickness (car) (plane) (boat)
Kailangan ko ng gamot para sa pagtatae / pagtitibi / sipon / ubo / mga kagat ng Insekto / sunburn / pagkahilo sa biyahe (kotse) (eroplano) (barko)
Kah-Ee-Lah-Ngahn Ko Nahng Gah-Mot
Pah-Rah Sah Pahg-Tah-Tah-E /
Pahg-Tee-Tee-Bi / Sec-Pun / Oo-Bo /
Mah-Ngah Kah-gaht Nahng
Een-Sek-To / Sunburn /
Pahg-Kah-Hee-Lo Sah Bee-Yah-He
(Kot-Che) (E-Rop-Plah-No) (Bahr-Ko)

How much / how many do I take?
Gaano karami / ilan ang iinumin ko?
Gah-Ah-No Kah-Rah-Mi / I-Lahn Ahng
I-I-Noo-Min Ko

101

F I L I P I N O

How often do I take it / them?
Gaano kadalas ko ito / ang mga ito iinumin?
Gah-Ah-No Kah-Dah-Lahs Ko Ee-To / Ahng Mah-Ngah Ee-To Ee-Ee-Noo-Meen

I am / he is / she is taking this medication
Iniinom ko / niya ang gamot na ito
I-Ni-I-Nom Ko / Ni-Ya Ang Ga-Mot Na I-To

How much does it cost?
Magkano ang bayad niya?
Mahg-Kah-No Ahng Bah-Yahd Nee-Yah

Can you recommend a good doctor / dentist?
Makakapagrekomenda ka bang isang mabuting doktor / dentista?
Mah-Kah-Kah-Pahg-Re-Ko-Men-Dah Kah Bahng Ee-Sahng Mah-Boo-Teeng Dok-Tor / Den-Tees-Tah

Is it suitable for children?
Bagay ba para sa mga bata?
Bah-Gahy Bah Pah-Rah Sah Mah-Ngah Bah-Tah

Doctor

I have a pain here / in my arm / leg / chest / stomach
Nakaramdam ako ng sakit dito / sa aking kamay / binti / dibdib / tiyan
Nah-Kah-Kah-Rahm-Dahm Ah-Ko Nahng Sah-Keet Dee-To / Sah A-Keeng Kah-Mahy / Been-Ti / Deeb-Deeb / Tee-Yahn

Please call a doctor, this is an emergency
Pakitawagan ang isang doktor, ito ay isang emergency
Pah-Kee-Tah-Wah-Gahn Ahng Ee-Sahng Doktor, Ee-To Ahy Ee-Sahng Emergency

I would like to make an appointment to see the doctor
Gusto kong gumawa ng isang appointment para magpakita sa doktor
Goos-To Kong Goo-Mah-Wah Nahng Ee-Sahng Appointment Pah-Rah Mahg-Pah-Kee-Tah Sah Dok-Tor

I am diabetic / pregnant
Diabetic / buntis ako
Diabetic / Boon-Tees Ah-Ko

I need a prescription for ...
Gusto ko ng reseta para sa ...
Goos-To Ko Nahng Re-Se-Tah Pah-Rah Sah...

Can you give me something to ease the pain?
Puwede bang bigyan ninyo ako ng pampaalis ng Sakit?
Poo-We-De Bahng Beeg-Yahn Neen-Yo Ah-Ko Nahhng Pahm-Pah-Ah-Lees Nahng Sah-Keet

I am / he is / she is allergic to penicillin
Allergic ako / siya sa penicillin
Allergic Ah-Ko / See-Yah Sah Penicillin

Does this hurt?
Masakit ba ito?
Mah-Sah-Keet Bah Ee-To

You must / he must / she must go to hospital
Kailangan mong / niyang maitakbo sa ospital
Kah-Ee-Lah-Ngahn Mong / Nee-Yahng Mah-EeTahk-Bo Sah Os-PeeTahl

Take these once / twice / three times a day
Inumin ang mga ito minsan / dalawang / tatlong beses sa isang araw
I-Noo-Meen Ahng Mah-Ngah Ee-To Meen-Sahn / Dah-Lah-Wahng / Taht-Long Be-Ses Sah Ee-sahng A-Rahw

I am / he is / she is taking this medication
Iniinom ko / niya ang gamot na ito
Ee-Nee-Ee-Nom Ko / Nee-Yah Ahng Gah-Mot Nah Ee-To

I have medical insurance
May medical insurance ako
Mahy Medical Insurance Ah-Ko

Dentist

I have toothache
Masakit ang ngipin ko
Mah-Sah-Keet Ahng Ngee-Peen Ko

My filling has come out
Naalis ang pasta ng ngipin
Nah-A-Lees Ahng Pahs-Tah Nahng Ngee-Peen

I do / do not want to have an injection first
Gusto / ayaw ko munang mainiksiyunan
Goos-To / Ah-Yahw Ko Moo-Nahng Mah-Ee-Neek-Cho-Nahn

EMERGENCIES

Help!
Tulong!
Too-Long

Fire!
Sunog!
Soo-Nog

Stop!
Hinto!
Heen-To

Call an ambulance / a doctor / the police / the fire brigade!
Tumawag ng ambulansiya / isang doktor / pulis / bombero!
Too-Mah-Wag Nang Am-Boo-Luhn-SeeYah / Ee-sahng Dok-Tor / Poo-Lees / Bom-Be-Ro

Please may I use a telephone?
Puwede ba akong makitawag?
Poo-We-De Bah Ah-Kong Mah-Kee Tah-Wag

I have had my traveller's cheques / credit cards / handbag / rucksack / (knapsack) / luggage / wallet / passport / mobile phone stolen
Ninakaw ang aking mga traveler's cheques / mga credit card / handbag / rucksack / knapsack / bagahe / pitaka / pasaporte / selpon
Nee-Nah-Kahw Ang A-Keeng Mah-Ngah Traveler's Cheques / Mah-Ngah Credit Card / Handbag / Rucksack / Knapsack / Bah-Gah-He / Pee-Tah-Ka / Pah-Sah-Porte / Sel-Pon

May I please have a copy of the report for my insurance claim?
Puwede bang bigyan ako ng kopya ng report para sa king paghahabol sa insurance?
Poo-We-De Bang Beeg-Yahn Ah-Ko Nahng Kop-Yah Nahng Report Pah-Ra Sah Ah-Keeng Pag-Hah-Hah-Bol Sah Insurance

Can you help me? I have lost my daughter / my son / my companion(s)
Matutulungan mo ba ako? Nawala ang anak ko / (mga) kasama ko
Mah-Too-Too-Loo-Ngan Mo Ba Ah-Ko? Nah-Wah-Lah Ang Ahnak Ko / (Mah-Ngah) Kah-Sah-Mah Ko

Please go away / leave me alone
Lumayo ka / Iwanan mo ako
Loo-Mah-Yo Ka / I-Wah-Nan Mo Ah-Ko

I'm sorry
Pasensiya ka na
Pah-Sen-See-Yah Ka Na

I want to contact the British / American / Canadian / Irish / Australian / New Zealand / South African consulate
Gusto kong kontakin ang konsulado ng British / American / Canadian / Irish / Australian / New Zealand / South African
Goos-To Kong Kon-Tah-Keen Ang Kon-Soo-Lah-Do Nang British / American/ Canadian / Irish / Australian / New Zealand / South African

I'm / we're / he is / she is ill / lost / injured
Ako / kami / siya ay may sakit / nawawala / nasugatan
Ah-Ko / Kah-Mee / See-Yah Ahy Mahy Sah-Keet / Nah-Wah-Wah-Lah / Nah-Soo-Gah-Tahn

They are ill / lost / injured
Sila ay may sakit / nawawala / nasugatan
See-Lah Ahy Mahy Sah-Keet / Nah-Wah-Wa-Lah / Nah-Soo-Gah-Tahn

INDONESIAN

I N D O N E S I A N

INTRODUCTION

The official language of the Republic of Indonesia is Bahasa Indonesia (meaning, simply, Indonesian Language), although many people, especially in big cities, speak English. While largely of Malay stock, the inhabitants of the Indonesian archipelago constitute a rich array of some 300 distinct cultures, each with its own individual language or dialect, including Javanese and Sundanese. Locals will be very enthusiastic about any effort on your behalf to learn the language.

Addresses for Travel and Tourist Information

Australia: Embassy of the Republic of Indonesia; 8 Darwin Avenue, Yarralumla, Canberra ACT 2600. Tel: 6250 8600; Fax: 6273 6017;
Web: www.kbri-canberra.org.au
Consulate of the Republic of Indonesia, 72 Queen's Road, Melbourne. Tel: 03 9525 2755; Fax: 03 9525 1588
Consulate of the Republic of Indonesia, Harry Chan Avenue, Darwin NT. Tel: 08 8941 0048; Fax: 08 8941 2709; Email: kridrw@indoconsdarwin.org.au

Canada: Embassy of the Republic of Indonesia, 55 Parkdale Avenue, Ottawa, Ontario K1Y 1E5. Tel: 613 724 1100; Fax: 613 724 1105;
Web: www.indonesia-ottawa.org

UK: Embassy of the Republic of Indonesia, 38 Grosvenor Square, London W1K 2HW. Tel: 020 7499 7661; Fax: 020 7491 4993;
Web: www.indonesianembassy.org.uk

USA: Embassy of the Republic of Indonesia, 2020 Massachusetts Ave, Washington DC 20036. Tel: 202 775 5200; Fax: 202 775 5365;
Email: information@embassyofindonesia.org;
Web: www.embassyofindonesia.org

Indonesia Facts

CAPITAL: Jakarta

CURRENCY: Rupiah (Rp)

OPENING HOURS: Banks: Most banks in Indonesia open Mon-Fri 0800-1500. Shops open from 0900-2100, daily. Sunday is a public holiday, but some shops are open at least part of the day.

TELEPHONES: To dial in, Tel: International Access Code + 62 + Area Code minus first zero. Outgoing, Tel: 001 and the Country Code.

EMERGENCY NUMBERS: Police, Tel: 110. Fire, Tel: 113. Ambulance, Tel: 118.

PUBLIC HOLIDAYS: 1 Jan – New Year's Day; Jan – Idul Adha (Hari Raya Qurban/Haji); Mid-Jan to Mid-Feb – Chinese New Year; 30 Mar – Nyepi Day; Apr – Prophet Muhammad Birthday; 14 Apr – Good Friday (Wafat Isa Almasih); 13 May – Waicak; 25 May – Ascension Day; 17 Aug – Independence Day; Aug – Mi'raj Nabi Muhammad (Muhammad Ascension Day); Oct – Hari Raya Puasa; 25 Dec – Christmas; Dec – Hari Raya Qurban

Technical Language Hints

- Indonesian is an easy language to read as each written letter translates directly into one sound.

INDONESIAN

INDONESIAN

Alphabet

A *Are*	B *Bey*
C *Say*	D *Day*
E *Ay*	F *Ef*
G *Ghay*	H *Haa*
I *E*	J *Jay*
K *Car*	L *El*
M *Am*	N *En*
O *Ow*	P *Pay*
Q *Qee*	R *Er*
S *Es*	T *Tay*
U *Oo*	V *Vay*
W *Way*	X *Eks*
Y *Yay*	Z *Zet*

Basic Words and Phrases

Yes
Ya
Ee-Yaa

No
Tidak
Tee-Duck

Please
Silakan
See-Lar-Kahn

Thank you
Terima kasih
Terr-Ree-Mar Cars-See

Hello
Halo
Harl-Low

Goodbye
Selamat jalan; sampai ketemu
Sir-Lar-Mud; Sum-Pie Keu-Teu-Moo

Excuse me
Permisi
Per-Mie-See

Sorry
Maaf
Mar-Arf

How
Bagaimana
Bar-Guy-Marn-Nhaa

When
Kapan
Cup-Punn

Why
mengapa
Merng-Up-Par

What
Apa
Are-Par

Who
Siapa
See-Yup-Par

That's O.K.
Tidak apa-apa
Tee-Duck Are-Par Are-Par

Perhaps
Mungkin
Moong-Keen

To
Untuk
Oon-Took

From
Kepada
Keu-Par-Dha

Here
Di sini
Dee-See-Knee

There
Di sana
Dee-Sha-Nha

I don't understand
Saya tidak mengerti; saya tidak tahu
Sha-Yaa Tee-Duck Merng-Earth-Tea;
Sha-Yaa Tee-Duck Ta Hu

I don't speak Bahasa Indonesia
Saya tidak bisa Bahasa Indonesia
Sha-Yaa Tee-Duck Bee-Sha
Bha-Haa-Sha Indo-Nay-See-Yaa

Do you speak English?
Apakah anda berbahasa Inggris?
Are-Par-Carh Arn-Dha
Beur-Bha-Haa-Sha Ink-Grease

Can you please write it down?
Bisakah anda menuliskannya?
Bee-Sha-Kah Arn-Dha
Meu-New-List-Kahn-Nya

Please can you speak more slowly?
Bisakah anda berbicara lebih pelan?
Bee-Sha-Kah Arn-Dha
Beur-Bee-Cha-Rhaa Leu-Bee Peu-Larn

Greetings

Good morning /
Good afternoon /
Good evening / Goodnight
Selamat pagi / Selamat siang /
Selamat petang / Selamat malam
Seu-Laa-Mud Par-Ghee / Seu-Laa-Mud
See-Young / Seu-Laa-Mud Peu-Tunk
Seu-Laa-Mud Maa Larm

Pleased to meet you
Senang bertemu anda
Seu-Nung Beur-Ter-Moo Arn-Dha

How are you?
Apa kabar?
Are-Par Car-Bar

Well, thank you. And you?
Baik, terima kasih. Anda?
Ba-Eek, Teu-Ree-Maa Kha-See. Arn-Dha

My name is ...
Nama saya ...
Nha-Maa Sha-Yaa ...

This is my friend / boyfriend / girlfriend / husband / wife / brother / sister
Ini teman saya / pacar saya / suami saya / isteri saya / saudara laki-laki saya / saudara perempuan saya
E-Knee Teu-Marn Sha-Yaa / Par-Char
Sha-Yaa / Sua-Me Sha-Yaa / Is-Ter-Ree
Sha-Yaa / Saw-Dha-Rhaa Laa-Kee –
Laa-Kee Sha-Yaa / Saw-Dha-Rhaa
Per-Reum-Poo-One Sha-Yaa

Where are you travelling to?
Kemana anda sedang bepergian?
Ker-Mhaa-Nha Arn-Dhaa Sir Dunk
Beu-Per-Ghee-Yarn

I am / we are going to ...
Saya / kami dalam perjalanan ke ...
Sha-Yaa / Car-Me Da-Lumb
Per-Jar-Larn-Nun Keu ...

How long are you traveling for?
Berapa lama anda akan bepergian?
Beur-Are-Par Lar-Maa Arn-Dha
Are-Kahn Beu-Per-Ghee-Yan

Where do you come from?
Dari manakah anda?
Dha-Ree Maa-Nha-Carh Arn-Dha

INDONESIAN

I N D O N E S I A N

I am / we are from Australia / Britain / Canada / America
Saya / kami dari Australia / Inggris / Kanada / Amerika
Sha-Yaa / Car-Me Dha-Ree
Aus-Tra-Lee-Yaa / Ink-Grease /
Car-Nha-Dha / Are-May-Ree-Car

We are on holiday
Kami sedang liburan
Kha-Me Seu-Dunk Lee-Boo-Run

This is our first visit here
Ini kunjungan pertama kami ke sini
E-Knee Koon-Joong-Ahn Per-Tha-Maa Car-Me Ker See-Knee

How old are you?
Berapakah usia anda?
Beur-Are-Par-Carh
Woo-See-Are Arn-Dha

I am ... years old
Usia saya ... tahun
Woo-See-Are Sha-Yaa ...Tha-Hoon

I am a businessman / business woman / doctor / journalist / manual worker / administrator / scientist / student / teacher
Saya seorang pengusaha / dokter / wartawan / pekerja kasar / pegawai pemerintah / ilmuwan / siswa / guru
Sha-Yaa Seu-Ooh-Rung Peng-Woo-Sha-Haa / Dock-Ter / Whar-Tha-One / Peu-Kerr-Jha Kha-Shar / Peu-Gaa-Why Peu-Meur-Rin-Tha / Ill-Moo-One / Sees-Wha / Goo-Roo

Would you like / may I have a cigarette?
Apakah anda ingin rokok / boleh saya minta rokok?
Are-Par-Carh Arn-Dha Ink-Ngeen Raw-Cock / Bow-Layh Sha-Yaa Mint-Tha Raw-Cock

Do you mind if I smoke?
Boleh saya merokok?
Bow-Layh Sha-Yaa Meur-Raw-Cock

Do you have a light?
Apakah anda punya korek?
Are-Par-Carh Arn-Dha Poon-Nyaa Co-Reg

I am waiting for my husband / wife / boyfriend / girlfriend
Saya sedang menunggu suami / istri / pacar saya
Sha-Yaa Sir-Dunk Mern-Noong-Goo Sew-Are-Me / Is-Ter-Ree / Par-Char Sha-Yaa

Days	
Monday Senin *Seu-Nin*	**Tuesday** Selasa *Seu-Laa-Sha*
Wednesday Rabu *Rhaa-Boo*	**Thursday** Kamis *Kha-Miss*
Friday Jumat *Joom-Art*	**Saturday** Sabtu *Sub-Too*
Sunday Minggu *Mink-Goo*	

Morning
Pagi
Par-Ghee

Afternoon
Siang
See-Young

Evening
Sore
So-Ray

Night
Malam
Maa-Lump

Yesterday / Today / Tomorrow
Kemarin / Hari ini / Besok lusa
Keu-Maa-Reen / Haa-Ree E-Knee /
Bay-Sock Lew-Sha

Numbers

Zero
Nol
Noal

One
Satu
Sha-Too

Two
Dua
Do-Wha

Three
Tiga
Tee-Gaa

Four
Empat
Uhm-Putt

Five
Lima
Lee-Maa

Six
Enam
Er-Numb

Seven
Tujuh
Too-Jooh

Eight
Delapan
Der-Laa-Parn

Nine
Sembilan
Serm-Bee-Larn

Ten
Sepuluh
Sir-Poo-Looh

Eleven
Sebelas
Sir-Beur-Lars

Twelve
Dua belas
Do-Wha Beur-Lars

Thirteen
Tiga belas
Tee-Gaa Beur-Lars

Fourteen
Empat belas
Uhm-Putt Beur-Lars

Fifteen
Lima belas
Lee-Maa Beur-Lars

Sixteen
Enam belas
Ern-Numb Beur-Lars

Seventeen
Tujuh belas
Too-Jooh Beur-Lars

Eighteen
Delapan belas
Der-Laa-Parn Beur-Lars

Nineteen
Sembilan belas
Serm-Bee-Larn Beur-Lars

Twenty
Dua puluh
Do-Wha Poo-Looh

Twenty-one
Dua puluh satu
Do-Wha Poo-Looh Sha-Too

Twenty-two
Dua puluh dua
Do-Wha Poo-Looh Do-Wha

Thirty
Tiga puluh
Tee-Gaa Poo-Looh

INDONESIAN

Forty
Empat puluh
Uhm-Putt Poo-Looh

Fifty
Lima puluh
Lee-Maa Poo-Looh

Sixty
Enam puluh
Ern-Numb Poo-Looh

Seventy
Tujuh puluh
Too-Jooh Poo-Looh

Eighty
Delapan puluh
Der-Laa-Parn Poo-Looh

Ninety
Sembilan puluh
Serm-Bee-Larn Poo-Looh

One hundred
Seratus
Sir-Rhaa-Toos

Five hundred
Lima ratus
Lee-Maa Rhaa-Toos

One thousand
Seribu
Sir-Ree-Boo

One million
Satu juta
Sha-Too Joo-Tha

Time

What time is it?
Pukul berapakah sekarang?
*Poo-Cool Beur-Are-Par-Carh
Sir-Kha-Rung*

It is ...
Sekarang pukul ...
Sir-Kha-Rung Poo-Cool ...

9.00
Sembilan
Serm-Bee-Larn

9.05
Sembilan lebih lima menit
*Serm-Bee-Larn Ler-Beeh Lee-Maa
Mern-Neet*

9.15
Sembilan seperempat
Serm-Bee-Larn Sir-Per-Uhm-Putt

9.20
Sembilan lebih dua puluh
*Serm-Bee-Larn Ler-Beeh Do-Wha
Poo-Looh*

9.30
Setengah sepuluh
Sir-Terng-Arh Sir-Poo-Loh

9.35
Sembilan lebih tiga puluh lima
*Serm-Bee-Larn Ler-Beeh Tee-Gaa
Poo-ooh Lee-Maa*

9.40
Sepuluh kurang dua puluh menit
*Sir-Poo-Looh Koo-Rung Do-Wha
Poo-Looh Mern-Neet*

9.45
Sepuluh kurang seperempat

Sir-Poo-Looh Koo-Rung
Sir-Per-Uhm-Putt

9.50
Sepuluh kurang sepuluh menit
Sir-Poo-Looh Koo-Rung Sir-Poo-Looh
Mern-Neet

9.55
Sepuluh kurang lima menit
Sir-Poo-Looh Koo-Rung Lee-Maa
Mern-Neet

12.00 / Midday / Midnight
Dua belas / siang / malam
Do-Wha Beur-Lars / See-Yang /
Maa-Larm

Money

I would like to change these traveller's cheques / this currency
Saya ingin menukar cek perjalanan / mata uang ini
Sha-Yaa Ink-Ngeen Mern-New-Car
Check Per-Jha-Larn-Narn / Maa-Tha
Uw-Wunk E-Knee

How much commission do you charge? (What is the service charge?)
Berapa komisi yang anda minta? (berapakah ongkos layanannya?)
Beur-Are-Par Co-Me-See Young Arn-Dha
Min-Thaa? (Beur-Are-Par Onk-Cost
Laa-Yarn-Narn-Nyar)

Can I obtain money with my MasterCard?
Bisakah saya menarik uang dengan MasterCard?
Bee-Sha-Carh Sha-Yaa Meu-Nha-Rick
Uw-Wunk Deung-Arn Mas-Ter-Card

Where is the nearest ATM?
Dimanakah ATM terdekat?
Dee-Maa-Nha-Carh Are-Te-Em
Ter-Dir-Cart

My name is ... Some money has been wired to here for me to collect
Nama saya ... Sejumlah uang telah dikirimkan ke sini untuk saya
Nha-Maa Sha-Yaa ... Sir-Joom-Laah
Uw-Wunk Tir-Laah Dee-Kee-Rim-Kahn
Ker See-Knee Oon-Took Sha-Yaa

ARRIVING AND DEPARTING

Airport

Excuse me, where is the check-in desk for ... airline?
Maaf, di manakah konter check-in untuk maskapai ...?
Mar-Arf, Dee Maa-Nha-Carh Counter
Check-In Oon-Took Mash-Kha-Pie ...

What is the boarding gate / time for my flight?
Berapakah nomor pintu masuk penerbangan saya? Jam berapakah saya harus masuk ke pesawat saya?
Beur-Are-Par-Carh No-More Pin-Too
Mar-Sook Pern-Ner-Bunk-Ngaan
Sha-Yaa? Jump Beur-Are-Par-Carh
Sha-Yaa Haa-Roos Maa-Sook Ker
Peu-Sha-What Sha-Yaa

How long is the delay likely to be?
Berapa lama kira-kira penundaan ini?
Beur-Are-Par Lar-Maa Kee-Rhaa
Kee-Rhaa Pern-Noon-Dha-Ahn E-Knee

INDONESIAN

Where is the duty-free shop?
Dimanakah toko bebas pajak?
Dee-Marn-Nar-Carh Tow-Co Bay-Bass Par-Juck

Which way is the baggage reclaim?
Manakah jalan untuk mengambil bagasi?
Maa-Nha-Carh Jha-Larn Uw-Took Meung-Arm-Bill Bha-Gaa-See

I have lost my luggage. Please can you help?
Saya telah kehilangan barang-barang saya. Bisakah anda membantu?
Sha-Yaa Ter-Laah Ker-Hee-Lung-Ahn Bha-Rung Bha-Rung Sha-Yaa. Bee-Sha-Carh Arn-Dha Merm-Bunn-Too

I am flying to ...
Saya dalam penerbangan ke ...
Sha-Yaa Dha-Larm Pern-Nerr-Bha-Ngaan Ker ...

Where can I get the bus to the city centre?
Dimanakah saya bisa naik bus ke pusat kota?
Dee-Maa-Nha-Carh Sha-Yaa Bee-Sha Nha-Eek Bees Ker Poo-Shat Co-Tha

Trains and Boats

Where is the ticket office / information desk?
Dimanakah tempat penjualan tiket / meja informasi?
Dee-Maa-Nha-Carh Term-Putt Pern-Joo-Whal-Larn Tee-Cat / May-Jha In-For-Maa-See

Which platform does the train / speedboat / ferry to ... depart from?
Dari jalur mana kereta api / perahu / feri ke ... diberangkatkan?
Dha-Ree Jha-Lure Maa-Nha Ker-Ray-Tha Are-Pee / Per-Rhaa-Hoo Beur-E-Could-Nyaa / Fair-Ree Ker ... Dee-Beur-Rung-Cut-Kahn

Where is platform ...?
Dimanakah jalur ...?
Dee-Maa-Nha-Carh Jha-Lure ...

When is the next train / boat to ...?
Kapan kereta api / perahu berikutnya menuju ... berangkat?
Kha-Punn Ker-Ray-Tha Are-Pee / Per-Rhaa-Hoo Beur-E-Could-Nyaa Mern-New-Joo ... Beur-Rung-Cut

Is there a later train / boat to ...?
Apakah itu kereta api / perahu terakhir ke ...?
Are-Par-Carh E-Too Ker-Ray-Tha Are-Pee / Per-Rhaa-Hoo Ter-Arc-Heer Ker ...

Notices and Signs

Gerbong makan
Gherr-Bunk Maa-Kahn
Buffet (Dining) car

Bus
Bees
Bus

Air minum / air tidak boleh diminum
Eye-Eer Me-Noom / Eye-Eer Tee-Duck Bow-Layh Dee-Me-Noom
Drinking / Non-drinking water

Pintu masuk
Pin-Too Maa-Sook
Entrance

Pintu keluar
Pin-Too Ker-Loo-Are
Exit

Rumah sakit
Roo-Maah Sha-Kit
Hospital

Informasi
In-For-Maa-See
Information

Barang tertinggal
(pengambilan bagasi)
*Bha-Rung Terr-Ting-Gal
(Perng-Arm-Bee-Larn Bha-Gaa-See)*
Left luggage (Baggage claim)

Lemari barang
Ler-Maa-Ree Bha-Rung
Luggage lockers

Kantor pos
Kahn-Torr Post
Post office

Jalur
Jha-Lure
Platform

Stasiun kereta api
Stha-Syun Ker-Ray-Tha Are-Pee
Railway (Railroad) station

Bandar udara
Bahn-Dhar Uw-Dha-Rhaa
Airport

Kantor polisi
Kahn-Torr Poll-Lee-See
Police station

Terminal
Ter-Me-Null
Port

Restoran
Rest-Tow-Run
Restaurant

Merokok / Dilarang merokok
*Meu-Rock-Cock /
Dee-Laa-Rung Meu-Rock-Cock*
Smoking / Non-smoking

Telepon
Te-Le-Pone
Telephone

Tempat penjualan tiket
Term-Putt Pern-Joo-Wall-Ahn Tee-Cat
Ticket office

Konter check-in
Corn-Terr Check-In
Check-in desk

Jadwal
Jhad-Do-Arl
Timetables (Schedules)

Toilet (kamar kecil)
Tow-E-Let (Kha-Mahr Ker-Chill)
Toilets (Restrooms)

Pria / Wanita
Pree-Yaa / Wha-Knee-Tha
Ladies / Gentlemen

Kereta bawah tanah
Ker-Ray-Tha Bha-Whah Tha-Nhah
Underground (Subway)

Ruang tunggu
Rue-Wunk Toong-Goo
Waiting room

Buying a Ticket

I would like a first-class / second-class single (oneway) / return (round-trip) ticket to ...
Saya ingin tiket kelas satu / kelas dua, sekali jalan / pulang pergi ke ...
Sha-Yaa Ink-Ngeen Tee-Cat Ker-Lars Sha-Too / Ker-Lars Do-Wha, Sir-Kha-Lee Jha-Lam / Poo-Lung Per-Ghee Ker ...

Is it an express (fast) train / bus?
Apakah ini kereta api / bus cepat?
Are-Par-Carh E-Knee Ker-Ray-Tha Are-Pee / Bees Che-Putt

Is my rail pass valid on this train / ferry / bus?
Apakah tiket saya berlaku untuk kereta api / feri / bis ini?
Are-Par-Carh Tee-Cat Sha-Yaa Beur-Laa-Koo Oon-Took Ker-Ray Tha Are-Pee / Fair-Ree / Bees E-Knee

I would like an aisle / window seat
Saya ingin tempat duduk dekat jendela / dekat lorong
Sha-Yaa E-Ngeen Term-Putt Do-Duke De-Cart Jearn-Day-Laa / Der-Cart Lo-Wrong

No smoking / smoking, please
Dilarang merokok / diizinkan merokok

Dee-Laa-Rung Mer-Rock-Cock / Dee-E-Zin-Kahn Mer-Rock-Cock

We would like to sit together
Kami ingin duduk bersama
Kha-Me E-Ngeen Do-Duke Beur-Sha-Maa

I would like to make a seat reservation
Saya ingin memesan tempat duduk
Sha-E-Ngeen Meu-Meu-Sun Term-Putt Do-Duke

I would like to reserve a couchette / sleeper for one person / two people / my family
Saya ingin memesan satu kursi tempat tidur untuk satu orang / dua orang / keluarga saya
Sha-Yaa E-Ngeen Meu-Meu-Sun Sha-Too Course-See Term-Putt Tea-Dure Oon-Took Sha-Too Ow-Rung / Do-Are Ow-Rung / Keu-Loo-Wharr-Gaa Sha-Yaa

I would like to reserve a cabin
Saya ingin memesan kabin
Sha-Yaa E-Ngeen Meu-Meu-Sun Cup-Bean

Timetables (Schedules)

Tiba
Tee-Bha
Arrive

Menelepon (Berhenti) pada ...
Meu-Neu-Lay-Phone (Beur-Heun-Tea) Par-Dar ...
Calls (Stops) at ...

Layanan katering
Laa-Yarn-Narn Cutter-Ring
Catering service

Ganti jam ...
Gun-Tea Jump ...
Change at ...

Melalui
Meu-Laa-Loo-E
Connection / Via

Setiap hari
Seu-Tee-Arp Har-Ree
Daily

Tiap 40 menit
Tea-Up Uhm-Putt Poo-Looh Mern-Neet
Every 40 minutes

Kelas satu
Keu-Lars Sha-Too
First class

Setiap jam
Sir-Tea-Up Jump
Hourly

Dianjurkan memesan tempat duduk
Dee-Ahn-Joor-Kahn Meu-Meu-Sun Term-Putt Do-Duk
Seat reservations are recommended

Kelas dua
Keu-Lars Do-Wha
Second class

Layanan ekstra dengan biaya
Laa-Yarn-Narn Extra Derng-Ahn Bee-Are-Yar
Supplement payable

Luggage

How much will it cost to send (ship) my luggage in advance?
Berapakah biaya untuk mengirimkan (mengapalkan) barang-barang saya?
Beur-Are-Par-Carh Bee-Are-Yaa Oon-Took Mung-Ngee-Rim Kahn (Mung-Ngaa-Paal-Kahn) Bha-Rung Bha-Rung Sha-Yaa

Where is the left luggage (baggage claim) office?
Dimanakah kantor untuk barang-barang yang tertinggal (pengambilan bagasi)?
Dee-Maa-Nha-Carh Kahn-Torr Oon-Took Bha-Rung Bha-Rung Young Terr-Tink-Gal (Peung-Arm-Bee-Larn Bha-Gaa-See)

What time do you open / close?
Pukul berapa anda buka / tutup?
Poo-Cool Beur-Are-Par Ahn-Dha Boo-Kaa / To-Toop

Where are the luggage trolleys (carts)?
Dimanakah kereta barang?
Dee-Maa-Nha-Carh Kerr-Ray-Tha Bha-Rung

Where are the lockers?
Dimanakah loker?
Dee-Maa-Nha-Carh Locker

I have lost my locker key
Saya kehilangan kunci loker
Sha-Yaa Keu-He-Lung-Ahn Koon-Chi Locker

INDONESIAN

On Board

Is this seat free?
Apakah tempat duduk ini kosong?
Are-Par-Carh Term-Putt Do-Duke E-Knee Core-Song

Excuse me, you are sitting in my reserved seat
Maaf, anda duduk di tempat yang saya pesan
Mar-Arf, Ahn-Dha Do-Duke Dee Term-Putt Young Sha-Yaa Peu-Sun

Which station is this?
Stasiun apa ini?
Sthaa-See-Yoon Are-Par E-Knee

What time is this train / bus / ferry / flight due to arrive / depart?
Pukul berapa kereta api / bus / feri / pesawat ini akan sampai / berangkat?
Poo-Cool Beur-Are-Par Kerr-Ray-Tha Are-Pee / Bees / Fair-Ree / Peu-Sha-What E-Knee Are-Kahn Sum-Pie / Beur-Rung-Cut

Travelling with Children

Do you have a high chair / babysitting service / cot?
Apakah anda memiliki kursi yang tinggi / layanan penjagaan bayi / tempat tidur bayi?
Are-Par-Carh Ahn-Dha Meu-Me-Lee-Qee Koor-See Young Tink-Ghee / La-Yarn-Ahn Pern-Jha-Gaa-Ahn Bha-Yee / Term-Putt Tea-Dure Buy-Yi

Where is the nursery / playroom?
Dimanakah kamar anak / ruang bermain?
Dee-Maa-Nha-Carh Kha-Maar Ahn-Nuck / Rue-Wunk Beur-Maa-Een

Where can I warm the baby's bottle?
Dimana saya bisa menghangatkan botol bayi?
Dee-Maa-Nha Sha-Yaa Bee-Sha Meng-Hung-Art-Kahn Bot-Toll Bha-Yee

Customs and Passports

Passports, please!
Mohon tunjukkan paspornya!
Mo-Horn Tune-Jook-Kahn Pass-Por-Nyaa

I have nothing / wine / spirits (alcohol) / tobacco to declare
Saya tak punya apa-apa / anggur / rokok untuk dilaporkan
Sha-Yaa Tuck Poo-Nyaa Are-Par Are-Par / Unk-Goore / Rock-Cock Oon-Took Dee-Laa-Por-Kahn

I will be staying for ... days / weeks / months
Saya akan tinggal selama ... hari / minggu / bulan
Sha-Yaa Are-Kahn Tink-Gaal Seu-Laa-Maa ... Haa-Ree / Ming-Goo / Boo-Larn

SIGHTSEEING

Asking the Way

Excuse me, do you speak English?
Maaf, apakah anda berbahasa Inggris?
Mar-Arf Are-Par-Carh Arn-Dha Beur-Bha-Haa-Sha Ink-Grease

Excuse me, can you help me please?

Maaf, bisakah anda membantu saya?
*Mar-Arf, Bee-Sha-Carh Arn-Dha
Meum-Barn-Too Sha-Yaa*

Where is the Tourist Information Office?
Di manakah kantor informasi wisata?
*Dee Maa-Nha-Carh Kahn-Torr
In-For-Maa-See We-Sha-Tha*

Excuse me, is this the right way to ...?
Maaf, apakah ini jalan yang benar menuju ...?
*Mar-Arf Are-Par-Carh E-Knee Jha-Larn
Young Beu-Nhar Meu-New-Joo ...*

... the cathedral / the tourist information office / the castle / the old town
Katedral / kantor informasi wisata / kastil / kota tua
*Cut-Te-Draal / Kahn-Torr
In-For-Maa-See We-Sha-Tha /
Kars-Till / Co-Tha Too-Wha*

Can you tell me the way to the railway (railroad) station / bus station / taxi rank (stand) / city centre (downtown) / beach?
Bisakah anda menunjukkan jalan ke stasiun kereta api / terminal bus / terminal taksi / pusat kota / pantai?
*Bee-Sha-Carh Ahn-Dha Meu-Noon-Jook-Kahn Jha-Larn Ker Stars-Syun
Kerr-Ray-Tha Are-Pee / Terr-Me-Nahl
Bees / Terr-Me-Nahl Tuck-See /
Poo-Shut Co-Tha / Parn-Tie*

First / second / left / right / straight ahead
Pertama / kedua / kiri / kanan / lurus
*Per-Tha-Maa / Keu-Do-Waa /
Qee-Ree / Kahn-Ahn / Loo-Roos*

At the corner / at the traffic lights
Di pojok / di lampu lalu lintas
*Dee-Poch-Jock / Dee Larm-Poo Laa-Loo
Lin-Tars*

Where is the nearest police station / post office?
Dimanakah kantor polisi / kantor pos terdekat?
*Dee-Maa-Nha-Carh Kahn-Torr
Poll-Lee-See / Kahn-Torr Poss
Ter-Deu-Cut*

Is it near / far?
Apakah jauh / dekat?
Are-Par-Carh Jha-Uhh / Duer-Cut

Do I need to take a taxi / catch a bus?
Apakah saya perlu naik taksi / bis?
*Are-Par-Carh Sha-Yaa Per-Loo Nha-Eek
Tuck-See / Bees*

Do you have a map?
Apakah anda punya peta?
*Are-Par-Carh Arn-Dha Poo-Nyaa
Pay-Tha*

Can you point to it on my map?
Bisakah anda menunjukkannya pada peta saya?
Bee-Sha-Carh Arn-Dha Mern-Noon-Jook-Kahn-Nyaa Par-Dar Pay-Tha Sha-Yaa

Thank you for your help
Terima kasih atas bantuannya
*Terr-Ree-Maa Kha-Seeh Are-Tars
Bunn-Too-One-Nyaa*

How do I reach the motorway / main road?
Bagaimanakah saya menuju jalan raya?
*Bha-Guy-Maa-Nha-Carh Sha-Yaa
Mern-New-Joo Jha-Larn Rhaa-Yaa*

I think I have taken the wrong turning
Saya pikir saya salah belok
Sha-Yaa Pee-Kirr Sha-Yaa Sha-Laah Bay-Lock

I am looking for this address
Saya sedang mencari alamat ini
Sha-Yaa Sir-Dunk Mern-Cha-Ree Are-Larm-Mud E-Knee

I am looking for the ... hotel
Saya sedang mencari hotel ...
Sha-Yaa Sir-Dunk Meun-Cha-Ree Hotel ...

How far is it to ... from here?
Seberapa jauhkah ke ...dari sini?
Seu-Beur-Are-Par Jha-Uhh-Carh Ker ... Dha-Ree See-Knee

Carry straight on for ... kilometres
Lurus hingga ... kilometer
Loo-Roos Hing-Gaa ... Qee-Low-Met-Terr

Take the next turning on the right / left
Tikungan berikutnya belok ke kanan / kiri
Tea-Koo-Ngahn Beur-Ree-Koot-Nyaa Bay-Lock Ker Kha-Nahn / Kee-Ree

Turn right / left at the next crossroads / traffic lights
Belok kanan / kiri di perempatan / lampu lalu lintas berikutnya
Bay-Lock Kha-Nahn / Kee-Ree Dee Per-Uhm-Putt-Than / Lump-Poo Laa-Loo Lin-Tars Beur-Ree-Coot-Nyaa

You are going in the wrong direction
Anda salah arah
Arn-Dha Sha-Laah Are-Rhaah

Where is the cathedral / church / museum / pharmacy?
Dimanakah katedral / gereja / museum / apotek?
Dee-Maa-Nha-Carh Cut-Tay-Drall / Gherr-Ray-Jha / Moo-See-Yoom / Are-Port-Tack

How much is the admission / entrance charge?
Berapakah biaya masuk?
Beur-Are-Par-Carh Be-Are-Yaa Maa-Shook

Is there a discount for children / students / senior citizens?
Apakah ada diskon untuk anak-anak / pelajar / manula?
Are-Par-Carh Are-Dha Disc-Corn Oon-Took Are-Nuck Are-Nuck / Per-Laa-Jhar / Maa-New-Laa

What time does the next guided tour (in English) start?
Pukul berapa tur berpandu (bahasa Inggris) dimulai?
Poo-Cool Beur-Are-Par Tour Beur-Punn-Do (Bha-Haa-Sha Ink-Grease) Dee-Moo-Lie

One / two adults / children, please
Satu / dua orang dewasa / anak-anak
Sha-Too / Do-Wha Ow-Rung Day-Wha-Sha / Are-Nuck Are-Nuck

May I take photographs here?
Bolehkah saya memotret di sini?
Bo-Layh-Carh Sha-Yaa Meu-Mote-Trait Dee See-Knee

INDONESIAN

At the Tourist Office

Do you have a map of the town / area?
Apakah anda punya peta kota / wilayah ini?
Are-Par kaah Arn-Dha Poo-Nyaa Pay-Tha Co-Tha / We-Lie-Yaah E-Knee

Do you have a list of accommodation?
Apakah anda punya daftar penginapan?
Are-Paa-Carh Arn-Dha Poon-Nyaa Darf-Thar Peu-Ngee-Narp-Punn

Can I reserve accommodation?
Bisakah saya memesan penginapan?
Bee-Sha-Carh Sha-Yaa Meu-Meu-Sun Peu-Ngee-Narp-Punn

ACCOMMODATION

Hotels

I have a reservation in the name of ...
Saya telah memesan atas nama ...
Sha-Yaa Teu-Larh Meu-Meu-Sun Are-Tars Nha-Maa ...

I wrote to / faxed / telephoned you last month / last week
Saya mengirim surat / mengirim faks / menelepon anda bulan lalu / minggu lalu
Sha-Yaa Meu-Ngee-Rim Sue-Rut / Meu-Ngee-Rim Fax / Meu-Neu-Lay-Phone Arn-Dha Boo-Larn Laa-Loo / Ming-Goo Laa-Loo

Do you have any rooms free?
Apakah anda punya kamar kosong?
Are-Pa-Carh Arn-Dha Poo-Nyaa Kha-Mar Course-Song

I would like to reserve a single / double room with / without bath / shower
Saya ingin memesan kamar single / double dengan / tanpa kamar mandi
Sha-Yaa E-Ngeen Meu-Meu-Sun Kha-Maar Single / Double Deu-Ngarn / Tun-Paa Kha-Mar Marn-Dee

I would like bed and breakfast / (room and) full board
Saya ingin tempat tidur dan sarapan / (kamar dan) makan tiga kali
Sha-Yaa E-Ngeen Term-Putt Tee-Duor Darn Sha-Rub-Punn / (Kha-Mar Darn) Maa-Karn Tee-Gaa Kha-Lee

How much is it per night?
Berapakah tarif per malam?
Beur-Are-Par-Carh Tha-Reef Per Maa-Larm

Is breakfast included?
Apakah termasuk sarapan?
Are-Paa-Carh Teur-Maa-Sook Sha-Rhaa-Punn

Do you have any cheaper rooms?
Apakah anda punya kamar yang lebih murah?
Are-Paa-Carh Arn-Dha Poon-Nyaa Kha-Mar Young Leu-Bee Moo-Rhaah

I would like to see / take the room
Saya ingin melihat / mengambil kamar itu
Sha-Yaa E-Ngeen Meu-Lee-Hut / Meung-Arm-Bill Kha-Mar E-Too

I would like to stay for ... nights
Saya akan menginap selama ... malam
Sha-Yaa Are-Kahn Meu-Ngee-Narp Sir-Larm-Maa ... Maa-Larm

INDONESIAN

The shower / light / tap / hot water doesn't work
Pancuran / lampu / kran / air hangatnya rusak
Punn-Chu-Run / Lump-Poo / Crun / Ar-Ear Hung-Art-Nyaa Roo-Suck

At what time / where is breakfast served?
Pukul berapa / dimana sarapan dihidangkan?
Poo-Cool Beur-Are-Par / Dee-Maa-Nha Sha-Rhaa-Punn Dee-He-Dunk-Kahn

What time do I have to check out?
Pukul berapa saya harus keluar?
Poo-Cool Beur-Are-Par Sha-Yaa Haa-Roose Keu-Loo-Whar

Can I have the key to room number ...?
Bisakah saya mengambil kunci kamar nomor...?
Bee-Sha-Carh Sha-Yaa Merng-Arm-Bill Coon-Chee Car-Mar Nor-More ...

My room number is ...
Nomor kamar saya adalah ...
Nor-More Car-Mar Sha-Yaa Are-Dhar-Larh ...

My room is not satisfactory / not clean enough / too noisy
Kamar saya tidak memuaskan / tidak bersih / terlalu berisik
Car-Mar Sha-Yaa Tee-Duck Meu-Moo-Us-Karn / Tee-Duck Beur-Seeh / Ter-Laa-Loo Beur-E-Seek

Please can I change rooms?
Bisakah saya pindah kamar?
Bee-Sha-Carh Sha-Yaa Peen-Dah Car-Mar

Where is the bathroom?
Dimanakah kamar mandi?
Dee-Maa-Nha-Carh Car-Mar Mun-Dee

Do you have a safe for valuables?
Apakah anda punya brankas untuk barang-barang berharga?
Are-Par-Carh Arn-Dha Poo-Nyaa Brunk-Cars Oon-Took Bar-Rung Bar-Rung Beur-Harg-Ghaa

Is there a laundry / do you wash clothes?
Apakah ada jasa pencucian pakaian / apakah anda menerima pencucian pakaian?
Are-Par-Carh Are-Dha Jar-Sha Pern-Choo-Chee-Arn Par-Kye-Arn / Are-Par-Carh Arn-Dha Meu-Neur-Ree-Mar Pern-Choo-Chee-Arn Par-Kye-Arn

I would like an air-conditioned room
Saya ingin kamar ber-AC
Shaa-Yaa E-Ngeen Car-Mar Beur-Are-Say

Do you accept traveller's cheques / credit cards?
Apakah anda menerima cek perjalanan / kartu kredit?
Are-Par-Carh Arn-Dha Meu-Neur-Ree-Mar Check Per-Jar-Laa-Nunn / Car-Too Credit

May I have the bill please?
Bisa minta bonnya?
Bee-Sha Meen-Tha Bon-Nyaa

Excuse me, I think there may be a mistake in this bill
Maaf, menurut saya ada kekeliruan dalam bon ini
Mar-Arf, Meu-Noo-Root Sha-Yaa Are-Dha Ker-Ker-Lee-Roo-Arn Dha-Lum Bon E-Knee

22

Youth Hostels

How much is a dormitory bed per night?
Berapakah biaya kamar asrama per malam?
Beur-Rhaa-Par-Carh Bee-Are-Yaa Car-Mar Us-Rhaa-Mar Per Mar-Lum

I am / am not an HI member
Saya anggota / bukan anggota HI
Sha-Yaa Arng-Go-Tha / Boo-Karn Arng-Go-Tha Har-Ee

May I use my own sleeping bag?
Bisakah saya memakai tas tidur saya sendiri?
Bee-Sha-Carh Sha-Yaa Meu-Mar-Kye Thas-Tee-Door Sha-yaa Sern-Dee-Ree

What time do you lock the doors at night?
Jam berapa anda mengunci pintu pada malam hari?
Jarm Beur-Are-Par Arn-Dha Merng-Oon-Chee Pin-Too Par-Dha Mar-Lum Haa-Ree

Camping

May I camp for the night / two nights?
Bolehkah saya berkemah selama semalam / dua malam?
Bow-Layh-Carh Sha-yaa Beur-Care-Marh Sue-Lar-Mar Sir-Mar-Lum / Doo-Are Mar-Lum

Where can I pitch my tent?
Dimakah saya bisa mendirikan tenda?
Dee-Maa-Nha-Carh Sha-Yaa Bee-Sha Mern-Dee-Ree-Carn Ten-Dar

How much does it cost for one night / week?
Berapa biayanya untuk semalam / seminggu?
Beur-Rhaa-Par Bee-Are-Yaa Oon-Took Sir-Mar-Lum / Sir-Meeng-Goo

Where are the washing facilities?
Dimanakah fasilitas mencuci?
Dee-Maa-Nha-Carh Far-See-Lee-Thas Mern-Choo-Chee

Is there a restaurant / supermarket / swimming pool on site / nearby?
Apakah ada restoran / supermarket / kolam renang di sini / di sekitar sini?
Ar-Par-Carh Are-Dha Rest-Tore-Run / Soo-Per-Mar-Kert / Cor-Lum Rer-Narng Dee See-Knee / Dee Sir-Key-Tha See-Knee

Do you have a safety deposit box?
Apakah anda punya kotak penyimpanan?
Are-Par-Carh Arn-Dha Poo-Nyar Core-Tuck Per-Nyeem-Par-Narn

EATING AND DRINKING

Cafés and Bars

I would like a cup of / two cups of / another coffee / tea
Saya ingin secangkir / dua cangkir / tambah kopi / teh
Sha-Yaa E-Ngeen Sir-Chunk-Keer / Doo-Are Chunk-Keer / Tum-Bah Core-Pee / Tayh

With / without milk / sugar
Dengan / tanpa susu / gula
Derng-Arn / Tarn-Par Soo-Soo / Goo-Laa

EATING AND DRINKING

I would like a bottle / glass / two glasses of mineral water / red wine / white wine, please
Saya ingin sebotol / segelas / dua gelas air mineral / anggur merah / anggur putih
Sha-Yaa E-Ngeen Sir-Bore-Toll / Ser-Geu-Lars / Doo-Are Gher-Las Eye-Eer Me-Ner-Rarl / Arng-Goor May-Rhaah / Arng-Goor Poo-Teeh

I would like a beer / two beers, please
Saya ingin satu / dua bir
Sha-yaa E-Ngeen Sha-Too / Doo-Are Beer

Please may I have some ice?
Saya minta es?
Sha-Yaa Mean-Tha Ays

Do you have any matches / cigarettes / cigars?
Apakah anda punya korek api / rokok / cerutu?
Are-Par-Carh Arn-Dha Poo-Nyar Core-Rack Are-Pee / Roar-Cock / Cha-Root-Too

Restaurants

Can you recommend a good / cheap restaurant in this area?
Bisakah anda memberitahukan restoran yang murah / bagus di wilayah ini?
Bee-Sha-Carh Arn-Dha Merm-Bury-Tha-Who-Karn Rest-Tore-Run Young Moor-Rah / Bar-Goose Dee We-Laa-Yah E-Knee

I would like a table for ... people
Saya butuh meja untuk ... orang
Sha-Yaa Boo-Tooh Mare-Jar Oon-Took ... Ore-Rung

Do you have a non-smoking area?
Apakah anda punya daerah bebas rokok?
Are-Par-Carh Arn-Dha Poo-Nyar Dha-Ay-Rah Bare-Bus Roar-Cock

Waiter / Waitress!
Pelayan!
Per-Laa-Yarn

Excuse me, please, may we order?
Maaf, bisa kami memesan?
Mar-Arf, Bee-Sha Car-Me Meu-Meu-Sun

Do you have a set menu / children's menu / wine list?
Apakah anda punya daftar menu standar / menu anak-anak / daftar anggur?
Are-Par-Carh Arn-Dha Poo-Nyar Duff-Tar May-Noo Stun-Dar / Meu-Noo Are-Knuck-Are-Knuck / Darf-Tar Arng-Goor

Do you have any vegetarian dishes?
Apakah anda punya hidangan untuk vegetarian?
Are-Par-Carh Arn-Dha Poo-Nyar Hee-Darng-Arn Oon-Took Fay-Gher-Tha-Ree-Arn

Do you have any local specialities?
Apakah anda punya makanan khas daerah?
Are-Par-Carh Arn-Dha Poo-Nyar Mar-Car-Narn Cush Dha-Ay-Rah

Are vegetables included?
Apakah termasuk sayuran?
Are-Par-Carh Ter-Mar-Sook Sha-You-Run

I
N
D
O
N
E
S
I
A
N

Could I have it well-cooked / medium / rare please?
Bisakah itu dimasak matang / agak matang / mentah?
Bee-Sha-Carh E-Too Dee-Mar-Suck Mar-Tongue / Are-Gark Mar-Tongue / Meurn-Tah

What does this dish consist of?
Terdiri dari apa saja hidangan ini?
Ter-Dee-Ree Dha-Ree Are-Par Sha-Jar Hee-Darng-Arn E-Knee

I am a vegetarian. Does this contain meat?
Saya vegetarian. Apakah ini mengandung daging?
Sha-Yaa Fay-Gher-Tha-Ree-Arn. Are-Par-Carh F-Knee Merng-Arn-Doong Dhar-Gheeng

I do not eat nuts / dairy products / meat / fish
Saya tidak makan kacang-kacangan / produk susu / daging / ikan
Sare-Yaa Tee-Duck Mar-Karn Car-Chung-Car-Chung-Arn / Proar-Duke Soo-Soo / Dhar-Gheeng / E-Karn

Not (very) spicy, please
Jangan (terlalu) pedas
Jung-Arn (Ter-Lar-Loo) Per-Dars

I would like the set menu, please
Saya ingin menu standar
Sha-Yaa E-Ngeen Meu-Noo Stun-Dar

We are still waiting to be served
Kami masih menunggu pesanan kami
Car-Me Mar-Seeh Meu-Noong Peu-Sar-Aan Car-Me

Please bring a plate / knife / fork
Bawakan piring / pisau / garpu
Bar-War-Karn Pee-Ring / Pee-Saw / Gar-Poo

Excuse me, this is not what I ordered
Maaf, ini bukan yang saya pesan
Mar-Arf, E-Knee Boo-Kahn Young Sha-Yaa Peu-Sun

May I have some / some more bread / water / coffee / tea?
Bisakah saya minta / tambah roti / air / kopi / teh?
Bee-Sha-Carh Sha-Yaa Meen-Tha / Tum-Bhah Raw-Tee / Eye-Eer / Core-Pee / Tayh

May I have the bill, please?
Bisa minta bonnya?
Bee-Sha Meen-Tha Bon-Nyar

Does this bill include service?
Apa bon ini sudah termasuk pelayanan?
Are-Par Bon E-Knee Soo-Dhah Ter-Mar-Sook Per-Lar-Yar-Narn

Do you accept traveller's cheques / MasterCard / US dollars?
Apakah anda menerima cek perjalanan / Master card / dolar AS?
Are-Par-Carh Arn-Dha Meu-Ner-Ree-Mar Check Per-Jar-Larn-Narn / Master Card / Door-Lar Are-May-Ree-Car

Can I have a receipt, please?
Bisakah saya minta kuitansinya?
Bee-Sha-Carh Sha-Yaa Meen-Tha Coo-We-Tarn-See-Nyar

Where is the toilet (restroom), please?
Dimanakah toilet (kamar kecil)?
Dee-Maa-Nha-Carh Toy-Let (Car-Mar Ker-Cheel)

INDONESIAN

On the Menu

Sarapan / Makan siang /
Makan malam
*Sha-Ra-Pun / Mar-Karn See-Young /
Mar-Karn Mar-Lum*
Breakfast / Lunch / Dinner

Hidangan pertama
Hee-Darng-Arn Per-Tha-Mar
First courses

Sup
Soup
Soups

Hidangan utama
Hee-Darng-Arn Oo-Tha-Mar
Main courses

Hidangan ikan
Hee-Darng-Arn E-Karn
Fish dishes

Hidangan daging
Hee-Darng-Arn Dha-Gheeng
Meat dishes

Daging sapi
Dha-Gheeng Sha-Pee
Beef

Bistik
Bee-Steak
Steak

Daging babi
Dha-Gheeng Bar-Bee
Pork

Daging sapi muda
Dha-Gheeng Sha-Pee Moo-Dha
Veal

Daging ayam
Dha-Gheeng Are-Yum
Chicken

Daging kambing
Dha-Gheeng Come-Bing
Lamb

Daging babi asap
Dha-Gheeng Bar-Bee Are-Sarp
Ham

Hidangan vegetarian
*Hee-Darng-Arn
Fay-Gher-Tha-Ree-Arn*
Vegetarian dishes

Sayuran
Sha-You-Run
Vegetables

Kentang goreng
Kern-Tunk Gore-Rang
Chips (french fries)

Kentang rebus / goreng / tumbuk
*Kern-Tunk Reu-Boos / Gore-Rang /
Toom-Book*
**Boiled / sauté / mashed
potatoes**

Nasi
Nha-See
Rice

Keju
Cay-Jew
Cheese

Makanan penutup
Mar-Car-Narn Peu-Noo-Toop
Desserts

Es krim
Ays-Cream
Ice cream

Kue-kue
Coo-Way-Coo-Way
Cakes

Kue pastel
Coo-Way Pars-Tell
Pastries

Buah
Boo-Arh
Fruit

Roti
Raw-Tee
Bread

Rol
Roll
Rolls

Roti panggang
Raw-Tee Punk-Gharng
Toast

Mentega
Mern-Tay-Gaa
Butter

Garam / merica
Ghar-Rum / Mer-Ree-Cha
Salt / pepper

Gula
Goo-Laa
Sugar

Makanan khas
Mar-Car-Narn Cars
Specialities

Makanan khas daerah
Mar Car Narn Cars Dhar-Ay-Rah
Local specialities

Menu standar
Mer-Noo Stun-Dar
Set Menu

Daftar anggur
Duff-Tar Arng-Goor
Wine list

Anggur merah
Arng-Goor Mare-Rah
Red wines

Anggur putih
Arng-Goor Poo-Teeh
White wines

Anggur pink
Arng-Goor Pink
Rosé wines

Sampanye
Sum-Par-Nyer
Sparkling wines

Bir
Beer
Beer

Anggur botol / Bir Tuang
Beer Bore-Toll / Beer Too-Wung
**Bottled beer / Draught
(draft) beer**

Minuman tanpa alkohol
Mc-Noo-Marn Tum-Par Arl-Core-Hall
Non-alcoholic drinks

Air mineral
Eye-Eer Me-Ner-Rarl
Mineral water

Jus buah
Joos Boo-Ah
Fruit juices

Jus jeruk
Joose Jer-Rook
Orange juice

Jus lemon
Juice Lair-Morn
Lemonade

Es
Ays
Ice

I
N
D
O
N
E
S
I
A
N

127

Kopi susu / kopi pahit / kopi espresso
Corp-Pee Soo-Soo / Corp-Pee Par-Heat / Corp-Pee Ays-Press-So
White coffee / black coffee / espresso coffee

Teh dengan susu / dengan lemon
Tayh Derng-Arn Soo-Soo / Derng-Arn Lair-Morn
Tea with milk / with lemon

Coklat (minuman)
Choke-Lut
Chocolate (drink)

Susu
Soo-Soo
Milk

Makanan ringan
Mar-Car-Narn Ring-Ahn
Snacks / Light meals

Salad
Sha-Lard
Salads

Roti lapis
Raw-Tee Laa-Piece
Sandwiches

Telur	Sosis
Teu-Loor	*Sore-Sees*
Eggs	**Sausage**

Telur rebus / goreng / orak-arik
Teu-Loor Rer-Boos / Gore-Rang / Or-Ruck-Are-Reek
Boiled / fried / scrambled eggs

Typical local dishes

Nasi goreng
Nar-See Go-Rang
Fried Rice

Gado-gado
Gha-Doe Gha-Doe
Vegetables in peanut butter sauce

Sate ayam
Sar-Tay Are-Yum
Barbecued diced chicken on skewer

Sup ayam
Soup Are-Yum
Spicy chicken soup

Mie goreng
Me Go-Rang
Fried Noodle

GETTING AROUND

Public Transport

Where is the bus stop / coach stop / nearest metro (subway) station?
Di manakah tempat pemberhentian bis / stasiun kereta api (bawah tanah) terdekat?
Dee-Maa-Nha-Carh Term-Part Perm-Beur-Hern-Tee-Arn Bees / Star-See-Oon Ker-Ray-Tha Are-Pee (Bar-Wah Tha-Nah) Teur-Deur-Cut

When is the next / last bus to ...?
Kapankah bis berikutnya / terakhir ke ...?

Car-Pun-Carh Bees Beur-Ree-Coot-Nyar / Ter-Ark-Hear Ker …

How much is the fare to the city centre (downtown) / railway station / airport?
Berapakah ongkos ke pusat kota / stasiun kereta api / bandara?
Beur-Ra-Paa-Carh Ong-Cores Ker Poo-Sart Core-Tha / Star-See-Oon Ker-Ray-Tha Are-Pee / Bun-Dha-Rhaa

Will you tell me when to get off?
Maukah Anda memberi tahu saya saatnya turun?
Mar-Oo-Carh Arn-Dha Merm-Beur-Ree Tha-Hoo Sha-Yaa Sha-Art-Nyar Too-Roon

Does this bus go to … ?
Apakah bis ini ke …?
Are-Par-Carh Bees E-Knee Ker …

Which number bus goes to … ?
Bis nomor berapakah yang menuju ke …?
Bees Nor-More Beur-Are-Paa-Carh Young Meu-Noo-Jew Ker …

May I have a single (oneway) / return (round-trip) / day ticket / book of tickets?
Saya mau beli tiket sekali jalan / pulang pergi / tiket harian / sebendel tiket
Sha-Yaa Mar-Oo Beur-Lee Tee-Cat Ser-Car-Lee Jar-Larn / Poo-Lung Per-Ghee / Tee-Cat Haa-Ree-Arn / Ser-Ben-Deul Tee-Cat

Taxis and Rickshaws

I would like to go to …
Saya ingin pergi ke …
Sha-Yaa E-Ngeen Per-Ghee Ker …

How much will it cost?
Berapakah ongkosnya?
Beur-Are-Par-Carh Ong-Cores-Nyar

Please may I stop here?
Bisakah saya berhenti di sini?
Bee-Sha-Carh Sha-Yaa Beur-Hern-Tee Dee See-Knee

I would like to order a taxi today / tomorrow / at 2pm to go from … to …
Saya ingin memesan taksi hari ini / besok / pukul 2 siang untuk pergi dari … ke…
Sha-Yaa E-Ngeen Meu-Meu-Sun Tuck-See Haa-Ree E-Knee / Bay-Soak Poo-Cool Doo-Are See-Arng Oon-Took Per-Ghee Dha-Ree … Ker …

Entertaiment

Can you recommend a good bar / nightclub?
Bisakah anda memberitahu bar / klub malam yang bagus?
Bee-Sha-Carh Arn-Dha Merm-Beur-Ree-Tha-Hoo Barr / Ker-Lub Mar-Lum Young Bar-Goose

Do you know what is on at the cinema (playing at the movies) / theatre at the moment?
Apakah anda tahu film apa yang sedang diputar di bioskop sekarang?
Are-Par-Carh Arn-Dha Tha-Hoo Fee-Lerm Are-Par Young Ser-Darng Dee-Poo-Tha Dee Bee-Yos-Cope Ser-Car-Rung

I would like to book (purchase) … tickets for the matinee / evening performance on Monday

Saya ingin memesan (membeli) …
tiket untuk pementasan siang / malam
pada hari Senin
*Sha-Yaa E-Ngeen Meu-Meu-Sun
(Merm-Beur-Ree) … Tee-Cat Oon-Took
Per-Man-Tha-Sun See-Arng /
Mar-Lum*

What time does the film / performance start?
Pukul berapa film / pementasan
dimulai?
*Poo-Cool Beur-Are-Par Fee-Lerm /
Per-Man-Thaa-Sun Dee-Moo-Lie*

COMMUNICATIONS

Post

How much will it cost to send a letter / postcard / this package to Britain / Ireland / America / Canada / Australia / New Zealand?
Berapakah ongkos mengirimkan
surat / kartu pos / paket ini ke
Inggris / Irlandia / Amerika /
Kanada / Australia / Selandia Baru?
*Beur-Are-Par Ong-Cores Merng-E-Reem-
Karn Soo-Rut / Car-Too Post / Par-Cat
E-Knee Ker Ink-Grease / Ear-Larn-Dee-
Yaa / Are-May-Ree-Car / Car-Nar-Dha /
Oz-Traa-Lee-Yaa / Sir-Larn-Dee-Yar
Bar-Roo*

I would like one stamp / two stamps
Saya butuh selembar perangko /
dua lembar perangko
*Sha-Yaa Boo-Tooh Ser-Lerm-Bar
Per-Rung-Co / Doo-Are Lerm-Bar
Per-Rung-Co*

I'd like ... stamps for postcards to send abroad, please
Saya butuh … perangko kartu pos
untuk dikirmkan ke luar negeri
*Sha-Yaa Boo-Tooh … Per-Rung-Co
Car-Too Pores Oon-Took Dee-Key-
Reem-Karn Ker Loo-Are Neu-Gher-Ree*

Phones

I would like to make a telephone call / reverse the charges to (make a collect call to) ...
Saya ingin menelepon / bebankan
biayanya pada …
*Sha-Yaa E-Ngeen Meu-Nail-Pone /
Beu-Bunn-Karn Bee-Are-Yarn-Nyar
Par-Dhaa …*

Which coins do I need for the telephone?
Koin mana yang saya butuhkan untuk
menelepon?
*Coin Maa-Nha Young Sha-Ya
Boo-Tooh-Karn Oon-Took
Meu-Nell-Pone*

The line is engaged (busy)
Sambungan sibuk
Sum-Boong-Arn See-Book

The number is ...
Nomornya adalah …
Nor-More-Nyar Are-Dha-Larh …

Hello, this is ...
Halo, ini …
Har-Low, E-Knee …

Please may I speak to ...?
Bisakah saya bicara dengan …?
*Bee-Sha-Carh Sha-Yaa Bee-Cha-Yar
Derng-Arn …*

He / she is not in at the moment. Can you call back?

Shat ini dia sedang tidak ada. Bisakah
anda menelepon kembali?
*Sha-Art E-Knee Dee-Are Ser-Darng
Tee-Duck Are-Dha. Bee-Sha-Carh
Arn-Dha Meu-Nell-Pone Kerm-Bar-Lee*

SHOPPING

Shops

Toko buku / toko alat tulis
*Toe-Cowe Boo-Coo / Toe-Cowe
Are-Lut Too-Lees*
Bookshop / Stationery

Penjual perhiasan / hadiah
*Pern-Jew Arl Per-Hee-Are-Sun / Har-
Dee-Ah*
Jeweller / Gifts

Sepatu
Sir-Par-Too
Shoes

Perangkat keras
Per-Rung-Cart Ker-Rus
Hardware

Penata rambut
Per-Nar-Tha Rum-Boot
Hairdresser

Pria / wanita
Pree-Yaa / Wha-Knee-Tha
(men's) / (women's)

Pembuat roti
Perm-Boo-Art Raw-Tee
Baker

Telepon
Teller-Pone
Phones

Supermarket
Soo-Per-Mar-Kert
Supermarket

Gerai Foto
Gher-Rye Fow-Towe
Photo-Shop

Biro perjalanan
Bee-Row Per-Jar-Laa-Narn
Travel agent

Apotek
Are-Pore-Take
Pharmacy

In the Shop

**What time do the shops
open / close?**
Pukul berapakah toko-toko itu
buka / tutup?
*Poo-Cool Beur-Are-Paa-Carh Toe-Cowe
Toe-Cowe E-Too Boo-Car / Too-Toop*

Where is the nearest market?
Dimanakah pasar terdekat?
*Dee-Maa-Nha-Carh Par-Sar
Ter-Der-Cart*

**Can you show me the one in
the window / this one?**
Bisa anda perlihatkan yang di
jendela itu / yang ini?
*Bee-Sha Arn-Dha Per-Lee-Hut-Karn
Young Dee Jern-Dare-Laa E-Too / Young
E-Knee*

Can I try this on?
Bisakah saya mencobanya?
*Bee-Sha-Carh Sha-Yaa
Mern-Chaw-Bar-Nyar*

INDONESIAN

What size is this?
Berapakah ukurannya?
Beur-Are-Par-Carh Oo-Coo-Run-Nyar

This is too large / too small / too expensive
Ini terlalu besar / terlalu kecil / terlalu mahal
E-Knee Ter-Lar-Loo Beu-Sarr / Ter-Lar-Loo Ker-Cheel / Ter-Lar-Loo Mar-Hull

Do you have any others?
Apakah anda punya yang lainnya?
Are-Par-Carh Arn-Dha Poo-Nyar Young Line-Nyar

My size is ...
Ukuran saya adalah...
Oo-Coo-Run Sha-Yaa Are-Dha-Larh ...

Where is the changing room / children's / cosmetic / ladieswear / menswear / food department?
Dimanakah ruang ganti / bagian anak-anak / kosmetik / pakaian wanita / pakaian pria / makanan?
Dee-Maa-Nha-Carh Roo-Arng Gun-Tee / Bar-Ghee-Arn Are-Knuck-Are-Knuck / Cos-Met-Teak / Par-Kye-Arn Wha-Knee-Tha / Par-Kye-Arn Pree-Yaa / Mar-Car-Narn

I would like ... a quarter of a kilo / half a kilo / a kilo of bread / butter / cheese / ham / this fruit
Saya butuh ... seperempat kilo / setengah kilo / sekilo roti / mentega / keju / daging babi asap / buah ini
Sha-Yaa Boo-Tooh ... Ser-Per-Erm-Part Key-Low / Ser-Terng-Ah Key-Low / Ser-Key-Low Raw-Tee / Mern-Tair-Gaa / Ker-Jew / Dhar-Gheeng Bar-Bee Are-Sarp / Boo-Ah E-Knee

How much is this?
Berapakah harganya?
Beur-Are-Par-Carh Harg-Ghaa-Nyar

I'll take this one, thank you
Saya ambil yang ini
Sha-Yaa Arm-Bill Young E-Knee

Do you have a carrier (shopping) bag?
Apakah anda punya tas belanja?
Are-Par-Carh Arn-Dha Poo-Nyar Tars Beu-Larn-Jar

Do you have anything cheaper / larger / smaller / of better quality?
Apakah anda punya sesuatu yang lebih murah / lebih besar / lebih kecil / dengan kualitas yang lebih baik?
Are-Par-Carh Arn-Dha Poo-Nyar Ser-Soo-Are-Too Young Ler-Beeh Moo-Rah / Ler-Beeh Beu-Sar / Ler-Beeh Ker-Cheel / Derng-Arn Coo-Are-Lee-Tars Young Ler-Beeh Bike

I would like a film / to develop this film for this camera
Saya perlu film / mencuci film untuk kamera ini
Sha-Yaa Per-Loo Fee-Lerm / Mern-Choo-Chee Fee-Lerm Oon-Took Car-Mare-Rhaa E-Knee

I would like some batteries, the same size as this old one
Saya perlu baterai, yang ukurannya sama dengan yang lama ini
Sha-Yaa Per-Loo But-Rare, Young Oo-Coo-Run-Nyar Sha-Mar Derng-Arn Young Laa-Mar E-Knee

Would you mind wrapping this for me, please?
Bisa dibungkus?
Bee-Sha Dee-Boong-Coose

Sorry, but you seem to have given me the wrong change
Maaf, sepertinya kembaliannya salah
Mar-Aarf, Ser-Per-Tee-Nyar Kerm-Bar-Lee-Arn-Nyar Sha-Larh

MOTORING

Car Hire (Rental)

I have ordered (rented) a car in the name of ...
Saya telah memesan (menyewa) mobil atas nama...
Sha-Yaa Ter-Larh Meu-Meu-Sun (Meu-Nyair-Wha) More-Bill Are-Tars Nar-Mar ...

How much does it cost to hire (rent) a car for one day / two days / a week?
Berapakah ongkos sewa mobil untuk sehari / dua hari / seminggu
Beur-Are-Par-Carh Ong-Cores Sair-Whar Mob-Bill Oon-Took Seu-Haa-Ree / Doo-Are Haa-Ree / Seu-Meeng-Goo

Is the tank already full of petrol (gas)?
Apakah bahan bakarnya penuh?
Are-Par-Carh Bar-Hun Bar-Car-Nyar Per-Nooh

Is insurance and tax included?
Apakah termasuk asuransi dan pajak?
Are-Par-Carh Ter-Mar-Sook Are-Soo-Run-See Darn Par-Juck

How much is the deposit?
Berapakah uang mukanya?
Beur-Are-Par-Carh Oo-Wunk Moo Car-Nyar

By what time must I return the car?
Jam berapa saya harus mengembalikan mobil ini?
Jarm Beur-Are-Par Sha-Yaa Har-Roose Merng-Uhm-Bar-Lee-Kahn More-Bill E-Knee

I would like a small / large / family / sports car with a radio / cassette player
Saya ingin mobil kecil / besar / keluarga / sport dengan radio / tape
Sha-Yaa E-Ngeen More-Bill Ker-Cheel / Beu Sarr / Keu-Loo-Are-Gaa / Sport Derng-Arn Rud-Dee-Yo / Tip

Do you have a road map?
Apakah anda punya peta jalan?
Are-Par-Carh Arn-Dha Poo-Nyar Pair-Tha Jar-Larn

Parking

How long can I park here?
Berapa lama saya bisa parkir di sini?
Beur-Are-Par Laa-Mar Sha-Yaa Bee-Sha Par-Keer Dee See-Knee

Is there a car park near here?
Apakah ada tempat parkir mobil di dekat sini?
Are-Par-Carh Are-Dha Term-Part Par-Keer More-Bill Dee Der-Cart See-Knee

At what time does this car park close?
Pukul berapa tempat parkir mobil ini tutup?
Poo-Cool Beur-Are-Par Term-Putt Par-Keer More-Bill E-Knee Too-Toop

MOTORING

INDONESIAN

Signs and Notices

Satu arah
Sha-Too Are-Rah
One way

Dilarang masuk
Dee-Laa-Rung Mar-Sook
No entry

Dilarang parkir
Dee-Laa-Rung Par-Keer
No parking

Pengalihan jalan
Perng-Are-Lee-Hun Jar-Larn
Detour (diversion)

Pemberhentian
Perm-Beur-Hern-Tee-Arn
Stop

Dahulukan
Dhar-Who-Loo-Karn
Give way (yield)

Jalan licin
Jar-Larn Lee-Cheen
Slippery road

Dilarang mendahului
*Dee-Laa-Rung
Mern-Dhar-Who-Loo-We*
No overtaking

Bahaya!
Bar-Har-Yar
Danger!

At the Filling Station

Unleaded (lead-free) / standard / premium / diesel

Rendah timbal (bebas timbal) / standar / bensin / solar
Rern-Dah Team-Barl (Bay-Bus Team-Barl) / Stun-Dar / Ben-Seen / Sore-Larr

Fill the tank please
Tolong isi tangkinya
Tore-Long E-See Tung-Key-Nyar

Do you have a road map?
Apakah anda punya peta jalan?
Are-Par-Carh Arn-Dha Poo-Nyar Pair-Tha Jar-Larn

How much is the car wash?
Berapakah ongkos mencuci mobil?
Beur-Are-Paa-Carh Ong-Cores Mern-Choo-Chi More-Bill

Breakdowns

I've had a breakdown at ...
Mobil saya mogok di ...
More-Bill Sha-Yaa More-Gock Dee...

I am a member of the [motoring organisation]
Saya anggota [organisasi motor]
Sha-Yaa Arng-Gore-Tha [Or-Gun-Knee-Shaa-See More-Tore]

I am on the road from ... to ...
Saya dalam perjalanan darat dari ... ke ...
Sha-Yaa Dhar-Lum Per-Jar-Larn-Narn Dhar-Rut Dha-Ree ... Ker ...

I can't move the car. Can you send a tow-truck?
Mobil saya mogok. Bisakah anda mengirim mobil derek?
More-Bill Sha-Yaa More-Gock. Bee-Sha-Carh Arn-Dha Merng-E-Reem Mo-Bill Dare-Reck

134

I have a flat tyre
Ban saya kempes
Barn Sha-Yaa Kerm-Pairs

The windscreen (windshield) has smashed / cracked
Kaca depan mobilnya retak / pecah
Car-Cha Der-Pun More-Bill-Nyar Re-Tuck / Per-Chah

There is something wrong with the engine / brakes / lights / steering / gearbox / clutch / exhaust
Ada masalah pada mesin / rem / lampu / kemudi / persneling / kopling / knalpot
Are-Dha Mar-Sha-lah Par-Dar Mer-Seen / Ram / Lum-Poo / Ker-Moo-Dee / Per-Snare-Ling / Cop-Ling / Kern-Narl-Pot

It's overheating
Mesin terlalu panas
Mer-Seen Ter-Laa-Loo Par-Nars

It won't start
Mesinnya tidak mau hidup
Meu-Seen-Nyar Tee-Duck Maa-Oo Hee-Doop

Where can I get it repaired?
Dimana saya bisa memperbaikinya?
Dee-Maa-Nha Sha-Yaa Bee-Sha Merm-Per-Bye-Key-Nyar

Can you take me there?
Bisakah anda mengantarkan saya ke sana?
Bee-Sha-Carh Arn-Dha Merng-Arn-Tart-Karn Sha-Yaa Ker Sha-Nar

Will it take long to fix?
Apakah lama memperbaikinya?
Are-Par-Carh Laa-Mar Merm-Per-Bye-Key-Nyar

How much will it cost?
Berapa ongkosnya?
Beur-Are-Par Ong-Cores-Nyar

Please can you pick me up / give me a lift?
Bisakah anda mengantarkan saya / memberi tumpangan?
Bee-Sha-Carh Arn-Dha Merng-Arn-Tart-Karn Sha-Yaa / Merm-Beur-Ree Toom-Pung-Arn

Accidents and Traffic Offences

Can you help me? There has been an accident
Bisakah anda membantu saya? Telah terjadi kecelakaan
Bee-Sha-Carh Arn-Dha Merm-Bun-Too Sha-Yaa? Ter-Larh Ter-Jar-Dee Ker-Cheur-Laa-Car-Arn

Please call the police / an ambulance
Tolong telepon polisi / ambulan
Tore-Long Teller-Pone Pore-Lee-See / Arm-Boo-Larn

Is anyone hurt?
Apakah ada yang terluka?
Are-Par-Carh Are-Dha Young Ter-Loo-Car

I'm sorry, I didn't see the sign
Maaf, saya tidak melihat rambu-rambu itu
Mar-Aarf, Sha-Yaa Tee-Duck Meu-Lee-Hut Rum-Boo- Rum-Boo E-Too

Must I pay a fine? How much?
Haruskah saya membayar denda? Berapa?
Har-Roos-Carh Sha-Yaa Merm-Bar-Yarr Dern Dha? Beur-Are-Par

Show me your documents
Tunjukkan surat-surat anda
*Toon-Juke-Karn Soo-Rut-Soo-Rut
Arn-Dha*

HEALTH

Pharmacy

**Do you have anything for a
stomach ache / headache / sore
throat / toothache?**
Apakah anda punya obat sakit perut /
sakit kepala / sakit tenggorokan /
sakit gigi
*Are-Par-Carh Arn-Dha Poo-Nyar Or-But
Suck-It Per-Root / Suck-It Ker-Par-Laa /
Suck-It Terng-Gore-Rock-Karn /
Suck-It Ghee-Ghee*

**I need something for diarrhoea /
constipation / a cold / a cough /
insect bites / sunburn / travel
(motion) sickness (car) (plane)
(boat)**
Saya butuh obat untuk diare /
sembelit / demam / batuk / gigitan
serangga / terbakar matahari / mabuk
perjalanan (darat, udara, laut)
*Sha-Yaa Boo-Tooh Or-But Oon-Took
Dee-Are-Ray / Serm-Beu-Leet /
Derm-Marm / Bar-Took / Ghee-Ghee-
Tarn Sir-Rung-Ghaa / Terr-Bar-Car
Mar-Tha-Haa-Ree / Mar-Book
Per-Jar-Larn-Narn (Dhaa-Rut,
Oo-Dhaa-Rhaa, Lar-Wood)*

**How much / how many do I
take?**
Berapa banyak yang harus saya
minum?
*Beur-Are-Paa Bar-Nyuck Young
Har-Roos Sha-Yaa Me-Noom*

How often do I take it / them?
Seberapa sering saya harus
meminumnya?
*Seu-Beur-Are-Paa Sir-Ring Sha-Yaa Har-
Roos Meu-Me-Noom-Nyar*

**I am / he is / she is taking this
medication**
Saya / dia / sedang memakai obat ini
*Sha-Yaa / Dee-Are / Ser-Darng
Meu-Mar-Kye Or-But E-Knee*

How much does it cost?
Berapa harganya?
Beur-Are-Par Harg-Ghaa-Nyar

**Can you recommend a good
doctor / dentist?**
Bisakah anda memberitahukan
dokter / dokter gigi yang bagus?
*Bee-Sha-Carh Arn-Dha Merm-Beur-Ree-
Tha-Who-Karn Dock-Ter / Dock-Ter
Ghee-Ghee Young Bar-Goose*

Is it suitable for children?
Apakah ini cocok untuk anak-anak?
*Are-Par-Carh E-Knee Chaw-Chalk
Oon-Took Are-Knuck-Are-Knuck*

Doctor

**I have a pain here / in my arm /
leg / chest / stomach**
Saya merasakan nyeri di sini / di
lengan / kaki / dada / perut saya
*Sha-Yaa Meu-Rhaa-Sha-Karn Nyer-Ree
Dee See-Knee / Dee Lerng-Arn /
Car-Key / Dha-Dha / Per-Root Sha-Yaa*

**Please call a doctor, this is an
emergency**
Tolong telepon dokter, ini darurat
*Tore-Long Teller-Pone Dock-Ter, E-Knee
Dhar-Roo-Rut*

I
N
D
O
N
E
S
I
A
N

I would like to make an appointment to see the doctor
Saya ingin daftar untuk menemui dokter
Sha-Yaa E-Ngeen Duff-Tar Oon-Took Meu-Neu-Moo-E Dock-Ter

I am diabetic / pregnant
Saya menderita diabetes / sedang hamil
Sha-Yaa Meun-Deur-Ree-Tha Dee-Are-Bet-Ters / Ser-Darng Har-Meal

I need a prescription for ...
Saya butuh resep untuk …
Sha-Yaa Boo-Tooh Re-Sep Oon-Took …

Can you give me something to ease the pain?
Bisakah anda memberi pereda nyeri?
Bee-Sha-Carh Arn-Dha Merm-Beur-Ree Per-Rer-Dar Nyer-Ree

I am / he is / she is allergic to penicillin
Saya / dia alergi pada penisilin
Sha-Yaa / Dee-Are Are-Lair-Ghee Par-Dar Penny-See-Lean

Does this hurt?
Sakit?
Sar-Kit

You must / he must / she must go to hospital
Anda harus / dia harus di bawa ke rumah sakit
Arn-Dha Har-Roose / Dee-Are Har-Roose Dee-Bar-War Ker Roo-Mah Sar-Kit

Take these once / twice / three times a day
Minumlah ini sekali / dua kali / tiga kali sehari

Me-Noom-Larh E-Knee Ser-Car-Lee / Doo-Are Car-Lee / Tee-Gaa Car-Lee Ser-Haa-Ree

I am / he is / she is taking this medication
Saya / dia sedang memakai obat ini
Sha-Yaa / Dee-Are Ser-Darng Meu-Mar-Kye Or-But E-Knee

I have medical insurance
Saya punya asuransi medis
Sha-Yaa Poo-Nyar Are-Soo-Run-See Met-Disk

Dentist

I have toothache
Saya sakit gigi
Sha-Yaa Sar-Kit Ghee-Ghee

My filling has come out
Saya habis muntah
Sha-Yaa Har-Bees Moon-Tah

I do / do not want to have an injection first
Saya ingin / tidak ingin disuntik dulu
Sha-Yaa E-Ngeen / Tee-Duck E-Ngeen Dee Soon-Teak Do-Loo

EMERGENCIES

Help!
Tolong!
Taw-Long

Fire!
Kebakaran!
Ker-Bar-Car-Run

Stop!
Berhenti!
Beur-Hern-Tee

Call an ambulance / a doctor / the police / the fire brigade
Telepon ambulan / dokter / polisi / pemadam kebakaran
Teller-Pone Arm-Boo-Larn / Dock-Ter / Pore-Lee-See / Peu-Mar-Dum Keu-Bar-Car-Run

Please may I use a telephone?
Bolehkah saya menggunakan telepon?
Bow-Layh-Carh Sha-Yaa Merng-Goo-Nar-Karn Teller-Pone

I have had my traveller's cheques / credit cards / handbag / rucksack / (knapsack) / luggage / wallet / passport / mobile phone stolen
Cek / kartu kredit / tas tangan / ransel / barang-barang / dompet / paspor / telepon genggam saya dicuri
Check / Car-Too Credit / Tars Tung-Arn / Run-Serl / Bar-Rung-Bar-Rung / Dorm-Pet / Pars-Pore / Teller-Pone Gherng-Gum Sha-Yaa Dee-Choo-Ree

May I please have a copy of the report for my insurance claim?
Bisakah saya mendapatkan salinan laporan untuk mengurus klaim asuransi saya?
Bee-Sha-Carh Sha-Yaa Mern-Dhar-Part-Karn Sha-Lee-Nun Laa-Pore-Run Oon-Took Merng-Oo-Roose Claim Are-Soo-Run-See Sha-Yaa

Can you help me? I have lost my daughter / my son / my companion(s)
Bisakah anda membantu saya? anak / teman saya hilang
Bee-Sha-Carh Arn-Dha Merm-Bun-Too Sha-Yaa? Are-Knuck / Ter-Marn Sha-Yaa Hee-Lung

Please go away / leave me alone
Pergilah / tinggalkan saya sendiri
Per-Ghee-Larh / Teeng-Gull-Karn Sha-Yaa Sern-Dee-Ree

I'm sorry
Saya ikut prihatin; Maaf
Sha-Yaa E-Coot Pre-Har-Teen; Mar-Aarf

I want to contact the British / American / Canadian / Irish / Australian / New Zealand / South African consulate
Saya ingin menghubungi konsulat Inggris / Amerika / Kanada / Irlandia / Australia / Selandia baru / Afrika selatan
Sha-Yaa E-Ngeen Merng-Hoo-Boong-E Con-Soo-Lut Ink-Grease / Are-May-Ree-Car / Car-Nar-Dar / Ear-Larn-Dee-Are / Oz-Thrar-Lee-Are / Ser-Larn-Dee-Yar Bar-Roo / Uf-Free-Car Ser-Laa-Tarn

I'm / we're / he is / she is ill / lost / injured
Saya / kami / dia sakit / tersesat / terluka
Sha-Yaa / Car-Me / Dee-Are Sar-Kit / Ter-Ser-Sart / Ter-Loo-Car

They are ill / lost / injured
Mereka sakit / tersesat / terluka
Meu-Ray-Car Sar-Kit / Ter-Ser-Sart / Ter-Loo-Car

KHMER

ខ្មែរ

K
H
M
E
R

INTRODUCTION

Khmer (or Cambodian) is the national language of the Kingdom of Cambodia and is also understood in many of its neighbouring countries, including Thailand, Laos and Vietnam. Possibly one of the oldest languages in South-East Asia, it is traditionally written in an Indian-derived alphabet. In addition to Khmer, the older generation of cambodians are likely to speak French, a leftover from the French rule in the 19th century, while the younger generation prefer to use English. Khmer is not an easy language to pick up but the numbers and basic greetings get you a long way for little effort!

Addresses for Travel and Tourist Information

Australia: Department of Foreign Affairs and Trade, Canberra ACT 2600.
Web: www.smarttraveller.gov.au/zw-cgi/view/Advice/Cambodia#content
Royal Embassy of Cambodia, 5 Canterbury Crescent, Deakin, ACT 2600.
Tel: 02 6273 1154/02 6273 1259; Fax: 02 6273 1053;
Email: cambodianembassy@ozemail.com.au;
Web: www.embassyofcambodia.org.nz/au.htm

Canada: There is no official Cambodian embassy in Canada. The nearest is in Washington (see USA).

UK: Royal Embassy of Cambodia, 28-32 Wellington Road, St. John's Wood, London NW8 9SP. Tel: 020 7483 9063; Fax: 020 7483 9061;
Email: cambodianembassy@btconnect.com;
Web: www.cambodianembassy.org.uk

USA: The Royal Embassy of Cambodia, 4530 16th Street NW, Washington DC 20011; Tel: 202 726 7742; Fax: 202 726 8381;
Email: cambodia@embassy.org; Web: embassy.org/cambodia

Cambodia Facts

CAPITAL: Phnom Penh

CURRENCY: Riel

OPENING HOURS: Banks: Open Mon-Fri, 0730-1130, 1400-1700. A few banks open on Saturday mornings. Post Offices and shops follow a similar pattern, closing for lunch, but most open until later in the evening.

TELEPHONES: To dial in, Tel: International Access Code + 855 + Area Code – first zero. Outgoing, Tel: 00 + Country Code.

EMERGENCY NUMBERS: General Emergency Tel: 117 (In Phnom Penh, ring 018 811593 for 24-hr English-speaking assistance). Hospital: Phnom Penh SOS International Medical Centre: Tel: 015 916685.

PUBLIC HOLIDAYS: Jan 1 – New Year's Day; Jan 7 – Victory Day (Celebration of the defeat of the Genocidal Regime – the Khmer Rouge in 1979); Feb 19-20 – Vietnamese & Chinese New Year; Apr 14-16 – Cambodian New Year; May 14 – Bonn Chroat Preah Nongkoal (the Royal Plughing Ceremony); Oct 30-Nov 1 – King Norodom Sihanouk's Birthday; Nov 9 – Celebration of 1953 Independence Day From France.

Technical Language Hints

- There are several notable dialects in use in Cambodia.

- English is quickly becoming Cambodia's second language but French pronunciation of English words is common.

- Khmer as spoken in the capital is well understood throughout the country, but there are sharp differences in accent in the far reaches of Cambodia which may mean that you have to listen particularly carefully. The most noticeable accent is found south of Phnom Penh, where combinations of hard consonants are slurred together (for example, "br" will become closer in sound to "p" and "sr" becomes "s").

K
H
M
E
R

Alphabet

Consonants

ក Gor	ខ Kor
គ Go	ឃ Ko
ង O	ច Jor
ឆ Qor	ជ Jo
ឈ Qo	ញ Nho
ដ Dor	ឋ Tor
ឌ Do	ឍ To
ណ Nor	ត Tor
ថ Tor	ទ To
ធ To	ន No
ប Bor	ផ Por
ព Bo	ភ Po
ម Mo	យ Yo
រ Ro	ល Lo

វ Vo	ស Sor
ហ Hor	ឡ Lor
អ Or	

Vowels

ា A / Ea	ិ E / I
ី Ei / I:	ឹ Eu / Eu
ឺ Eu: / Eu:	ុ O / U
ូ O: / U:	ួ Uo / Uo
ើ Ae / Eu	ឿ Eu: / Eu:
ៀ Ea / Ea	េ E / E
ែ Ae / Ea	ៃ Ay / Ei
ោ Ao: / Ou:	ៅ Ao / Ou
ំ Om / Um	+ Orm / Om
ាំ Am / Uam	ះ Ah / Iah

NB: Vowels with colons: long vowels (should be pronounced longer)

Basic Words and Phrases

Yes
បាទ / ចាំ
Bat / Jas

No
អត់ទេ
Ort Te

Please
សូមមេត្តា
Som Me Ta

Thank you
អរគុណ
Or Kun

Hello
សួស្តី
Suo Sdei

Goodbye
ជំរាបលា
Chum Riab Lia

Excuse me
អត់ទោស
Ort Ios

Sorry
សុំទោស
Som Tos

How
យ៉ាងម៉េច
Yang Mej

When
ពេលណា
Pel Na

Why
ហេតុអ្វី
Het Ah Vei

What
អ្វី
Avei

Who
អ្នកណា
Nak Na

That's O.K.
មិនអីទេ
Men Ei Te

Perhaps
ប្រហែល
Bro Hel

To
ទៅ
Teuv

From
មកពី
Mok Pi

Here
ទីនេះ
Ti Nis

There
ទីនោះ
Ti Nos

I don't understand
ខ្ញុំអត់យល់ទេ
Khnom Ort Youl Te

I don't speak Khmer
ខ្ញុំមិនចេះនិយាយភាសាខ្មែរ
Knhom Min Jeh Ni Yeay Peasa Kmai

Do you speak English?
តើអ្នកនិយាយភាសាអង់គ្លេសទេ?
Tei Nak Ni Yeay Pia Sa An Glai Te

Can you please write it down?
តើអ្នកអាចសរសេរវាបានទេ?
Tei Nak Ahj Sor Se Vea Ban Te

Please can you speak more slowly?
តើអ្នកអាចនិយាយអោយយឺតបានទេ?
Tei Nak Ahj Ni Yeay Ouy Yeut Ban Te

Greetings

Good morning /
Good afternoon /
Good evening / Goodnight
អរុណសួស្តី / ទិវាសួស្តី / សាយ័ណ្ហសួស្តី / រាត្រីសួស្តី
Arun Suo Sdei / Ti Via Suo Sdei /
Say Yun Suo Sdei / Ria Trei Suo Sdei

Pleased to meet you
សប្បាយរីករាយបានស្គាល់អ្នក
Sa Bay Ri Reay Ban Skorl Nuk

How are you?
តើអ្នកសុខសប្បាយទេ?
Tei Nak Sok Sa Bay Te

Well, thank you. And you?
សុខស្បាយ អរគុណអ្នក ចុះអ្នកវិញ?
Sok Sa Bay Or Kun Nak Jos Nak Vinh

My name is ...
ឈ្មោះរបស់ខ្ញុំ គឺ ...
Chmos Ro Bos Khnom Keu...

143

KHMER

This is my friend / boyfriend / girlfriend / husband / wife / brother / sister

នេះគឺជាមិត្ត / មិត្តប្រុស / មិត្តស្រី / ប្តី / ប្រពន្ធ / បងប្អូនប្រុស / បងប្អូនស្រី របស់ខ្ញុំ

Ni Keu Jia Mit / Mit Bros / Mit Srey / Pdey / Bror Pun / Bong Paoun Bros / Bang Paoun Srey Ro Bos Khnom

Where are you travelling to?

តើអ្នកធ្វើដំណើរកំសាន្តទៅកន្លែងណា?

Tei Nak Tveu Dom Nei Kom San Tov Korn Laeng Na

I am / we are going to ...

ខ្ញុំ / យើង ចង់ទៅ ...

Khnom / Yeung Jong Tov ...

How long are you travelling for?

តើអ្នកធ្វើដំណើរកំសាន្តសំរាប់រយៈពេលប៉ុន្មាន?

Tei Nak Tveu Dom Neur Kom San Som Rab Ro Yak Pel Pun Man

Where do you come from?

តើអ្នកមកពីណា?

Tei Nak Mok Pi Na

I am / we are from Australia / Britain / Canada / America

ខ្ញុំ / យើងមកពីអូស្ត្រាលី / អង់គ្លេស / កាណាដា / អាមេរិកកាំង

Khnom / Yeung Mok Pi Au Stra Li / An Glai / Ka Na Da / A Me Ri Kang

We are on holiday

យើងវិស្សមកាល

Yeung Vi Sa Mak Kal

This is our first visit here

នេះគឺជាការធ្វើទស្សនាលើកទីមួយនៅទីនេះ

Nis Keu Jia Ka Tveu Tos Sna Leuk Ti Mouy Nov Ti Nis

How old are you?

តើអ្នកអាយុប៉ុន្មាន?

Tei Nak A Youk Pun Man

I am ... years old

ខ្ញុំអាយុ ... ឆ្នាំ

Khnom A Youk ... Chnam

I am a businessman / business woman / doctor / journalist / manual worker / administrator / scientist / student / teacher

ខ្ញុំគឺជាអ្នកជំនួញ / អ្នកជំនួញស្រី / វេជ្ជបណ្ឌិត / អ្នកកាសែត / កម្មករ / អ្នករដ្ឋបាល / អ្នកវិទ្យាសាស្ត្រ / និស្សិត / គ្រូបង្រៀន

Khnom Keu Jia Nak Chum Nouy / Nak Chum Nouy Srey / Vi Jiak Bun Det / Nak Ka Set / Kam Ma Kor / Nak Rat Ta Bal / Nak Vi Tyia Sas / Ni Set / Krou Bong Rian

Would you like / may I have a cigarette?

តើអ្នកចង់ជក់ / តើអ្នកអាចអោយខ្ញុំមួយដើមបានទេ?

Tei Nak Jong Juk / Tei Nak Ahj Ouy Khnom Ba Rey Mouy Derm Ban Te

Do you mind if I smoke?

តើអ្នកប្រកាន់ទេបើខ្ញុំជក់បារី?

Tei Nak Bror Kan Te Bei Khnom Juk Ba Rey

Do you have a light?

តើអ្នកមានដែកកេះទេ?

Tei Nak Mian Daek Kes Te

I am waiting for my husband / wife / boyfriend / girlfriend

ខ្ញុំកំពុងរង់ចាំប្តីរបស់ខ្ញុំ / ប្រពន្ធ / មិត្តប្រុស / មិត្តស្រី

Khnom Kom Pong Rong Jam Pdei Ro Bos Khnom / Bro Pun / Met Bros / Met Srey

**K
H
M
E
R**

Days

Monday
ថ្ងៃចន្ទ
Tngay Jan

Tuesday
ថ្ងៃអង្គារ
Tngay An Kia

Wednesday
ថ្ងៃពុធ
Tngay Put

Thursday
ថ្ងៃព្រហស្បតិ៍
Tngay Bro Hoh

Friday
ថ្ងៃសុក្រ
Tngay Sok

Saturday
ថ្ងៃសៅរ៍
Tngay Sao

Sunday
ថ្ងៃអាទិត្យ
Tngay Ah Tit

Morning
ពេលព្រឹក
Pel Preuk

Afternoon
ពេលរសៀល
Pel Ro Seal

Evening
ពេលល្ងាច
Pel Lngaj

Night
ពេលយប់
Pel Yub

Yesterday / Today / Tomorrow
ម្សិលមិញ / ថ្ងៃនេះ / ថ្ងៃស្អែក
Msil Minh / Tngay Nis / Tngay Saek

Numbers

Zero
សូន្យ
Son

One
មួយ
Mouy

Two
ពីរ
Pi

Three
បី
Bey

Four
បួន
Boun

Five
ប្រាំ
Pram

Six
ប្រាំមួយ
Pram Mouy

Seven
ប្រាំពីរ
Pram Pi

Eight
ប្រាំបី
Pram Bey

Nine
ប្រាំបួន
Pram Boun

Ten
ដប់
Dob

Eleven
ដប់មួយ
Dob Mouy

Twelve
ដប់ពីរ
Dob Pi

Thirteen
ដប់បី
Dob Bey

Fourteen
ដប់បួន
Dob Boun

Fifteen
ដប់ប្រាំ
Dob Pram

Sixteen
ដប់ប្រាំមួយ
Dob Pram Mouy

Seventeen
ដប់ប្រាំពីរ
Dob Pram Pi

Eighteen
ដប់ប្រាំបី
Dob Pram Bey

Nineteen
ដប់ប្រាំបួន
Dob Pram Boun

Twenty
ម្ភៃ
Mo Pey

Twenty-one
ម្ភៃមួយ
Mo Pey Mouy

Twenty-two
ម្ភៃពីរ
Mo Pey Pi

Thirty
សាមសិប
Sam Seb

Forty
សែសិប
Sae Seb

Fifty
ហាសិប
Ha Seb

Sixty
ហុកសិប
Hok Seb

Seventy
ចិតសិប
Jet Seb

**K
H
M
E
R**

Eighty
ប៉ែតសិប
Pet Seb

Ninety
កៅសិប
Kao Seb

One hundred
មួយរយ
Mouy Roy

Five hundred
ប្រាំរយ
Pram Rouy

One thousand
មួយពាន់
Mouy Poin

One million
មួយលាន
Mouy Lian

Time

What time is it?
តើម៉ោងប៉ុន្មាន?
Tei Moung Pun Man

It is ...
ម៉ោង ...
Moung ...

9.00
ប្រាំបួន
Pram Boun

9.05
ប្រាំបួនប្រាំនាទី
Pram Boun Pram Nia Ti

9.15
ប្រាំបួនដប់ប្រាំនាទី
Pram Boun Dob Pram Nia Ti

9.20
ប្រាំបួនម្ភៃនាទី
Pram Boun Mopey Nia Ti

9.30
ប្រាំបួនសាមសិបនាទី
Pram Boun Sam Seb Nia Ti

9.35
ប្រាំបួនសាមសិបប្រាំនាទី
Pram Boun Sam Seb Pram Nia Ti

9.40
ប្រាំបួនសែសិបនាទី
Pram Boun Sae Seb Nia Ti

9.45
ប្រាំបួនសែសិបប្រាំនាទី
Pram Boun Sae Seb Pram Nia Ti

9.50
ប្រាំបួនហាសិបនាទី
Pram Boun Ha Seb Nia Ti

9.55
ប្រាំបួនហាសិបប្រាំនាទី
Pram Boun Ha Seb Pram Nia Ti

12.00 / Midday / Midnight
ម៉ោងដប់ពីរ / ថ្ងៃត្រង់ / អាធ្រាត
Moung Dob Pi / Tngay Trong / Ah Triat

Money

I would like to change these traveller's cheques / this currency
ខ្ញុំចង់ប្ដូរសែកទេសចរណ៍ទាំងនេះ / របិយបណ្ណនេះ
Khnom Jong Pdo Saek Tes Jor Tiaing Nis / Rob Pey Ban Nis

How much commission do you charge? (What is the service charge?)
តើអ្នកយកកំរៃជើងសារប៉ុន្មាន? (តើថ្លៃសេវាប៉ុន្មាន?)
Tei Nak Yok Kom Rei Yeung Sa Pun Man (Tei Tlai Se Va Bom Rei Pun Man)

Can I obtain money with my MasterCard?
តើខ្ញុំអាចបើកប្រាក់ជាមួយម៉ាស្ទ័រកាតរបស់ខ្ញុំបានទេ?
Tei Khnom Ahj Beik Prak Jia Mouy Ma Steur Kat Ro Bos Khnom Ban Te

146

Where is the nearest ATM?
តើមានស៊ីមATMដែលជិតបំផុតនៅកន្លែងណា?
*Tei Ma Sin ATM Dael Jit Bom Put Neuv
Kan Laeng Na*

My name is ... Some money has been wired to here for me to collect
ឈ្មោះខ្ញុំ ... មីកប្រាក់មូលទ្មេមត្រូវបានផ្ញេមកមិនេះដើម្បី
ឪោយខ្ញុំបកបើក
*Chmos Khnom Keu...Teuk Prak Mouy
Jum Noun Treuv Ban Pte Mok Ti Nis
Dem Bei Ouy Khnom Mok Beik*

Airport

Excuse me, where is the check-in desk for ... airline?
អត់ទោស តើកន្លែងឆែកអ៊ុងសំរាប់ក្រុមហ៊ុនឃុនហោ ...
នៅទីណា?
*Ort Tos Tei Korn Laeng Chaek In Som
Rab Krom Hun Yun Hoh ... Neuv Ti Na*

What is the boarding gate / time for my flight?
តើទ្រកចូលយន្តហោះលេខប៉ុន្មាន /
តើមាងចូលយន្តហោះនៅម៉ោងប៉ុន្មានសំរាប់ការហោះ
ហ៊ាររបស់ខ្ញុំ?
*Tei Jrok Jol Yun Hoh Laek Pun Man /
Tei Moung Jol Yun Hoh Neuv Moung
Pun Man Som Rab Ka Hoh Hey Ro
Bos Khnom*

How long is the delay likely to be?
តើការពន្យាពេលមានរយៈពេលប៉ុន្មាន?
*Tei Ka Pun Yeah Pel Mian Ro Yak Pel
Pun Man*

Where is the duty free shop?
តើហាងទំនិញរចឥូននៅកន្លែងណា?
*Tei Hang Tom Nij Roj Pun Nov Korn
Laeng Na*

Which way is the baggage reclaim?
តើផ្លូវណាទៅយកអីវ៉ាន់?
Tei Pleuv Na Teuv Yok Ei Van

I have lost my luggage. Please can you help?
ខ្ញុំបានបាត់វ៉ាលីសរបស់ខ្ញុំ។ សូមអ្នកជួយខ្ញុំផង?
*Khnom Ban But Va Lis Ro Bos Khnom
Som Nak Juy Khnom Phorng*

I am flying to ...
ខ្ញុំចេញដងទៅ...
Khnom Jaej Dom Nae Teuv...

Where can I get the bus to the city centre?
តើកន្លែងណាដែលខ្ញុំអាចជិះឡានក្រុងដើម្បីទៅទីប្រជុំជន?
*Tei Korn Laeng Na Del Khnom Ahj Ji
Lan Krong Dem Bei Teuv Ti Pror Jum
Jun*

Trains and Boats

Where is the ticket office / information desk?
តើការិយាល័យលក់សំបុត្រនៅកន្លែងណា /
ទីស្នាក់ការពេតិមានៅកន្លែងណា?
*Tei Ka Ri Ya Lay Lork Som But Neuv
Korn Laeng Na / Ti Snak Ka Poro Mian
Neuv Korn Laeng Na*

Which platform does the train / speedboat / ferry to ... depart from?
តើកន្លែងចេញដងនេះសំរាប់រងភ្លើង / ទូកលឿន /
នាវាចែលងទៅ ... នៅឯណា?
*Tci Korn Laeng Jenh Dom Nei Som Rab
Rot Pleung / Touk Leun / Nia Via Jum
Long Teuv... Neuv Ek Na*

K H M E R

Where is platform ... ?
តើកន្លែងឈរចាំចេញដើរនៅកន្លែងណា ...?
Tei Korn Laeng Chor Jam Jenh Dom Nei Neuv Korn Laeng Na ...

When is the next train / boat to ... ?
តើនៅពេលណាមានរថភ្លើង / កាណុតបន្ទាប់ចេញទៅ ...?
Tei Neuv Pel Na Man Rot Pleung / Ka Not Bun Tup Jenh Tov ...

Is there a later train / boat to ... ?
តើមានរថភ្លើង / កាណុតបន្ទាប់ទៀតទៅ ...?
Tei Mian Rot Pleung / Ka Not Bun Tep Tiat Teuv ...

Notices and Signs

ឡានមានបរិភោគអាហារ
Lan Mian Bom Rei Ah Ha
Buffet (Dining) car

ឡានក្រុង
Lan Krong
Bus

ទឹកបរិសុទ្ធ / គ្រឿងផេសជ្ជៈ
Teuk Bor Ri Sot / Kreung Phae Sa Jek
Drinking / Non-drinking water

ច្រកចូល
Jrork Jol
Entrance

ច្រកចេញ
Jrork Jenh
Exit

មន្ទីរពេទ្យ
Mun Ti Pet
Hospital

ព័ត៌មាន
Poro Mian
Information

អីវ៉ាន់មិនបពួល (អីវ៉ាន់ត្រូវប្រកាស)
Ei Van Men Bun Jol
(Ei Van Treuv Pror Kas)
Left luggage (Baggage claim)

សោរាំលីស
Sor Va Lis
Luggage lockers

ប្រៃសណីយ៍
Prei Sa Ni
Post office

កន្លែងឈរ
Korn Laeng Chor
Platform

ចំណតរថភ្លើង (ផ្លូវរទេះភ្លើង)
Jam Nort Rot Pleung
(Pleuv Rot Pleung)
Railway (Railroad) station

ព្រលានយន្តហោះ
Pro Lian Yun Hoh
Airport

ស្ថានីយ៍ប៉ូលីស
Satan Ni Polis
Police station

កំពង់ផែ
Kom Pong Pae
Port

ភោជនីយដ្ឋាន
Phnoj Ni Tan
Restaurant

ជក់បារី / អត់ជក់បារី
Juk Ba Rey / Ort Juk Ba Rey
Smoking / Non smoking

ទូរស័ព្ទ
Tour Sab
Telephone

ការិយាល័យលក់សំបុត្រ
Ka Ri Ya Lay Lork Som But
TIcket offIce

កន្លែងឆែកអ៊ិន
Korn Laeng Chaek In
Check-in desk

តារាងពេលវេលា (តារាងពេលវេលា)
Ta Rang Pel Via Lia
Timetables (Schedules)

បន្ទប់ទឹក (បង្គន់)
Bun Tub Teuk (Bong Kun)
Toilets (Restrooms)

សុភានារី / សុភាបុរស
So Piap Nia Ri / So Piap Bo Ros
Ladies / Gentlemen

រថភ្លើងក្រោមដី (រថភ្លើងក្រោមដី)
Rot Pleung Krom Dei
Underground (Subway)

បន្ទប់រង់ចាំ
Bun Tub Rong Jam
Waiting room

Buying a Ticket

I would like a first-class / second-class single (oneway) / return (round trip) ticket to ...
ខ្ញុំចង់បានសំបុត្រមួយតែទៅថ្នាក់ទី១ /
សំបុត្រមួយតែទៅថ្នាក់ទីពីរ (សំបុត្រទៅអត់មក)/
សំបុត្រទៅមក (ទៅមក) ទៅ...
Khnom Jong Ban Som But Mouy Tae Teuv Tnak Ti Mouy / Som But Mouy Tae Teuv Tnak Ti Pi (Sam But Teuv Ort Mok) / Som But Teuv Mok (Teuv Mok) / Teuv...

Is it an express (fast) train / bus?
តើវាជារថភ្លើង / ឡានក្រុងល្បឿនលឿន?
Tei Via Jia Rot Pleung / Lan Krong Lbeun Leurn

Is my rail pass valid on this train / ferry / bus?
តើកាតរបស់ខ្ញុំមានសុពលភាពសំរាប់រទេះភ្លើង /
នាវាចំលង / ឡានក្រុងនេះទេ?
Tei Kat Ro Bos Khnom Mian So Pol Piap Som Rab Rot Pleung / Nia Via Jom Lorng / Lan Krong Nis Te

I would like an aisle / window seat
ខ្ញុំចង់បានកន្លែងអង្គុយជិតច្រកផ្លូវដើរ / ជិតបង្អួច
Khnom Jong Ban Korn Laeng Ang Kouy Jit Jrok Pleuv Del / Jit Bang Ouj

No smoking / smoking, please
ហាមជក់បារី / អាចជក់បារីបាន
Ham Juk Ba Rey / Ahj Juk Ba Rey Ban

We would like to sit together
យើងចង់អង្គុយជិតគ្នា
Yeung Jong Ang Kouy Jit Knia

I would like to make a seat reservation
ខ្ញុំចង់កក់សំបុត្រ
Khnom Jong Kork Som But

KHMER

I would like to reserve a
couchette / sleeper for one
person / two people / my family
ខ្ញុំចង់កក់កន្លែងគេងនៅលើរថភ្លើង / សំរាប់
មួយនាក់ / ពីរនាក់ / គ្រួសារ
*Khnom Jong Kork Korn Laeng Keng
Nov Leu Rot Pleung / Som Rab Mouy
Nak / Pi Nak / Krour Sa*

I would like to reserve a cabin
ខ្ញុំចង់កក់កៅអីនៅក្នុងបន្ទប់
*Khnom Jong Kork Kao Ei Nov Knong
Bun Tub*

Timetables (Schedules)

មកដល់
Mok Dol
Arrive

ឈប់នៅ...
Chub...
Calls (Stops) at ...

សេវាកម្មផ្ដល់អាហារ
Se Va Kam Pdol Ah Hah
Catering service

ប្ដូរនៅ ...
Pdo Neuv ...
Change at ...

ការទាក់ទង / កាត់តាម
Ka Tak Tong / Kat Tam
Connection / Via

ប្រចាំថ្ងៃ
Pro Cham Tgnai
Daily

រាល់៤០នាទី
Ral Sae Seb Nia Ti
Every 40 minutes

លំដាប់ទី១
Lom Dab Ti Mouy
First class

រាល់ម៉ោង
Ral Moung
Hourly

ត្រូវកក់សំបុត្រទុកជាមុន
Treuv Kork Som But Tok Jia Mon
**Seat reservations are
recommended**

លំដាប់ទីពីរ
Lum Dab Ti Pi
Second class

បង់បន្ថែម
Bong Bun Taem
Supplement payable

Luggage

How much will it cost to
send (ship) my luggage in
advance
តើអស់ថ្លៃប៉ុន្មានសំរាប់ការផ្ញើវ៉ាលីសតាមកប៉ាល់ជាមុន?
*Tei Os Dom Lai Pun Man Som Rab Ka
Pnhei Ei Van Tam Ka Pal Jia Mun*

Where is the left luggage
(baggage claim) office?
តើការិយាល័យ(ប្រកាសអីវ៉ាន់ (ប្រកាសអីវ៉ាន់)
នៅកន្លែងណា?
*Tei Ka Ri Ya Lay Bro Kas Ei Van
Neuv Korn Laeng Na*

What time do you open / close?
តើអ្នកបើក / បិទនៅម៉ោងប៉ុន្មាន?
*Tei Nak Beik / Bet Neuv Moung Pun
Man*

Where are the luggage trolleys (carts) ?
តើរទេះរុញអីវ៉ាន់នៅឯណា?
Tei Ro Tes Ruj Ei Van Neuv Korn Laeng Na

Where are the lockers?
តើមេសោនៅឯណា?
Tei Me Sor Neuv Korn Laeng Na

I have lost my locker key
ខ្ញុំបាត់កូនសោ
Khnom Ban But Korn Sor

On Board

Is this seat free?
តើកៅអីនេះទំនេរទេ?
Tel Kao Ei Ni Tum Ne Te

Excuse me, you are sitting in my reserved seat
អត់ទោស អ្នកកំពុងអង្គុយ
នៅកៅអីរបស់ខ្ញុំដែលបានកក់ទុក
Ort Tos Nak Kom Pong Ang Kouy Neuv Korn Laeng Ro Bos Khnom Del Ban Kork Tok

Which station is this?
តើនេះគឺជាស្ថានីយ៍មួយណា?
Tei Ni Keu Jia Stan Ni Mouy Na

What time is this train / bus / ferry / flight due to arrive / depart?
តើម៉ោងប៉ុន្មានរថភ្លើង / ឡានក្រុង / នាវាទិលល / យន្តហោះ ត្រូវមកដល់ / ត្រូវចេញដំណើរ?
Tei Moung Pun Man Rot Pleung / Lan Krong / Nia Via Jam Long / Yun Hoh Trov Mok Dol / Trov Jeh Dom Nei

Travelling with Children

Do you have a high chair / babysitting service / cot?
តើអ្នកមានកៅអីខ្ពស់ / សេវាកម្មកូនក្មេង / គ្រែតូចទេ?
Tei Nak Mian Kao Ei Khpos / Se Va Kam Korn Kmeng / Kre Toh Te

Where is the nursery / playroom?
តើកន្លែងមើលក្មេង / បន្ទប់លេងនៅណា?
Tei Korn Laeng Meul Kmeng / Bun Tub Leng Neuv Ei Na

Where can I warm the baby's bottle?
តើកន្លែងណាដែលខ្ញុំអាចកំដៅដប់ទឹកដោះគោបាន?
Tei Korn Laeng Na Del Khnom Ahj Kom Dao Dob Teuk Dos Ko Ban

Customs and Passports

Passports, please!
សូមមេត្តាបង្ហាញលិខិតឆ្លងដែន
Som Me Ta Bang Hanh Li Khet Chlang Den

I have nothing / wine / spirits (alcohol) / tobacco to declare
ខ្ញុំអត់មានអី / ស្រា /
ប្រេីងស្រវឹង (អាកុលគោល) / ថ្នាំជក់ត្រូវប្រកាសទេ
Khnom Ort Mian Ah Vei / Sra / Kreurng Sro Veung (Al Gol) / Tnam Juk Treuv Pro Kas Te

I will be staying for ... days / weeks / months
ខ្ញុំនឹងស្នាក់នៅសំរាប់រយៈពេល...ថ្ងៃ / អាទិត្យ / ខែ
Khnom Neung Snak Nov Sam Rab Ro Yak Pel Tngay / Ah Tit / Khae

K
H
M
E
R

KHMER

SIGHTSEEING

Asking the Way

Excuse me, do you speak English?
អត់ទោស តើអ្នកនិយាយភាសាអង់គ្លេសទេ?
Ort Tos Tei Nak Ni Yeay Pia Sa Ang Glay Te

Excuse me, can you help me please?
អត់ទោស តើអ្នកអាចជួយខ្ញុំបានទេ?
Ort Tos Tei Nak Ahj Juy Khnom Ban Te

Where is the Tourist Information Office?
តើការិយាល័យបរិមាណសំរាប់ភ្ញៀវទេសចរនៅឯណា?
Tei Ka Ri Ya Lai Poro Mian Som Rab Piev Tes Jor Neuv Korn Laeng Na

Excuse me, is this the right way to ... ?
អត់ទោស តើផ្លូវនេះត្រូវទេដើម្បីទៅ... ?
Ort Tos Tei Pleuv Nis Treuv Te Dem Bei Teuv...

... the cathedral / the tourist information office / the castle / the old town
... ព្រះវិហារ / ការិយាល័យ
ពតិមាណសំរាប់ភ្ញៀវទេសចរ / បន្ទាយ / ទីក្រុងចាស់
... Pras Vi Hia / Ka Ri Ya Lay Poro Mian Som Rab Piev Tes Jor / Bang Deay / Ti Krong Jas

Can you tell me the way to the railway (railroad) station / bus station / taxi rank (stand) / city centre (downtown) / beach?
តើអ្នកអាចនិយាយប្រាប់ខ្ញុំពីផ្លូវទៅ
ស្ថានីយរថភ្លើង (រថភ្លើង) / ចំណតឡានក្រុង /
ចំណតតាក់ស៊ី (ចំណត) / ទីប្រជុំជន (កណ្តាលក្រុង) /
មាតសមុទ្រ?
Tei Nak Ahj Ni Yeay Prab Khnom Pi Pleuv Teuv Satan Ni Rot Pleung (Rot Pleung) / Jom Not Lan Krong / Jom Not Tak Si / Ti Pro Jum Jun (Kang Dal Krong) / Mat Sa Mut

First / second / left / right / straight ahead
ទីមួយ / ទីពីរផ្នែក / ផ្នែក / ស្តាំ / ឆ្ពោះទៅត្រង់
Ti Mouy / Ti Pi / Chveng / Sdam / Chpos Teuv Trong

At the corner / at the traffic lights
នៅកាច់ជ្រុង / នៅភ្លើងស្តុប
Neuv Kaj Jrong / Neuv Pleung Stop

Where is the nearest police station / post office?
តើស្ថានីយប៉ូលីស / ប្រៃសណីយ៍ជិតបំផុតនៅឯណា?
Tei Satan Ni Po Lis / Pres Sni Jit Bun Put Neuv Ek Na

Is it near / far?
តើវានៅជិត / ឆ្ងាយទេ?
Tei Via Neuv Jit / Chgay Te

Do I need to take a taxi / catch a bus?
តើខ្ញុំត្រូវជិះតាក់ស៊ី / ជិះឡានក្រុងទេ?
Tei Khnom Trov Jis Tak Si / Jis Lan Krong Te

Do you have a map?
តើអ្នកមានផែនទីទេ?
Tei Nak Mian Pen Ti Te

Can you point to it on my map?
តើអ្នកអាចចង្អុលបង្ហាញវានៅលើផែនទីរបស់ខ្ញុំបានទេ?
Tei Nak Ahj Jong Ol Bong Haj Neuv Lei Pen Ti Ro Bos Khnom Ban Te

Thank you for your help
អរគុណសំរាប់ការជួយរបស់អ្នក
Or Kun Som Rab Ka Juy Ro Bos Nak

How do I reach the motorway / main road?
តើធ្វើដូចម្ដេចខ្ញុំអាចទៅដល់ផ្លូវធំ / ផ្លូវធំ?
Tei Tveu Doj Mdej Khnom Ahj Teuv Dol Pleuv Tom / Pleuv Tom

I think I have taken the wrong turning
ខ្ញុំគិតថាខ្ញុំបត់ខុសហើយ
Khnom Kit Ta Khnom But Khoh Haj

I am looking for this address
ខ្ញុំកំពុងរកអាសយដ្ឋាននេះ
Khnom Kom Pong Rok Ah Saj Tan Nis

I am looking for the ... hotel
ខ្ញុំកំពុងរកសណ្ឋាគារ ...
Khnom Kom Pong Rok Sun Tha Kia...

How far is it to ... from here?
តើមានចំងាយប៉ុន្មានពីទីនេះទៅ ... ?
Tei Mian Jam Ngay Pun Man Pi Ti Nis Teuv ...

Carry straight on for ... kilometres
ឆ្ពោះទៅត្រង់ ... គីឡូម៉ែត្រ
Chpos Teuv Trang ... Ki Lo Met

Take the next turning on the right / left
បន្ទាប់មកបត់ស្ដាំ / ឆ្វេង
Bun Tab Mok Bort Sdam / Chveng

Turn right / left at the next crossroads / traffic lights
បត់ស្ដាំ / បត់ឆ្វេងនៅផ្លូវវ៉ាក់បែក / ភ្លើងស្តុបបន្ទាប់
Bort Sdam / Bort Chveng Neuv Pleuv Bom Baek / Pleung Stop Bun Tab

You are going in the wrong direction
អ្នកកំពុងតែទៅខុសផ្លូវ
Nak Kom Pong Te Teuv Khoh Pleuv

Where is the cathedral / church / museum / pharmacy?
តើព្រះវិហារ / ព្រះវិហារគ្រឹស្ត / សារមន្ទីរ / ឱសថស្ថាននៅកន្លែងណា?
Tei Pras Vi Hia / Pras Vi Hia Kreus / Sa Ra Mon Tis / Or Sot Stan Neuv Korn Laeng Na

How much is the admission / entrance charge?
តើថ្លៃចូលទៅសួនប៉ុន្មាន?
Tei Tlai Jol Tos Sna Pun Man

Is there a discount for children / students / senior citizens?
តើមានការបញ្ចុះថ្លៃសំរាប់ក្មេង / កូនសិស្ស / មនុស្សចាស់ទេ?
Tei Mian Ka Bun Jos Tlai Som Rab Kmeng / Korn Seus / Mnos Jas Te

What time does the next guided tour (in English) start?
តើការឥេស្សនាបន្ទាប់មាន មគ្គទេសក៍ (អង់គ្លេស) ចាប់ផ្តើមនៅម៉ោងប៉ុន្មាន?
Tei Ka Tos Sna Bun Tab Mian Mak Ko Tes (Pia Sa Ang Glai) Jam Pdem Neuv Moung Pun Mian

One / two adults / children, please
មនុស្សពេញ / ក្មេង មួយ / ពីរនាក់
Mnos Thom / Kmeng Mouy / Pi Nak

May I take photographs here?
តើខ្ញុំអាចថតរូបនៅទីនេះបានទេ?
Tei Khnom Ahj Tort Rob Neuv Ti Nis Ban Te

K
H
M
E
R

KHMER

At the Tourist Office

Do you have a map of the town / area?
តើអ្នកមានផែនទីនៃទីក្រុង / តំបន់ទេ?
Tei Nak Mian Pen Ti Ney Ti Krong / Dom Bun Te

Do you have a list of accommodation?
តើអ្នកមានបញ្ជីរាយនាមកន្លែងស្នាក់នៅទេ?
Tei Nak Mian Bun Ji Raj Niam Korn Laeng Snak Neuv Te

Can I reserve accommodation?
តើខ្ញុំអាចកក់កន្លែងស្នាក់នៅបានទេ?
Tei Khnom Ahj Kok Korn Laeng Snak Nov Ban Te

ACCOMMODATION

Hotels

I have a reservation in the name of ...
ខ្ញុំបានកក់ទុកដោយដាក់ឈ្មោះ ...
Khnom Ban Kork Tok Doj Dak Chmos...

I wrote to / faxed / telephoned you last month / last week
ខ្ញុំបានរស / ហ្វាក់ / ទូរស័ព្ទ
អោយអ្នកពីខែមុន / អាទិត្យមុន
Khnom Ban Sor Se / Fax / Tou Ro Sab Ouy Nak Pi Khae Mun / Ah Tit Mun

Do you have any rooms free?
តើអ្នកមានបន្ទប់ទំនេរទេ?
Tei Nak Mian Bun Tub Tum Ne Te

I would like to reserve a single / double room with / without bath / shower
ខ្ញុំចង់កក់បន្ទប់សំរាប់មនុស្សម្នាក់ /
បន្ទប់សំរាប់មនុស្សពីរនាក់ជាមួយ /
មិនមានបន្ទប់ទឹក / ទឹកផ្កាឈូក

Khnom Jong Kork Bun Tub Som Rab Mnos Mnak / Bun Tub Som Rab Mnos Pi Nak Jia Mouy / Min Mian Bun Tub Teuk / Teuk Phka Chouk

I would like bed and breakfast / (room and) full board
ខ្ញុំបានបន្ទប់និងអាហារពេលព្រឹក / (បន្ទប់និង)
អាហារពេញមួយថ្ងៃ
Khnom Jong Ban Bun Tub Neung Ah Hah Pel Preuk / (Bun Tub Neung) Ah Hah Pej Mouy Tngay

How much is it per night?
តើថ្លៃប៉ុន្មានក្នុងមួយយប់?
Tei Tlai Pun Man Knong Mouy Yub

Is breakfast included?
តើរួមទាំងអាហារពេលព្រឹក?
Tei Rum Tiang Ah Hah Pel Preuk

Do you have any cheaper rooms?
តើអ្នកមានបន្ទប់ណាថោកជាងនេះទេ?
Tei Nak Mian Bun Tub Na Tork Jiang Nis Te

I would like to see / take the room
ខ្ញុំចង់មើល / យកបន្ទប់នេះ
Khnom Jong Meul / York Bun Tub Nis

I would like to stay for ...nights
ខ្ញុំចង់ស្នាក់នៅសំរាប់ ...យប់
Khnom Jong Snak Nov Som Rab ...Yub

The shower / light / tap / hot water doesn't work
ទឹកផ្កាឈូក / ភ្លើង / ចំបុយទឹក /
ម៉ាស៊ីនទឹកក្ដៅមិនដំនើរការ
Teuk Phka Chouk / Pleung / Jom Buey Tek / Ma Sin Teuk Kdao Min Dom Neur Ka

At what time / where is breakfast served?
តើម៉ោងប៉ុន្មាន /
នៅកន្លែងណាអាហារពេលព្រឹកត្រូវបានបំរើ?
Tei Moung Pun Man / Neuv Korn Laeng Na Ah Ha Pel Preuk Trov Ban Bom Rei

What time do I have to check out?
តើកោះប៉ុន្មានខ្ញុំត្រូវចេញ?
Tei Moung Pun Man Khnom Treuv Jenh

Can I have the key to room number ... ?
តើអ្នកអាចឱ្យកូនសោលេខបន្ទប់ ... ?
Tei Nak Ahj Ouy Korn Sor Lek Bun Tub ...

My room number is ...
លេខបន្ទប់របស់ខ្ញុំ ...
Lek Bun Tub Ro Bos Khnom Keu ...

My room is not satisfactory / not clean enough / too noisy.
បន្ទប់របស់ខ្ញុំមិនគួរអោយពេញចិត្ត /
មិនស្អាត / ឬសំលេងខ្លាំងណាស់
Bun Tub Ro Bos Khnom Min Kour Ouy Pinh Jet / Min Saart / Leu Som Leng Nas

Please can I change rooms?
តើខ្ញុំអាចប្តូរបន្ទប់បានទេ
Tei Khnom Ahj Pdo Bun Tub Ban Te

Where is the bathroom?
តើបន្ទប់ទឹកនៅកន្លែងណា?
Tei Bun Tub Teuk Neuv Korn Laeng Na

Do you have a safe for valuables?
តើអ្នកមានសេវាសុវត្ថិភាពសំរាប់របស់មានតំលៃទេ?
Tei Nak Mian Se Va So Vat Piap Som Rab Ro Bos Mian Dom Lai Te

Is there a laundry / do you wash clothes?
តើមានសេវាបោកអ៊ុត / តើអ្នកមានសេវាបោកខោអាវទេ?

Tei Mian Se Va Bork Ort / Tei Nak Mian Se Va Bork Khoh Ao Te

I would like an air-conditioned room
ខ្ញុំចង់បានបន្ទប់ម៉ាស៊ីនត្រជាក់
Khnom Jong Ban Bun Tub Ma Sin Tror Jaek

Do you accept traveller's cheques / credit cards?
តើអ្នកទទួលយកសែកទេសចរណ៍ / ឬក្រេឌីតកាតទេ?
Tei Nak To Tuol York Saek Tes Jork / Krae Dit Kat Te

May I have the bill please?
តើអាចអោយវិក័យប័ត្រខ្ញុំបានទេ?
Tei Ahj Ouy Vi Kay But Khnom Ban Te

Excuse me, I think there may be a mistake in this bill
អត់ទោស ខ្ញុំគិតថាវិកយ័ប្រ័ត្រនេះគិតខុស
Ort Tos Khnom Kit Tha Vi Kay But Nis Kit Khoh

Youth Hostels

How much is a dormitory bed per night?
តើគ្រែសយយន្ទមួយយប់ប៉ុន្មាន?
Tei Krae Soy Yun Tun Mouy Yub Pun Man

I am / am not an HI member
ខ្ញុំជា / មិនមែនជា សមាជិកសណ្ឋាគារយុវវ័យ HI ទេ
Khnom Jia / Min Men Jia Sa Ma Jeuk Sorn Ta Kia Yu Vak Jun Hi Te

May I use my own sleeping bag?
តើខ្ញុំអាចប្រើភ្ជុបបៅ៉ប់កេងរបស់ខ្ញុំបានទេ?
Tei Khnom Ahj Brei Pouy Don Dob Keng Ro Bos Khnom Ban Te

K
H
M
E
R

155

KHMER

What time do you lock the doors at night?

តើម៉ោងប៉ុន្មានអ្នកចាក់សោទ្វារនៅពេលយប់?

Tei Moung Pun Man Nak Jak Sor Tvia Neuv Pel Yub

Camping

May I camp for the night / two nights?

តើខ្ញុំអាចបោះជំរុំមួយយប់ / ពីរយប់បានទេ?

Tei Khnom Ahj Bos Jum Rum Mouy Yub / Pi Yub Ban Te

Where can I pitch my tent?

តើកន្លែងណាខ្ញុំអាចបោះតង់បាន

Tei Korn Laeng Na Khnom Ahj Bos Tang Ban

How much does it cost for one night / week?

តើអស់ថ្លៃប៉ុន្មានសំរាប់មួយយប់ / មួយអាទិត្យ?

Tei Oh Tlay Pun Man Som Rab Mouy Yub / Mouy A Tit

Where are the washing facilities?

តើសេវាកម្មបោកខោអាវនៅកន្លែងណា?

Tei Se Va Kam Bork Khor Ao Neuv Korn Laeng Na

Is there a restaurant / supermarket / swimming pool on site / nearby?

តើមានភោជនីយដ្ឋាន / ផ្សារទំនើប / ប៊ុស្សីនទឹក នៅកន្លែងនេះ / នៅជិតនេះទេ?

Tei Mian Pnhoj Ni Tan / Psa Tom Neub / Pi Sin Teuk Neuv Korn Laeng Nis / Neuv Jit Nis Te

Do you have a safety deposit box?

តើអ្នកមានទូដែកទេ?

Tei Nak Mian Tou Daek Te

EATING AND DRINKING

Cafés and Bars

I would like a cup of / two cups of / another coffee / tea

ខ្ញុំចង់បានកាហ្វេ / តែ / មួយពែង / ពីរពែង

Khnom Jong Ban Ka Fae / Tae / Mouy Peng / Pi Peng

With / without milk / sugar

ជាមួយ / អត់មានទឹកដោះគោ / ស្ករ

Jia Mouy / Ort Mian Teuk Doh Ko / Skor

I would like a bottle / glass / two glasses of mineral water / red wine / white wine, please

ខ្ញុំចង់បានទឹកសុទ្ធ / ស្រាក្រហម / ស្រាសមួយដប / មួយកែវ / ពីរកែវ

Khnom Jong Ban Teuk Sort / Sra Kroh Horm / Sra Sor Mouy Dob / Mouy Keo / Pi Keo

I would like a beer / two beers, please

ខ្ញុំចង់បានប៊ីយ៉ែរមួយកំប៉ុង / ពីរកំប៉ុង

Khnom Jong Ban Bi Yaer Mouy Kom Pong / Pi Kom Pong

Please may I have some ice?

សូមទឹកកកបន្តិច?

Som Teuk Koh Bun Tej

Do you have any matches / cigarettes / cigars?

ខ្ញុំចង់បានឈើគូស / បារី / ស៊ីហ្គា

Khnom Jong Ban Cheu Kuos / Ba Rey / Ci Ga

Restaurants

Can you recommend a good / cheap restaurant in this area?

តើអ្នកអាចណែនាំភោជនីយដ្ឋានល្អ / ថោកនៅក្នុងតំបន់នេះបានទេ?

*Tei Nak Aj Nae Nam Pnhoj Ni
Tan Laor / Tork Neuv Knong Dom Bun
Nis Ban Te*

I would like a table for ... people
ខ្ញុំចង់បានតុសំរាប់ ... នាក់
Khnom Jong Ban Tok Som Rab ... Nak

Do you have a non-smoking area?
តើមានកន្លែងអត់ជក់បារីទេ?
Tei Mian Korn Laeng Ort Juk Ba Rey Te

Waiter / Waitress!
អ្នកប់រើប្រុស / អ្នកប់រើស្រី
Nak Bam Rei Bros / Nak Bam Rei Srey

Excuse me, please may we order?
អត់ទោស យើងចង់កម៉ង់បានទេ?
Ort Tos Yeung Jong Kom Mang Ban Te

Do you have a set menu / children's menu / wine list?
តើអ្នកមានអ៊ីនុយញ៉ុត / ម៉ឺនុយសំរាប់កូនក្មេង / ស្យៅវភៅបញ្ជីស្រាទេ?
Tei Nak Mian Me Nuy Chut / Me Nuy Som Rab Korn Kmeng / Saov Peuv Bun Ji Sra Te

Do you have any vegetarian dishes?
តើអ្នកមានម្ហូបបួសទេ?
Tei Nak Mian Ma Hob Bos Te

Do you have any local specialities?
តើអ្នកមានម្ហូបពិសេសប្រចាំតំបន់ទេ?
Tei Nak Mian Ma Hob Pi Ses Pro Jam Dom Bun Te

Are vegetables included?
តើរួមបញ្ចូលទាំងបន្លែទេ?
Tei Rum Bun Jol Tiang Bun Lae Te

Could I have it well cooked / medium / rare please?
ខ្ញុំចង់បានវាចោយឆ្អិន / ឆ្អិនល្មម / មិនសូវឆ្អិន?
Khnom Jong Ban Via Ouy Chaet / Chaet Lmaum / Min Seuv Chaet

What does this dish consist of?
តើម្ហូបនេះមានគ្រឿងផ្សំអ្វី?
Tei Ma Hob Nis Mlan Kreung Psom Ah Vey Khlah

I am a vegetarian. Does this contain meat?
ខ្ញុំជាអ្នកញ៉ាំអាហារបួស ។ តើនេះមានជាតិសាច់ទេ?
*Khnom Jia Nak Yam Ah Ha Bos.
Tel Nis Mian Jiat Saj Te*

I do not eat nuts / dairy products / meat / fish
ខ្ញុំអត់ញ៉ាំគ្រាប់ធ្ងួនជាតិ / ផលិតផលដែលធ្វើពីទឹកដោះគោ / សាច់ / សាច់ត្រី
Khnom Ort Nham Krob Tun Jiat / Por Let Pol Dael Tveu Pi Teuk Dos Ko / Saj / Saj Trey

Not (very) spicy, please
អត់ហឹរខ្លាំង
Ort Heul Klaing

I would like the set menu, please
ខ្ញុំចង់បានម៉ឺនុយញ៉ុត
Khnom Jong Ban Me Nuy Chut

We are still waiting to be served
យើងកំពុងរង់ចាំការបំរើ
Yeung Kom Pong Rong Jam Ka Bum Rei

Please bring a plate / knife / fork
សូមយកចាន / កាំបិត / សម
Som Yok Jan / Kam Bet / Sorm

Excuse me, this is not what I ordered
អត់ទោស ខ្ញុំអត់បានកម៉ង់វាទេ
Ort Tos Khnom Ort Ban Kom Mang Te

K
H
M
E
R

K H M E R

May I have some / some more bread / water / coffee / tea?
ខ្ញុំសុំ / សុំថែមនំបុ័ង / ទឹក / កាហ្វេ / តែ បានទេ?
Knhum Som / Som Them Nompang / Tek / Kaphe / Te Ban Te

May I have the bill, please?
សូមគិតលុយ
Som Kit Luy

Does this bill include service?
តើវិក័យប័ត្រនេះមានគិតថ្លៃសេវាដែរឬទេ?
Tei Vikaiybat Nis Mean Kit Thlai Seva De Reu Te

Do you accept traveller's cheques / MasterCard / US dollars?
តើអ្នកទទួលយក traveller's Cheques / MasterCard / ដុល្លាអាមេរិក ដែរឬទេ?
Tei Nak Tortuol Yok Traveller's Cheques / MasterCard / Dollar Americ De Reu Te

Can I have a receipt, please?
សូមអោយវិកាយបុត្រមកខ្ញុំបានទេ?
Som Ouy Vi Kay But Mok Khnom Ban Te

Where is the toilet (restroom) , please?
តើបង្គន់ (បន្ទប់ទឹក) នៅឯណា ?
Tei Bangkun (Bantobtek) Nov E Na

On the Menu

អាហារពេលព្រឹក / អាហារពេលថ្ងៃត្រង់ / អាហារពេលល្ងាច
Ah Ha Pel Preuk / Ah Ha Pel Tgnay Trang / Ah Ha Pel Lgnaj
Breakfast / Lunch / Dinner

ម្ហូបទី១
Ma Hob Ti Mouy
First courses

ស៊ុប
Soub
Soups

អង់ត្រេ (អាហារញ៉ាំលេង)
Ang Trae (Ah Ha Nham Laeng)
Main courses

ម្ហូបសាច់ត្រី
Ma Hob Saj Trey
Fish dishes

ម្ហូបសាច់ (គោ ជ្រូក ...)
Ma Hob Saj (Ko Jrok...)
Meat dishes

សាច់គោ	ប៊ិស្តិក
Saj Ko	*Bi Staek*
Beef	**Steak**

សាច់ជ្រូក	សាច់គោ
Saj Chrok	*Saj Ko*
Pork	**Veal**

សាច់មាន់	សាច់ចៀម
Saj Moin	*Saj Jaem*
Chicken	**Lamb**

ហ្ស៊ីបុង (ហែម)
Haem
Ham

ម្ហូបបួស
Ma Hob Bos
Vegetarian dishes

បន្លែ
Bun Lae
Vegetables

K H M E R

ជំទ្បុងបារាំងចៀន
Dom Loung Ba Riang Jian
Chips (french fries)

ស្ងោរ / ឆា / កិនអោយម៉ត់ជំទ្បុងបារាំង
Sngor / Cha / Kin Ouy Mort Dom Long Ba Riang
Boiled / sauté / mashed potatoes

បាយ
Baj
Rice

ប្រម៉ាំ
Fro Ma
Cheese

បង្អែម
Bong Em
Desserts

ការ៉េម
Ka Rem
Ice cream

នំបាវ៉ាង (នំខេក)
Num Khet
Cakes

នំ
Num
Pastries

ផ្លែឈើ
Plae Cheu
Fruit

នំប៉័ង
Num Piang
Bread

ដុំ
Dom
Rolls

ថូស (នំប៉័ងករំ)
Tos
Toast

បឺរ
Beur
Butter

អំបិល / ម្រេច
Am Bil / Mrej
Salt / pepper

ស្ករ
Skor
Sugar

ម្ហូបពិសេស
Ma Hob Pi Ses
Specialities

ម្ហូបពិសេសប្រចាំតំបន់
Ma Hob Pi Ses Bro Jam Dom Bun
Local specialities

ម្ហូបឈុត
Ma Hob Chut
Set Menu

បញ្ជីរាយមុខស្រា
Bun Ji Ray Mok Sra
Wine list

ស្រាក្រហម
Sra Kro Hom
Red wines

ស្រាស
Sra Sor
White wines

ស្រារ៉ូស
Sra Ros
Rosé wines

ស្រាឡាយ
Sra Lay
Sparkling wines

បៀរ
Bi Yaer
Beer

បៀរដប / ទុប៊ីបៀរថ្មី
Bi Yaer Dob / To Bi Yaer To
Bottled beer / Draught (draft) beer

គេសជ្ជៈអត់មានជាតិស្រវឹង
Peas Yuk Ort Mian Jiat Sroh Veung
Non-alcoholic drinks

ទឹកបរិសុទ្ធ
Teuk Bor Ri Sot
Mineral water

ទឹកផ្លែឈើ
Teuk Plae Cheu
Fruit juices

ទឹកក្រូច
Teuk Kroj
Orange juice

159

KHMER

កេសជ្ជៈទឹកក្រូចឆ្មា
Pias Yak Teuk Kroj Chma
Lemonade

ទឹកកក
Teuk Koh
Ice

កាហ្វេទឹកដោះគោ / កាហ្វេខ្មៅ / កាហ្វេអេសប្រេសសូ
*Ka Fae Teuk Dos Ko /
Ka Fae Kmao / Ka Fae Es Pres So*
**White coffee / black coffee /
espresso coffee**

តែជាមួយទឹកដោះគោ / ជាមួយក្រូចឆ្មា
*Tae Jia Mouy Teuk Dos Ko /
Jia Mouy Kroj Chma*
Tea with milk / with lemon

សុកូឡា (កេសជ្ជៈ)
Teuk So Ko La
Chocolate (drink)

ទឹកដោះគោ
Teuk Dos Ko
Milk

អាហារសំរន់ / អាហារញុំាំលេង
*Ah Ha Som Rorn / Ah Ha Nham
Laeng*
Snacks / Light meals

សាឡាដ	សាន់វិច
Salad	*San Vij*
Salads	**Sandwiches**

ពងមាន់	សាច់ក្រក
Pong Moin	*Saj Kroh*
Eggs	**Sausage**

ស្ងោរ / ឆា / គុសពងមាន់
Sgor / Cha / Kous Pong Moin
Boiled / fried / scrambled eggs

Typical local dishes

ស៊ុបជូ
Soup Jou
Sour soup

សាច់មាន់ផ្អំឆ្អិនឆ្អែត
Saj Moin Jom In Chaet
Well-cooked chicken

ស៊ុប
Soup
Soup

អណ្ដើកាំង
Orn Daek Lang
Grilled turtle

GETTING AROUND

Public Transport

**Where is the bus stop /
coach stop / nearest metro
(subway) station?**
តើណាតឡានក្រុងមួយណាដែលនៅជិតស្ថានីយរថភ្លើង
ក្រោមដីជាងគេ?
*Tei Jom Nort Lan Krong Mouy Na Del
Neuv Jit Stan Ni Rot Pleung Krom Dey
Jiang Ke*

When is the next / last bus to ...?
តើនៅពេលណាមានឡានក្រុងបន្ទាប់ /
ចុងក្រោយទៅ... ?
*Tei Neuv Pel Na Mian Lan Krong Bun
Tub / Jong Kroy Teu ...*

**How much is the fare to the
city centre (downtown) / railway
station / airport?**
តើតំលៃឡានដិនៃទៅទីប្រជុំជន (កណ្ដាលក្រុង) /
ស្ថានីយរថភ្លើង / ព្រលានយន្តហោះថ្លៃប៉ុន្មាន?

Tei Dom Lai Yian Yum Nis Teuv Ti Pror Jum Jun (Kang Dal Krong) / Stan Ni Rot Pleung / Bro Laen Yun Hoh Tlai Pun Man

Will you tell me when to get off?

តើអ្នកនឹងប្រាប់ខ្ញុំនៅពេលដែលខ្ញុំត្រូវចុះ?

Tei Nak Neung Prab Khnom Neuv Pel Del Khnom Trov Jos

Does this bus go to ...?

តើឡានក្រុងនេះទៅ ...?

Tei Lan Krong Ni Teuv...

Which number bus goes to ...?

តើឡានក្រុងលេខប៉ុន្មានទៅ ...?

Tei Lan Krong Lae Pun Man Teuv ...

May I have a single oneway / return (round trip) / day ticket / book of tickets?

ខ្ញុំចង់បានសំបុត្រតែទៅ / សំបុត្រទៅមក (ទៅមក) / សំបុត្រមួយថ្ងៃ / សៀវភៅសំបុត្របានទេ?

Khnom Jong Ban Som But Tae Teuv / Som But Teuv Mok (Teuv Mok) / Som But Mouy Tngay / Siao Peuv Som But Ban Te

Taxis and Rickshaws

I would like to go to ...

ខ្ញុំចង់ទៅ ...

Khnom Jong Teuv ...

How much will it cost?

តើវាអស់ថ្លៃប៉ុន្មាន?

Tei Via Os Tlai Pun Man

Please may I stop here?

តើខ្ញុំអាចឈប់នៅទីនេះបានទេ?

Tei Khnom Ahj Chub Neuv Ti Ni Ban Te

I would like to order a taxi today / tomorrow / at 2pm to go from ... to ...

ខ្ញុំចង់ហៅតាក់ស៊ីថ្ងៃនេះ / ថ្ងៃស្អែក / នៅម៉ោង២រសៀល ចេញពី ... ទៅ ...

Khnom Jang Hao Tak Si Tngay Ni / Tngay Saek / Nov Moung Pi Ro Sial Jej Pi ... Teuv ...

Entertainment

Can you recommend a good bar / nightclub?

តើអ្នកអាចណែនាំ / ណែក្លឹបណាល្អបានទេ?

Tei Nak Aj Nae Nam Ba / Nal Klub Na Laor Ban Te

Do you know what is on at the cinema (playing at the movies) / theatre at the moment?

តើអ្នកដឹងថាគេលេងរឿងអ្វីនៅរោងកុន / រោងល្ខោននៅខណៈពេលនេះ?

Tei Nak Deung Ta Ke Laeng Reung A Vei Neuv Rong Korn / Rong Lakhorn Neu Kha Nak Pel Nis

I would like to book (purchase) ... tickets for the matinee / evening performance on Monday

ខ្ញុំចង់កក់ (ទិញ) ... សំបុត្រសម្រាប់អនុសំវរិបរ៍ ការសំដែងពេលព្រឹក / ពេលល្ងាចនៅថ្ងៃច័ន្ទ

Khnom Jong Kork(Tinh) Som But Tok Mun Som Rab Ka Som Daeng Pel Preuk / Pel Lngej Neuv Tngay Jan

What time does the film / performance start?

តើម៉ោងប៉ុន្មានចាប់ផ្ដើមលេខ?

Tei Moung Pun Man Reung / Ka Sam Daeng Jab Pdem

K
H
M
E
R

K
H
M
E
R

COMMUNICATIONS

Post

How much will it cost to send a letter / postcard / this package to Britain / Ireland / America / Canada / Australia / New Zealand?

តើអស់ថ្លៃប៉ុន្មានដើម្បីផ្ញើសំបុត្រ / កាតប៉ុស្តាល់ / កញ្ចប់នេះទៅអង់គ្លេស / អៀរឡង់ / អាមេរិកកាំង / កាណាដា / អូស្ត្រាលី / ញូស៊ីឡេន

Tei Os Tlai Pun Man Dem Bei Pnhei Som But / Kat Po Stal / Korn Job Nis Teuv Ang Glay / Ir Lang / A Me Rik Kiang / Ka Na Da / Oh Stra Li / New Seu Len

I would like one stamp / two stamps

ខ្ញុំចង់បានតែមមួយ / តែមពីរ

Khnom Jong Ban Taem Mouy / Taem Pi

I'd like ... stamps for postcards to send abroad, please

ខ្ញុំចង់បាន ... តែមសំរាប់កាតប៉ុស្តាល់ដើម្បីផ្ញើទៅក្រៅប្រទេស

Khnom Jang Ban ... Taem Som Rab Kat Po Stal Dem Bei Phnei Teuv Krao Pro Tes

Phones

I would like to make a telephone call / reverse the charges to (make a collect call to) ...

ខ្ញុំចង់ទូរស័ព្ទទៅ ... / ចង់អោយ ភាគីខាងអ្នកទទួលជាអ្នកបង់ប្រាក់

Khnom Jong Touro Sub Teuv ... / Jong Ouy Pia Ki Kang Nak To Tuol Jia Nak Bang Brak

Which coins do I need for the telephone?

តើខ្ញុំត្រូវប្រើកាក់មួយណាដើម្បីទូរស័ព្ទ?

Tei Khnom Treuv Brei Kak Mouy Na Daem Bei Touro Sab

The line is engaged (busy)

បណ្ដាញទូរស័ព្ទជាប់រវល់

Born Daj Touro Sab Yub Ro Vol

The number is ...

លេខគឺ ...

Lek Keu ...

Hello, this is ...

សួស្ដី / នេះគឺជា ...

Suo Sdei / Nis Keu Jia ...

Please may I speak to ...?

តើខ្ញុំអាចនិយាយជាមួយ ...?

Tei Khnom Ahj Ni Yeay Jia Mouy ...

He / she is not in at the moment. Can you call back?

គាត់ / នាងអត់នៅទេ ។ តើអ្នកអាចទូរស័ព្ទមកម្ដងទៀតបានទេ?

Kort / Niang Ort Neuv Te Pel Nis Tei Nak Ahj Touro Sab Mok Mdorg Tiat Ban Te

SHOPPING

Shops

ហាងលក់សៀវភៅ / គ្រឿងសំភារៈការិយាល័យ

Hang Lork Siao Peuv / Kreung Ka Ri Ya Lai

Bookshop / Stationery

ជាងទង / អំណោយ

Jiang Taung / Om Nouy

Jeweller / Gifts

ស្បែកជើង
Sbaek Jeung
Shoes

គ្រឿងហាតវៃ
Kreung Hat Vae
Hardware

ជាងអ៊ិតពាក់
Jiang Ort Sork
Hairdresser

របស់បុរស / របស់ស្ត្រី
Ro Bos Bu Ros / Ro Bos Srey
men's / women's

អ្នកធ្វើនំ
Nak Tveu Num
Baker

ទូរសព្ទ
Touro Sab
Phones

ផ្សារទំនើប
Psa Tom Neub
Supermarket

ហាងថតរូប
Hang Tort Roub
Photo-Shop

ភ្នាក់ងារទេសចរណ៍
Pnak Ngia Tes Jor
Travel agent

ឱសថស្ថាន (ហ្វាម៉ាស៊ី)
Or Sort Stan (Fa Ma Si)
Pharmacy

In the Shops

What time do the shops open / close?
តើម៉ោងប៉ុន្មានកេបើកហាង / បិទហាង?
Tei Moung Pun Man Ke Beik Hang / Bet Hang

Where is the nearest market?
តើផ្សារដែលនៅជិតបំផុតនៅកន្លែងណា?
Tei Psa Del Neuv Jit Bom Put Nov Korn Laeng Na

Can you show me the one in the window / this one?
តើអ្នកអាចបង្ហាញខ្ញុំអាមួយនៅក្នុងកញ្ចក់បានទេ / អាមួយនេះ?
Tei Nak Ahj Bong Hanh Ah Mouy Neuv Knong Korn Jork Ban Te / Ah Mouy Nis

Can I try this on?
តើខ្ញុំអាចលេសអាមួយនេះបានទេ?
Tei Khnom Ahj Lo Ah Mouy Nis Ban Te

What size is this?
តើអាមួយនេះខ្នាតអី?
Tei Ah Mouy Nis Khnat Ei

This is too large / too small / too expensive.
អាមួយនេះធំណាស់ / តូចណាស់ / ថ្លៃណាស់ ។
Ah Mouy Nis Tom Nas / Toj Nas / Tlai Nas

Do you have any others?
តើអ្នកមានអាផ្សេងទៀតទេ?
Tei Nak Mian Ah Pseng Tiat Te

My size is ...
ទំហំរបស់ខ្ញុំគឺ ...
Tom Hum Ro Bos Khnom Keu ...

KHMER

Where is the changing room/ children's / cosmetic / ladieswear / menswear / food department?

តើមានបន្ទប់ផ្លាស់ខោអាវ / មជ្ឈមណ្ឌលកុមារ / គ្រឿងសំអាង / ខោអាវស្រ្តី / ខោអាវប្រុស / មជ្ឈមណ្ឌលអាហារនៅកន្លែងណា?

Tei Bun Tub Khor Ao / Maj Chak Mun Dol Ko Ma / Kreung Sam Ang / Khor Ao Srey / Khor Ao Bo Ros / Maj Chak Mun Dol Ah Ha Neuv Korn Laeng Na

I would like ... a quarter of a kilo / half a kilo / a kilo of bread / butter / cheese / ham / this fruit

ខ្ញុំចង់បានទំប៉ុង / បឺរ / ប្រមា / ហែម (សាច់ជ្រូកបុស) / ផ្លែឈើនេះពីរកាន្លះ / កន្លះគីឡូ / មួយគីឡូ

Khnom Jong Ban Num Piang / Beur / Fro Ma / Haem (Saj Sam Bong) / Plae Cheu Nis Pi Kham Korn Lah / Korn Lah Ki Lo / Mouy Ki Lo

How much is this?

តើអាមួយនេះថ្លៃប៉ុន្មាន?

Tei Ah Mouy Nis Tlai Pun Man

I'll take this one, thank you

ខ្ញុំយកអាមួយនេះ អរគុណ

Khnom Yok Ah Mouy Nis, Or Kun

Do you have a carrier (shopping) bag?

តើអ្នកមានថង់យួរដែរទេ?

Tei Nak Mian Tong Yuor Dai Te

Do you have anything cheaper / larger / smaller / of better quality?

តើអ្នកមានអាផ្សេងទៅកជាង / ធំជាង / តូចជាង / ល្អជាងនេះ?

Tei Nak Mian Ah Pseng Tork Jiang Nis / Tom Jiang Nis / Toj Jiang Nis / Laor Jiang Nis

I would like a film / to develop this film for this camera

ខ្ញុំចង់បានហ្វីលមួយដុំ / ចង់លាងហ្វីលសំរាប់ម៉ាស៊ីនថតរូបនេះ

Khnom Jong Ban Fil Mouy Dom / Jong Liang Fil Som Rab Ma Sin Tot Rob Nis

I would like some batteries, the same size as this old one

ខ្ញុំចង់បានថ្មដែលមានខ្នាតដូចអាមួយនេះ

Khnom Jong Ban Tmor Del Mian Khnat Doj Ah Mouy Nis

Would you mind wrapping this for me, please?

សូមអ្នកជួយខ្ចប់អោយខ្ញុំងបានទេ?

Som Nak Juy Khjob Ouy Khnom Phorng Ban Te

Sorry, but you seem to have given me the wrong change

សូមទោស អ្នកអាប់លុយអោយខ្ញុំច្រឡំហើយ

Som Tos Nak Ab Luy Ouy Khnom Jroh Lom Hei

MOTORING

Car Hire (Rental)

I have ordered (rented) a car in the name of ...

ខ្ញុំបានជួលឡានដោយដាក់ឈ្មោះ ...

Khnom Ban Jul Lan Douy Dak Chmos ...

How much does it cost to hire (rent) a car for one day / two days / a week?

តើជួលឡានសំរាប់មួយថ្ងៃ / ពីរថ្ងៃ / មួយអាទិត្យអស់ថ្លៃប៉ុន្មាន?

Tei Jul Lan Som Rab Mouy Tngay / Pi Tngay / Mouy Ah Tit Os Tlai Pun Man

Is the tank already full of petrol (gas)?
តើវាមានប្រេង (ហ្គាស) ពេញហើយឬ?
Tei Vea Mian Preng (Gaz) Penh Hei Reu

Is insurance and tax included? How much is the deposit?
តើថ្លៃធានារ៉ាប់រង និង ពន្ធត្រូវបានមេបពូលហើយឬ?
តើថ្លៃកក់ប៉ុន្មាន?
Tei Tlai Tia Nia Rab Rong Neung Pun Treuv Ban Bun Jul Hei Reu. Tei Tlai Koh Pun Man

By what time must I return the car?
តើខ្ញុំត្រូវ ប្រគល់ឡានទៅម៉ោងប៉ុន្មាន?
Tei Khnom Treuv Pro Kul Lan Neuv Moung Pun Man

I would like a small / large / family / sports car with a radio / cassette player
ខ្ញុំចង់បានឡានតូច / ឡានធំ / ឡានសំរាប់គ្រួសារ / ឡាកស្ព័រជាមួយវិទ្យុ / ម៉ាស៊ីនបាក់កាសែត
Khnom Jong Ban Lan Toj / Lan Tom / Lan Som Rab Krour Sa / Lan Spor Jia Mouy Vi Tyu / Ma Sin Jak Kas Saet

Do you have a road map?
តើអ្នកមានផែនទីផ្លូវទេ?
Tei Nak Miun Pen Ti Pleuv Te

How long can I park here?
តើខ្ញុំអាចចតនៅទីនេះរយ:ពេលប៉ុន្មាន?
Tei Khnom Ahj Jort Neuv Ti Nis Ro Yak Pel Pun Man

Is there a car park near here?
តើមានចំណតរថយន្តនៅជិតនេះទេ?
Tei Mian Jom Nort Rot Yun Neuv Jit Nis Te

At what time does this car park close?
តើចំណតរថយន្តបិទនៅម៉ោងប៉ុន្មាន?
Tei Jom Nort Rot Yun Bet Neuv Moung Pun Man

តែទៅ
Tae Teuv
One way

ហាមចូល
Ham Jul
No entry

ហាមចត
Ham Jort
No parking

ផ្លូវវាង (ការបត់ចែក)
Pleuv Viang
Detour (diversion)

ឈប់
Chub
Stop

បើកផ្លូវអោយ (អោយទៅមុន)
Beik Pleuv Ouy (Ouy Teuv Mun)
Give way (yield)

ផ្លូវរអិល
Pleuv Ro El
Slippery road

ហាមវា
Ham Va
No overtaking

គ្រោះថ្នាក់
Kros Tnak
Danger!

K
H
M
E
R

At the Filling Station

Unleaded (lead free) / standard / premium / diesel
ប្រេងម៉ាស៊ីនឥតមានជាតិសំណ / ធម្មតា / ពិសេសជាងធម្មតា / ប្រេងម៉ាហ្សូត
Praeng Ma Zot Ort Mian Jiat Sam Nor / Tam Mda / Bi Ses Jing Tam Mda / Brenh Ma Zot

Fill the tank please
ចាក់សាំង
Jak Sang

Do you have a road map?
តើអ្នកមានផែនទីផ្លូវទេ?
Tei Nak Mian Pen Ti Pleuv Te

How much is the car wash?
តើលាងឡានតម្លៃប៉ុន្មាន?
Tei Liang Lan Tlai Pun Man

Breakdowns

I've had a breakdown at ...
ខ្ញុំខូចឡានៅ ...
Khnom Khoj Lan Neuv ...

I am a member of the [motoring organisation]
ខ្ញុំជាសមាជិកនៃ [អង្គការត្រួតពិនិត្យ]
Khnom Keu Jia Sa Ma Jik Ney [An Ka Trourt Pi Nit]

I am on the road from ... to ...
ខ្ញុំនៅតាមបណ្ដោយផ្លូវពី ...ទៅ ...
Khnom Nov Tam Bun Douy Plov Pi ... Tov ...

I can't move the car. Can you send a tow truck?
ឡានរបស់ខ្ញុំមិនអាចបើកបបាន ។ តើអ្នកអាច បញ្ជូនឡានលូសណ្ដោងមកបានទេ?

I have a flat tyre
រថយន្តរបស់ខ្ញុំបែកកង់
Rot Yun Ro Bos Khnom Baek Kong

The windscreen (windshield) has smashed / cracked
កញ្ចក់រថយន្តបានបែកខ្ទេច
Korn Juk Rot Yun Ban Baek Kteij

There is something wrong with the engine / brakes / lights / steering / gearbox / clutch / exhaust
វាមានបញ្ហាជាមួយម៉ាស៊ីន / ហ្វ្រាំង / ភ្លើង / ចង្កូត / ប្រអប់ស្ដី / អំប្រីយ៉ា / បំពង់សីម៉ាំង
Vea Mian Pan Ha Jia Mouy Ma Sin / Friang / Pleung / Jong Kort / Bror Ob Speu / Am PriYa / Bom Pong Seu Miang

It's overheating
វាក្ដៅខ្លាំងពេក
Vea Kdao Kliang Paek

It won't start
វាអត់ឆេះទេ
Vea Ort Ches Te

Where can I get it repaired?
តើខ្ញុំអាចជួសជុលវានៅកន្លែងណា?
Tei Khnom Ahj Jous Jul Vea Neuv Korn Laeng Na

Can you take me there?
តើអ្នកអាចនាំខ្ញុំទៅទីនោះបានទេ?
Tei Nak Ahj Nem Khnom Teuv Ti Nos Ban Te

Will it take long to fix?
តើចំនាយពេលយូរដែរឬទេដើម្បីជួសជុលវា?
Tei Jom Nay Pel Yu Te Dem Bei Tveu Via

How much will it cost?
តើនឹងអស់ថ្លៃប៉ុន្មាន?
Tei Neung Os Tlai Pun Man

Please can you pick me up / give me a lift?
តើអ្នកអាចជួយមកទូលខ្ញុំផងបានទេ?
Tei Nak Ahj Juy Mok To Toul Khnom Phorng Ban Te

Can you help me? There has been an accident
តើអ្នកអាចជួយខ្ញុំផងបានទេ? មានគ្រោះថ្នាក់កើតឡើង
Tei Nak Ahj Juy Khnom Ban Te. Mian Kros Tnak Ket I eung

Please call the police / an ambulance
សូមទូរស័ព្ទហៅប៉ូលីស / ឡានសង្គ្រោះ
Som Touro Sab Hao Po Lis / Lan Song Kros

Is anyone hurt?
តើមានអ្នករបួសរបួសទេ?
Tei Mian Nak Rong Ro Bos Te

I'm sorry, I didn't see the sign
ខ្ញុំសូមទោស ខ្ញុំអត់បានឃើញផ្លាកសញ្ញា
Khnom Som Tos Khnom Ört Khuenh Plak Sun Nha

Must I pay a fine? How much?
តើខ្ញុំត្រូវបង់ប្រាក់ពិន័យនេះទេ? ថ្លៃប៉ុន្មាន?
Tei Khnom Treuv Bong Prak Pak Pi Ney Te. Tlai Pun Man

Show me your documents
បង្ហាញខ្ញុំនូវឯកសាររបស់អ្នក
Bong Hanh Khnom Neuv Ek Ka Sa Ro Bos Nak

Do you have anything for a stomach ache / headache / sore throat / toothache?
តើអ្នកមានថ្នាំសំរាប់ជំងឺក្រពះ / ឈឺក្បាល / ឈឺបំពង់ក / ឈឺធ្មេញទេ?
Tei Nak Mian Tnam Som Rab Jum Ngeu Kror Pias / Cheu Kbal / Cheu Bom Pong Kor / Cheu Tmenh Te

I need something for diarrhoea / constipation / a cold / a cough / insect bites / sunburn / travel (motion) sickness (car) (plane) (boat)
ខ្ញុំត្រូវការថ្នាំសំរាប់រាគ / ទល់លាមក / ផ្តាសាយ / ក្អក / សត្វល្អិតខាំ / រោះកក់ដោយថ្ងៃ / ពុល (ឡាន) (យន្តហោះ) (កាណូត)
Khnom Treuv Ka Tnam Som Rab Riak / Tol La Mok / Pda Say / Kaor / Sat Laet Kham / Ro Liak Kom Dao Tngay / Pol (Lan) (Yun Hoh) (Ka Not)

How much / how many do I take?
តើខ្ញុំត្រូវញាំវាប៉ុន្មានគ្រាប់?
Tei Khnom Treuv Nham Via Pun Man Krob

How often do I take it / them?
តើខ្ញុំត្រូវញាំវាប៉ុន្មានដង?
Tei Khnom Treuv Nham Via Pun Man Daung

I am / he is / she is taking this medication
ខ្ញុំ / គាត់ / នាង កំពុងប្រើថ្នាំនេះ
Khnom / Kiat / Niang / Kom Pong Brei Tnam Nis

How much does it cost?
តើអស់ថ្លៃប៉ុន្មាន?
Tei Os Tlai Pun Man

**K
H
M
E
R**

Can you recommend a good doctor / dentist?

តើអ្នកអាចណែនាំខ្ញុំនូវវេជ្ជបណ្ឌិត / ពេទ្យធ្មេញល្អបានទេ?
Tei Nak Ahj Nae Nem Khnom Neuv Vi Jak Bun Det / Pet Tmenh Laor Ban Te

Is it suitable for children?

តើវាសាកសមសំរាប់កូនក្មេងទេ?
Tei Via Sak Som Jia Mouy Kmeng Te

Doctor

I have a pain here / in my arm / leg / chest / stomach

ខ្ញុំឈឺត្រង់នេះ / ឈឺដៃ / ឈឺជើង / ឈឺទ្រូង / ឈឺក្រពះ
Khnom Cheu Trong Nis / Cheu Dai / Cheu Jeung / Cheu Troung / Cheu Kror Pias

Please call a doctor, this is an emergency

សូមហៅវេជ្ជបណ្ឌិត នេះគឺជាការបន្ទាន់
Som Hao Vi Jak Bun Det, Nis Keu Jia Ka Bun Tun

I would like to make an appointment to see the doctor

ខ្ញុំចង់ណាត់ជួបវេជ្ជបណ្ឌិត
Khnom Jong Nat Jub Vi Jak Bun Det

I am diabetic / pregnant

ខ្ញុំមានរោគទឹកនោមផ្អែម / មានផ្ទៃពោះ
Khnom Mian Rok Teuk Num Paem / Mian Ptei Pos

I need a prescription for ...

ខ្ញុំត្រូវការវេជ្ជបញ្ជាសំរាប់ ...
Khnom Treu Ka Vi Jak Bun Jia Som Rab ...

Can you give me something to ease the pain?

តើអ្នកអាចអោយថ្នាំខ្ញុំដើម្បីបំបាត់ការឈឺចាប់បានទេ?
Tei Nak Ahj Ouy Tnam Khnom Dem Bei Bom Bat Ka Cheu Jab Ban Te

I am / he is / she is allergic to penicillin

ខ្ញុំ / គាត់ / នាង មានប្រតិកម្មជាមួយនឹងថ្នាំប៉េនីស៊ីលីន
Khnom / Kiat / Niang Mian Bro Ti Kam Jia Mouy Neung Tnam Pe Ni Si Lin

Does this hurt?

តើវាធ្វើអោយឈឺចាប់ទេ?
Tei Via Tveu Ouy Cheu Jab Te

You must / he must / she must go to hospital

អ្នក / គាត់ / នាង ត្រូវទៅមន្ទីរពេទ្យ
Nak / Kiat / Niang Treuv Tov Mun Ti Pet

Take these once / twice / three times a day

ញាំទាំងអស់នេះ មួយ / ពីរ / បីដង ក្នុងមួយថ្ងៃ
Nham Tiang Os Nis Mouy / Pi / Bey Dong Knong Mouy Tngay

I am / he is / she is taking this medication

ខ្ញុំ / គាត់ / នាង កំពុងប្រើប្រាស់ថ្នាំនេះ
Khnom / Kiat / Niang Kom Pong Brey Tnam Nis

I have medical insurance

ខ្ញុំមានធានារ៉ាប់រងសុខភាព
Khnom Mian Tia Nia Rab Rong Sok Piap

**K
H
M
E
R**

Dentist

I have toothache
ខ្ញុំឈឺធ្មេញ
Khnom Cheu Tmenh

My filling has come out
របស់បំពេញបានចេញ
Ro Bos Bom Penh Ban Jenh

I do / do not want to have an injection first
ខ្ញុំចង់ / មិនចង់ចាក់ថ្នាំមុន
Khnom Jong / Min Jong Jak Tnam Mun

EMERGENCIES

Help!
ជួយផង
Juy Phorng

Fire!
ភ្លើងឆេះ
Pleung Ches

Stop!
ឈប់
Chub

Call an ambulance / a doctor / the police / the fire brigade!
ហៅឡានសង្គ្រោះ / វេជ្ជបណ្ឌិត / ប៉ូលីស /
ក្រមពន្លត់អគ្គិភ័យ
Hao Lan Song Kros / Vi Jak Bun Det / Po Lis / Krom Pun Lort Ah Ki Pey

Please may I use a telephone?
តើខ្ញុំអាចប្រើប្រាស់ទូរស័ព្ទនេះបានទេ?
Tei Khnom Ahj Prei Pras Touro Sab Nis Ban Te

I have had my traveller's cheques / credit cards / handbag / rucksack / (knapsack) / luggage / wallet / passport / mobile phone stolen
ខ្ញុំត្រូវបានគេលួចសែកទេសចរណ៍ / ក្រេឌីតកាត /
កាបូបយួរដៃស្រី / កាបូបស្ពាយក្រោយ /
កាបូបស្ពាយក្រោយ / វ៉ាលីស / កាបូបកាន់ដៃ /
លិខិតឆ្លងដែន / ទូរស័ព្ទដៃ
Khnom Treuv Ban Ke Luoj Saek Tes Joh / Krae Dit Kat / Ka Bob Yuo Dai Srey / Ka Bob Spay Krouy / Ka Bob Spay Krouy / Va Lis / Ka Bob Kan Dai / Li Khet Chlang Daen / Touro Sab Dai

May I please have a copy of the report for my insurance claim?
តើខ្ញុំអាចបានឯកសាររបាយការណ៍មួយច្បាប់ពីរបាយការណ៍សំរាប់ប្រកាសទានារ៉ាប់រងរបស់ខ្ញុំបានទេ?
Tei Khnom Ahj Ban Ek Ka Sa Ko Pi Mouy Jbab Pi Ro Bay Ka Som Rab Bror Kas Tia Nia Rab Rong Ro Bos Khnom Ban Te

Can you help me? I have lost my daughter / my son / my companion(s)
តើអ្នកអាចជួយខ្ញុំបងបានទេ? ខ្ញុំបានបាត់កូនស្រី /
កូនប្រុស / ដៃគូរបស់ខ្ញុំ
Tei Nak Ahj Juy Khnom Ban Te. Khnom Ban But Korn Srey / Korn Kros / Dai Kuu Ro Bos Khnom

Please go away / leave me alone
សូមចេញឲ្យឆ្ងាយ / ទុកឲ្យខ្ញុំនៅម្នាក់ឯង
Som Jenh Ouy Chngay / Tok Ouy Khnom Neuv Mnak Ek

I'm sorry
ខ្ញុំសូមទោស
Khnom Som Tos

EMERGENCIES

KHMER

I want to contact the British / American / Canadian / Irish / Australian / New Zealand / South African consulate

ខ្ញុំចង់ទាក់ទងទៅកុងស៊ុលអង់គ្លេស /
អាមេរិកកាំង / កាណាដា / អៀឡ្យង់ /
អូស្រ្តាលី / ញូសីឡែន / អាហ្វ្រិកខាងត្បូង
Khnom Jŏng Tak Tong Teuv Kong Sul
Ang Glae / Ah Mae Rik Kiang / Ka Na
Da / Er Lan / Os Stra Li / New Seu Len /
Ah Frek Khang Tbong

I'm / we're / he is / she is ill / lost / injured

ខ្ញុំ / យើង / គាត់ / នាង ឈឺ /
វង្វេងផ្លូវ / រងរបួស ។
Khnum / Yoeung / Koit /
Neang Chheu / Vongveng Plov /
Rong Robuos

They are ill / lost / injured

ពួកគេឈឺ / វង្វេងផ្លូវ / រងរបួស ។
Puok Ke Chheu / Vongveng Plov / Rong
Robuos

170

LAO
ລາວ

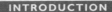

INTRODUCTION

L A O

Laotian and Lao dialects are closely related to Thai, and along with French form the main languages in the Lao People's Democratic Republic. As you would expect, there are varying dialects in the country but the most widely-used is Vientiane, which is the one this guide uses for transliteration. English is understood in tourist areas whilst French is spoken by many born prior to 1950.

Addresses for Travel and Tourist Information

UK: There is no official Laos embassy in the UK. The nearest is in Paris, Tel: 33 1455 30298; Fax: 33 1472 75789;
Email: ambalaoparis@wanadoo.fr; Web: www.laoparis.com

USA & Canada: Embassy of the Lao People's Democratic Republic, 2222 S. Street, NW Washington, DC 20008. Tel: 202 332 6416;
Fax: 202 332 4923; Web: www.laoembassy.com

Laos Facts

CAPITAL: Vientiane

CURRENCY: Lao Kip

OPENING HOURS: Most offices open between 0830-1700 with a lunch hour between 1200-1300. Public offices and banks close at 1530 every day and at weekends. Post Offices are open until 1200 on Saturdays.

TELEPHONES: To dial in, Tel: International Access Code + 856. Outgoing, Tel: 00 + Country Code.

EMERGENCY NUMBERS: Police, Tel: 191; Fire, Tel: 190; Ambulance, Tel: 195.

PUBLIC HOLIDAYS: Jan 1 – New Year's Day; May 1 – Labour Day; Apr 14-16 – Lao New Year's Days; Dec 2 – Independence Day.

Technical Language Hints

- There are 30 consonants in Lao script, but only 20 different sounds; and there are 28 vowels and dipthongs.

- Read Lao from left to right, and you will notice that vowels can be written above, below, before or after the consonants.

- Lao is another monosyllabic, tonal language, similar in sound to some dialects of Thai and Chinese.

**L
A
O**

Alphabet

Consonants

| ກ | ຂ |
| Kor | Kor |

| ຄ | ງ |
| Khor | Ngor |

| ຈ | ສ |
| Jor | Sor |

| ຊ | ຍ |
| Saw | Yor |

| ດ | ຕ |
| Dor | Tor |

| ຖ | ທ |
| Thor | Thor |

| ນ | ບ |
| Nor | Bor |

| ປ | ຜ |
| Por | Phor |

| ພ | ຟ |
| Phor | For |

| ຝ | ມ |
| For | Mor |

| ຢ | ລ |
| Nhor | Lor |

| ວ | ຫ |
| Vor | Hor |

| ອ | ຮ |
| Or | Hor |

special consonants

| ໜ | ໝ |
| Nor | Mor |

| ຫຍ | ຫລ |
| Ngor | Lor |

| ຫວ | |
| Vor | |

Vowels

| Xະ | Xາ |
| A | A |

| Xິ | Xີ |
| I | Ee |

| Xຶ | Xື |
| Ue | Ue |

| Xຸ | Xູ |
| U | Oo |

| ເXາະ | ເXอ |
| or | Or |

| ໄX | ໃX |
| Ai | Ai |

| ໂX | Xໍ |
| O | Or |

Basic Words and Phrases

Yes	**No**
ໄດ້	ບໍ່
Dai	Bor

Please	**Thank you**
ກະລຸນາ	ຂອບໃຈ
Kalouna	Khorb Jai

Hello	**Goodbye**
ສະບາຍດີ	ລາກ່ອນ
Sabaidi	La Korn

Excuse me
ຂໍໂທດ
Kor Thod

Sorry
ຂໍໂທດ
Kor Thod

How
ແນວໃດ
Neo Dai

When
ເວລາໃດ
Vela Dai

Why
ເປັນຫຍັງ
Pen Gneng

What
ແມ່ນຫຍັງ
Men Gnang

Who
ແມ່ນໃผ
Men Phai

That's O.K.
ບໍ່ເປັນຫຍັງ
Bor Pen Gnang

Perhaps
ບາງທີ
Bang Thi

To
ຈາກ
Jaark

From
ເຖິງ
Theung

Here
ຢູ່ນີ້
You Ni

There
ຢູ່ພຸ້ນ
You Phoun

I don't understand
ຂ້ອຍບໍ່ເຂົ້າໃຈ
Khoi Bor Khaow Jai

I don't speak Lao
ຂ້ອຍເວົ້າພາສາລາວບໍ່ໄດ້
Khoi Vao Phasaa Lao Bor Dai

Do you speak English?
ເຈົ້າເວົ້າพาสาอังกิดบໍ?
Jao Vaophasaa Angkit Dai Bor

Can you please write it down?
ເຈົ້າກະລຸນາຂຽນໃຫ້ເບິ່ງໄດ້ບໍ?
Jao Kalouna Khian Hai Beung Dai Bor

Please can you speak more slowly?

ເຈົ້າກະລຸນາເວົ້າຕື້ມອີກ
ຊ້າໆແດ່ໄດ້ບໍ?
Jao Kalouna Vao Tuem Ik Sa Sa Dae Dai Bor

Greetings

Good morning /
Good afternoon /
Good evening / Goodnight
ສະບາຍດີຕອນເຊົ້າ / ສະບາຍດີຕອນສວຍ /
ລາຕຣີສະຫວັດ
*Sabaidi Ton Xao / Sabaidi Ton Svai /
Ratrisavat*

Pleased to meet you
ຍິນດີທີ່ໄດ້ພົບເຈົ້າ
Gnin Di Thi Dai Phob Jao

How are you?
ເຈົ້າສະບາຍດີບໍ?
Jao Sa Bai Di Bor

Well, thank you. And you?
ດີ, ຂອບໃຈ. ເຈົ້າເດເປັນແນວໃດ?
Di Khorb Jai. Jao Dea Pen Neo Dai

My name is ...
ຊື່ຂອງຂ້ອຍແມ່ນ ...
Xue Khong Kaoi Maen ...

This is my friend / boyfriend /
girlfriend / husband / wife /
brother / sister
ນີ້ແມ່ນເພື່ອນຂອງຂ້ອຍ / ແฟน / ແฟน /
ผัว / ເມย / ອ້าย ຫຼືນ້ອງຊาย / ເອື້ອย ຫຼື
ນ້ອງສาว
*Ni Mean Phuan Khong Khoi / Faen /
Fean / Phoua / Mia / Ai Lue Non Sail /
Auid Lue Non Sound*

Where are you travelling to?
ເຈົ້າເດີນທາງໄປໃส?
Jao Deun Thang Pai Sai

I am / we are going to ...
ຂ້ອຍ / ພວກເຮົາຈະໄປທີ່ ...
Khoi / Phouark Hao Ja Pai Thii ...

How long are you travelling for?
ເຈົ້າເດີນທາງດົນປານໃດ?
Jao Deun Thaang Don Paan Dai

Where do you come from?
ເຈົ້າມາຈາກໃສ?
Jao Maa Jaark Sai

I am / we are from Australia / Britain / Canada / America
ຂ້ອຍ / ພວກເຮົາມາຈາກອົດສຕາລີ / ອັງກິດ / ການາດາ / ອາເມຣິກາ
Khoi / Phouark Haoa Maa Jaark Ostrali / Angkit / Kanada / Amaerika

We are on holiday
ພວກເຮົາຢູ່ໃນຊ່ວງພັກຜ່ອນ
Phourk Haow You Nai Xouang Phak Phon

This is our first visit here
ນີ້ແມ່ນການມາຢາມຢາມຄັ້ງທຳອິດຂອງພວກເຮົາ
Ni Maen Kane Maa Yiam Yam Khang Tham It Khong Phouark Hao

How old are you?
ເຈົ້າອາຍຸເທົ່າໃດ?
Jao Ayou Thao Dai

I am ... years old
ຂ້ອຍ ... ປີ
Khoi ... Pi

I am a businessman / business woman / doctor / journalist / manual worker / administrator / scientist / student / teacher
ຂ້ອຍເປັນນັກທຸລະກິດ / ນັກທຸລະກິດຍິງ / ທ່ານໝໍ / ນັກຂ່າວ / ກຳມະກອນ / ຜູ້ບໍລິຫານ / ນັກວິທະຍາສາດ / ນັກສຶກສາ / ອາຈານ
Khoi Pen Nak Thourakit / Nak Thourakit Gning / Thaan Mor / Nak Khaow / Kammakone / Phou Bolihane / Nak Vithagnasat / Naksueksaa / Ajane

Would you like / may I have a cigarette?
ທ່ານ ຕ້ອງການ / ຂ້ອຍຂໍ ຢາສູບແດໄດ້ບໍ?
Jao Tong Kane / Khoi Khor Yasoub Dae Dai Bor

Do you mind if I smoke?
ຈະເປັນການລົບກວນ ເຈົ້າບໍ ຖ້າຂ້ອຍ ສູບຢາ?
Ja Pen Kane Lopkouane Jao Bor Thaa Khoi Soub-Ya

Do you have a light?
ທ່ານ ມີໄຟແຊ້ກບໍ?
Jao Mi Fai Xaek Bor

I am waiting for my husband / wife / boyfriend / girlfriend
ຂ້ອຍລໍຖ້າຜົວຂອງຂ້ອຍ / ເມຍ / ເພື່ອນຊາຍ / ເພື່ອນຍິງ
Khoi Lor Thaa Phoua Khong Khoi / Mia / Pheuane Xay / Pheuane Gning

Days

Monday ວັນຈັນ Van Jan	**Tuesday** ວັນອັງຄານ Van Ang Khane
Wednesday ວັນພຸດ Van Phout	**Thursday** ວັນພະຫັດ Van Pha-Hat
Friday ວັນສຸກ Van Souk	**Saturday** ວັນເສົາ Van Sao

Sunday
ວັນອາທິດ
Van Athit

Morning
ຕອນເຊົ້າ
Ton-Xao

Afternoon
ຕອນສວຍ
Tone Svai

Evening
ຕອນແລງ
Tone Laeng

Night
ຕອນກາງຄືນ
Tone Kaang Khuene

Yesterday / Today / Tomorrow
ມື້ວານ / ມື້ນີ້ / ມື້ອື່ນ
Mue Vaan / Mue Ni / Mue Uene

Numbers

Zero
ສູນ
Soune

One
ນຶ່ງ
Nueng

Two
ສອງ
Song

Three
ສາມ
Saam

Four
ສີ່
Sii

Five
ຫ້າ
Haa

Six
ຫົກ
Hok

Seven
ເຈັດ
Jet

Eight
ແປດ
Paed

Nine
ເກົ້າ
Kao

Ten
ສິບ
Sip

Eleven
ສິບເອັດ
Sip Aet

Twelve
ສິບສອງ
Sip Song

Thirteen
ສິບສາມ
Sip Saam

Fourteen
ສິບສີ່
Sip Sii

Fifteen
ສິບຫ້າ
Sip Haa

Sixteen
ສິບຫົກ
Sip Hok

Seventeen
ສິບເຈັດ
Sip Jet

Eighteen
ສິບແປດ
Sip Paed

Nineteen
ສິບເກົ້າ
Sip Kao

Twenty
ຊາວ
Xao

Twenty-one
ຊາວເອັດ
Xao Aet

Twenty-two
ຊາວສອງ
Xao Song

Thirty
ສາມສິບ
Saam Sip

Forty
ສີ່ສິບ
Sii Sip

Fifty
ຫ້າສິບ
Haa Sip

Sixty
ຫົກສິບ
Hok Sip

Seventy
ເຈັດສິບ
Jet Sip

Eighty
ແປດສິບ
Paed Sip

Ninety
ເກົ້າສິບ
Kao Sip

One hundred
ນຶ່ງຮ້ອຍ
Nueng Hoi

Five hundred
ຫ້າຮ້ອຍ
Haa Hoi

L
A
O

L A O

One thousand
ນຶ່ງພັນ
Nueng Phan

One million
ນຶ່ງລ້ານ
Nueng Laan

Time

What time is it?
ເວລາຈັກໂມງແລ້ວ?
Vela Jak Mong Laew

It is ...
ດຽວນີ້ແມ່ນ ...
Diao Nii Maen ...

9.00
ເກົ້າໂມງ
Kao Mong

9.05
ເກົ້າໂມງປາຍຫ້າ
Kao Mong Pai Haa

9.15
ເກົ້າໂມງປາຍສິບຫ້າ
Kao Mong Pai Sip Haa

9.20
ເກົ້າໂມງປາຍຊາວ
Kao Mong Pai Xao

9.30
ເກົ້າໂມງເຄິ່ງ (ເກົ້າໂມງສາມສິບ)
Kao Mong Kheung (Kao Mong Saam Sip)

9.35
ເກົ້າໂມງປາຍສາມສິບຫ້າ
Kao Mong Pai Saam Sip Haa

9.40
ເກົ້າໂມງປາຍສີ່ສິບ
Kao Mong Pai Sii Sip

9.45
ເກົ້າໂມງປາຍສີ່ສິບຫ້າ
Kao Mong Pai Sii Sip Haa

9.50
ເກົ້າໂມງປາຍຫ້າສິບ
Kao Mong Pai Haa Sip

9.55
ເກົ້າໂມງປາຍຫ້າສິບຫ້າ
Kao Mong Pai Haa Sip Haa

12.00 / Midday / Midnight
ສິບສອງໂມງ / ທ່ຽງ / ທ່ຽງຄືນ
Sip Song Mong / Thiang / Thiang Khuene

Money

I would like to change these traveller's cheques / this currency
ຂ້ອຍຢາກປ່ຽນ ເຊັກທຣາແວັລເລີ່ / ເງິນ
Khoi Yark PianXaek Traveller / Ngeune

How much commission do you charge? (What is the service charge?)
ເຈົ້າເກັບຄ່າຄອມມິດຊັນ ເທົ່າໃດ?
(ຈ່າຍສາລັບຄ່າບໍລິການອັນໃດ?)
Jao Kaep Khaa Khommixan Thao Dai (Jai Samlap Khaa Bolikane An Dai)

Can I obtain money with my MasterCard?
ຂ້ອຍສາມາດໃຊ້ ບັດມັດສເຕີກາດ ເພື່ອຖອນເອົາເງິນສົດໄດ້ບໍ່?

Khoi Samard Xai Bat Master Khad
Phuea Thone Ao Ngeune Sot Dai Bor

Where is the nearest ATM?
ຕູ້ ເອ ທີ ແອັມ ທີ່ໃກ້ທີ່ສຸດຢູ່ບ່ອນໃດ?
Tou Ae- Thi- Aem Thi You Kai Thii
Sout You Bone Dai

**My name is ... Some money
has been wired to here for
me to collect**
ຂ້ອຍຊື່ຂ້ອຍແມ່ນ...ມີເງິນຈຳນວນ
ນຶ່ງໄດ້ຝາກມາໃຫ້ຂ້ອຍຢູ່ທີ່ນີ້
Xue Khoi Maen... Mi Ngeune Jam
Nouane Nueng Dai Faark Maa Hai
Khoi You Thii Ni

Airport

**Excuse me, where is the
check-in desk for ... airline?**
ຂໍໂທດ, ບ່ອນກວດຄົນເຂົ້າເມືອງ
ສຳລັບ... ສາຍການບິນຢູ່ໃສ?
Khor Thod, Bone Kouat Khon Khao
Muang Samlap ... Saii Kane Bin You
Sai

**What is the boarding gate /
time for my flight?**
ປະຕູຂຶ້ນຍົນແມ່ນເບີໃດ /
ເວລາບິນຂອງຂ້ອຍແມ່ນເວລາຈັກໂມງ?
Patou Khuen Yon Maen An Dai / Vela
Bin Khongkhoi Maen Vela Jak Mong

**How long is the delay likely to
be?**
ການເລື່ອນເວລາອັນນີ້ຈະດົນປານໃດ?
Kane Lueane Vela Anni Ja Don Paan
Dai

Where is the duty-free shop?
ຮ້ານຄ້າປອດພາສີຢູ່ໃສ?
Hankhaa Pord Phasi You Sai

**Which way is the baggage
reclaim?**
ໄປເອົາຫິບເດິນທາງໃດຢູ່ບ່ອນໃດ?
Pai Ao Hib Deune Thaang You Bone
Dai

**I have lost my luggage. Please
can you help?**
ຫິບເດິນທາງຂອງຂ້ອຍເສຍ.
ກະລຸນາຊ່ວຍຂ້ອຍແດ່?
Hib Deune Thaang Khongkhoi Sia.
Kalouna Xouai Khoi Dae

I am flying to ...
ຂ້ອຍຈະບິນໄປ ...
Khoi Ja Bin Pai ...

**Where can I get the bus to
the city centre?**
ຂ້ອຍສາມາດໄປເອົາລົດເມໄດ້
ທາງໃດເພື່ອເຂົ້າໄປໃນເມືອງ?
Khoi Samard Pai Ao Lot Mae Dai
Thaang Dai Phuea Khao Pai Nai
Muang

Trains and Boats

**Where is the ticket office /
information desk?**
ບ່ອນຂາຍປີ້ຢູ່ໃສ / ບ່ອນສອບຖາມຢູ່ໃສ?
Bone Khai Pi You Sai /
Bone Sorb Thaam You Sai

**Which platform does the
train / speedboat / ferry to ...
depart from?**
ອັນໃດແມ່ນບ່ອນທີ່ລົດໄຟ / ເຮືອດ່ວນ /
ກຳປັ່ນໄປ...ອອກຈາກ?
An Dai Mean Bonc Thii Lot Fai /
Huea Douane / Kampan Pai ... Onk
Jark

L
A
O

L A O

Where is platform ...?
ບ່ອນຂື້ນຢູ່ໃສ ...?
Bone Khuen You Sai ...

When is the next train / boat to?
ເວລາໃດລົດໄຟຂະບວນຕໍ່ໄປ / ເຮືອຈະ
ອອກເດີນທາງໆໄປ?
Vela Dai Lot Fai Kha Bouane Tor Pai / Muea Ja Ork Deune Thaang Pai

Is there a later train / boat to ...?
ມີລົດໄຟ / ເຮືອຈະອອກເດີນທາງໆໃນຖ້ຽວຕໍ່
ໄປບໍ...
Mi Lot Fai / Huea Ja Ork Deune Thaang Nai Thiao Tor Pai Bor ...

Notices and Signs

ຕູ້ລົດໄຟທ້ອງອາຫານ (ຫ້ອງອາຫານ)
Tou Lot Pai Hong Aharn (Hong Aharn)
Buffet (Dining) car

ລົດເມ
Lot Mae
Bus

ນ້ຳດື່ມ / ນ້ຳໃຊ້
Namdueum / Nam Xai
Drinking / Non-drinking water

ທາງເຂົ້າ
Thaang Khao
Entrance

ທາງອອກ
Thaang Ork
Exit

ໂຮງໝໍ
Hong Mor
Hospital

ຂໍ້ມູນ
Khor Moune
Information

ບ່ອນຝາກເຄື່ອງ (ຮັບເອົາເຄື່ອງ)
Bone Fark Khuang (Bone Hap Khuang)
Left luggage (Baggage claim)

ບ່ອນເກັບເຄື່ອງ
Bone Kep Khuang
Luggage lockers

ໄປສະນີ
Pai Sa Ni
Post office

ບ່ອນລໍຖ້າ
Bone Lor Thaa
Platform

ສະຖານີລົດໄຟ
Sa Thana Ni Lot Fai
Railway (Railroad) station

ສະໜາມບິນ
Sa Nam Bin
Airport

ສະຖານີຕຳຫຼວດ
Sa Than Ni Tam Loaud
Police station

ທ່າເຮືອ
Thaa Huea
Port

ຮ້ານອາຫານ
Haan Ahane
Restaurant

ສູບຢາໄດ້ / ຫ້າມສູບຢາ
Soubya Dai / Ham Soub Ya
Smoking / Non-smoking

ໂທລະສັບ
Tho La Sab
Telephone

ບ່ອນຂາຍບັດເດິນທາງ
Bone Khai Bat Deune Thaang
Ticket office

ບ່ອນກວດເຄກະສານເດິນທາງ
*Bone Kouat Aekasaan Deune
Thaang*
Check-in desk

ຕາຕະລາງເວລາ (ຕາຕະລາງ)
Tatalaang Vela (Ta Ta Lang)
Timetables (Schedules)

ຫ້ອງນ້ຳ (ຫ້ອງສຸຂາ)
Hong Nam (Houng Soou Khaa)
Toilets (Restrooms)

ຍິງ / ຊາຍ
Gning / Xai
Ladies / Gentlemen

ລົດໄຟໃຕ້ດິນ
Lot Fai Tai Din
Underground (Subway)

ຫ້ອງລໍຖ້າ
Hong Lor Thaa
Waiting room

Buying a Ticket

**I would like a first-class /second-
class single (oneway) / return
(round-trip) ticket to ...**

ຂ້ອຍຢາກໄດ້ປີ້ຊັ້ນນຶ່ງ / ຊັ້ນສອງ
(ເດີນທາງຖ້ຽວດຽວ) / ກັບ (ໄປ-ກັບ)
ເພື່ອໄປ...
*Khoi Yank Dai Pi Xan Neuung / Xan
Song (Deune Thaang Thiao Diaol) /
Kap (Pai – Kap) Phua Pai...*

**Is it an express (fast) train /
bus?**
ອັນນີ້ແມ່ນລົດໄຟ / ລົດເມດ່ວນ (ໂຊ) ບໍ່?
*An Ni Meang Lot Fai / Lotmae
Douane (Vai) Bor*

**Is my rail pass valid on this
train / ferry / bus?**
ບັດຂຶ້ນລົດຂອງຂ້ອຍໃຊ້ໄດ້ກັບ
ລົດໄຟ / ເຮືອຂ້າມຟາກ / ລົດເມໄດ້ບໍ່?
*Bat Khuen Lot Khong Khai Xai Dai
Kap Lot Fai / Huea Kham Fark / Lot
Mae Dai Bor*

**I would like an aisle /
window seat**
ຂ້ອຍຢາກໄດ້ບ່ອນນັ່ງທີ່ຢູ່ໃກ້ທາງຍ່າງ /
ຕິດກັບປ່ອງຢ້ຽມ
*Khoi Yaarh Dai Bone Nang Thi You
Kai Thaang Gnaang / Tid Dap Pong
Yiam*

No smoking / smoking, please
ຫ້າມສູບຢາ / ສູບຢາໄດ້
Ham Soub Ya / Soub Ya Dai

We would like to sit together
ພວກເຮົາຢາກນັ່ງນຳກັນ
Phouark Hao Yaark Nang Nam Kan

**I would like to make a seat
reservation**
ພວກເຮົາຢາກຈອງບ່ອນນັ່ງ
Phouark Hao Yaark Jong Bone Nang

**I would like to reserve a
couchette / sleeper for one
person / two people / my family**

L
A
O

ພວກເຮົາຢາກຈອງຕູ້ງຍາວ / ຕູ້ນອນສຳລັບນຶ່ງ
ຄົນ / ສອງຄົນ / ຄອບຄົວຂອງຂ້ອຍ
Phouak Hao Yark Jong Tang Gnao /
Tou Nonesam Lap Nueng Khon /
Song Kon / Khorb Kaua Khong Khoi

I would like to reserve a cabin
ຂ້ອຍຢາກຈອງຕູ້ເດີນທາງ
Khoi Yark Jong Tou Deune Thaang

Timetables (Schedules)

ມາຮອດ
Ma Hord
Arrive

ເອີ້ນ (ຢຸດ) ທີ່
Eun (Yout) Thii
Calls (Stops) at ...

ການບໍລິການຈັດຫາ
Kane Bori Kaan Jat Haa
Catering service

ປ່ຽນທີ່
Pian Thi
Change at ...

ການຕິດຕໍ່ / ໂດຍທາງ
Kane Tit Tor / Doi Thaang
Connection / Via

ທຸກມື້
Touk Mue
Daily

ທຸກໆ 40 ນາທີ
Thouk Thouk Sii Sip Nathi
Every 40 minutes

ຊັ້ນທີ່ນຶ່ງ
Xan Thi Nueung
First class

ທຸກໆຊົ່ວໂມງ
Thouk Thouk Xoua Mong
Hourly

ການຈອງບ່ອນແມ່ນ
ຖືກຮັບຮອງແລ້ວ
Kane Jong Bone Maen
Thuek Haphong Laew
**Seat reservations are
recommended**

ຊັ້ນທີ່ສອງ
Xan Thi Song
Second class

ສາມາດຈ່າຍເພີ້ມໄດ້
Samard Jaii Pheum Dai
Supplement payable

Luggage

**How much will it cost to send
(ship) my luggage in advance?**
ການສົ່ງຫີບເດີນທາງ (ຂົນສົ່ງ)
ລ່ວງໜ້າຂອງຂ້ອຍລາຄາເທົ່າໃດ?
Kane Faark Hib Deune Thang
(Khon Song) Louang Naa Khong
Khoi Lakhaa Thao Dai

**Where is the left luggage
(baggage claim) office?**
ຫ້ອງການຮັບຜິດຊອບຄົນເຄື່ອງເດີນທາງ
(ຮຽກຮ້ອງເລື່ອງເຄື່ອງເດີນທາງ)?
Hong Kane Hap Phit Sorb Khon
Kheuang Deune Thaang (Hiak Hong
Leuang Kheuang Deune Thaang)

**What time do you open /
close?**
ເຈົ້າເປີດ / ປິດຈັກໂມງ?
Jao Peud / Pid Jak Mong

Where are the luggage trolleys (carts)?
ລົດສຳລັບຂົນເຖື່ອງຢູ່ໃສ (ລົ້)?
Lor Samlap Khon Kheuang You Sai (Lor)

Where are the lockers?
ຕູ້ເກັບເຄື່ອງຂົວຄາວຢູ່ໃສ?
Tou Kep Kheuang Xoua-Khao You Sai

I have lost my locker key
ຂ້ອຍເຮັດກະແຈຕູ້ນີ້ເສຍ
Khoi Het Kajae Tou Ni Sia

On Board

Is this seat free?
ບ່ອນນັ່ງນີ້ຫວ່າງບໍ?
Bone Nang Ni Vaang Bor

Excuse me, you are sitting in my reserved seat
ຂໍໂທດ, ເຈົ້າ (ທ່ານ) ນັ່ງຢູ່ບ່ອນ
ຂອງຂ້ອຍທີ່ຈອງໄວ້
Khor Thod, Jao (Thaan) Nang You Bone Thii Khoi Jong Vai

Which station is this?
ນີ້ແມ່ນສະຖານນີໃດ?
Ni Maen Sathaani Dai

What time is this train / bus / ferry / flight due to arrive / depart?
ລົດໄຟ / ລົດເມ / ກຳປັ່ນ / ຍົນ
ຈະອອກຈັກໂມງ / ມາຮອດຈັກໂມງ?
Lot Fai / Lot Mae / Kampan / Gnon Ja Ork Jak Mong / Maa Hord Jak Mong

Travelling with Children

Do you have a high chair / babysitting service / cot?
ທ່ານມີຕັ່ງສູງ / ບໍລິການດູແລເດັກນ້ອຍ /
ຕຽງພັບບໍ?
Thaan Mi Tang Soung / Bolikane Doulae Deknoi / Tiang Phab Bor

Where is the nursery / playroom?
ອະນຸບານຢູ່ໃສ / ຫ້ອງສຳລັບເດັກຫຼິ້ນ?
Anoubane You Sai / Hong Samlap Dek Lin You Sai

Where can I warm the baby's bottle?
ຂ້ອຍສາມາດອຸ່ນນົມເດັກໄດ້ຢູ່ບ່ອນໃດ?
Khoi Samard Oun Nom Dek Dai You Bone Dai

Customs and Passports

Passports, please!
ກະລຸນາເອົາປັດສປໍ !
Khor Paspor Dae

I have nothing / wine / spirits (alcohol) / tobacco to declare
ຂ້ອຍບໍ່ມີຫຍັງ / ເຫຼົ້າວາຍ /
(ເຫຼົ້າ) / ຢາສູບທີ່ຈະແຈ້ງ
Khoi Bor Mi Gnang / Laow Vain / (Laow) / Yasoub Thii Ja Jaeng

I will be staying for ...days / weeks / months
ຂ້ອຍຈະຢູ່ ... ວັນ / ອາທິດ / ເດືອນ
Khoi Ja You ... Van / Athit / Deuane

SIGHTSEEING

Asking the Way

Excuse me, do you speak English?
ຂໍໂທດ, ທ່ານເວົ້າພາສາອັງກິດບໍ?
Khor Thod, Thaan Vao Phasaa Angkit Dai Bor

L
A
O

183

L
A
O

Excuse me, can you help me please?
ຂໍໂທດ, ເຈົ້າ ສາມາດຊ່ວຍຂ້ອຍໄດ້ບໍ່?
Khor Thod, Jao Samard Xouai Khoi Dai Bor

Where is the Tourist Information Office?
ຫ້ອງການທີ່ໃຫ້ຂໍມູນການທ່ອງທ່ຽວຢູ່ໃສ
Hong Kane Thii Hai Khor Moune Kane Thong Thiao You Sai

Excuse me, is this the right way to ...?
ຂໍໂທດ, ທາງແມ່ນໄປ...ຖືກບໍ່?
Khor Thod Thaang Nii Maen Pai ... Thuek Bor

...the cathedral / the tourist information office / the castle / the old town
... ໂບດ / ຫ້ອງການທີ່ໃຫ້ຂໍມູນການ ທ່ອງທ່ຽວ / ທີ່ຍາສາດ / ເມືອງເກົ່າ
... Bod / Hongkane Thii Hai Khor Moune Kane / Thong Thiao / Hor Pasard Mueang Kaow

Can you tell me the way to the railway (railroad) station / bus station / taxi rank (stand) / city centre (downtown) / beach?
ເຈົ້າ (ທ່ານ) ສາມາດບອກທາງໄປສະຖານ ບິລົດໄຟ / ສະຖານີລົດເມ / ລົວລົດແຕັກຊິ (ບ່ອນຈອດ) / ໃຈກາງເມືອງ (ກາງເມືອງ) / ແຄມທະເລ?
Jao (Thaan) Samard Bork Thaang Pai Sathaani Lotfai / Sathaani Lotmae / Khiou Lot Tak-Si (Bone Jord) / Jai Kaang Meuang (Kaang Meuang) / Khaem Thalae

First / second / left / right / straight ahead
ທຳອິດ / ທີສອງ / ຊ້າຍ / ຂວາ / ຊື່ໄປໜ້າ
Tham It / Thi Song / Xai / Khoua / Xue Pai Naa

At the corner / at the traffic lights
ຢູ່ທີ່ມຸມ / ຢູ່ໄຟຈາລະຈອນ
You Thii Moum / You Fai Jalajorn

Where is the nearest police station / post office?
ສະຖານີບິຕຳຫຼວດທີ່ໃກ້ທີ່ສຸດ / ໄປສະນີຢູ່ໃສ?
Sathaanii Tamlouad Thii Kai Thii Sout / Pai Sani You Sai

Is it near / far?
ມັນໃກ້ / ໄກບໍ່?
Man Kai / Kaii Bor

Do I need to take a taxi / catch a bus?
ຂ້ອຍຕ້ອງໃຊ້ແທັກຊິ / ຂຶ້ນລົດເມບໍ່?
Khoi Tong Xai Tak Si / Khueun Lot Mae Bor

Do you have a map?
ເຈົ້າມີແຜນທີ່ບໍ່?
Jao Mi Phaen Thii Bor

Can you point to it on my map?
ເຈົ້າຈະຊີ້ບອກຢູ່ໃນແຜນທີ່ຂອງຂ້ອຍແດ່?
Jao Jong Xi Bork You Nai Phaen Thii Khong Khoi Dae

Thank you for your help
ຂອບໃຈສຳລັບຄວາມຊ່ວຍເຫຼືອຂອງທ່ານ
Khorb Jai Samlap Khouam Xouai Luea Khong Thaan

How do I reach the motorway / main road?
ຂ້ອຍຈະໄປທາງດ່ວນ / ເສັ້ນທາງຫຼວງແນວໃດ?
Khoi Ja Pai Hord Thaang Douane / Sen Thaang Louang Neow Dai

I think I have taken the wrong turning

184

ຂ້ອຍຄິດວ່າຂ້ອຍລ້ວຫາງຜິດແລ້ວ
Khoi Khit Va Khoi Tong Liao Thaang Phit Leow

I am looking for this address
ຂ້ອຍກາລັງຊອກຫາທີ່ຢັບນີ້ຢູ່
Khoi Kam Lang Xork Haa Thii You An Ni You

I am looking for the ... hotel
ຂ້ອຍກາລັງຊອກຫາໂຮງແຮມ...
Khoi Kam Lang Xork Haa Hong Haem ...

How far is it to ... from here?
ຈາກບ່ອນນີ້ໄປ... ໄກບໍ?
Gnang Ja Tong Pai Xue Lik ... Kilomaet

Carry straight on for ... kilometres
ຍັງຈະຕ້ອງໄປຊື່ອີກ ... ກິໂລແມັດ
Gnang Ja Tong Pai Xue lik ... Kilomaet

Take the next turning on the right / left
ຕໍ່ໄປແມ່ນໃຫ້ລ້ຽວທາງຂວາ / ຊ້າຍ
Tor Pai Tong Hai Liao Thaang Khoua / Xai

Turn right / left at the next crossroads / traffic lights
ລ້ຽວທາງຂວາ / ຊ້າຍທີ່ຢູ່ທາງຂ້າມ / ໄຟສັນຍານຈາລະຈອນທາງໜ້າ
Liao Thaang Khoua / Xai You Thaang Khaam / Fai Sangnaan Jalajone Thaang Naa

You are going in the wrong direction
ເຈົ້າກາລັງໄປທາງຜິດ
Jao Kamlang Pai Thaang Phit

Where is the cathedral / church / museum / pharmacy?

ໂບດສາຄັນ / ໂບດ / ທີ່ພິພິດທະພັນ / ຮ້ານຂາຍຢາຢູ່ໃສ?
Bod Samkhan / Bod / Hor Phi-Phit-Ta-Phan / Han Khaii Yaa You Sai

How much is the admission / entrance charge?
ຄ່າທຳນຽມໃນ
ການເຂົ້າ / ຫາງເຂົ້າແມ່ນເທົ່າໃດ?
Khaa Thamniam Nai Kane Khaow / Khaa Khaow Maen Thao Dai

Is there a discount for children / students / senior citizens?
ມີການລົດລາຄາເສຳລັບ
ເດັກ / ນັກຮຽນ / ຄົນອະວຸໂສບໍ?
Mi Kane Lot Lakhaa Samlab Dek / Nak-Hian / Khon Avouso Bor

What time does the next guided tour (in English) start?
ການນຳທ່ຽວຄັ້ງຕໍ່ໄປຈະເລີມ
ເວລາໃດ (ທີ່ເປັນພາສາອັງກິດ)
Kane Namthiao Khang Tor Pai Ja Leum Vela Dai (Thii Pen Phasaa Angkit)

One / two adults / children, please
ນຶ່ງ / ຜູ້ໃຫຍ່ສອງຄົນ / ເດັກ
Nueng / Phou Gnai Song Khon / Dek

May I take photographs here?
ຂ້ອຍຖ່າຍຮູບຢູ່ບ່ອນນີ້ໄດ້ບໍ?
Khoi Thai Houb You Bone Ni Dai Bor

At the Tourist Office

Do you have a map of the town / area?
ເຈົ້າມີແຜນທີ່ຂອງເມືອງ / ບໍລິເວນນີ້ບໍ?
Jao Mi Phaen Thii Khong Muang / Borlivaen Ni Bor

185

Do you have a list of accommodation?
ເຈົ້າມີລາຍລະອຽດຂອງຫໍພັກອາໃສບໍ່?
Jao Mi Lai-La–Lad Thi Pak A Sai Bor

Can I reserve accommodation?
ຂ້ອຍສາມາດຈອງຫໍພັກອາໃສບໍ່?
Khoi Samard Jong Thii Phak Asai Bor

ACCOMMODATION

Hotels

I have a reservation in the name of ...
ຂ້ອຍໄດ້ຈອງໃນນາມຊື່ຂອງ ...
Khoi Dai Jong Nai Naam Xue Khong ...

I wrote to / faxed / telephoned you last month / last week
ຂ້ອຍໄດ້ຂຽນເຖິງ / ແຟັກເຖິງ / ໂທຫາເຈົ້າ ເດືອນທີແລ້ວ / ອາທິດທີຜ່ານມາ
Khoi Dai Khian Theung / Faek Heung / Tho Haa Jao Deuane Thii Laew / Athit Thii Phaan Me

Do you have any rooms free?
ເຈົ້າມີຫ້ອງຫວ່າງບໍ່?
Jao Mi Hong Vaang Bor

I would like to reserve a single / double room with / without bath / shower
ຂ້ອຍຢາກຈອງຫ້ອງດ່ຽວ / ຄູ່ທີ່ມີ / ບໍ່ມີຫ້ອງອາບນ້ຳ / ບ່ອນອາບນ້ຳ
Khoi Yaark Jong Hong Diao / Khou Thii Mi / Bor Mi Hong Aarb Nam / Bone Aarb Nam

I would like bed and breakfast / (room and) full board
ຂ້ອຍຢາກໄດ້ບ່ອນນອນແລະອາຫານເຊົ້າ / (ຫ້ອງແລະ) ອາຫານຄົບຊຸດ
Khoi Yaark Dai Bone None Lae Ahane Xao / (Hong Lae) Ahane Khop Xout

How much is it per night?
ລາຄາຕໍ່ຄືນແມ່ນເທົ່າໃດ?
Lakhaa Tor Khuene Maen Thao Dai

Is breakfast included?
ມີອາຫານເຊົ້າຮວມນຳບໍ່?
Mi Ahane Xao Houam Nam Bor

Do you have any cheaper rooms?
ເຈົ້າມີຫ້ອງລາຄາຖືກກວ່ານີ້ບໍ່?
Jao Mi Hong Lakhaa Thuek Koua Ni Bor

I would like to see / take the room
ຂ້ອຍຢາກເຫັນ / ໄດ້ຫ້ອງ
Khoi Yaark Hen / Dai Hong

I would like to stay for ... nights
ຂ້ອຍຢາກພັກ ... ຄືນ
Khoi Yaark Phak ...Khuen

The shower / light / tap / hot water doesn't work
ບ່ອນອາບນ້ຳ / ໄຟ / ກ໊ອກນ້ຳ / ບໍ່ຮ້ອນ ໃຊ້ງານບໍ່ໄດ້
Bone Aab Nam / Fai / Kock Nam / Nam Hone Xai Viak Bor Dai

At what time / where is breakfast served?
ເວລາໃດ / ບ່ອນໃດຈະມີອາຫານເຊົ້າ?
Vela Dai / Bone Dai Ja Mi Ahane Xao

What time do I have to check out?
ເວລາໃດຂ້ອຍຈະຕ້ອງແຈ້ງອອກ?
Vela Dai Khoi Ja Tong Jaeng Ork

Can I have the key to room number ... ?
ຂ້ອຍຂໍເອົາກະແຈຫ້ອງ ໝາຍເລກ ... ໄດ້ບໍ່?

Khoi Khor Ao Kajae Hong
Mai Laek ... Dai Bor

My room number is ...
ໝາຍເລກຫ້ອງຂ້ອຍແມ່ນ ...
Mai Laek Hong Khoi Maen ...

**My room is not satisfactory /
not clean enough / too noisy**
ຂ້ອຍບໍ່ພໍໃຈຫ້ອງພັກ /
ບໍ່ສະອາດພຽງພໍ / ສຽງດັງຫຼາຍ
*Khoi Bor Phor Jai Hong Phak / Bor
Saad Phiangphor / Sieng Dang Lai*

Please can I change rooms?
ກະລຸນາປ່ຽນຫ້ອງໃຫ້ຂ້ອຍແດ່ໄດ້ບໍ່?
Kalouna Pian Hong Hai Khoi Dai Bor

Where is the bathroom?
ຫ້ອງອານບໍ່ຢູ່ໃສ?
Hong Aam Nam You Sai

**Do you have a safe for
valuables?**
ເຈົ້າມີຕູ້ເຊັບສາໄລບເກັບຂອງມີຄ່າບໍ່?
*Jao Mi Tou Xep Samlab Kep Khong
Mi Khaa Bor*

**Is there a laundry / do you
wash clothes?**
ຢູ່ພຸ້ນມີຮ້ານຊັກລີດ / ເຈົ້າຊັກເຄື່ອງບໍ່?
*You Phoun Mi Han Xak Liid / Jao
Xak Kheuang Bor*

**I would like an air-conditioned
room**
ຂ້ອຍຢາກໄດ້ຫ້ອງທີ່ມີແອເຢັນ
Khoi Yaark Dai Hong Thii Mi Ae Yen

**Do you accept traveller's
cheques / credit cards?**
ເຈົ້າຮັບທຣາແວລເລີ່ເຊັກ / ບັດເຄຼດິດບໍ່?
*Jao Hap Tra-Veller Xaek /
Bat Khredit Bor*

May I have the bill please?
ຂ້ອຍຂໍໃບບິນໄດ້ບໍ່?
Khoi Khor Bai Bin Dai Bor

**Excuse me, I think there may
be a mistake in this bill**
ຂໍໂທດ, ຂ້ອຍຄິດວ່າໃບບິນນີ້ມີບ່ອນຜິດ
*Khor Thod, Khoi Khit Va Bai Bin Ni
Mi Bone Phit*

Youth Hostels

**How much is a dormitory bed
per night?**
ລາຄາບ່ອນນອນຕິນນຶ່ງໃນຫໍພັກນີ້ເທົ່າໃດ?
*La Ka Born Norn Born Neung Nai
Hor Pak Ni Thao Dai*

I am / am not an HI member
ຂ້ອຍແມ່ນ / ຂ້ອຍບໍ່ແມ່ນ HI ສະມາຊິກ
*Khoi Maen / Khoi Bor Maen Het I
Sa Ma Xik Khong*

**May I use my own sleeping
bag?**
ຂ້ອຍຢາກໃຊ້ຖົງນອນຂອງຂ້ອຍເອງ
ໄດ້ບໍ່?
*Khoi Yak Xai Thong Non Khongkhoi
Eng Dai Bor*

**What time do you lock the
doors at night?**
ເຈົ້າລ໋ອກປະຕູຕອນກາງຄືນຈັກໂມງ?
*Jao Lock Patou Ton Kang Kheun Jak
Mong*

Camping

**May I camp for the night / two
nights?**
ຂ້ອຍສາມາດພັກຂ້ວຄາວ
ນຶ່ງຄືນ / ສອງຄືນໄດ້ບໍ່?
*Khoi Samad Phak Xua Khao Neung /
Song Kheun Dai Bor*

EATING AND DRINKING

Where can I pitch my tent?
ຂ້ອຍສາມາດປຸກເຕັ້ນຂອງຂ້ອຍຢູ່ໃສ?
Khoi Samad 'Pouk Ten Khongkhaoi
You Sai

How much does it cost for one night / week?
ລາຄາສຳລັບນຶ່ງຄືນ / ອາທິດເທົ່າໃດ?
La Kha Sum Lab Neung Kheun /
Ar Thid Thao Dai

Where are the washing facilities?
ເຄື່ອງລ້າງຕ່າງໆຢູ່ໃສ?
Kheung Larng Tung Tung You Sai

Is there a restaurant / supermarket / swimming pool on site / nearby?
ມີຮ້ານອາຫານ / ຮ້ານສັບພະສິນຄ້າ / ສະ
ລອຍນໍ້າຢູ່ໃນສະຖານທີ່ນີ້ / ຢູ່ໃກ້ບໍ?
Mee Harn Arharn / Harn Sab Pha
Sin Kha / Sa Loy Nam You Nai Sa
Tharn Thee Phak / You Kai Bor

Do you have a safety deposit box?
ເຈົ້າມີຕູ້ເພື່ອເກັບເງິນທີ່ປອດໄພບໍ?
Jao Meek Up Pheu Kep Nguen Thee
Pot Phai Bor

EATING AND DRINKING

Cafés and Bars

I would like a cup of / two cups of / another coffee / tea
ຂ້ອຍຢາກໄດ້ກາເຟ / ຊາ / ນຶ່ງ / ສອງ
ຈອກອີກ
Khoi Yak Dai Ka Fey / Xa /
Neung / Song Jork Ik

With / without milk / sugar
ກັບ / ບໍ່ມີນົມ / ນໍ້າຕານ
Kup / Bor Mee Nom / Namtan

I would like a bottle / glass / two glasses of mineral water / red wine / white wine, please
ກະລຸນາເອົານໍ້າແຮ່ນຶ່ງ / ສອງຂວດ / ຈອກ /
ເຫົ້າອາຍແດງ / ອາຍຂາວ
Kalouna Ao Nam Hair Neung /
Song Khuat / Jork /
Rao Wine Daeng / Wine Khao

I would like a beer / two beers, please
ກະລຸນາເອົາເບຍນຶ່ງຂວດ / ສອງຂວດ
Kalouna Ao Beer Neung Khuat /
Song Khuat

Please may I have some ice?
ກະລຸນາເອົານໍ້າກ້ອນໃຫ້ຂ້ອຍແດ່?
Kalouna Ao Nam Kone Hai Khoi
Dae

Do you have any matches / cigarettes / cigars?
ເຈົ້າມີໄຟແຊ້ກ / ຢາສູບ / ຊິກາບໍ?
Jao Mee Fay Xaek / Ya Soub /
Xe Ka Bor

Restaurants

Can you recommend a good / cheap restaurant in this area?
ເຈົ້າແນະນຳຮ້ານອາຫານດີ /
ຖືກໃນບໍລິເວນນີ້ໃຫ້ໄດ້ບໍ?
Jao Nae Num Harn Ar Harn Dee /
Theuk Nai Bor Li Wene Nee Hai Dai
Bor

I would like a table for ... people
ຂ້ອຍຢາກໄດ້ໂຕະສຳລັບ ... ຄົນ
Khoi Yak Dai Toh Sumlab ... Kone

L
A
O

Do you have a non-smoking area?
ເຈົ້າຢູ່ລະຫຍາມທີ່ ຫ້າມສູບຢາບໍ່?
Jao You Sa Tharn Thee Harm
Soub Ya Bor

Waiter / Waitress!
ພະນັກງານບໍລິການຊາຍ / ພະນັກງານ
ບໍລິການຍິງ!
Pa Nak Gnan Bor Li Karn Xai /
Pa Nak Gnan Borlikarn Gning

Excuse me, please may we order?
ຂໍໂທດ, ພວກເຮົາສັ່ງອາຫານໄດ້ບໍ່?
Kor Thod, Phuak Phourk Haow Sang
Arhan Dai Bor

Do you have a set menu / children's menu / wine list?
ເຈົ້າມີອາຫານເປັນຊຸດ / ອາຫານຂອງເດັກ /
ລາຍການເຫຼົ້າວາຍບໍ່?
Jao Mee Arhan Pen Sout / Arhan Khong
Dek / Lai Karm Rao Vaine Bor

Do you have any vegetarian dishes?
ເຈົ້າມີອາຫານມັງສາລິລະບໍ່?
Jao Mee Arhan Mangsalila Bor

Do you have any local specialities?
ເຈົ້າມີອາຫານພື້ນບ້ານພິເສດບໍ່?
Jao Mee Arhan Pheunban Pi Set Bor

Are vegetables included?
ມີຜັກລວມນຳບໍ່?
Mee Phak Luam Nam Bor

Could I have it well-cooked / medium / rare please?
ກະລຸນາເຮັດໃຫ້ສຸກແທ້ໆ / ສຸກກາງໆ /
ດິບໃຫ້ຂ້ອຍໄດ້ບໍ່?
Ka Loo Na Het Hai Sook Tae Tae /
Sook Kang Kang / Deep Hai Koy
Dui Bor

What does this dish consist of?
ໃນອາຫານນີ້ມີຫຍັງແດ່?
Nai Arhanne Mee Yang Dae

I am a vegetarian. Does this contain meat?
ຂ້ອຍເປັນຄົນກິນມັງສາລິລະ.
ອັນນີ້ມີຊີ້ນບໍ່?
Khoi Pen Khon Kin Mangsalila.
Un Ni Mee Seen Bor

I do not eat nuts / dairy products / meat / fish
ຂ້ອຍບໍ່ກິນໝາກຖົ່ວດິນ /
ເຄື່ອງທີ່ເຮັດຈາກນົມ / ຊີ້ນ / ປາ
Khoi Bor Kin Mak Thoi Deen / Keung
Thee Het Jak Nom / Sine / Pa

Not (very) spicy, please
ກະລຸນາເຮັດບໍ່ເຜັດ (ເຜັດໜ້ອຍ)
Kalouna Het Bor Pet (Pet Lai)

I would like the set menu, please
ກະລຸນາເອົາອາຫານເປັນຊຸດໃຫ້ຂ້ອຍ
Ka Loo Na Ao Arhan Pen Sout Hai
Khoi

We are still waiting to be served
ພວກເຮົາກຳລັງລໍຖ້າເສີມອາຫານ
Phourk Haow Kam Lung Lor Tha
Serb Arhan

Please bring a plate / knife / fork
ກະລຸນາເອົາຈານ / ມີດ / ສ້ອມ
Kalouna Ao Jan / Meed / Sorm

Excuse me, this is not what I ordered
ຂໍໂທດ, ອັນນີ້ບໍ່ແມ່ນອັນທີ່ຂ້ອຍສັ່ງ
Kor Thod, Un Nee Bor Maen Khoi
Sang

L A O

189

May I have some / some more bread / water / coffee / tea?
ຂ້ອຍຊໍເຂົ້າຈີ່ / ນ້ຳ / ກາເຟ /
ຊາຕື່ມ / ຕື່ມອີກໄດ້ບໍ?
Khoi Kor Kao Jee / Nam / Ka Fey / Xa Teum / Teum Ik Dai Bor

May I have the bill, please?
ຂ້ອຍຊໍໃບບິນໄດ້ບໍ?
Khoi Kor Bai Bin Dai Bor

Does this bill include service?
ໃນໃບບິນນີ້ລວມທັງຄ່າບໍລິການແລ້ວບໍ?
Nai Bai Bin Nee Luam Thang Karn Bor Li Karn Laeo Bor

Do you accept traveller's cheques / MasterCard / US dollars?
ເຈົ້າຮັບເຊັກທ່ອງທ່ຽວ /
ບັດມັດສະເຕີ ກາດໆ/ ເງິນໂດລາຍ່?
Jao Hap Xek Thongtheo / Bad MasterCard / Nguen Dollar Bor

Can I have a receipt, please?
ຂ້ອຍຊໍໃບຮັບໄດ້ບໍ?
Khoi Kor Bai Hab Dai Bor

Where is the toilet (restroom), please?
ກະລຸນາບອກຂ້ອຍແດ່ວ່າຫ້ອງນ້ຳ
(ຫ້ອງນ້ຳ) ຢູ່ໃສ?
Kalouna Bork Khoi Dae Va (Hong Nam) Hong Nam Yu Sai

On the Menu

ອາຫານເຊົ້າ / ອາຫານຕອນສວາຍ /
ອາຫານຕອນແລງ
Arhan Sao / Arhan Ton Suay / Arhan Ton Laeng
Breakfast / Lunch / Dinner

ອາຫານສັ່ງທໍາອິດ ຊຸບ
Arhan Tham It   Soup
First courses Soups

ອາຫານຫຼັກ
Arhan Lak
Main courses

ອາຫານທີ່ມີປາ
Arhan Thee Mee Pa
Fish dishes

ອາຫານທີ່ມີຊີ້ນ
Arhan Thee Mee Sine
Meat dishes

ຊີ້ນງົວ   ສະເຕັກ
Sin Ngua   Stek
Beef   Steak

ໝູ ຊີ້ນ   ງົວອ່ອນ
Mou Sine   Ngua Orn
Pork   Veal

ໄກ່   ແກະ
Kai   Kae
Chicken   Lamb

ແຮມ
Ham
Ham

ອາຫານມັງສາລິລະ
Arhan Mangsalila
Vegetarian dishes

ຜັກຕ່າງໆ
Pak Tarng Tarng
Vegetables

ມັນຝຣັ່ງຈືນກອບ (ມັນຝຣັ່ງຈືນ)
Manfalang Jeun Korp (Manfalang Feun)
Chips (french fries)

ຕົ້ມ / ຊຶດເຕ່ / ມັນຝຣັ່ງບົດ
Tom / Saute / Man Falang Bot
Boiled / sauté / mashed potatoes

ເຂົ້າ
Kao
Rice

ເນຍ
Neuy
Cheese

ຂອງຫວານ
Khong Varn
Desserts

ກະແລ້ມ
Kaleum
Ice cream

ເຄັກ
Kek
Cakes

ຂະໜົມອົບ
Kha Nom Ob
Pastries

ໝາກໄມ້
Mak Mai
Fruit

ເຂົ້າຈີ່
Khao Ji
Bread

ເຂົ້າຈີ່ມົນ
Khao Jee Mon
Rolls

ເຂົ້າຈີ່ປິ້ງ
Khao Jee Ping
Toast

ເບີເຄືອ
Bur Keua
Butter

ເກືອ / ໝິກໄທ
Keu / Pik Thai
Salt / pepper

ນ້ຳຕານ
Nam Tan
Sugar

ລາຍການພິເສດ
Arhan Pee Set
Specialities

ລາຍການພິເສດພື້ນບ້ານ
Lai Karn Pee Set Peun Barn
Local specialities

ອາຫານເປັນຊຸດ
Arhan Pen Sout
Set Menu

ລາຍການເຫົ້າວາຍ
Lai Karn Rao Vaine
Wine list

ເຫົ້າວາຍແດງ
Rao Vaine Daeng
Red wines

ເຫົ້າວາຍຂາວ
Rao Vaine Khao
White wines

ເຫົ້າວາຍໂຣສ
Rao Vaine Rose
Rosé wines

ເຫົ້າວາຍທີ່ມີດີກຣີສູງ
Rao Vaine Thee Mee Degree Soung
Sparkling wines

ເບຍ
Beer
Beer

ເບຍຂວດ / ເບຍເຢັນ (ໄຄຍຄົວເບຍ)
Beer Khout/Beer Yen (Kai Kau Beer)
Bottled beer / Draught (draft) beer

ເຄື່ອງດື່ມທີ່ບໍ່ມີເຫົ້າ
Keung Deum Thee Bor Mee Rao
Non-alcoholic drinks

ນ້ຳແຮ່
Nam Hair
Mineral water

ນ້ຳໝາກໄມ້
Nam Mak Mai
Fruit juices

ນ້ຳໝາກກ້ຽງ
Nam Mak Kieng
Orange juice

LAO

L A O

Lemonade
ນ້ຳໂລ້ໂມນັດ
Lemonade

ນ້ຳກ້ອນ
Nam Korn
Ice

ກາເຟນົມ / ກາເຟດຳ /
ກາເຟເອສແປຣດໂຊ
*Ka Fey Nom / Ka Fey Dam /
Ka Fey Espresso*
**White coffee / black coffee /
espresso coffee**

ຊາກັບນົມ / ຊາກັບໝາກນາວ
Xa Kap Nom / Xa Kap Mak Nao
Tea with milk / with lemon

ເຄື່ອງດື່ມລົດຊອກໂກແລັດ (ເຄື່ອງດື່ມ)
*Keung Deum Lot Chocolate
(Keung Deum)*
Chocolate (drink)

ນ້ຳນົມ
Nam Nom
Milk

ອາຫານຫວ່າງໆ / ອາຫານເບົາ
Arhan Vang / Arhan Bao
Snacks / Light meals

ສະລັດ
Salat
Salads

ແຊນວິດ
Sandwiche
Sandwiches

ໄຂ່
Khai
Eggs

ໄສ້ກອກ
Sai Kok
Sausage

ໄຂ່ຕົ້ມ / ຈືນ / ຂົ້ວ
Khai Tom / Jeun / Khua
**Boiled / fried / scrambled
eggs**

Typical local dishes

ສະລັດຜັກລວມ
Sa Lad Phak Luam
Mixed salad

ໝາກຮຸ່ງ
Mak Houng
Papaya

ຊຸບເຜັດ
Soup Phet
Spicy soup

ໄກ່ອົບ
Kai Ob
Baked chicken

ເຂົ້າໜຽວ
Kao Neo
Sticky rice

ນ້ຳປາ
Nam Pa
Fish sauce

GETTING AROUND

Public Transport

**Where is the bus stop / coach
stop / nearest metro (subway)
station?**
ສະຖານີລົດເມ / ບ່ອນຈອດລົດຫ້ອຍ / ລົດ
ໄຟໃຕ້ດິນທີ່ໃກ້ທີ່ສຸດ (ລົດໄຟໃຕ້ດິນ) ຢູ່ໃສ?
*Sathanee Lot Mey / Born Jort Lot
Noy / Lot Fai Tai Dine Tee Kai Tee
Sout (Lot Fai Tai Dine) You Sai*

**When is the next / last bus
to ...?**
ເວລາໃດລົດເມຄັນຕໍ່ໄປ / ສຸດທ້າຍໄປ...?
*Vey La Dai Lot Mey Khan Tor Pai /
Sout Thai Pai ...*

How much is the fare to the city centre (downtown) / railway station / airport?

ຄ່າໂດຍສານໄປໃນໃຈກາງເມືອງ (ໃນເມືອງ) / ສະຖານີລົດໄຟ / ສະໜາມບິນເທົ່າໃດ?
Kha Doy San Pai Nai Jai Kang Meung (Nai Meung) / Sa Tha Nee Lot Fai / Sa Nam Bine Thoi Pai

Will you tell me when to get off?

ເຈົ້າບອກຂ້ອຍແຕ່ວ່າເວລາໃດທີ່ຈະລົງ?
Jao Bok Khoi Dae Va Vela Dai Thee Ja Long

Does this bus go to ...?

ລົດເມຄັນນີ້ໄປ... ບໍ?
Lot Mey Khan Nee Pa... Bor

Which number bus goes to ...?

ລົດເມຄັນໃດໄປ...?
Lot Mey Khan Dai Pai...

May I have a single (oneway) / return (round-trip) / day ticket / book of tickets?

ຂ້ອຍຕ້ອງການປີ້ເດີນທາງຖ້ຽວດຽວ (ເດີນທາງຖ້ຽວລູ) / ກັບ (ໄປແລະກັບ) / ປີ້ເດີນທາງມາຍໝີ / ປີ້ມຂອງປີ້ເດີນທາງໄດ້ບໍ?
Khoi Tong Karn Pee Deune Thew Deo (Deun Than Khan Deo) / Kap (Pai Lae Kap) / Pee Deune Thaang Lai Meu / Peum Kong Pee Deune Thaang Dai Bor

I would like to go to ...

ຂ້ອຍຢາກໄປທີ່ ...
Khoi Yak Pai Thee ...

How much will it cost?

ລາຄາມັນເທົ່າໃດ?
La Kha Man Thao Dai

Please may I stop here?

ກະລຸນາໃຫ້ຂ້ອຍລົງຢູ່ນີ້ໄດ້ບໍ?
Kalouna Hai Khoi Long You Nee Dai Bor

I would like to order a taxi today / tomorrow / at 2pm to go from ... to ...

ຂ້ອຍຢາກຈອງລົດແຕັກຊີມື້ນີ້ / ມື້ອື່ນ / ໃນເວລາ 2 ໂມງສວຍທີ່ໄປຈາກ ... ເຖິງ ...
Khoi Yak Jong Lot Taxi Meu Nee / Meu Eun / Nui Ve La Song Mong Souy Thee Pai Jak ...Then ...

Can you recommend a good bar / nightclub?

ເຈົ້າແນະນຳບາຣ / ນາຍຄລັບທີ່ດີໄດ້ບໍ?
Jao Nae Nam Bar / Nai Club Thee Dee Dai Bor

Do you know what is on at the cinema (playing at the movies) / theatre at the moment?

ເຈົ້າຮູ້ບໍ່ວ່າຮູບເງົາເລື່ອງໃນຢູ (ຫຼິ້ມ ເລື່ອງຫຍັງ) / ໂຮງລະຄອນກຳລັງຫຼິ້ນຢູ່ບໍ?
Jao Hoo Bor Va Houp Ngnao Leung Yang (Leen Leung Yang) / Hong La Khorn Kam Lang Leen You Bor

I would like to book (purchase) ... tickets for the matinee / evening performance on Monday

ຂ້ອຍຢາກຈອງ (ຊື້) ປີ້...ເພື່ອການສະ ແດງມາຕິເນ / ຕິນນີ້ ໃນວັນຈັນ
Khoi Yak Jong (Seu) Pee... Peu Karn Sa Daeng Martiney / Kheun Nee Nai Van Jan

What time does the film / performance start?
ຈະເລີ່ມສາຍໜັງເວລາຈັກໂມງ?
Ja Leum Sai Nang Vey La Jak Mong

COMMUNICATIONS

Post

How much will it cost to send a letter / postcard / this package to Britain / Ireland / America / Canada / Australia / New Zealand?
ລາຄາສົ່ງຈົດໝາຍ / ປິດສະກາດ / ເຄື່ອງສິ່ງ ໄປອັງກິດ / ໄອແລນ / ອາເມຣິກາ / ການນາດາ / ອົດສຕຣາລີ / ນິວຊີແລນ ເທົ່າໃດ?
Lak Kha Song Jotmai / Post Card / Keung Song Pai An Kit / Ai Land / America / Canada / Australia / Newzealand Thao Dai

I would like one stamp / two stamps
ຂ້ອຍຢາກໄດ້ສະແຕມອັນນຶ່ງ / ສອງອັນ
Khoi Yak Dai Stemp Aunt Neung / Song Aunt

I'd like ... stamps for postcards to send abroad, please
ຂ້ອຍຢາກໄດ້ສະແຕມ...ເພື່ອຕິດໂປສະການ ດສແລະສົ່ງຮຽບທີ່ຕ່າງໆປະເທດ
Khoi Yak Dai Stamp... Peu Tit Postcard Lae Song Heun Thee Tang Pa Thet

Phones

I would like to make a telephone call / reverse the charges to (make a collect call to) ...
ຂ້ອຍຢາກໂທລະສັບ / ເພື່ອຈອງທີ່ ແລະ(ເກັບເງິນຄ່າໂທທີ່)...
Khoi Yak Tholasap / Pai Keb Ngun Thee Lae (Kep Ngun Kha Tho Thee) ...

Which coins do I need for the telephone?
ຫຼຽນແບບໃດທີ່ຂ້ອຍຕ້ອງການ ເພື່ອໂທລະສັບ?
Leeun Baep Dai Thee Khoi Tong Karn Peu Tholasap

The line is engaged (busy)
ສາຍໂທລະສັບບໍ່ຫວ່າງ (ຄາສາຍ)
Sai Tholasap Bor Vang (Kha Saii)

The number is ...
ໝາຍເລກແມ່ນ ...
Mai Lek Maen ...

Hello, this is ...
ສະບາຍດີ, ນີ້ແມ່ນ...
Sa Bai Dee, Nee Maen ...

Please may I speak to ...?
ກະລຸນາໃຫ້ຂ້ອຍລົມກັບ ...ໄດ້ບໍ?
Kalouna Hai Khoi Lom Kap ... Dai Bor

He / she is not in at the moment. Can you call back?
ດຽວນີ້ລາວບໍ່ຢູ່. ເຈົ້າໂທມາອີກໄດ້ບໍ?
Deo Nee Lao You Bor. Jao Tho Mar Ik Dai Bor

SHOPPING

Shops

ຮ້ານຂາຍປຶ້ມ / ຮ້ານຂາຍເຄື່ອງຂຽນ
Harn Khai Peum /
Harn Khai Kheung Kheeun
Bookshop / Stationery

ຮ້ານຂາຍເຄື່ອງເພັດ /
ຮ້ານຂາຍຂອງຂວັນ
Harn Khai Kheung Pet /
Harn Khai Khong Khoun
Jeweller / Gifts

ຮ້ານຂາຍເກີບ
Harn Khai Kerb
Shoes

ຮ້ານຂາຍເຄື່ອງໂລຫະ
Harn Khai Keung Lo Ha
Hardware

ຊ່າງເສີມສວຍຂອງ
San Serm Suay
Hairdresser

(ຜູ້ຍິງ) / (ຂອງຜູ້ຊາຍ)
(Khong Poo Sai) / (Khong Poo Ying)
(men's) / (women's)

ຄົນເຮັດເຂົ້າຈີ່
Kon Het Khao Jee
Baker

ໂທລະສັບ
Tho La Sap
Phones

ຮ້ານສັບພະສິນຄ້າ
Harn Sap Pa Sine Kha
Supermarket

ຮ້ານຖ່າຍຮູບ
Harn Khai Houp
Photo-Shop

ອົງການທ່ອງທ່ຽວ
Ong Karn Thong Theo
Travel agent

ຮ້ານຂາຍຢາ
Harn Khai Ya
Pharmacy

In the Shops

What time do the shops open / close?
ຮ້ານຂາຍຢາເປີດ / ປິດເວລາໃດ?
Harn Khai Ya Perd / Pid Vey La Dai

Where is the nearest market?
ຕະຫຼາດທີໃກ້ທີ່ສຸດຢູ່ໃສ?
Ta Lad Thee Kai Thee Sout You Sai

Can you show me the one in the window / this one?
ເຈົ້າສະແດງໃຫ້ຂ້ອຍເຫັນໂຕທີ່ຢູ່ໃນ ປ່ອງຢ້ຽມ / ນີ້ ບໍ?
Jao Sa Daeng Hai Khoi Hen Toh Thee You Nai Pong Yeum/ Nee Bor

Can I try this on?
ເຈົ້າລອງອັນນີ້ໄດ້ບໍ?
Jao Long Un Nee Dai Bor

What size is this?
ຂະຫນາດຊ່ຳໃດ?
Kha Nat Sum Dai

This is too large / too small / too expensive.
ອັນນີ້ໃຫຍ່ໂພດ / ນ້ອຍໂພດ / ແພງໂພດ
Un Nee Yai Pod / Noy Pod / Paeng Pod

Do you have any others?
ເຈົ້າມີອັນອື່ນອີກບໍ?
Jao Mee Aunt Eun Ik Bor

My size is ...
ຂະໜາດຂອງຂ້ອຍແມ່ນ...
Kha Nat Khong Khoi Maen

Where is the changing room / children's / cosmetic / ladieswear / menswear / food department?
ຫ້ອງປ່ຽນເຄື່ອງຢູ່ໃສ / ພະແນກເດັກ / ເຄື່ອງ
ສຳອາງ / ຊຸດໃນຂອງຜູ້ຍິງ / ຊຸດຊັນໃນ
ຂອງຜູ້ຊາຍ / ພະແນກອາຫານຢູ່ໃສ?
Hong Peeun Kheung You Sai / Pha Naek Dek / Kheung Sam Ang / Sout San Nai Khong Poo Ying / Sout San Nai Khong Poo Sai / Pha Naek Arhan You Sai

I would like ... a quarter of a kilo / half a kilo / a kilo of bread / butter / cheese / ham / this fruit
ຂ້ອຍຢາກໄດ້... ສາມຂີດເຄິ່ງ / ເຄິ່ງກິໂລ /
ໜຶ່ງກິໂລເຂົ້າຈີ່ / ນໍ້າມັນເບີ / ເບຍ / ແຮມ /
ໝາກໄມ້ອັນນີ້
Khoi Yak Dai... ... Sam Khit Keung / Keung Kilo / Neung Kilo Khao Jee / Nam Man Bur / Neui / Ham / Mak Mai Un Nee

How much is this?
ລາຄາອັນນີ້ເທົ່າໃດ?
La Kha Un Nee Thao Dai

I'll take this one, thank you
ຂ້ອຍຊິເອົາອັນນີ້, ຂອບໃຈ
Khoi Xe Ao Un Nee, Kop Jai

Do you have a carrier (shopping) bag?
ເຈົ້າມີອັນເຫື່ອຖົງ (ຊື້ເຄື່ອງ)ບໍ່?
Jao Mee Un Heuo Bor Thong (Xeu Kheung Bor)?

Do you have anything cheaper / larger / smaller / of better quality?
ລາຄາຖຶກກວ່າ (ເຊິ່ງ) ໃຫຍ່ກວ່າ ນ້ອຍກວ່າ / ຄຸນນະພາບດີກວ່າ?

ເຈົ້າມີສິນຄ້າທີ່ມີປະສິດທິພາບຖຶກກວ່ານີ້ /
ໃຫຍ່ກວ່າ / ນ້ອຍກວ່າ / ດີກວ່ານີ້ບໍ່?
Jao Mee Sine Kha Thee Mee Pa Sit Thi Phab Theuk Kua Nee / Yai Kua / Noy Kua / Dee Kua Nee Bor?

I would like a film / to develop this film for this camera
ຂ້ອຍຢາກໄດ້ຟິມ / ລ້າງຮູບ
Khoi Yak Dai Film / Larng Houp

I would like some batteries, the same size as this old one
ຂ້ອຍຢາກໄດ້ຖ່ານໄຟສາຍ, ຂະໜາດຊ້ຳ
ໂຕເກົ່ານີ້
Khoi Yak Dai Than Fai Sai, Kha Nat Sam Toh Kao Nee

Would you mind wrapping this for me, please?
ກະລຸນາຫໍ່ໃຫ້ຂ້ອຍແດ່ໄດ້ບໍ່?
Kalouna Hor Hai Khoi Dae Dai Bor

Sorry, but you seem to have given me the wrong change
ຂໍໂທດ, ຂ້ອຍຄິດວ່າເຈົ້າທອນ
ເງິນໃຫ້ຂ້ອຍຜິດ
Khor Thod, Koy Kit Wa Jao Thorn Ngun Hai Koy Pit

MOTORING

Car Hire (Rental)

I have ordered (rented) a car in the name of ...
ຂ້ອຍໄດ້ຈອງ (ເຊົ່າ) ລົດທີ່ອອກຊື່...
Khoi Dai Jong (Xao) Lot Thee Ork Seu ...

How much does it cost to hire (rent) a car for one day / two days / a week?
ລາຄາເຊົ່າຈ້າງ (ເຊົ່າ) ລົດສຳລັບນຶ່ງວັນ /
ສອງມື້ / ອາທິດນຶ່ງເທົ່າໃດ?

La Kha Wa Jang (Xao) Lot Sam LabWan Neung / Song Meu / Ar Thit Neung Thao Dai

Is the tank already full of petrol (gas)?
ຖັງນ້ຳມັນ (ແກັດສ)ເຕັມແລ້ວບໍ່?
Thung Nam Mun (Gas) Tem Leo Bor?

Is insurance and tax included? How much is the deposit?
ມີການລວມຂອງປະກັນໄພແລະ ພາສີແລ້ວບໍ່? ຄ່າມັດຈຳເທົ່າໃດ?
Mee Karn Luam Khong Pa Kan Phai Lae Pa See Leo Bor? Kha Mat Jum Thao Dai

By what time must I return the car?
ເວລາໃດທີ່ຂ້ອຍຕ້ອງສົ່ງລົດຄືນ?
Vey La Dai Thee Khoi Tong Song Lot Kheun

I would like a small / large / family / sports car with a radio / cassette player
ຂ້ອຍຢາກໄດ້ລົດ ສປອດທີ່ນ້ອຍ / ໃຫຍ່ / ສຳລັບຄອບຄົວ / ທີ່ມີເກະຍຸ / ເທັບ
Khoi Yak Dai Lot Sa Port Thee Noy / Yai / Sum Lab Khop Khua / Thee Mee Vi Tha You / Thep

Do you have a road map?
ເຈົ້າມີແຜນທີ່ຫົນທາງບໍ່?
Jao Mee Phanthee Hon Than Bor

How long can I park here?
ຂ້ອຍສາມາດຈອດຢູ່ນີ້ໄດ້ດົນຊ່ຳໃດ?
Khoi Su Mat Jot You Nee Dai Done Sum Dai

Is there a car park near here?
ມີບ່ອນສຳລັບຈອດລົດຢູ່ໃກ້ໆນີ້ບໍ່?
Mee Born Sum Lab Jot Lot You Kai Kai Nee Bor

At what time does this car park close?
ບ່ອນຈອດລົດນີ້ຈະປິດເວລາຈັກໂມງ?
Born Jot Lot Nee Ja Pit Vey La Jak Mong

ທາງເລນດຽວ
Thung Lane Deo
One way

ຫ້າມເຂົ້າ
Harm Khao
No entry

ຫ້າມຈອດ
Harm Jort
No parking

ທາງລ້ຽວ (ທາງໄປທາຍສາຍ)
Thang Leo (Thang Lai Sai)
Detour (diversion)

ຢຸດ
Yout
Stop

ໃຫ້ທາງ (ໃຫ້ໄປກ່ອນ)
Hai Thang (Hui Pai Korn)
Give way (yield)

ທາງມື່ນ
Thang Meun
Slippery road

ບໍ່ໃຫ້ແຊງ
Bor Hai Xeng
No overtaking

ອັນຕະລາຍ!
Un Ta Lai
Danger!

At the Filling Station

Unleaded (lead-free) / standard / premium / diesel
ບໍ່ມີທາດຊືນ (ບໍ່ມີຊືນ) / ມາດຕະຖານ / ດີທີ່ສຸດ / ນ້ຳມັນດິເຊວ
Bor Mee Thad Seun (Bor Mee Thad Seun) / Mad Tha Than / Dee Thi Soud / Nam Man Dee Sel

Fill the tank please
ກະລຸນາຕື່ມນ້ຳມັນໃສ່ຖັງ
Ka Loo Na Teum Nam Man Sai Thang

Do you have a road map?
ເຈົ້າມີແຜນທີ່ຫົນທາງບໍ່?
Jao Mee Pand Thee Hon Thang Bor

How much is the car wash?
ລ້າງລົດລາຄາເທົ່າໃດ?
Lang Lot La Kha Thao Dai

Breakdowns

I've had a breakdown at ...
ຂ້ອຍຕ້ອງຈອດທີ່...
Khoi Tong Jort Thee ...

I am a member of the [motoring organisation]
ຂ້ອຍເປັນສະມາຊິກຂອງ [ສະມາຄົມລົດຍົນ]

Khoi Pen Sa Ma Xik Khong [Sa Ma Kom Lot Yon]

I am on the road from ... to ...
ຂ້ອຍຢູ່ໃນທາງລະຫວ່າງ ... ຫາ ...
Khoi You Nai La Wang ... Ha ...

I can't move the car. Can you send a tow-truck?
ຂ້ອຍຍ້າຍລົດບໍ່ໄດ້. ເຈົ້າສົ່ງ ລົດລາກມາໄດ້ບໍ່?
Khoi Yai Lot Bor Dai. Jao Song Lot Ma Dai Bor

I have a flat tyre
ລົດຂ້ອຍຢາງແຕກ
Lot Khoi Yarng Taek

The windscreen (windshield) has smashed / cracked
ກະຈົກບັງລົມ (ແກ້ວບັງລົມ) ໄດ້ແຕກມຸ່ນ / ແຕກຮ້າວ
Kam Bang Lom (Keo Bang Lom) Dai Taek Moun / Taek Hao

There is something wrong with the engine / brakes / lights / steering / gearbox / clutch / exhaust
ມີເຄື່ອງຈັກຜິດປົກກະຕິໜຶ່ງທີ່ເພຍເຊິ່ງແມ່ນ / ເບກ / ໄຟ / ພວງມະໄລລົດ / ກະປຸກເກຍ / ຄາດ / ທໍ່ໄອເສຍ
Mee Keung Jak Aunt Dai Aunt Neung Thii Phey Cheung Mean / Bek / Fai / Phoung Ma Lai Lot / Ka Puk Kai / Kad / Thor Khoun

It's overheating
ມັນຮ້ອນເກີນໄປ
Man Horn Keun Pai

It won't start
ມັນຕິດບໍ່ໄດ້
Man Tit Bor Dai

Where can I get it repaired?
ຂ້ອຍສາມາດໄປແປງຢູ່ບ່ອນໃດໄດ້?
Khoi Sa Mat Pai Paeng You Born Dai Daii

Can you take me there?
ເຈົ້າໄປສົ່ງຂ້ອຍບ່ອນນັ້ນໄດ້ບໍ້?
Jao Pai Song Khoi Born Nan Dai Bor

Will it take long to fix?
ຈະສ້ອມແປງມັນດົນບໍ້?
Ja Sorm Paeng Mun Don Bor

How much will it cost?
ລາຄາເທົ່າໃດ?
La Kha Thao Dai

Please can you pick me up / give me a lift?
ກະລຸນາຍົກຂ້ອຍຂຶ້ນແດ່ /
ເອົາອ້ມຍົກໃຫ້ຂ້ອຍແດ່?
Kaloona Yok Koy Keun Dae / Ao Aunt Yok Hai Koy Dae

Accidents and Traffic Offences

Can you help me? There has been an accident
ເຈົ້າສາມາດຊ່ວຍຂ້ອຍໄດ້ບໍ້?
ຢູ່ຫັ້ນເກີດອຸບັດຕິເຫດ
Jao Sa Mad Xouy Koy Dai Bor?
You Han Keut Ou Bat Ti Het

Please call the police / an ambulance
ກະລຸນາເອີ້ນຕຳຫຼວດ / ລົດພະຍາບານ
Kalouna Eun Tam Luat / Lot Pa Ya Barn

Is anyone hurt?
ມີໃຜໄດ້ຮັບບາດເຈັບ
Mee Pai Dae Dai Hap Bat Jep

I'm sorry, I didn't see the sign
ຂ້ອຍຂໍໂທດ, ຂ້ອຍບໍ່ເຫັນປ້າຍສັນຍານນີ້
Khoi Kor Thod, Koy Bor Hen Pai San Yarn Nee

Must I pay a fine? How much?
ຂ້ອຍຕ້ອງຈ່າຍຄ່າປັບໄໝບໍ້? ເທົ່າໃດ?
Khoi Tong Jai Kha Pap Mai Bor? Thao Dai

Show me your documents
ເອົາເອກະສານຂອງເຈົ້າໃຫ້ຂ້ອຍເບິ່ງແດ່
Ao Ae Ka Sarn Kong Jao Hai Khoi Beung Dae

Pharmacy

Do you have anything for a stomach ache / headache / sore throat / toothache?
ເຈົ້າມີຫຍັງສຳລັບບັນເທົາອາການ
ເຈັບທ້ອງ / ເຈັບຫົວ / ເຈັບຄໍ / ເຈັບແຂ້ວ?
Jao Mee Yang Bor Sam Lab Ban Thao Ar Karn Jeb Thong / Jeb Hua / Jeb Khor / Jeb Kheo

I need something for diarrhoea / constipation / a cold / a cough / insect bites / sunburn / travel (motion) sickness (car) (plane) (boat)
ຂ້ອຍຕ້ອງການບາງຢ່າງສຳລັບອາການ
ເຈັບຍ້ອນຖອກທ້ອງ / ທ້ອງຜູກ /
ໄຂ້ຫວັດ / ໄອ / ແມງໄມ້ກັດ / ແດດໄໝ /
ວິນວຽນ (ລົດ) (ຍົນ) (ເຮືອ)
Khoi Tong Karn Bang Yang Sam Lab Ar Karn Jeb Yorn Thok Thong / Thong Pouk / Khai Vat / Ai / Meng Mai Kat / Daet Mai / Veen Hua (Lot) (Yon) (Heu)

**L
A
O**

How much / how many do I take?
ຂ້ອຍຄວນຈະໃຊ້ຢາຫຼາຍຊ່ຳໃດ / ແນວໃດ?
Khoi Khoun Ja Xay Ya Lai Xam Dai / Neo Dai

How often do I take it / them?
ຂ້ອຍຄວນຈະກິນຢາ / ໃຊ້ມັນ ເລື້ອຍຊ່ຳໃດ?
Khoi Khoun Ja Kin Ya / Xai Mun Leui Leui Xum Dai

I am / he is / she is taking this medication
ຂ້ອຍ / ລາວໃຊ້ວິທີປິ່ນປົວນີ້
Khoi / Lao Xai Vi Thee Pin Pua Nee

How much does it cost?
ລາຄາມັນເທົ່າໃດ?
La Ka Man Thao Dai

Can you recommend a good doctor / dentist?
ເຈົ້າແນະນຳທ່ານໝໍ / ໝໍປົວແຂ້ວ ທີ່ດີໃຫ້ຂ້ອຍໄດ້ບໍ?
Jao Nae Num Than Mor / Mor Pua Kheo Thee Dee Hai Khoi Dai Bor

Is it suitable for children?
ມັນເໝາະສົມກັບເດັກນ້ອຍຫຼືບໍ?
Mum Morh Som Kab Dek Noy Leu Bor

Doctor

I have a pain here / in my arm / leg / chest / stomach
ຂ້ອຍໄດ້ຮັບບາດເຈັບຢູ່ນີ້ / ຢູ່ແຂນຂອງ ຂ້ອຍ / ຂາ / ເອິກ / ທ້ອງ
Khoi Dai Hab Bat Jeb You Nee / You Khen Khong Khoi / Kha / Euk / Thong

Please call a doctor, this is an emergency
ກະລຸນາໂທຫາທ່ານໝໍ, ອັນນີ້ແມ່ນ ກໍລະນີສຸກເສີນ
Kalouna Tho Ha Tharn Mor, Un Nee Maen Kor La Nee Souk Seun

I would like to make an appointment to see the doctor
ຂ້ອຍຢາກນັດທ່ານໝໍພົບກັບທ່ານໝໍ
Khoi Yak Nat Than Phob Kab Than Mor

I am diabetic / pregnant
ຂ້ອຍເປັນເບົາວານ / ຖືພາ
Khoi Pen Bao Varn / Theu Pha

I need a prescription for ...
ຂ້ອຍຕ້ອງການໃບສັ່ງຢາສຳລັບ ...
Khoi Tong Karn Bai Sang Ya Sam Lab ...

Can you give me something to ease the pain?
ເຈົ້າເອົາອັນໃດອັນນຶ່ງໃຫ້ຂ້ອຍເພື່ອບັນ ເທົາຄວາມເຈັບປວດໄດ້ບໍ?
Jao Ao Aunt Dai Aunt Neung Hai Khoi Pheu Ban Thao Khoum Jeb Pout Dai Bor

I am / he is / she is allergic to penicillin
ຂ້ອຍ / ລາວແພ້ຢາເປນີຊິລິນ
Khoi / Lao Pae Ya Peniciline

Does this hurt?
ມັນຈະເຈັບບໍ?
Mun Ja Jeb Bor

You must / he must / she must go to hospital
ເຈົ້າ / ລາວຈະຕ້ອງ / ລາວຈະຕ້ອງ ໄປໂຮງໝໍ
Jao / Lao Ja Tong / Lao Ja Tong / Pai Hong Mor

Take these once / twice / three times a day
ກິນນີ້ / ສອງ / ສາມຄັ້ງຕໍ່ມື້
Kin Neung / Song / Sam Khang Tor Meu

I am / he is / she is taking this medication
ຂ້ອຍ / ລາວໃຊ້ຢາ/ ລາວໃຊ້ຢາ ປິ່ນປົວແບບນີ້
Khoi / Lao Xai Karn / Lao Xai Karn Pin Pua Baeb Nee

I have medical insurance
ຂ້ອຍມີການປະກັນສຸຂະພາບ
Khoi Mee Karn Pa Kan Sou Kha Phab

Dentist

I have toothache
ຂ້ອຍເຈັບແຂ້ວ
Khoi Jeb Kheo

My filling has come out
ບ່ອນອັດແຂ້ວຂອງຂ້ອຍອອກແລ້ວ
Khoi Ard Kheo Khong Koy Ork Leo

I do / do not want to have an injection first
ຂ້ອຍຕ້ອງການ / ບໍ່ຕ້ອງການ ສັກຢາກ່ອນ
Khoi Tong Karn / Bor Tong Karn Sak Ya Korn

EMERGENCIES

Help!
ຊ່ອຍແດ່!
Xuay Dae

Fire!
ໄຟໄໝ້!
Fai Mai

Stop!
ຢຸດ!
Yout

Call an ambulance / a doctor / the police / the fire brigade!
ເອີ້ນລົດພະຍາບານ / ທ່ານໝໍ / ຕຳຫຼວດ / ກອງດັບເພີງ!
Ern Lot Pha Ya Barn / Tharn Mor / Tam Luat / Kong Dap Pheung

Please may I use a telephone?
ກະລຸນາໃຫ້ຂ້ອຍໃຊ້ໂທລະສັບໄດ້ບໍ່?
Kalouna Hai Koy Xai Tho La Sab Dai Bor

I have had my traveller's cheques / credit cards / handbag / rucksack / (knapsack) / luggage / wallet / passport / mobile phone stolen
ເຊັກເດີນທາງ / ບັດເຄຼດິດ / ຖົງພາຍ / ຖົງເປ້ / (ຖົງເປ້ຂອງນັກເດີນທາງ) / ຫີບເຄື່ອງຂອງ / ກະເປົາເງິນ / ປັດສປໍ / ໂທລະສັບມືຖືຂອງຂ້ອຍຖືກລັກ
Xek Deun Thang / Bat Crey Dit / Thong Phai / Thong Paey / (Thong Paey Khong Nak Deun Thang) / Heep Keung Khong / Ka Pao / Pad Sa Por / Tho La Sab Meu Theu Khong Khoi Theuk Lak

May I please have a copy of the report for my insurance claim?
ຂ້ອຍຂໍສຳເນົາຂອງການລາຍງານ ການຮຽກເກັບປະກັນໄພໄດ້ບໍ່?
Khoi Khor Sum Nao Khong Karn Lai Nguan Karn Heak Kep Pa Kan Phai Dai Bor

L A O

201

**L
A
O**

Can you help me? I have lost my daughter / my son / my companion(s)
ເຈົ້າຊ່ວຍຂ້ອຍໄດ້ບໍ? ລູກສາວ / ລູກຊາຍ / ເພື່ອນຮ່ວມທາງຂອງຂ້ອຍເສຍ
Jao Xuay Koy Dai Bor? Look Sao / Look Xai / Pheun Huam Thang Khong Khoi Sia

Please go away / leave me alone
ກະລຸນາໄປໄກຈາກຂ້ອຍ / ປ່ອຍ ຂ້ອຍຢູ່ຄົນດຽວ
Kalouna Pai Kai Jak Khoi / Poy Khoi You Kon Deo

I'm sorry
ຂ້ອຍຂໍໂທດ
Khoi Kor Thot

I want to contact the British / American / Canadian / Irish / Australian / New Zealand / South African consulate
ຂ້ອຍຕ້ອງການຕິດຕໍ່ກັບຫ້ອງການກົງສຸນ ຂອງອັງກິດ / ອາເມລິກາ / ການາດາ / ໄອຣ໌ແລນ / ອົດສຕາລີ / ນິວຊີແລນ / ອາເມລິກາໃຕ້
Khoi Tong Karn Tit Tor Kab Hong Karn Kong Soun Kong Ang Kit / America / Canada / Irish / Australia / New Zealand / Ah Merica Tai

I'm / we're / he is / she is ill / lost / injured
ຂ້ອຍ / ພວກເຮົາ / ລາວຜູ້ຊີງ ເຈັບ / ລາວຜູ້ຊາຍເຈັບ / ເສຍ / ບາດເຈັບ
Khoi / Phouk Hao / Lao Poo Nging Jeb / Lao Poo Sai Jeb / Sia / Bat Jeb

They are ill / lost / injured
ພວກເຂົາເຈັບ / ເສຍ / ບາດເຈັບ
Phouk Kao Jeb / Sia / Bat Jeb

202

MALAY
MELAYU

INTRODUCTION

Perched on the South China Sea, Malaysia is divided into two regions, West, also known as Peninsular Malaysia, and East Malaysia which shares Borneo with Brunei and Indonesia. There are 13 states and 2 federal territories (Kuala Lumpur and Labuan). Kuala Lumpur is the capital city.

The official language is Malay, known as Bahasa Melayu and is understood throughout the country, but there is also a mixture of English, Chinese, Mandarin and Hakka dialects, Cantonese, Tamil and numerous tribal languages.

Addresses for Travel and Tourist Information

Australia: Malaysia Tourism Promotion Board, Level 2, 171 Clarence Street, Sydney, New South Wales. Tel: 2 9299 4441/2/3; Fax: 2 9262 2026; Email: mtpb.sydney@tourism.gov.my

Canada: Malaysia Tourism Promotion Board, 1590-1111, West Georgia Street, Vancouver. Tel: 604 689 8899/Tel: 1 888 689 6872 (Toll-Free); Fax: 604 689 8804; Email: mtpb.vancouver@tourism.gov.my

UK: Malaysia Tourism Promotion Board, 57 Trafalgar Square, London WC2N 5DU. Tel: 020 7930 7932; Fax: 020 7930 9015; Email: mtpb.london@tourism.gov.my

USA: Malaysia Tourism Promotion Board, 818 West Seventh Street, Suite 970, California, Los Angeles. Tel: 213 689 9702; Fax: 213 689 1530; Email: mtpb.la@tourism.gov.my

MALAY

Malaysia Facts

CAPITAL: Kuala Lumpur

CURRENCY: Ringgit (1 RM = 100 sen)

OPENING HOURS: Department stores and supermarkets are usually open from 1000-2200 and shops 0930-1900. In Kuala Lumpur as well as in most major towns, there are several 24-hour stores. Bank hours: Mon-Fri from 1000-1500, Sat 0930-1130.

TELEPHONES: To dial in, Tel: 00 +60 + Area Code minus first zero. Outgoing, Tel: 00 and the Country Code.

EMERGENCY NUMBERS: Police / Ambulance Tel: 999; Fire Tel: 994

PUBLIC HOLIDAYS: Jan 1 – New Year's Day (except Johor, Kelantan, Terengganu, Kedah and Perlis); Apr 13 – Good Friday; May1 – Labour Day; May 9 – Vesak Day (except for Federal Territory of Labuan); June 6 – Birthday of Yang di-Pertuan Agong (King); July 23 – Maal Hijrah; Aug 31– National Day; Dec 25 – Christmas Day

Technical Language Hints

- Pronunciation of Malay is easy – there are no surprises as it reads very similarly to English.

- Keep on the lookout for English words to help understanding. They are frequently used in everyday language, often either with a simple change in spelling (k is substituted for c, for example) or in speech, with "lah" added onto the end of a word.

MALAY

**M
A
L
A
Y**

Alphabet	
A *Are*	B *Ber*
C *Char*	D *Der*
E *Err*	F *Fa*
G *Ger*	H *Ha*
I *Ee*	J *Jer*
K *Car*	L *Laa*
M *Mar*	N *Nar*
O *Oo*	P *Per*
Q *Ker*	R *Rar*
S *Sar*	T *Ter*
U *Woo*	V *Ver*
W *Waa*	X *There is no X in Malay*
Y *Ee*	Z *Zzz*

Basic Words and Phrases

Yes
Ya
Ee-Ya

No
Tidak
Tee-Duck

Please
Tolong
Tow-Long

Thank you
Terima kasih
Ter-Ree-Ma Car-Sayh

Hello
Apa khabar
Are-Par Car-Bar

Goodbye
Selamat tinggal
Sir-Lar-Mart Ting-Garl

Excuse me
Maaf
Mar-Arf

Sorry
Maaf
Mar-Arf

How
Bagaimana
Bar-Guy-Maa-Naa

When
Bila
Bee-Laa

Why
Kenapa
Ker-Naa-Paa

What
Apa
Aa-Paa

Who
Siapa
See-Aa-Paa

That's O.K.
Tidak mengapa
Tee-Dark Meng-A-Paa

Perhaps
Mungkin
Moong-Kin

To
Ke
Ker

From
Dari
Daa-Ree

Here
Sini
See-Nee

There
Sana
Saa-Naa

I don't understand
Saya tidak faham
Saa-Yaa Tee-Dark Far-Harm

I don't speak Malay
Saya tidak boleh bertutur bahasa Melayu
Saa-Yaa Tee-Dark Bow-Layh Ber-Too-Towr Baa-Haa-Saa Mer-Laa-You

Do you speak English?
Bolehkah anda bertutur bahasa Inggeris?
Bow-Layh-Car Arn-Daa Ber-Too-Towr Baa-Haa-Saa Ing-Gir-Race

Can you please write it down?
Bolehkah anda tulis di sini?
Bow-Layh-Car Arn-Daa Too-List Dee See-Nee

Please can you speak more slowly?
Bolehkah anda bercakap lebih perlahan?
Bow-Layh-Car Arn-Daa Ber-Cha-Carp Ler-Bay Per-Laa-Harn

Greetings

Good morning /
Good afternoon /
Good evening / Goodnight
Selamat pagi / Selamat tengah hari / Selamat petang / Selamat malam

Sir-Laa-Mart Par-Gee / Sir-Laa-Mart Terng-Aah Haa-Ree / Sir-Laa-Mart Per-Tarng / Sir-Laa-Mart Mar-Larm

Pleased to meet you
Saya gembira bertemu dengan anda
Saa-Yaa Gum-Bee-Raa Ber-Ter-Moo Derng-An Arn-Daa

How are you?
Apa khabar?
Are-Par Car-Bar

Well, thank you. And you?
Terima kasih. Anda ialah?
Ter-Ree-Ma Car-Sayh. Arn-Daa E-Ya-Laah

My name is ...
Nama saya ialah...
Naa-Maa Sa-Yaa E-Ya-Laah...

This is my friend / boyfriend / girlfriend / husband / wife / brother / sister
Ini kawan saya / teman lelaki saya / teman wanita saya / suami saya / isteri saya / abang saya / kakak saya
E-Nee Car-Waan Sar-Yaa / Ter-Marn Ler-Laa-Kee Sar-Yaa / Ter-Marn Waa-Nee-Taa Sar-Yaa / Sua-Mee Sar-Yaa / Is-Ter-Ree Sar-Yaa / Are-Barng Sar-Yaa / Car-Kaak Sar-Yaa

Where are you travelling to?
Ke mana anda hendak pergi?
Ker Mar-Naa Arn-Daa Hern-Duck Per-Gee

I am / we are going to...
Saya / kami hendak ke...
Sar-Yaa / Car-Mee Hern-Duck Ker...

**M
A
L
A
Y**

MALAY

How long are you travelling for?
Berapa lama anda akan pergi?
Ber-Raa-Par Lar-Mar Arn-Daa Are-Karn Per-Gee

Where do you come from?
Anda dari mana?
Arn-Daa Daar-Ree Mar-Nar

I am / we are from Australia / Britain / Canada / America
Saya / kami dari Australia / Britain / Kanada / Amerika
Sar-Yaa / Car-Mee Daar-Ree Australia / Britain / Car-Naa-Daa / Are-Mer-Ree-Car

We are on holiday
Kami sedang bercuti
Car-Mee Ser-Darng Ber-Choo-Tee

This is our first visit here
Ini pertama kali kami ke sini
Ee-Nee Per-Tar-Mar Car-Lee Car-Mee Ker See-Nee

How old are you?
Berapakah umur anda?
Ber-Raa-Par-Kaah Oo-Moor Arn-Daa

I am... years old
Saya berumur... tahun
Sar-Yaa Ber-Oo-Moor...Tar-Hoon

I am a businessman / business woman / doctor / journalist / manual worker / administrator / scientist / student / teacher
Saya seorang usahawan / usahanita / doktor / wartawan / pekerja lembur / pentadbir / saintis / pelajar / guru
Sar-Yaa Sir-Oo-Rung Oos-Har-One / Oos-Har-Nii-Taa / Doc-Toor / Waar-Tar-One / Per-Ker-Jar Lamb-Boor / Pen-Tard-Biir / Sa-In-Tease / Per-Lar-Jar / Goo-Roo

Would you like / may I have a cigarette?
Mahukah anda / bolehkah saya ambil sebatang rokok?
Mar-Hoo-Kaah Arn-Daa / Bow-Layh-Kaah Sar-Yaa Um-Bail Sir-Bar-Tongue Row-Coke

Do you mind if I smoke?
Boleh saya merokok?
Bow-Layh Sar-Yaa Mur-Row-Coke

Do you have a light?
Anda ada pemetik api?
Arn-Daaa Are-Daa Per-Mer-Tick Are-Pee

I am waiting for my husband / wife / boyfriend / girlfriend
Saya sedang menunggu suami / isteri / teman lelaki / teman wanita saya
Sar-Yaa Ser-Dung Mer-Noong-Goo Soo-A-Mee / Is-Ter-Ree / Ter-Marn Ler-Laa-Kee / Ter-Marn Waa-Nee-Taa Sar-Yaa

Days

Monday
Isnin
East-Nin

Tuesday
Selasa
Ser-Lar-Sar

Wednesday
Rabu
Rar-Boo

Thursday
Khamis
Kaa-Miss

Friday
Jumaat
Joo-Maa-Art

Saturday
Sabtu
Sub-Too

Sunday
Ahad
Are-Hart

208

Morning
Pagi
Par-Gee

Afternoon
Tengah hari
Terng-Ah Haaree

Evening
Petang
Per-Tarng

Night
Malam
Mar-Larm

Yesterday / Today / Tomorrow
Semalam / Hari ini / Esok
Ser-Mar-Larm / Haree Ee-Nee / A-Soak

Numbers

Zero
Sifar
See-Far

One
Satu
Sar-Too

Two
Dua
Doo-Aa

Three
Tiga
Tee-Gaa

Four
Empat
Erm-Part

Five
Lima
Lee-Mar

Six
Enam
Err-Num

Seven
Tujuh
Too-Jooh

Eight
Lapan
Lar-Parn

Nine
Sembilan
Surm-Bee-Larn

Ten
Sepuluh
Ser-Poo-Looh

Eleven
Sebelas
Ser-Bur-Laars

Twelve
Dua belas
Doo-Aa Bur-Laars

Thirteen
Tiga belas
Tee-Gaa Bur-Laars

Fourteen
Empat belas
Erm-Part Bur-Laars

Fifteen
Lima belas
Lee-Mar Bur-Laars

Sixteen
Enam belas
Err-Num Bur-Laars

Seventeen
Tujuh belas
Too-Jooh Bur-Laars

Eighteen
Lapan belas
Lar-Pun Bur-Laars

Nineteen
Sembilan belas
Surm-Bee-Larn Bur-Laars

Twenty
Dua puluh
Doo-Aa Poo-Looh

Twenty-one
Dua puluh satu
Doo-Aa Poo-Looh Sar-Too

Twenty-two
Dua puluh dua
Doo-Aa Poo-Looh Doo-Aa

Thirty
Tiga puluh
Tee-Gaa Poo-Looh

Forty
Empat puluh
Erm-Part Poo-Looh

Fifty
Lima puluh
Lee-Mar Poo-Looh

M
A
L
A
Y

209

Sixty
Enam puluh
Err-Num Poo-Looh

Seventy
Tujuh puluh
Too-Jooh Poo-Looh

Eighty
Lapan puluh
Lar-Pun Poo-Looh

Ninety
Sembilan puluh
Serm-Bee-Larn Poo-Looh

One hundred
Seratus
Ser-Rar-Toos

Five hundred
Lima ratus
Lee-Maa Rar-Toos

One thousand
Satu ribu
Sar-Too Ree-Boo

One million
Satu juta
Sar-Too Joo-Taa

Time

What time is it?
Pukul berapa sekarang?
Poo-Cool Ber-Rar-Paa Ser-Car-Rarng

It is ...
Sekarang pukul ...
Ser-Car-Rarng Poo-Cool ...

9.00
Sembilan
Serm-Bee-Larn

9.05
Sembilan lima minit
Serm-Bee-Larn Lee-Maa Mee-Neet

9.15
Sembilan suku
Serm-Bee-Larn Soo-Koo

9.20
Sembilan dua puluh
Serm-Bee-Larn Doo-Aa Poo-Looh

9.30
Sembilan setengah
Serm-Bee-Larn Ser-Terng-Aah

9.35
Sembilan tiga puluh lima
*Serm-Bee-Larn Tee-Gaa Poo-Looh
Lee-Maa*

9.40
Sembilan empat puluh
Serm-Bee-Larn Erm-Part Poo-Looh

9.45
Sembilan empat puluh lima
*Serm-Bee-Larn Erm-Part Poo-Looh
Lee-Maa*

9.50
Sembilan lima puluh
Serm-Bee-Larn Lee-Maa Poo-Looh

9.55
Sembilan lima puluh lima
*Serm-Bee-Larn Lee-Maa Poo-Looh
Lee-Maa*

12.00 / Midday / Midnight
Dua belas / Tengah hari /
Tengah malam
*Doo-Aa Ber-Laars / Terng-Ah Haaree /
Terng-Ah Mar-Larm*

Money

I would like to change these traveller's cheques / this currency
Saya mahu tukar cek pengembaraan ini / mata wang ini
Sar-Yaa Mar-Hoo Too-Car Check Perng-Erm-Baa-Raa-An Ee-Nee / Mar-Taa Waa-Ng Ee-Nee

How much commission do you charge? (What is the service charge?)
Berapa komisyen yang anda kenakan? (Berapa bayaran khidmatnya?)
Ber-Rar-Paa Commission Young Arn-Daa Ker-Naa-Karn (Ber-Rar-Paa Baa-Yaa-Rarn Hid-Mart-Nya)

Can I obtain money with my MasterCard?
Bolehkah saya dapatkan wang dari MasterCard saya?
Bow-Layh-Car Sar-Yaa Daar-Part-Karn Waa-Ng Daa-Ree Mastercard Sar-Yaa

Where is the nearest ATM?
Di manakah mesin ATM yang terdekat?
Dee Maa-Naa-Kah May-Sayn ATM Young Ter-Der-Kart

My name is ... Some money has been wired to here for me to collect
Nama saya... Saya mahu mengambil wang yang dikirimkan kepada saya di sini
Naa-Maa Sar-Yaa... Sar-Yaa Maa-Hoo Meerng-Arm-Bill Waa-Ng Young Dee-Kee-Reem-Karn Kee-Paa-Daa Sar-Ya Dee See-Nee

Airport

Excuse me, where is the check-in desk for ... airline?
Maaf, di mana kaunter mendaftar untuk pesawat ...
Mar-Arf, Dee Mar-Naa Counter Mern-Duft-Tar Oon-Took Per-Saa-Waart ...

What is the boarding gate / time for my flight?
Apakah pintu masuk / masa untuk penerbangan saya?
Are-Paa-Kaah Pin-Too Maa-Sook / Maa-Saa Oon-Took Pern-Ner-Barng-Arn Saa-Yaa

How long is the delay likely to be?
Berapa lama lagi akan ditunda?
Ber-Rar-Paa Lar-Maa Lar-Gee Are-Karn Dee-Toon-Daa

Where is the duty-free shop?
Di manakah kedai bebas cukai?
Dee Maa-Naa-Kaah Ker-Dye Bay-Bus Choo-Kye

Which way is the baggage reclaim?
Ke mana arah ke kaunter menuntut bagasi?
Ker Maa-Naa Are-Raah Ker Counter Mer-Noon-Toot Bar-Gar-See

I have lost my luggage. Please can you help?
Saya kehilangan beg. Boleh anda tolong?
Sar-Yaa Ker-Hee-Larng-Arn Beg. Bow-Layh Arn-Daa Tow-Loong

MALAY

MALAY

I am flying to...
Saya akan terbang ke...
Sar-Yaa Are-Karn Ter-Barng Ke...

Where can I get the bus to the city centre?
Di mana boleh saya ambil bas ke pusat bandar?
Dee Maa-Naa Bow-Layh Sar-Yaa Arm-Bill Bus Ker Poo-Sart Barn-Daar

Trains and Boats

Where is the ticket office / information desk?
Di mana pejabat tiket / meja pertanyaan?
Dee Maa-Naa Per-Jaa-Bart Ticket / May-Jaa Per-Tarn-Yar-Aan

Which platform does the train / speedboat / ferry to ... depart from?
Keretapi / bot laju / feri ke... akan berlepas dari platform yang mana?
Ker-Ray-Taa-Pee / Boat Laa-Joo / Ferry Ker... Are-Karn Ber-Ler-Pass Daa-Ree Platform Young Maa-Naa

Where is platform ...?
Di mana platform...
Dee Maa-Naa Platform...

When is the next train / boat to ...?
Bilakah keretapi / bot yang berikutnya akan ke...
Bee-Laa-Kaah Ker-Ray-Taa-Pee / Boat Young Ber-Ee-Koot-Nyaa Are-Karn Ker...

Is there a later train / boat to ...?
Adakah keretapi / bot yang selepas ini?
Are-Der-Kaah Ker-Ray-Taa-Pee / Boat Young Ser-Ler-Pass Ee-Nee

Notices and Signs

Kereta buffet (Hidangan)
Ker-Ray-Taa Buffet (Hee-dung-arn)
Buffet (Dining) car

Bas
Bus
Bus

Air minum / air yang tidak boleh diminum
Are-Ayr Mee-Noom / Are-Ayr Young Tee-Dark Bow-Layh Dee-Mee-Noom
Drinking / Non-drinking water

Pintu masuk
Pin-Too Maa-Sook
Entrance

Pintu keluar
Pin-Too Ke-Loo-Are
Exit

Hospital
Hospital
Hospital

Informasi
Infor-Maa-See
Information

Bagasi yang tertinggal (Tuntut bagasi)
Baa-Gaa-See Young Ter-Ting-Garl (Toon-Toot Bar-Gaa-See)
Left luggage (Baggage claim)

Almari bagasi
Al-Maa-Ree Baa-Gaa-See
Luggage lockers

Pejabat pos
Per-Jaa-Bart Post
Post office

Platform
Platform
Platform

Stesen kereta api
Station Ker-Ray-Taa-Pee
Railway (Railroad) station

Lapangan terbang
Laa-Parng-Aan Ter-Barng
Airport

Balai polis
Bar-Lye Police
Police station

Pelabuhan
Per-Laa-Boo-Harn
Port

Restoran
Rest-Tore-Rarn
Restaurant

Merokok / Tidak merokok
Mur-Row-Coke /
Tee-Dark Mur-Row-Coke
Smoking / Non-smoking

Telefon
Telephone
Telephone

Pejabat tiket
Per-Jaa-Bart Ticket
Ticket office

Meja mendaftar
May-Jer Mern-Duff-Tar
Check-in desk

Jadual
Jaa-Doo-Aall
Timetables (Schedules)

Tandas
Tarn-Dust
Toilets (Restrooms)

Tandas wanita / Tandas lelaki
Tarn-Dust Waa-Nee-Tar / Tarn-Dust
Ler-Laa-Key
Ladies / Gentlemen

Kereta api bawah tanah
Ker-Ray-Taa-Pee Baa-Waah
Taa-Naah
Underground (Subway)

Bilik menunggu
Bee-Lick Mer-Noong-Goo
Waiting room

Buying a ticket

I would like a first-class / second-class single (oneway) / return (round-trip) ticket to ...
Saya mahu tiket kelas pertama / kelas kedua sehala / dua hala ke ...
Saa-Yaa Maa-Who Ticket Ker-Lars
Per-Taa-Maa / Ker-Lars Ker-Doo-Aa
Ser-Haa-Laa / Doo-Aa Haa-Laa Ker ...

Is it an express (fast) train / bus?
Adakah ini kereta api / bas ekspress?
Are-Daa-Kaah Ee-Nee Ker-Ray-Taa-Pee /
Bus Express

**M
A
L
A
Y**

213

**M
A
L
A
Y**

Is my rail pass valid on this train / ferry / bus?
Adakah pas saya sah untuk kereta api / feri / bas ini?
Are-Daa-Kah Pass Saa-Yaa Saah Oon-Took Ker-Ray-Taa-Pee / Ferry / Bus Ee-Nee

I would like an aisle / window seat
Saya mahu tempat duduk lorong / tingkap
Saa-Yaa Maa-Who Term-Part Doo-Dook Low-Roong / Ting-Cup

No smoking / smoking, please
Maaf, tidak boleh merokok / merokok
Maa-Aarf, Tee-Dark Bow-Layh Mur-Row-Coke / Mur-Row-Coke

We would like to sit together
Kami mahu duduk bersama
Car-Mee Maa-Who Doo-Dook Ber-Saa-Maa

I would like to make a seat reservation
Saya mahu membuat tempahan tempat duduk
Saa-Yaa Maa-Who Merm-Boo-Art Term-Paa-Harn Term-Part Doo-Dook

I would like to reserve a couchette / sleeper for one person / two people / my family
Saya mahu membuat tempahan bagi kursandar / tempat tidur untuk seorang / dua orang / keluarga saya
Saa-Yaa Maa-Who Merm-Boo-Art Term-Paa-Harn Baa-Gee Koor-Sarn-Daar / Term-Part Tee-Dour Oon-Took Ser-Oo-Rung / Doo-Aa Oo-Rung / Ker-Loo-Are-Gaa Saa-Yaa

I would like to reserve a cabin
Saya mahu membuat tempahan sebuah kabin
Saa-Yaa Maa-Who Merm-Boo-Art Term-Paa-Harn Ser-Boo-Ah Cabin

Timetables (Schedules)

Ketibaan
Ker-Tee-Baa-Aarn
Arrive

Hentian di...
Hern-Tee-Aan Dee...
Calls (Stops) at ...

Khidmat catering
Hid-Mart Catering
Catering service

Tukar di
Too-Car Dee...
Change at ...

Sambungan / Melalui
Sarm-Boong-An / Mer-Laa-Loo-Ee
Connection / Via

Setiap Hari
Ser-Tee-Arp Haa-Ree
Daily

Setiap 40 minit
Ser-Tee-Arp 40 Mee-Neet
Every 40 minutes

Kelas pertama
Ker-Last Per-Taa-Maa
First class

Setiap jam
Ser-Tee-Arp Jarm
Hourly

214

Dicadangkan untuk menempah tempat duduk
Dee-Cha-Darng-Karn Oon-Took Mer-Nerm-Parh Term-Part Doo-Dook
Seat reservations are recommended

Kelas kedua
Ker-Last Ker-Doo-Aa
Second class

Tambahan mesti dibayar
Tum-Baa-Harn Meers-Tee Dee-Bar-Yaar
Supplement payable

Luggage

How much will it cost to send (ship) my luggage in advance?
Berapa harga untuk menghantar beg saya dahulu?
Ber-Rar-Paa Haar-Gaa Oon-Took Merng-Harn-Tar Bag Saa-Yaa Daa-Who-Loo

Where is the left luggage (baggage claim) office?
Di manakah pejabat untuk menuntut bagasi?
Dee Maa-Naa-Kaah Per-Jaa-Bart Oon-Took Mer-Noon Toot Baa-Gaa-See

What time do you open / close?
Jam berapa anda buka / tutup?
Jarm Ber-Raa-Paa Arn-Daa Boo-Car / Too-Toop

Where are the luggage trolleys (carts)?
Di manakah troli bagasi?
Dee Maa-Naa-Kaah Trolley Baa-Gaa-See

Where are the lockers?
Di mana almari?
Dee Maa-Naa Al-Maa-Ree

I have lost my locker key
Kunci almari saya hilang
Koon-Chee Al-Maa-Ree Saa-Yaa Hee-Lung

On Board

Is this seat free?
Tidak ada orang duduk di sini?
Tee-Dark Are-Daa Oo-Rung Doo-Dook Dee See-Nee

Excuse me, you are sitting in my reserved seat
Maaf, anda duduk di kerusi yang saya sudah tempah
Mar-Arf, Arn-Daa Doo-Dook Dee Ker-Roo-See Young Saa-Yaa Soo-Daah Term-Paah

Which station is this?
Ini stesen yang mana?
Ee-Nee Station Young Maa-Naa

What time is this train / bus / ferry / flight due to arrive / depart?
Pukul berapa kereta api / bas / feri / pesawat ini akan tiba / berangkat?
Poo-Cool Ber-Raa-Paa Ker-Ray-Tar-Are-Pee / Bus / Ferry / Per-Saa-Wart Ee-Nee Are-Karn Tee-Baa / Ber-Aang-Kart

M A L A Y

Travelling with Children

Do you have a high chair / babysitting service / cot?
Adakah anda ada kerusi tinggi / khidmat jagaan anak / katil bayi?
Are-Daa-Kaah Arn-Daa Are-Daa Ker-Roo-See Ting-Gee / Hid-Mart Jaa-Gaa-Aan Are-Nark / Car-Teel Baa-Ee

Where is the nursery / playroom?
Di manakah bilik kanak-kanak / bilik permainan?
Dee Maa-Naa-Kaah Bee-Leek Car-Nark-Car-Nark / Bee-Leek Per-Maa-In-Narn

Where can I warm the baby's bottle?
Di mana boleh saya hangatkan botol bayi?
Dee Maa-Naa Bow-Layh Saa-Yaa Harng-Art-Karn Bo-Toll Baa-Ee

Customs and Passports

Passports, please!
Pasport!
Passport

I have nothing / wine / spirits (alcohol) / tobacco to declare
Saya tidak ada apa-apa / wain / alcohol / rokok untuk diisytiharkan
Saa-Yaa Tee-Dark Are-Daa Are-Par Are-Par / Wine / Alcohol / Row-Coke Oon-Took Dee-Isyy-Tee-Haar-Karn

I will be staying for ... days / weeks / months
Saya akan tinggal untuk ...hari / minggu / bulan
Saa-Yaa Are-Karn Ting-Garl Oon-Took ...Har-Ree / Ming-Goo / Boo-Laan

Asking the Way

Excuse me, do you speak English?
Maaf, anda boleh berbahasa Inggeris?
Mar-Arf, Arn-Daa Bow-Layh Ber-Baa-Haa-Saa Ing-Ger-Riis

Excuse me, can you help me please?
Maaf, boleh tolong saya?
Mar-Arf, Bow-Layh Tow-Long Saa-Yaa

Where is the Tourist Information Office?
Di mana Pejabat Penerangan Pelancong?
Dee Maa-Naa Per-Jaa-Bart Per-Neer-Rung-Aan Per-Larn Choong

Excuse me, is this the right way to ...?
Maaf, adakah ini jalan yang betul ke...
Mar-Arf, Are-Daa-Kaah Ee-Nee Jar-Larn Young Ber-Tool Ker...

... the cathedral / the tourist information office / the castle / the old town
... gereja / pejabat penerangan pelancong / istana / bandar lama
... Ger-Ray-Jaa / Per-Jaa-Bart Per-Ner-Rung-Aan Per-Larn-Choong / Is-Taa-Naa / Barn-Daar Laa-Maa

Can you tell me the way to the railway (railroad) station / bus station / taxi rank (stand) / city centre (downtown) / beach?
Boleh anda tunjukkan saya arah ke stesen kereta api / stesen bas / perhentian teksi / pusat bandar / pantai?

216

Bow-Layh Arn-Daa Toon-Jook-Karn Saa-Yaa Are-Raah Ker Station Ker-Ray-Tar-Pee / Station Bus / Per-Hern-Tee-Aan Taxi / Poo-Saat Barn-Daar / Parn-Thai

First / second / left / right / straight ahead
Pertama / kedua / kiri / kanan / jalan terus
Per-Taa-Maa / Ker-Doo-Aa / Kee-Ree / Kaa-Narn / Jar-Larn Ter-Oos

At the corner / at the traffic lights
Di simpang / di lampu trafik
Dee Sim Parng / Dee Laarm-Poo Traffic

Where is the nearest police station / post office?
Di manakah balai polis / pejabat pos yang berdekatan?
Dee Maa-Naa-Kaah Bar-Lye Police / Per-Jaa-Bart Post Young Ber-Der-Kaa-Tarn

Is it near / far?
Adakah ia dekat / jauh?
Are-Daa-Kaah Ee-Yaa Der-Kart / Jaa-Ooh

Do I need to take a taxi / catch a bus?
Perlukah saya naik teksi / bas?
Per-Loo-Kaah Saa-Yaa Naa-Eek Taxi / Bus

Do you have a map?
Anda ada peta?
Arn-Daa Are-Daa Per-Taa

Can you point to it on my map?
Bolehkah anda tunjukkan di peta saya?
Bow-Layh-Kaah Arn-Daa Toon-Jook-Karn Dee Per-Taa Saa-Yaa

Thank you for your help
Terima kasih kerana menolong
Ter-Ree-Maa Car-Sayh Ker-Rar-Na Mer-No-Loong

How do I reach the motorway / main road?
Bagaimana saya hendak ke jalan raya / jalan raya utama?
Baa-Guy-Maa-Naa Saa-Yaa Hern-Duck Ker Jaa-Larn Rar-Yaa / Jaa-Larn Rar-Yaa Oo-Taa-Maa

I think I have taken the wrong turning
Saya fikir saya sudah tersalah jalan
Saa-Yaa Pee-Kayr Saa-Yaa Soo-Daah Ter-Saa-Laah Jaa-Laan

I am looking for this address
Saya sedang mencari alamat ini
Saa-Yaa Ser-Darng Mern-Char-Ree Are-Laa-Mat Ee-Nee

I am looking for the ... hotel
Saya sedang mencari hotel...
Saa-Yaa Ser-Darng Mern-Charee Hotel...

How far is it to ... from here?
Berapa jauhkah ...dari sini?
Ber-Rar-Par Jaa-Ooh-Kaah Ker ... Daa-Ree See Nee

Carry straight on for ... kilometres
Jalan terus sejauh ...kilometer
Jar-Larn Ter-Roos Ser-Jaa-Ooh ... Kilometre

Take the next turning on the right / left
Di hadapan, belok kiri / kanan
Dee Haa-Daa-Parn, Bay Loke Kee-Ree / Kaa-Narn

M A L A Y

217

MALAY

Turn right / left at the next crossroads / traffic lights
Belok kanan / kiri di simpang / lampu trafik yang berikutnya
Bay-Loke Kaa-Narn / Kee-Ree Dee Sim-Parng / Laam-Poo Traffic Young Ber-Ee-Coat-Nya

You are going in the wrong direction
Anda menuju ke arah yang salah
Arn-Daa Mer-Noo-Joo Ker Are-Rah Young Sar-Laah

Where is the cathedral / church / museum / pharmacy?
Di manakah gereja / gereja / muzium / farmasi?
Dee Maa-Naa-Kaah Gerr-Ray-Jaa / Gerr-Ray-Jaa / Moo-Zee-Oom / Far-Maa-See

How much is the admission / entrance charge?
Berapa bayaran masuk?
Ber-Raa-Paa Baa-Yaa-Rarn Maa-Sook

Is there a discount for children / students / senior citizens?
Adakah diskaun bagi kanak-kanak / pelajar / warga tua?
Are-Daa-Kaah Discount Baa-Gee Car-Nack-Car-Nack / Per-Laa-Jar / War-Gaa Too-Aa

What time does the next guided tour (in English) start?
Pukul berapa guided tour (Inggeris) berikutnya akan bermula?
Poo-Cool Ber-Raa-Paa Guided Tour (Ing-Ger-Rees) Ber-Ree-Coat-Nya Are-Karn Ber-Moo-Laa

One / two adults / children, please
Satu / dua orang dewasa / kanak-kanak
Saa-Too / Doo-Aa Owe-Rung Day-Waa-Saa / Car-Nack-Car-Nack

May I take photographs here?
Bolehkah saya ambil gambar di sini?
Bow-Layh-Kaah Saa-Yaa Um-Bail Gum-Baar Dee See-Nee

At the Tourist Office

Do you have a map of the town / area?
Anda ada peta bandar / kawasan ini?
Arn-Daa Are-Daa Per-Taa Bund-Daar / Car-Waa-Son Ee-Nee

Do you have a list of accommodation?
Anda ada senarai tempat penginapan?
Arn-Daa Are-Daa Ser-Naa-Rye Term-Part Peng-Ee-Naa-Paan

Can I reserve accommodation?
Bolehkah saya menempah tempat penginapan?
Bow-Layh-Kaah Saa-Yaa Mer-Nerm-Paah Term-Part Peng-Ee-Naa-Paan

ACCOMMODATION

Hotels

I have a reservation in the name of ...
Saya ada tempahan atas nama ...
Saa-Yaa Are-Daa Term-Paa-Haan Are-Tars Nar-Mar ...

I wrote to / faxed / telephoned you last month / last week

Saya telah menulis / faks / telefon anda bulan lepas / minggu lepas
Saa-Yaa Ter-Laah Mer-Noo-Lees / Fax / Telephone Arn-Daa Boo-Larn Ler-Pass / Meeng-Goo Ler-Pass

Do you have any rooms free?
Ada bilik yang kosong?
Are-Daa Bee-Leek Young Co-Song

I would like to reserve a single / double room with / without bath / shower
Saya mahu tempah satu / dua bilik dengan / tanpa tab mandi / paip mandi
Saa-Yaa Mar-Who Tem-Paah Sar Too / Doo-Aa Bee-Lake Derng-Aan / Tarn-Paa Tub Marn-Dee / Pipe Marn-Dee

I would like bed and breakfast / (room and) full board
Saya mahu bilik dan sarapan / (bilik dan) makanan lengkap
Saa-Yaa Mar-Who Bee-Layk Darn Sar-Rar-Parn / (Bee-Layk Darn) Mar-Car-Narn Lerng-Carp

How much is it per night?
Berapa harga untuk satu malam?
Ber-Rar-Paa Haar-Gaa Oon-Took Sar-Too Mar-Larm

Is breakfast included?
Adakah termasuk sarapan?
Are-Daa-Kaah Ter-Mar-Sook Sar-Rar-Parn

Do you have any cheaper rooms?
Ada bilik yang lebih murah?
Are-Daa Bee-Layk Young Ler-Bayh Moo-Raah

I would like to see / take the room
Saya mahu melihat / menempah bilik itu

Saa-Yaa Mar-Who Mer-Lee-Hart / Mer-Nerm-Paah Bee-Layk Ee-Too

I would like to stay for ...nights
Saya mahu menginap untuk ...malam
Saa-Yaa Mar-Who Merng-Ee-Narp Oon-Took ...Mar-Larm

The shower / light / tap / hot water doesn't work
Paip mandi / lampu / paip / air panas rosak
Pipe Marn-Dee / Larm-Poo / Pipe / Are-Ayr Par-Nars Row-Sark

At what time / where is breakfast served?
Pukul berapa / di mana sarapan dihidangkan?
Poo-Cool Ber-Rar-Paa / Dee Mar-Naa Sar-Rar-Parn Dee-Hee-Darng-Karn

What time do I have to check out?
Pukul berapa harus saya keluar?
Poo-Cool Ber-Rar-Paa Har-Rose Saa-Yaa Ker-Loo-Aar

Can I have the key to room number ... ?
Boleh saya dapatkan kunci bilik nombor ... ?
Bow-Layh Saa-Yaa Dar-Part-Karn Koon-Chee Bee-Layk Norm-Boor ...

My room number is ...
Nombor bilik saya ...
Norm-Boor Bee-Layk Saa-Yaa ...

My room is not satisfactory / not clean enough / too noisy
Bilik saya tidak memuaskan / tidak cukup bersih / terlalu bising
Bee-Layk Saa-Yaa Tee-Dark Mer-Moo-Arss-Karn / Tee-Dark Choo-Kope Ber-Sayh / Ter-Laa-Loo Bee-Singh

M
A
L
A
Y

219

**M
A
L
A
Y**

Please can I change rooms?
Maaf, bolehkah saya tukar bilik?
Mar-Arf, Bow-Layh-Kaah Saa-Yaa Too-Car Bee-Layk

Where is the bathroom?
Di mana bilik mandi?
Dee Mar-Naa Bee-Layk Marn-Dee

Do you have a safe for valuables?
Adakah anda ada peti simpanan untuk barang berharga?
Are-Daa-Kah Arn-Daa Are-Daa Per-Tee Seem-Paa-Narn Oon-Took Bar-Rarng Ber-Har-Gaa

Is there a laundry / do you wash clothes?
Adakah terdapat tempat mencuci pakaian / anda mencuci pakaian?
Are-Daa-Kaah Ter-Daa-Part Term-Part Men-Choo-Chee Par-Car-Yarn / Arn-Daa Men-Choo-Chee Par-Car-Yarn

I would like an air-conditioned room
Saya mahu bilik berhawa dingin
Saa-Yaa Mar-Who Bee-Lake Ber-Haa-Waa Ding-Een

Do you accept traveller's cheques / credit cards?
Anda terima cek pengembaraan / kad kredit?
Arn-Daa Ter-Ree-Maa Check Perng-Erm-Baa-Raa-Arn / Card Credit

May I have the bill please?
Boleh saya dapatkan bil?
Bow-Layh Saa-Yaa Daa-Part-Karn Bill

Excuse me, I think there may be a mistake in this bill
Maaf, saya rasa ada kesilapan pada bil ini?

Mar-Arf, Saa-Yaa Rar-Saa Are-Daa Ker-See-Laa-Parn Par-Daa Bill Ee-Nee

Youth Hostels

How much is a dormitory bed per night?
Berapa harga sebuah katil dormitori untuk satu malam?
Ber-Rar-Par Haar-Gaa Ser-Boo-Aah Car-Tail Dormitory Oon-Took Saa-Too Mar-Lum

I am / am not an HI member
Saya seorang / bukan seorang ahli HI
Saa-Yaa Ser-Oo-Rarng / Boo-Karn Ser-Oo-Rarng Aah-Lee HI

May I use my own sleeping bag?
Bolehkah saya gunakan beg tidur saya?
Bow-Layh-Kah Saa-Yaa Goo-Naa-Karn Bag Tee-Dour Saa-Yaa

What time do you lock the doors at night?
Pukul berapa anda kunci pintu pada waktu malam?
Poo-Cool Ber-Rar-Par Arn-Daa Koon-Chee Pin-Too Paa-Daa Wark-Too Mar-Larm

Camping

May I camp for the night / two nights?
Bolehkah saya berkhemah untuk malam ini / dua malam?
Bow-Layh-Kaah Saa-Yaa Ber-Kay-Maarh Oon-Took Mar-Larm Ee-Nee / Doo-Aa Mar-Larm

**M
A
L
A
Y**

Where can I pitch my tent?
Di mana boleh saya dirikan khemah saya?
Dee Mar-Naa Bow-Layh Saa-Yaa Dee-Ree-Karn Kay-Maarh Saa-Yaa

How much does it cost for one night / week?
Berapa harga untuk satu malam / minggu?
Ber-Rar-Paa Haar-Gaa Oon-Took Saa-Too Mar-Larm / Meeng-Goo

Where are the washing facilities?
Di mana kemudahan membasuh?
Dee Maa-Naa Ke-Moo-Daa-Harn Merm-Baa-Soh

Is there a restaurant / supermarket / swimming pool on site / nearby?
Adakah terdapat restoran / pasaraya / kolam renang di sini / yang berdekatan?
Are-Daa-Kaah Ter-Daa-Part Rest-Tore-Run / Paa-Sar-Raa-Ya / Kor-Larm-Rer-Narng Dee-See-Nee / Young Ber Der-Kaa-Tarn

Do you have a safety deposit box?
Anda ada peti simpanan?
Arn-Daa Are-Daa Per-Tee Sim-Par-Narn

Cafés and Bars

I would like a cup of / two cups of / another coffee / tea
Saya mahu secawan / dua cawan / satu lagi kopi / teh
Saa-Yaa Mar-Who Ser-Char-Waan / Doo-Aa Char-Waan / Saa-Too Laa-Gee Ko-Pee / Tayh

With / without milk / sugar
Dengan / tanpa susu / gula
Derng-Arn / Tarn-Paa Soo-Soo / Goo-Laa

I would like a bottle / glass / two glasses of mineral water / red wine / white wine, please
Saya mahu sebotol / segelas / dua gelas air mineral / wain merah / wain putih
Saa-Yaa Mar-Who Ser-Bo-Toll / Ser-Ger-Lars / Doo-Aa Ger-Lars Are-Ayr Mineral / Wine May-Raah / Wine Poo-Tayh

I would like a beer / two beers, please
Saya mahu sebotol bir / dua botol bir
Saa-Yaa Mar-Who Ser-Bo-Toll Biir / Doo-Aa Bo-Toll Biir

Please may I have some ice?
Boleh saya minta air batu?
Bow-Layh Saa-Yaa Mint-Taa Are-Ayr Baa-Too

Do you have any matches / cigarettes / cigars?
Adakah anda ada sebatang mancis / rokok / cerut?
Are-Daa-Kah Arn-Daa Are-Daa Scr Bar Tarng Marn-Cheese / Row-Coke / Cher-Root

Restaurants

Can you recommend a good / cheap restaurant in this area?
Bolehkah anda cadangkan sebuah restoran yang bagus / murah di kawasan ini?
Bow-Layh-Kah Arn-Daa Char-Darng-Karn Ser-Boo-Ah Rest-Tor-Rarn Young Bar-Ghost / Moo-Rarh Dee Kar-Waa-Sarn Ee-Nee

221

**M
A
L
A
Y**

I would like a table for ... people
Saya mahu meja untuk ...orang
*Saa-Yaa Mar-Who May-Jar Oon-Took
...O-Rarng*

**Do you have a non-smoking
area?**
Adakah ada kawasan tanpa merokok
di sini?
*Are-Daa-Kaah Are-Daa Kar-Waa-Son
Tarn-Paa Mer-Row-Coke Dee See-Nee*

Waiter / Waitress!
Pelayan / Pelayan
Per-Laa-Yarn / Per-Laa-Yarn

**Excuse me, please may we
order?**
Maaf, boleh kami buat pesanan?
*Mar-Arf, Bow-Layh Car-Mee Boo-Art
Per-Saa-Narn*

**Do you have a set menu /
children's menu / wine list?**
Anda ada menu set /
menu kanak-kanak / senarai wain?
*Arn-Daa Are-Daa Menu Set / Menu
Car-Nack-Car-Nack / Ser-Naa-Rye Wine*

**Do you have any vegetarian
dishes?**
Adakah anda ada makanan
sayur-sayuran?
*Are-Daa-Kaah Arn-Daa Are-Daa
Mar-Car-Narn Sar-Your-Sar-Your-Aan*

**Do you have any local
specialities?**
Adakah anda ada makanan tempatan?
*Are-Daa-Kaah Arn-Daa Are-Daa
Mar-Car-Narn Term-Par-Tarn*

Are vegetables included?
Adakah termasuk sayur-sayuran?
*Are-Daa-Kaah Ter-Maa-Sook
Sar-Your-Sar-Your-Aan*

**Could I have it well-cooked /
medium / rare please?**
Boleh saya minta dimasak penuh /
sederhana masak / setengah masak?
*Bow-Layh Saa-Yaa Mint-Taa Dee-Mar-
Sark Per-Nooh / Ser-Der-Haa-Naa
Mar-Sark / Ser-Terng-Aah Mar-Sark*

What does this dish consist of?
Apa yang ada dalam hidangan ini?
*Are-Paa Young Are-Daa Dar-Lum
Hee-Darng-An Ee-Nee*

**I am a vegetarian. Does this
contain meat?**
Saya seorang pemakan sayur. Adakah
ini ada daging?
*Saa-Yaa Ser-Oo-Rarng Per-Mar-Karn
Saa-Your. Are-Daa-Kah Ee-Nee Are-Daa
Dar-Geeng*

**I do not eat nuts /
dairy products / meat / fish**
Saya tidak makan kacang / produk
tenusu / daging / ikan
*Saa-Yaa Tee-Dark Mar-Karn
Kar-Chang / Pro-Duuk Ter-Noo-Soo /
Dar-Geeng / Ee-Karn*

Not (very) spicy, please
Jangan (terlalu) pedas
Jarng-Aan (Ter-Laa-Loo) Per-Dast

I would like the set menu, please
Saya mahu menu set
Saa-Yaa Mar-Who Menu Set

We are still waiting to be served
Kami masih menunggu untuk dilayan
*Car-Mee Mar-Sayh Mer-Noong-Goo
Oon-Took Dee-Laa-Yarn*

Please bring a plate / knife / fork
Tolong bawa satu pinggan / pisau / garfu
Tow-Long Bar-Waa Saa-Too Ping-Garn / Pee-Sarw / Gar-Foo

Excuse me, this is not what I ordered
Maaf, ini bukan yang saya pesan
Mar-Arf, Ee-Nee Boo-Karn Young Saa-Yaa Per-Sarn

May I have some / some more bread / water / coffee / tea?
Saya mahu sedikit / sedikit lagi roti / air / kopi / teh?
Saa-Yaa Mar-Who Ser-Dee-Keet / Ser-Dee-Keet Lar-Gee Row-Tee / Are-Ayr / Ko-Pee / Tayh

May I have the bill, please?
Tolong beri bil saya?
Tow-Long Ber-Ree Bill Saa-Yaa

Does this bill include service?
Adakah bil ini termasuk bayaran perkhidmatan?
Are-Daa-Kaah Bill Ee-Nee Ter-Maa-Sook Bar-Yar-Rarn Per-Hid-Maa-Tarn

Do you accept traveller's cheques / MasterCard / US dollars?
Adakah anda terima cek pengembaraan / MasterCard / mata wang Amerika?
Are-Daa-Kaah Am-Daa Ter-Ree-Maa Check Peng-Erm-Baa-Raa-An / MasterCard / Maa-Taa Warng Are-Mer-Ree-Kaa

Can I have a receipt, please?
Boleh saya dapatkan resitnya?
Bow-Layh Saa-Yaa Dar-Part-Karn Ree-Sit-Nnya

Where is the toilet (restroom), please?
Di mana tandas?
Dee Maa-Naa Tarn-Dast

On the Menu

Sarapan / makan tengah hari / makan malam
Sar-Rar-Parn / Mar-Karn Terng-Ah-Haa-Ree / Mar-Karn Mar-Larm
Breakfast / Lunch / Dinner

Hidangan pertama
Hee-Darng-Aan Per-Tar-Maa
First courses

Sup
Soup
Soup

Hidangan utama
Hee-Darng-Aan Oo-Taa-Maa
Main courses

Lauk ikan
Laa-Oak Ee-Karn
Fish dishes

Lauk daging
Laa-Ouk Dar-Geeng
Meat dishes

Daging lembu
Dar-Geeng Lump-Boo
Beef

Stik
Steak
Steak

M
A
L
A
Y

223

MALAY

Daging babi
Dar-Geeng Bar-Bee
Pork

Daging anak lembu
Dar-Geeng Are-Nack Lump-Boo
Veal

Ayam
Are-Yum
Chicken

Kambing
Come-Bing
Lamb

Daging babi
Dar-Geeng Bar-Bee
Ham

Lauk sayur-sayuran
Laa-Oak Sar-Your-Sar-Your-Raan
Vegetarian dishes

Sayur-sayuran
Sar-Your-Sar-Your-Raan
Vegetables

Kentang goreng
Kern-Tarng Go-Raing
Chips (french fries)

Rebus / saute / kentang hancur
Rer-Boos / Soo-Tay / Kern-Tarng Harn-Choor
Boiled / sauté / mashed potatoes

Nasi
Naa-See
Rice

Keju
Kay-Juu
Cheese

Pencuci mulut
Pern-Choo-Chee Moo-Loot
Desserts

Ais krim
Ice Cream
Ice cream

Kek
Cake
Cakes

Pastri
Pastry
Pastries

Buah-buahan
Boo-Aah-Boo-Aah-Han
Fruit

Roti
Row-Tee
Bread

Gulung
Goo-Low-Ng
Rolls

Roti bakar
Row-Tee Bar-Car
Toast

Mentega
Mern-Tay-Gaa
Butter

Garam / lada hitam
Gaa-Rarm / Laa-Daa Hee-Tum
Salt / pepper

Gula
Goo-Laa
Sugar

Keistimewaan
Ke-Is-Tee-May-Waa-Aan
Specialities

Keistimewaan tempatan
Ke-Is-Tee-May-Waa-Aan Term-Part-Tarn
Local specialities

Menu set
Menu Set
Set Menu

Senarai wain
Se-Naa-Rye Wine
Wine list

Wain merah
Wine May-Rarh
Red wines

Wain putih
Wine Poo-Tayh
White wines

Wain Rose
Wine Rose
Rosé wines

Wain berbuih
Wine Ber-Boo-Eh
Sparkling wines

Bir
Biir
Beer

Bir dalam botol / arak dalam tong
(draf) bir
*Biir Dar-Lum Bo-Toll / Are-Rug
Dar-Lum Tong (Draft) Biir*
**Bottled beer /
Draught (draft) beer**

Minuman tanpa alkohol
Mee-Nuum-Maan Tarn-Paa Alcohol
Non-alcoholic drinks

Air mineral
Are-Ayr Mineral
Mineral water

Jus buah-buahan
Juice Boo-Ah-Boo-Aah-Harn
Fruit juices

Jus oren
Juice O-Ren
Orange juice

Jus lemon   Ais
Juice Lemon   *Ice*
Lemonade   Ice

Kopi putih / kopi hitam /
Kopi Ekspresso
*Ko-Pee Poo-Tch / Ko-Pee Hee-Tarm /
Ko-Pee Espresso*
**White coffee / black coffee /
espresso coffee**

Teh susu / dengan lemon
Tayh Soo-Soo / Derng-An Lemon
Tea with milk / with lemon

Air cokelat
Are-Ayr Chocolate
Chocolate (drink)

Susu
Soo-Soo
Milk

Snek / makanan ringan
Snack / Mar-Kaa-Naan Reeng-An
Snacks / Light meals

Salad
Salad
Salads

Sandwic
Sandwich
Sandwiches

Telur
Ter-Lowr
Eggs

MALAY

MALAY

Sosej
Sausage
Sausage

Telur rebus / goreng / hancur
Ter-Lowr Rer-Boos / Go-Raing / Harn-Choor
Boiled / fried / scrambled eggs

Typical Local Dishes

Nasi lemak dengan ikan bilis dan telur
Naar-See Ler-Muck Derng-Arn E-Karn Bee-Lees Darn Ter-Loor
Coconut rice with fried fish and egg

Nasi Goreng
Naar-See Go-Rayng
Fried Rice

Mee Hoon Sup
Me Hun Soup
Vermicelli in tangy soup

Mee Rebus
Me-Rer-Boos
Yellow noodle in bean gravy

Tahu Goreng
Tar-Who Go-Rayng
Fried tofu

GETTING AROUND

Public Transport

Where is the bus stop / coach stop / nearest metro (subway) station?
Di mana stesen bas / stesen koc / stesen keretapi bawah tanah yang berdekatan?
Dee Maa-Naa Station Bus / Station Coach / Station Ke-Ray-Taa-Pee Baa-Waah Taa-Naah Young Ber-Der-Kar-Tarn

When is the next / last bus to ... ?
Bilakah bas yang berikutnya / akhir ke... ?
Bee-Laa-Kah Bus Young Ber-Ee-Kuut-Nya / Are-Heer Ker...

How much is the fare to the city centre (downtown) / railway station / airport?
Berapa tambang ke pusat bandar / stesen keretapi / lapangan terbang?
Ber-Rar-Paa Tarm-Barng Ker Poo-Sart Barn-Daar / Station Ker-Ray-Taa-Pee / Laa-Paang-An Ter-Baang

Will you tell me when to get off?
Boleh anda beritahu saya bila harus berhenti?
Bow-Layh Arn-Daa Ber-Ree-Taa-Who Saa-Yaa Bee-Laa Haar-Rose Ber-Hern-Tee

Does this bus go to ... ?
Adakah bas ini ke... ?
Are-Daa-Kaah Bus Ee-Nee Ker...

Which number bus goes to ... ?
Bas nombor apa ke...?
Bus Norm-Bor Are-Paa Ker...

May I have a single (oneway) / return (round-trip) / day ticket / book of tickets?
Saya mahu membeli satu tiket sehala / dua hala / tiket sehari / sebuku tiket?

Saa-Yaa Mar-Who Merm-Ber-Lee
Saa-Too Ticket Ser-Haa-Laa / Doo-Aa
Haa-Laa / Ticket Se-Haa-Ree /
Ser Boo-Koo Ticket

Taxis and Rickshaws

I would like to go to ...
Saya mahu ke...
Saa-Yaa Mar-Who Ker...

How much will it cost?
Berapa harganya?
Ber-Rar-Paa Har-Gaa-Nya

Please may I stop here?
Maaf, boleh saya berhenti di sini?
Mar-Arf, Bow-Layh Saa-Yaa
Ber-Hern-Tee Dee See-Nee

**I would like to order a taxi
today / tomorrow / at 2pm to
go from ... to ...**
Saya mahu tempah teksi hari ini /
esok / pada jam 2 petang dari ...ke...
Saa-Yaa Mar-Who Term-Paah Taxi
Haa-Ree Ee-Nee / Ay-Sok / Paa-Daa
Jarm 2 Per-Tung Daa-Ree ...Ker ...

Entertainment

**Can you recommend a good
bar / nightclub?**
Boleh anda cadangkan sebuah bar /
kelab malam yang bagus?
Bow-Layh Arn-Daa Cha-Darng-Karn
Ser-Boo-Ah Bar / Club Mar-Larm Young
Bar-Ghost

**Do you know what is on at the
cinema (playing at the movies) /
theatre at the moment?**

Adakah anda tahu apa yang sedang
ditayangkan di pawagam / teater
sekarang?
Are-Daa-Kaah Arn-Daa Tar-Who
Are-Paa Young Ser-Dung Dee-Taa-Young-
Karn Dee Paa-Waa Garm /
Theatre Ser-Kaa-Rung

**I would like to book (purchase)
... tickets for the matinee /
evening performance on
Monday**
Saya mahu tempah (membeli) ...tiket
untuk persembahan tengah hari /
malam pada hari Isnin
Saa-Yaa Mar-Who Term-Paah
(Merm-Ber-Lee) ...Ticket Oon-Took
Per-Serm-Baah-Haan Terng-Ah-Haree /
Mar-Larm Paa-Daa Haa-Ree Isnin

**What time does the film /
performance start?**
Pukul berapa filem / persembahan
itu bermula?
Poo-Cool Ber-Rar-Paa Film / Per-Serm-
Baah-Haan Ee-Too Ber-Moo-Laa

COMMUNICATIONS

Post

**How much will it cost to send
a letter / postcard / this package
to Britain / Ireland / America /
Canada / Australia /
New Zealand?**
Berapa harga untuk pos surat /
poskad / pakej ini ke Britain /
Ireland / Amerika / Kanada /
Australia / New Zealand?
Ber-Rar-Paa Har-Gaa Oon-Took Post
Soo-Raat / Postcard / Package Ee-Nee
Ker Britain / Ireland / Are-Mee-Ree-Ka /
Canada / Australia / New Zealand

M A L A Y

227

M A L A Y

I would like one stamp / two stamps
Saya mahu beli sekeping stem / dua keping stem
Saa-Yaa Mar-Who Ber-Lee Ser-Ker-Peeng Stamp / Doo-Aa Ker-Peeng Stamp

I'd like ... stamps for postcards to send abroad, please
Saya mahu beli ...stem untuk hantar sekeping poskad ke luar negeri
Saa-Yaa Mar-Who Ber-Lee ...Stamp Oon-Took Hunt-Tar Ser-Ker-Ping Postcard Ker Luar Ner-ger-ree

Phones

I would like to make a telephone call / reverse the charges to (make a collect call to) ...
Saya mahu buat panggilan telefon / panggilan yang dibayar oleh penerima ke ...
Saa-Yaa Mar-Who Boo-Art Pang-Gee-Laan Telephone / Pang-Gee-Laan Young Dee-Baa-Yaar Oo-Layh Per-Ner-Ree-Maa Ker ...

Which coins do I need for the telephone?
Duit syiling yang mana untuk buat panggilan telefon?
Doo-It Syilling Young Mar-Naa Oon-Took Boo-Art Pang-Gee-Laan Telephone

The line is engaged (busy)
Talianya sibuk
Tar-Lee-Aan-Nyaa See-Book

The number is ...
Nombornya ...
Norm-Bor-Nya ...

Hello, this is ...
Hello, saya ...
Hello, Saa-Yaa ...

Please may I speak to ...?
Boleh saya bercakap dengan ...?
Bow-Layh Saa-Yaa Ber-Char-Karp Derng-Aan ...

He / she is not in at the moment. Can you call back?
Dia tidak ada sekarang. Boleh telefon sekali lagi?
Deer Tee-Dark Are-Daa Ser-Kar-Rarng. Bow-Layh Telephone Ser-Car-Lee Laa-Gee

SHOPPING

Shops

Kedai buku / kedai alat tulis
Ker-Dye Boo-Koo / Ker-Dye Are-Lart Too-Lees
Bookshop / Stationery

Penjual barang kemas / hadiah
Pern-Joo-Arl Bar-Rarng Ker-Mars / Har-Dee-Aah
Jeweller / Gifts

Kasut
Car-Soot
Shoes

Perkakas
Per-Car-Kaas
Hardware

Pendandan rambut
Pern-Darn-Darn Rarm-Boat
Hairdresser

228

Lelaki / wanita
Ler-Laa-Kee / Waa-Nee-Taa
(men's) / (women's)

Pembuat roti
Perm-Boo-Art Row-Tee
Baker

Telefon
Telephone
Phones

Pasaraya
Par-Sar-Raa-Yaa
Supermarket

Kedai gambar
Ker-Dye Garm-Bar
Photo-Shop

Agen pelancongan
Agent Per-Larn-Choong-An
Travel agent

Farmasi
Far-Mar-See
Pharmacy

M A L A Y

In the Shops

What time do the shops open / close?
Pukul berapa kedai-kedai buka / tutup?
Poo-Cool Ber-Rar-Par Ker-Dye-Ker-Dye Boo-Kaa / Too-Toop

Where is the nearest market?
Di mana pasar yang berdekatan?
Dee Mar-Naa Par-Sar Young Ber-Der-Car-Tarn

Can you show me the one in the window / this one?
Boleh anda tunjukkan saya yang di tingkap ini / yang ini?
Bow-Layh Arn-Daa Toon-Jook-Karn Saa-Yaa Young Dee Teeng-Cup Ee-Nee / Young Ee-Nee

Can I try this on?
Boleh saya cuba yang ini?
Bow-Luyh Saa-Yaa Choo-Baa Young Ee-Nee

What size is this?
Saiz apa yang ini?
Size Are-Paa Young Ee-Nee

This is too large / too small / too expensive
Ini terlalu besar / terlalu kecil / terlalu mahal
Ee-Nee Ter-Laa-Loo Ber-Sar / Ter-Laa-Loo Ker-Chail / Ter-Laa-Loo Mar-Harl

Do you have any others?
Anda ada yang lain?
Arn-Daa Are-Daa Young Laa-In

My size is ...
Saiz saya ...
Size Saa-Yaa ...

Where is the changing room / children's / cosmetic / ladieswear / menswear / food department?
Di mana bilik tukar baju / bahagian kanak-kanak / kosmetik / pakaian wanita / pakaian lelaki / makanan?
Dee Mar-Naa Bee-Leek Too-Car Baa-Joo / Bar-Haa-Gee-Aan Car-Nack-Car-Nack / Cosmetic / Par-Car-Yarn Waa-Nee-Taa / Par-Car-Yarn Ler-Laa-Kee / Mar-Car-Narn

229

**M
A
L
A
Y**

I would like ... a quarter of a kilo / half a kilo / a kilo of bread / butter / cheese / ham / this fruit
Saya mahu membeli ...suku kilo / setengah kilo / satu kilo roti / mentega / keju / daging babi / buah ini
Saa-Yaa Mar-Who Merm-Ber-Lee ...Soo-Koo Kilo / Ser-Terng-Aah Kilo / Saa-Too Kilo Row-Tee / Mern-Tay-Gaa / Kay-Joo / Dar-Geeng Bar-Bee / Boo-Ah Ee-Nee

How much is this?
Berapa harga ini?
Ber-Rar-Paa Haar-Gaa Ee-Nee

I'll take this one, thank you
Saya ambil yang ini, terima kasih
Saa-Yaa Arm-Bail Young Ee-Nee, Ter-Ree-Maa Car-Sayh

Do you have a carrier (shopping) bag?
Anda ada beg?
Arn-Daa Are-Daa Bag

Do you have anything cheaper / larger / smaller / of better quality?
Anda ada lagi yang lebih murah / lebih besar / lebih kecil / lebih bermutu
Arn-Daa Are-Daa Laa-Gee Young Ler-Bayh Moo-Raah / Ler-Bayh Ber-Sar / Ler-Bayh Ker-Chail / Ler-Bayh Ber-Moo-Too

I would like a film / to develop this film for this camera
Saya mahu beli filem / cuci filem ini untuk kamera ini
Saa-Yaa Mar-Who Ber-Lee Film / Choo-Chee Film Ee-Nee Oon-Took Camera Ee-Nee

I would like some batteries, the same size as this old one
Saya mahu beli bateri, sama saiz dengan yang lama ini
Saa-Yaa Mar-Who Ber-Lee Battery, Sar-Maa Size Derng-Aan Young Lar-Maa Ee-Nee

Would you mind wrapping this for me, please?
Boleh anda bungkuskan untuk saya?
Bow-Layh Arn-Daa Boong-Koos-Karn Oon-Took Saa-Yaa

Sorry, but you seem to have given me the wrong change
Maaf, saya rasa anda beri saya wang tukar yang salah
Maar-Arf, Saa-Yaa Rar-Saa Arn-Daa Ber-Ree Saa-Yaa Warng Too-Car Young Sar-Laah

MOTORING

Car Hire (Rental)

I have ordered (rented) a car in the name of ...
Saya telah tempah (sewa) sebuah kereta atas nama ...
Saa-Yaa Ter-Laah Term-Paah (Say-Waa) Ser-Boo-Aah Ker-Ray-Ter Are-Tas Nar-Maa ...

How much does it cost to hire (rent) a car for one day / two days / a week?
Berapa harga untuk sewa (sewa) sebuah kereta untuk sehari / dua hari / seminggu?
Ber-Rar-Paa Har-Gaa Oon-Took Say-Waa (Say-Waa) Ser-Boo-Ah Ker-Ray-Taa Oon-Took Ser-Haa-Ree / Doo-Aa Har-Ree / Ser-Mingg-Goo

Is the tank already full of petrol (gas)?
Adakah tangki sudah penuh dengan minyak?
Are-Daa-Kaah Tarng-Kee Soo-Daah Per-Nooh Derng-Aan Meen-Yak

Is insurance and tax included? How much is the deposit?
Sudahkah termasuk insuran dan cukai? Berapa wang pendahuluannya?
Soo-Daah-Kaah Ter-Maa-Sook Insurance Darn Choo-Kye? Ber-Rar-Paa Warng Pern-Daa-Hoo-Loo-Arn-Nya

By what time must I return the car?
Pukul berapa harus saya pulangkan kereta ini?
Poo-Cool Ber-Rar-Paa Har-Roos Saa-Yaa Poo-Lang-Karn Ker-Ray-Taa Ee-Nee

I would like a small / large / family / sports car with a radio / cassette player
Saya mahu sebuah kereta kecil / besar / keluarga / sukan dengan sebuah radio / pemain kaset
Saa-Yaa Mar-Who Ser-Boo-Aah Ker-Ray-Taa Ker-Chail / Ber-Sar / Ker-Loo-Ar-Gaa / Soo-Karn Derng-An Ser-Boo-Ah Radio / Per-Maa-In Cassette

Do you have a road map?
Anda ada peta jalan?
Arn-Daa Are-Daa Per-Taa Jar-Larn

Parking

How long can I park here?
Berapa lama boleh saya letak kereta di sini?
Ber-Raa-Paa Lar-Maa Bo-Layh Saa-Yaa Ler-Taak Ker-Ray-Taa Dee Sec-Nee

Is there a car park near here?
Adakah tempat meletak kereta dekat sini?
Are-Daa-Kaah Term-Part Mer-Ler-Tark Ker-Ray-Taa Der-Card See-Nee

At what time does this car park close?
Pukul berapa tempat meletak kereta ini tutup?
Poo-Cool Ber-Rar-Paa Term-Part Mer-Ler-Tark Ker-Ray-Taa Ee-Nee Too-Toop

Signs and Notices

Sehala
Ser-Haa-Laa
One way

Tidak boleh masuk
Tee-Dark Bo-Layh Mar-Sook
No entry

Tidak boleh letak kereta
Te-Dark Bo-Layh Ler-Tuck Ker-Ray-Taa
No parking

Lencongan
Len-Choung-Arn
Detour (diversion)

Berhenti
Ber-Hern-Tee
Stop

Beri laluan
Ber-Ree Lar-Loo-Arn
Give way (yield)

Jalan licin
Jar-Larn Lee-Cheen
Slippery road

M A L A Y

Tidak boleh memotong
Tee-Dark Bo-Layh Mer-Mor-Tong
No overtaking

Bahaya!
Bar-Haa-Yaa
Danger!

At the Filling Station

Unleaded (lead-free) / standard / premium / diesel
Tanpa plumbum / biasa / premium / diesel
Tarn-Paa Plume-Boom / Bee-A-Saa / Premium / Diesel

Fill the tank please
Tolong, isikan minyak
Tow-Long, Ee-See-Karn Meen-Yak

Do you have a road map?
Anda ada peta jalan?
Arn-Daa Are-Daa Per-Taa Jar-Larn

How much is the car wash?
Berapa harga untuk mencuci kereta?
Ber-Rar-Paa Har-Gaa Oon-Took Mern-Choo-Chee Ker-Ray-Taa

Breakdowns

I've had a breakdown at ...
Kereta saya rosak di...
Ker-Ray-Taa Saa-Yaa Ro-Sark Dee...

I am a member of the [motoring organisation]
Saya ahli [persatuan kenderaan]
Saa-Yaa Arh-Lee [Per-Saa-Too-Arn Kern-Der-Raa-Arn]

I am on the road from ... to ...
Saya dalam perjalanan dari ... ke ...
Saa-Yaa Dar-Larm Per-Jar-Laa-Narn Dar-Ree ... Ker ...

I can't move the car. Can you send a tow-truck?
Kereta saya tidak boleh bergerak. Tolong hantar lori tarik?
Ker-Ray-Taa Saa-Yaa Tee-Dark Bo-Layh Ber-Ger-Ruck. Tow-Long Harn-Tar Lorry Taa-Reek

I have a flat tyre
Tayar saya pancit
Tar-Yar Saa-Yaa Parn-Chit

The windscreen (windshield) has smashed / cracked
Kaca depan kereta pecah / retak
Car-Chaa Der-Parn Ker-Ray-Taa Per-Charh / Rer-Tark

There is something wrong with the engine / brakes / lights / steering / gearbox / clutch / exhaust
Ada sesuatu yang rosak pada enjin / brek / lampu / stering / kotak gear / klac / ekzos
Are-Daa Ser-Soo-A-Too Young Ro-Sark Par-Daa Engine / Brake / Larm-Poo / Stering / Ko-Tark Gear / Clutch / Exhaust

It's overheating
Ia terlalu panas
Ee-Yaa Ter-Laa-Loo Par-Naas

It won't start
Ia tidak mahu hidup
Ee-Yaa Tee-Dark Mar-Who Hee-Doop

Where can I get it repaired?
Di mana boleh saya membaikinya?
Dee Mar-Naa Bo-Layh Saa-Yaa Merm-Baa-E-Kee-Nya

Can you take me there?
Bolehkah anda bawa saya ke sana?
Bo-Layh-Kaah Arn-Daa Bar-Waa Saa-Yaa Ker Sar-Naa

Will it take long to fix?
Adakah lama untuk membaikinya?
Are-Daa-Kaah Laa-Maa Oon-Took Merm-Baa-Ee-Kee-Nya

How much will it cost?
Berapa harganya?
Ber-Rar-Paa Har-Gaa-Nya

Please can you pick me up / give me a lift?
Bolehkah anda mengambil / menumpang saya
Bow-Layh-Kaah Arn-Daa Merng-Arm-Bill / Mern-Noom-Pang Saa-Yaa

Accidents and Traffic Offences

Can you help me? There has been an accident
Bolehkah anda tolong saya? Ada kemalangan berlaku
Bow-Layh-Kah Arn-Daa Tow-Long Saa-Yaa? Are-Daa Ker-Mar-Lang-Arn Ber-Laa-Koo

Please call the police / an ambulance
Tolong panggilkan polis / ambulan
Tow-Long Parng-Gill-Karn Police / Ambulance

Is anyone hurt?
Ada sesiapa yang cedera?
Are-Daa Sir-See-Are-Pa Young Cher-Der-Raa

I'm sorry, I didn't see the sign
Maaf, saya tidak nampak papan tanda itu
Mar-Arf, Saa-Yaa Tee-Dark Narm-Park Par-Pun Tarn-Daa Ee-Too

Must I pay a fine? How much?
Perlukah saya bayar denda? Berapa?
Per-Loo-Kaah Saa-Yaa Bar-Yaar Dern-Daa? Ber-Rar-Paa

Show me your documents
Tunjukkan dokumen anda
Toon-Jook-Karn Document Arn-Daa

HEALTH

Pharmacy

Do you have anything for a stomach ache / headache / sore throat / toothache?
Anda ada ubat untuk sakit perut / pening / sakit tekak / sakit gigi?
Arn-Daa Are-Daa Oo-Bart Oon-Took Sar-Keet Per-Root / Per-Ning / Sar-Keet Ter-Kark / Sar-Keet Gee-Gee

I need something for diarrhoea / constipation / a cold / a cough / Insect bites / sunburn / travel (motion) sickness (car) (plane) (boat)
Saya perlukan ubat untuk cirit-birit / sembelit / selsema / batuk / gigitan serangga / sunburn / sakit dalam perjalanan (kereta) (pesawat) (bot)
Saa-Yaa Per-Loo-Karn Oo-Bart Oon-Took Chee-Reet-Bee-Reet / Serm-Ber-Leet / Sel-Ser-Maa / Bar-Tock / Gee-Gee-Tarn Ser-Rarng-Gaa / Sunburn / Sar-Keet Dar-Lam Per-Jar-Lar-Narn (Ker-Ray-Taa)(Per-Sar-Wart)(Boat)

M A L A Y

233

**M
A
L
A
Y**

How much / how many do I take?
Berapa / berapa banyak perlu saya ambil?
Ber-Rar-Paa / Ber-Rar-Paa Barn-Yark Per-Loo Saa-Yaa Arm-Bill

How often do I take it / them?
Berapa kali perlu saya ambilnya?
Ber-Rar-Paa Car-Lee Per-Loo Saa-Yaa Arm-Bill-Nyar

I am / he is / she is taking this medication
Saya / dia / dia sedang ambil ubat ini
Saa-Yaa / Dee-Yaa / Dee-Yaa Ser-Darng Arm-Bill Oo-Bart Ee-Nee

How much does it cost?
Berapa harganya?
Ber-Rar-Paa Har-Gaa-Nyar

Can you recommend a good doctor / dentist?
Bolehkah anda cadangkan seorang doktor / doktor gigi yang bagus?
Bow-Layh-Kah Arn-Daa Char-Darng-Karn Ser-Oo-Rarng Doctor / Doctor Gee-Gee Young Bar-Ghost

Is it suitable for children?
Sesuaikah untuk kanak-kanak?
Ser-Soo-Aai-Kaah Oon-Took Car-Nark-Car-Nark

Doctor

I have a pain here / in my arm / leg / chest / stomach
Saya rasa sakit di sini / di lengan saya / kaki / dada / perut
Saa-Yaa Rar-Saa Sar-Keet Dee See-Nee / Dee Lerng-Arn Saa-Yaa / Car-Kee / Daa-Daa / Per-Root

Please call a doctor, this is an emergency
Tolong panggil doktor, ini satu kecemasan
Tow-Long Parng-Gill Doctor, Ee-Nee Saa-Too Ker-Cher-Maa-Sarn

I would like to make an appointment to see the doctor
Saya mahu buat temu janji dengan doktor
Saa-Yaa Maa-Who Boo-Art Ter-Moo Jarn-Jee Derng-Arn Doctor

I am diabetic / pregnant
Saya seorang pesakit kencing manis / hamil
Saa-Yaa Ser-Oo-Rarng Per-Saa-Keet Kern-Ching Mar-Nees / Har-Meel

I need a prescription for ...
Saya perlu ubat untuk ...
Saa-Yaa Per-Loo Oo-Bart Oon-Took ...

Can you give me something to ease the pain?
Bolehkah anda berikan saya ubat untuk kurangkan rasa sakit?
Bow-Layh-Kah Arn-Daa Ber-Ree-Karn Saa-Yaa Oo-Bart Oon-Took Koo-Rarng-Karn Raa-Saa Saa-Keet

I am / he is / she is allergic to penicillin
Saya / dia / dia ada alahan dengan penicillin
Saa-Yaa / Dee-Aa / Dee-Aa Are-Daa Are-Laa-Harn Derng-Aan Penicillin

Does this hurt?
Sakit?
Sar-Keet

You must / he must / she must go to hospital
Anda mesti / dia mesti / dia mesti pergi ke hospital
Arn-Daa Mers-Tee / Dee-Aa Mers-Tee / Dee-Aa Mers-Tee Per-gee Ker Hospital

Take these once / twice / three times a day
Ambil ini sekali / dua kali / tiga kali sehari
Arm-Bill Ee-Nee Ser-Kaa-Lee / Doo-Aa Kaa-Lee / Tee-Gaa Kaa-Lee Ser-Haree

I am / he is / she is taking this medication
Saya / dia / dia sedang ambil ubat ini
Saa-Yaa / Dee-Aa / Dee-Aa Ser-Darng Arm-Bill Oo-Bart Ee-Nee

I have medical insurance
Saya mempunya insuran perubatan
Saa-Yaa Merm-Poon-Ya-Ee Insurance Per-Oo-Bart-Tarn

Dentist

I have toothache
Gigi saya sakit
Gee-Gee Saa-Yaa Sar-Keet

My filling has come out
Tampalannya terkeluar
Tarm-Par-Laan-Nyar Ter-Ker-Loo-Ar

I do / do not want to have an injection first
Saya mahu / tidak mahu suntikan terlebih dahulu
Saa-Yaa Mar-Who / Tee-Dark Mar-Who Soon-Tick-Karn Ter-Ler-Bayh Dar-Who-Loo

EMERGENCIES

Help!
Tolong!
Tow-Long

Fire!
Kebakaran!
Ker-Bar-Kar-Rarn

Stop!
Berhenti!
Ber-Hern-Tee

Call an ambulance / a doctor/ the police / the fire brigade!
Telefon ambulan / doktor / polis / bomba!
Telephone Ambulance / Doctor / Police / Bomb-Baa

Please may I use a telephone?
Bolehkah saya gunakan telefon?
Bow-Layh-Kah Saa-Yaa Goo-Naa-Karn Telephone

I have had my traveller's cheques / credit cards / handbag / rucksack / (knapsack) / luggage / wallet / passport / mobile phone stolen
Cek pengembaraan / kad kredit / beg tangan / beg gendong / beg pakaian / beg duit / passport / telefon bimbit saya dicuri
Check Perng-Erm-Bar-Raa-An / Card Credit / Bag Tarng-An / Bag Gain-Dong / Bag Par-Kai-An / Bag Doo-It / Passport / Telephone Beem-Bit Saa-Yaa Dee-Choo-Ree

M A L A Y

235

M A L A Y

May I please have a copy of the report for my insurance claim?
Bolehkah saya dapatkan salinan laporan untuk tuntutan insuran saya?
Bow-Layh-Kah Saa-Yaa Dar-Part-Karn Sar-Lee-Narn Lar-Po-Run Oon-Took Toon-Too-Tarn Insurance Saa-Yaa

Can you help me? I have lost my daughter / my son / my companion(s)
Bolehkah anda tolong saya? Anak perempuan saya / anak lelaki saya / teman (teman-teman) saya hilang
Bow-Layh-Kah Arn-Daa Tow-Long Saa-Yaa? Are-Nark Per-Rerm-Poo-Arn Saa-Yaa / Are-Nark Ler-Laa-Kee Saa-Yaa / Ter-Marn (Termarn-Termarn) Saa-Yaa Hee-Larng

Please go away / leave me alone
Pergi dari sini / biarkan saya seorang diri
Per-Gee Daa-Ree See-Nee / Bee-Yaa-R-Karn Saa-Yaa Ser-Oo-Rarng Dee-Ree

I'm sorry
Saya minta maaf
Saa-Yaa Meen-Taa Mar-Arf

I want to contact the British / American / Canadian / Irish / Australian / New Zealand / South African consulate
Saya mahu hubungi konsul British / Amerika / Kanada / Irish / Australia / New Zeland / Afrika Selatan
Saa-Yaa Mar-Who Who-Boong-Ee Consul British / Are-Mee-Ree-Kaa / Canada / Irish / Australia / New Zealand / Are-Free-Car Sir-Laar-Tarn

I'm / we're / he is / she is ill / lost / injured
Saya / kami / dia / dia sakit / hilang / cedera
Saa-Yaa / Car-Mee / Dee-Aa / Dee-Aa Sar-Keet / Hee-Larng / Cher-Der-Raa

They are ill / lost / injured
Mereka sakit / hilang / cedera
Mer-Ray-Car Sar-Keet / Hee-Larng / Cher-Der-Ra

THAI
ภาษาไทย

INTRODUCTION

T H A I

INTRODUCTION

Thai is a member of the Tai language family, and is the chief language of Thailand. It has four main regional dialects and Lao, Chinese, Malay, and Mon-Khmer (related to Khmer/Cambodian) are also spoken. English is taught in secondary schools and colleges and is also used in commerce and government, and at major tourist destinations.

Addresses for Travel and Tourist Information

Australia: Tourism Authority of Thailand, 2nd floor, 75 Pitt Street, Sydney, NSW 2000 Australia. Tel: 02 9247 7549; Fax: 02 9251 2465; Email: info@Thailand.Net.Au; Web: www.thailand.net.au

Canada: Royal Thai Consulate-General, 1040 Burrard Street, Vancouver BC, Canada V6Z 2R9. Tel: 604 687 1143; Fax: 604 687 4434; Email: info@thaicongenvancouver.org; Web: www.thaicongenvancouver.org

UK: Tourism Authority of Thailand (Office Address): 3rd floor, Brook House, 98-99 Jermyn Street, London WC1Y 2EE. Tel: 0870 900 2007; Fax: 01344 876680; Web: www.thaismile.co.uk

USA: Royal Thai Embassy, 1024 Wisconsin Avenue NW, Suite 401, Washington DC 20007. Tel: 202 944 3600; Fax: 202 944 3611; Email: info@thaiemdc.org; Web: www.thaiemdc.org/index.htmo

Thailand Facts

CAPITAL: Bangkok

CURRENCY: Baht (I Baht = 100 satang).

OPENING HOURS: Banks are usually open Mon-Fri 0930-1530, and closed Sat and Sun, but some are open on Saturday mornings. Stores open Mon-Sat 0800-1700. Large shops and department stores are open from 1000-2100.

TELEPHONES: To dial in, Tel: International Access Code +66. Outgoing. Tel: 001 and the Country Code.

EMERGENCY NUMBERS: Police, Tel: 191; Fire, Tel: 199; Tourist Police: 195.

PUBLIC HOLIDAYS: Jan 1 – New Year's Day; Feb 14 – Makha Bucha* (Full Moon Day); Apr 6 – Chakri Memorial Day; Apr 12 – 14 – Songkran Festival (Thai New Year); May 1 – National Labor Day; May 5 – Coronation Day; May 13 – Wisakha Bucha* (Full Moon Day); July 11 – Asanha Bucha* (Full Moon Day); July 12 – Buddhist Lent Day*; Aug 12 – H.M. The Queen's Birthday; Oct 23 – Chulalongkorn Day; Dec 5 – H.M. The King's Birthday; Dec 10 – Constitution Day; Dec 31 – New Year's Eve.

*These are religious holidays and vary from year to year according to the lunar cycle.

Technical Language Hints

- Thai grammar is thankfully very easy. There are no changes for tense, gender or plurals, and there is no word for "a" or "the".

- Read Thai from left to right, and notice that the vowels may be written "around" the words, before, after, above or below.

To be polite, a syllable is added on to the end of sentences. A female speaker would add "kha" and a male speaker would add "khrap" or (less formal) "khap". It's important to do this, as you may otherwise seem rude. This has been indicated for you in the text.

**T
H
A
I**

Basic Words and Phrases

Yes
ใช่
Chai

No
ไม่ใช่
Mai Chai

Please
ได้โปรด
Dai Proad

Thank you
ขอบคุณครับ / ค่ะ
Kob Khun Krub / Ka

Hello
สวัสดีครับ / ค่ะ
Sawasdee Krub / Ka

Goodbye
ลาก่อน
La Korn

Excuse me
ขอโทษครับ / ค่ะ
Kor Thoad Krub / Ka

Sorry
ขอโทษ
Khor Toad

How
อย่างไร
Yarng Rai

When
เมื่อไหร่
Mua Rai

Why
ทำไม
Tham Mai

What
อะไร
Ar Rai

Who
ใคร
Krai

That's O.K.
ไม่เป็นไร
Mai Pen Rai

Perhaps
บางที
Bang Thee

To
ถึง
Thueng

From
จาก
Jark

Here
ที่นี่
Theenee

There
ที่นั่น
Theenan

I don't understand
ผม / ฉันไม่เข้าใจ
Phom / Chan Mai Kao Jai

I don't speak Thai
ผม / ฉันพูดภาษาไทยไม่ได้
*Phom / Chan Phood Phasa Thai
Mai Dai*

Do you speak English?
คุณพูดภาษาอังกฤษได้ไหม
Khun Phood Pasa Angrid Dai Mai

Can you please write it down?
คุณจะเขียนให้ได้ไหมครับ / ค่ะ
*Khun Ja Kian Hai Pom Dai Mai
Krub / Ka*

**Please can you speak more
slowly?**
กรุณาพูดช้ากว่านี้ได้ไหมครับ / ค่ะ
*Garuna Pood Cha Gwa Nee Dai Mai
Krub / Ka*

Greetings

**Good morning /
Good afternoon /
Good evening / Goodnight**
อรุณสวัสดิ์ / สวัสดีตอนบ่าย / สวัสดีตอนเย็น /
ราตรีสวัสดิ์
*Arunsawad / Sawasdee Ton Bai /
Sawasdee Ton Yen / Ratree Saward*

Pleased to meet you
ยินดีที่ได้รู้จักคุณครับ / ค่ะ
*Yhin Dee Thee Dai Roo Jak Khun
Krub / Ka*

How are you?
คุณสบายดีหรือครับ / ค่ะ
Khun Sabaidee Rue Krub / Ka

Well, thank you. And you?
ผม / ฉันสบายดี ขอบคุณครับ / ค่ะ แล้วคุณละ
*Phom / Chan Sabaidee Kob Khun
Krub / Ka Laew Khun La*

My name is...
ผม / ฉันชื่อ ...
Phom / chan chue...

**This is my friend / boyfriend /
girlfriend / husband / wife /
brother / sister**
นี่คือเพื่อนชาย / เพื่อนหญิง / สามี / ภรรยา /
พี่ชาย พี่สาว / น้องชาย น้องสาวของผม / ฉัน
*Nee Kue Puan Chai / Puan Ying /
Samee / Panlaya / Peechai Peesao / Nong
Chai Nong Sao Khong Pom / Chan*

Where are you traveling to?
คุณกำลังจะเดินทางไปที่ไหน
*Khun Gumlung Ja Dern Tharng Pai
Thee Nai*

I am / we are going to ...
ผม / ฉัน / เรากำลังจะไป ...
Phom / Chan / Rao Gumlung Ja Pai ...

How long are you traveling for?
คุณจะเดินทางนานเท่าไหร่
Khun Ja Dern Tang Naan Thao Rai

Where do you come from?
คุณมาจากที่ไหน
Khun Ma Jak Thee Nai

**I am / we are from Australia /
Britain / Canada / America**
ผม / ฉัน / เรามาจากประเทศออสเตรเลีย /
สหราชอาณาจักร / แคนาดา / สหรัฐอเมริกา
*Phom / Chan / Rao Ma Jak Prathed
Australia / Saharach Arnajak /
Canada / Saharad America*

We are on holiday
เราอยู่ในวันหยุด
Rao Yoo Nai Wan Yood

This is our first visit here
เรามาเที่ยวที่นี่เป็นครั้งแรก
Rao Ma Thiao Thee Nee Pen Krung Raek

How old are you?
คุณอายุเท่าไหร่
Khun Aryoo Thao Rai

I am ... years old
ผม / ฉันอายุ ... ปี
Phom / Chan Aryoo ... Pee

**I am a businessman / business
woman / doctor / journalist /
manual worker / administrator /
scientist / student / teacher**
ผม / ฉันเป็นนักธุรกิจ / นักธุรกิจหญิง / หมอ /
นักข่าว / กรรมกร / ผู้บริหาร / นักวิทยาศาสตร์ /
นักเรียน / ครู
*Phom / Chan Pen Nak Thurakij /
Nak Thurakij Ying / Mor / Nakkao /
Kamakorn / Phoo Borihan / Nak
Vittayasad / Nak Rean/ Kru*

**Would you like / may I have a
cigarette?**
คุณอยากได้ / ผม / ฉันขอบุหรี่หนึ่งมวนได้ไหม
*Khun Yaak Dai / Phom / Chan Kor
Boori Nueng Muan Dai Mai*

Do you mind if I smoke?
คุณจะว่าอะไรไหมถ้าผม / ฉันจะสูบ
*Khun Ja Wa Arai Mai Tar Phom / Chan
Ja Soob*

Do you have a light?
คุณมีไฟไหม
Khun Mee Fai Mai

**I am waiting for my husband /
wife / boyfriend / girlfriend**
ผม / ฉันกำลังรอสามี / ภรรยา / เพื่อนชาย /
เพื่อนหญิงของผม / ฉัน
*Phom / Chan Gumlung Ror Samee /
Panlaya / Puan Chai / Puan Ying Khong
Phom / Chan*

T
H
A
I

THAI

Days

Monday
วันจันทร์
Wan Jaan

Tuesday
วันอังคาร
Wan Angkarn

Wednesday
วันพุธ
Wan Phood

Thursday
วันพฤหัสบดี
Wan Paruehard

Friday
วันศุกร์
Wan Sook

Saturday
วันเสาร์
Wan Sao

Sunday
วันอาทิตย์
Wan Arthid

Morning
เขา
Chao

Afternoon
บ่าย
Bai

Evening
เย็น
Yaen

Night
กลางคืน
Glang Kuen

Yesterday / Today / Tomorrow
เมื่อวานนี้ / วันนี้ / พรุ่งนี้
Mua Warn Nee / Wan Nee / Prung Nee

Numbers

Zero
ศูนย์
Soon

One
หนึ่ง
Nueng

Two
สอง
Song

Three
สาม
Sam

Four
สี่
See

Five
ห้า
Haa

Six
หก
Hok

Seven
เจ็ด
Jed

Eight
แปด
Paed

Nine
เก้า
Kao

Ten
สิบ
Sip

Eleven
สิบเอ็ด
Sib Ed

Twelve
สิบสอง
Sib Song

Thirteen
สิบสาม
Sib Sam

Fourteen
สิบสี่
Sib See

Fifteen
สิบห้า
Sib Haa

Sixteen
สิบหก
Sib Hok

Seventeen
สิบเจ็ด
Sib Jed

Eighteen
สิบแปด
Sib Paed

Nineteen
สิบเก้า
Sib Kao

Twenty
ยี่สิบ
Yee Sib

Twenty-one
ยี่สิบเอ็ด
Yee Sib Ed

Twenty-two
ยี่สิบสอง
Yee Sib Song

Thirty
สามสิบ
Sam Sib

Forty
สี่สิบ
See Sib

Fifty
ห้าสิบ
Haa Sib

Sixty
หกสิบ
Hok Sib

Seventy
เจ็ดสิบ
Jed Sib

Eighty
แปดสิบ
Paed Sib

Ninety
เก้าสิบ
Kao Sib

One hundred
หนึ่งร้อย
Nueng Roi

Five hundred
ห้าร้อย
Haa Roi

One thousand
หนึ่งพัน
Nueng Paan

One million
หนึ่งล้าน
Nueng Laan

Time

What time is it?
ตอนนี้เป็นเวลากี่นาฬิกา
Ton Nee Pen Vela Gee Narika

It is ...
ขณะนี้เป็นเวลา ...
Kananee Pen Vela ...

9.00
เก้านาฬิกา
Kao Narika

9.05
เก้านาฬิกาห้านาที
Kao Narika Haa Nathee

9.15
เก้านาฬิกาสิบห้านาที
Kao Narika Sib Haa Nathee

9.20
เก้านาฬิกายี่สิบนาที
Kao Narika Yee Sib Haa Nathee

9.30
เก้านาฬิกาสามสิบนาที
Kao Narika Sam Sib Nathee

9.35
เก้านาฬิกาสามสิบห้านาที
Kao Narika Sam Sib Haa Nathee

9.40
เก้านาฬิกาสี่สิบนาที
Kao Narika See Sib Nathee

9.45
เก้านาฬิกาสี่สิบห้านาที
Kao Narika See Sib Haa Nathee

9.50
เก้านาฬิกาห้าสิบนาที
Kao Narika Haa Sib Nathee

9.55
เก้านาฬิกาห้าสิบห้านาที
Kao Narika Haa Sib Haa Nathee

12.00 / Midday / Midnight
สิบสองนาฬิกา / เที่ยงวัน / เที่ยงคืน
Sib Song Narika / Thiang Wan / Thiang Kuen

Money

I would like to change these traveller's cheques / this currency
ผม / ฉันต้องการแลกเปลี่ยนเช็คนักเดินทาง / สกุลเงินนี้
Phom / Chan Tong Karn Laek Plian Check Nakderntang / Sakul Ngern Nee

How much commission do you charge? (What is the service charge?)
คุณจะคิดค่าคอมฯ เท่าไหร่ (คิดค่าธรรมเนียมบริการเท่าไหร่)
Khun Ja Kid Ka Com Thao Rai (Kid Ka Thamniam Borikarn Thao Rai)

Can I obtain money with my MasterCard?
ผม / ฉันจะแลกเงินโดยใช้บัตรมาสเตอร์การ์ดได้ไหม
Phom / Chan Ja Laek Ngern Doai Chai Bud MasterCard Dai Mai

243

T
H
A
I

ARRIVING AND DEPARTING

THAI

Where is the nearest ATM?
ดูเอทีเอ็มที่ใกล้ที่สุดอยู่ที่ไหน
Thu Atm Thee Glai Thee Sud Yoo Thee Nai

My name is ... Some money has been wired to here for me to collect
ผม / ฉันชื่อ ... มีการโอนเงินจำนวนหนึ่งมาให้ผม / ฉันที่นี่
Phom / Chan Chue ... Me Garn Oan Ngernn Jumnuan Nueng Ma Hai Phom / Chan Thee Nee

ARRIVING AND DEPARTING

Airport

Excuse me, where is the check-in desk for ... airline?
ขอโทษครับ / ค่ะ
เคาน์เตอร์เช็คอินของสายการบิน ... อยู่ที่ไหนครับ / ค่ะ
Kor Toad Krub / Ka Counter Checkin Khong Sai Garn Bin Yoo Thee Nai Krub / Ka

What is the boarding gate / time for my flight?
ขอทราบเกต / เวลาขึ้นเครื่องสำหรับไฟลท์ของผม / ฉันได้ไหม
Kor Sarp Gate / Vela Kuen Kruang Sumrap Flight Kon Phom / Chan Dai Mai

How long is the delay likely to be?
ไม่ทราบว่าเครื่องจะดีเลย์นานไหม
Mai Sarb Wa Kruang Ja Delay Naan Mai

Where is the duty-free shop?
ร้านค้าดิวตี้ฟรีอยู่ที่ไหนครับ / ค่ะ
Ranka Duty Free Yoo Thee Nai Krub / Ka

Which way is the baggage reclaim?
จะสามารถไปรับกระเป๋าเดินทางได้ที่ไหน
Ja Samard Pai Rub Krapao Dern Thang Dai Thee Nai

I have lost my luggage. Please can you help?
ผม / ฉันทำกระเป๋าหาย กรุณาช่วยผม / ฉันได้ไหมครับ / ค่ะ
Phom / Chan Thum Krapao Hai Karuna Chuai Phom / Chan Dai Mai Krub / Ka

I am flying to ...
ผม / ฉันกำลังบินไปที่ ...
Phom / Chan Gumlung Bin Pai Thee ...

Where can I get the bus to the city centre?
ผม / ฉันจะหารถไปใจกลางเมืองได้ที่ไหน
Phom / Chan Ja Haa Rhod Pai Jai Klang Muang Dai Thee Nai

Trains and Boats

Where is the ticket office / information desk?
ที่จำหน่ายตั๋ว / ประชาสัมพันธ์อยู่ที่ไหน
Thee Jumnai Tua / Pracha Samphun Yoo Thee Nai

Which platform does the train / speedboat / ferry to ... depart from
รถไฟ / เรือยนต์เร็ว / เรือรับส่งข้ามฟากที่จะไปยัง ... ออกจากชานชาลาไหน
Rhodfai / Rua Yon Raew / Rua Rub Song Kam Faak Thee Ja Pai Yung ... Ok Jark Chanchala Nai

Where is platform ...?
ชานชาลา ... อยู่ที่ไหน
Chanchala ... Yoo Thee Nai

244

When is the next train / boat to ... ?
รถไฟ / เรือที่จะเดินทางไปยัง ... จะออกตอนกี่โมง
Rhodfai / Rua Thee Ja Dern Tang Pai Yung ... Ja Ok Torn Gee Moang

Is there a later train / boat to ... ?
มีรถไฟ / เรือเที่ยวต่อไปยัง...ไหม
Mee Rhodfai / Rua Thiao Tor Pai Yung ... Mai

Notices and Signs

รถขายอาหาร (รับประทานอาหาร) ในขบวนรถไฟ
Rhod Kai Arhaan (Rubpratan Arhaan) Nai Kabuan Rhodfai
Buffet (Dining) car

รถโดยสาร
Rhod Doai Sarn
Bus

น้ำดื่ม / น้ำใช้
Nam Duem / Nam Chai
Drinking / Non-drinking water

ทางเข้า
Tang Kao
Entrance

ทางออก
Tang Ok
Exit

โรงพยาบาล
Roang Payaban
Hospital

ประชาสัมพันธ์
Pracha Samphun
Information

ที่พักสัมภาระ (ที่รับกระเป๋า)
Thee Pak Samphara (Thee Rub Krapao)
Left luggage (Baggage claim)

ล็อกเกอร์เก็บของ
Locker Geb Khong
Luggage lockers

ที่ทำการไปรษณีย์
Thee Thamkarn Praisanee
Post office

ชานชาลา
Chan Cha La
Platform

สถานี (ราง) รถไฟ
Sathan Nee (Rang) Rhod Fai
Railway (Railroad) station

สนามบิน
Sanam Bin
Airport

สถานีตำรวจ
Sa Tarn Nee Tum Ruad
Police station

ท่าเรือ
Thar Rua
Port

ภัตตาคาร
Phud Takarn
Restaurant

สูบ / ไม่สูบบุหรี่
Soob / Mai Soob Boori
Smoking / Non-smoking

T
H
A
I

โทรศัพท์
Thorasarb
Telephone

ที่จำหน่ายตั๋ว
Te Jumnai Tua
Ticket office

เคาน์เตอร์เช็คอิน
Counter Check-In
Check-in desk

ตารางเวลา (กำหนดการ)
Tarang Vela (Gumnodkarn)
Timetables (Schedules)

สุขา (ห้องน้ำ)
Sookaa (Hong Nam)
Toilets (Restrooms)

ห้องน้ำหญิง / ห้องน้ำชาย
Hong Nam Ying / Hong Nam Chai
Ladies / Gentlemen

รถไฟ (ใต้ดิน)
Rhodfai (Tai Din)
Underground (Subway)

ห้องรับรอง
Hong Rubrong
Waiting room

Buying a ticket

I would like a first-class / second-class single (oneway) / return (round-trip) ticket to ...
ผม / ฉันต้องการซื้อตั๋วเที่ยวเดียว /
ไป-กลับชั้นหนึ่ง / ชั้นสองไปยัง ...
Phom / Chan Tong Garn Sue Tua Thiao Diao / Pai Glub Chan Nueng / Chan Song Pai Yung ...

Is it an express (fast) train / bus?
นี่คือรถไฟ / รถโดยสารด่วนพิเศษ (เร็ว) ใช่ไหม
Nee Kua Rhodfai / Rod Doai Sarn Duan Pee Sed (Raew) Chai Mai

Is my rail pass valid on this train / ferry / bus?
บัตรโดยสารรถไฟของผม / ฉันใช้ได้กับรถไฟ / เรือรับ
ส่งข้ามฟาก / รถโดยสารคันนี้หรือไม่
Baad Doai Sarn Rhodfai Khong Phom / Chan Chai Dai Gub Rhodfai / Rua Rub Song Kam Fak / Rhod Doai Sarn Kan Nee Rue Mai

I would like an aisle / window seat
ผม / ฉันอยากได้ที่นั่งติดทางเดิน / ริมหน้าต่าง
Phom / Chan Yaak Dai Thee Nung Id Tang Dern / Rim Na Tang

No smoking / smoking, please
ผม / ฉันอยากได้ที่นั่งในโซนสูบบุหรี่ / ไม่สูบบุหรี่
Phom / Chan Yaak Dai Thee Nung Nai Zone Soob Boori/Mai Soob Boori

We would like to sit together
เราอยากได้ที่นั่งที่อยู่ติดกัน
Rao Yaak Dai Thee Nung Thee Yoo Tid Kaan

I would like to make a seat reservation
ผม / ฉันต้องการจองที่นั่ง
Phom / Chan Tong Garn Jong Thee Nung

I would like to reserve a couchette / sleeper for one person / two people / my family
ผม / ฉันต้องการจองทั่ง /
ปรับนอนสำหรับหนึ่งท่าน / สองท่าน / ทั้งครอบครัว
Phom / Chan Tong Garn Jo Thee Nung / Prab Noan Samrub Nueng Tharn / Song Tharn / Thung Krob Krua

I would like to reserve a cabin
ผม / ฉันต้องการจองห้องโดยสาร
*Phom / Chan Tong Garn Jong Hong
Doai Sarn*

Timetables (Schedules)

ขาเข้า
Ka Kao
Arrive

การโทร (หยุด) ที่ ...
Karn Toe (Yood) Thee ...
Calls (Stops) at ...

บริการจำหน่ายอาหาร
Borkarn Jam Nai Arhaan
Catering service

เปลี่ยนแปลงที่ ...
Plian Plang Thee ...
Change at ...

การเชื่อมต่อ / ผ่าน
Karn Chuam Tor / Paan
Connection / Via

ทุก ๆ วัน
Thook Thook Waan
Daily

ทุก ๆ 40 นาที
Thook Thook See Sib Nathee
Every 40 minutes

ชั้นหนึ่ง
Chan Nueng
First class

ทุก ๆ ชั่วโมง
Thook Thook Chua Moang
Hourly

ขอแนะนำให้ทำการจองที่นั่ง
*Kor Nae Num Hai Thum
Garn Jong Thee Nung*
**Seat reservations are
recommended**

ชั้นสอง
Chan Song
Second class

ท่านสามารถชำระค่าบริการเสริมได้
*Thun Samart Chamra Ka Borigarn
Serm Dai*
Supplement payable

Luggage

**How much will it cost to send
(ship) my luggage in advance?**
ต้องจ่ายค่าขนสงกระเป๋าเดินทาง (ส่งทางเรือ)
ล่วงหน้าเป็นจำนวนเงินเท่าไหร่
*Tong Jai Ka Kon Song Krapaoderntang
(Song Tang Rua) Luang Na Pen Jam
Nuan Ngern Thao Rai*

**Where is the left luggage
(baggage claim) office?**
สำนักงานบริการรับกระเป๋าเดินทางคืนตั้งอยู่ที่ไหน
*Sam Nak Ngarn Borikarn Rab Krapao
Dern Tang Kuen Tung Yoo Thee Nai*

What time do you open / close?
คุณเปิด / ปิดในเวลาทำการกี่โมง
*Khun Perd / Pid Nai Vela Thum Karn
Gee Mong*

**Where are the luggage trolleys
(carts)?**
รถเข็นกระเป๋าเดินทางอยู่ที่ไหน
*Rhod Ken Krapao Dern Tang Yoo
Thee Nai*

**T
H
A
I**

Where are the lockers?
ตู้ล็อกเกอร์อยู่ที่ไหน
Too Locker Yoo Thee Nai

I have lost my locker key
ผม / ฉันทำกุญแจตู้ล็อกเกอร์หาย
Phom / Chan Thum Koonjae Locker Hai

On Board

Is this seat free?
ที่นั่งนี้ว่างไหม
Thee Nung Nee Wang Mai

Excuse me, you are sitting in my reserved seat
ขอโทษครับ / ค่ะ คุณกำลังนั่งตรงที่ที่ผม / ฉันจองไว้
Kor Thod Krub / Ka Khun Gumlung Nang Trong Thee Thee Phom / Chan Jorng Wai

Which station is this?
นี่คือสถานีไหน
Nee Kue Satannee Nai

What time is this train / bus / ferry / flight due to arrive / depart?
รถไฟ / รถโดยสาร / เรือรับส่งข้ามฟาก /
เที่ยวบินมีกำหนดมาถึง / ออกเดินทางกี่โมง
Rhod Fai / Rhod Doai Saan / Rua Rub Song Kam Fak / Thiao Bin Mee Gumnoad Ma Thueng / Ok Dern Tang Gee Moang

Travelling with Children

Do you have a high chair / babysitting service / cot?
คุณมีเก้าอี้สูง / เก้าอี้นั่ง / เปลสำหรับเด็กไหม
Khun Mee Gao Ie Soong / Gao Ee Naang / Plae Samrub Dek Mai

Where is the nursery / playroom?
เนอเซอรี่ / ห้องนั่งเล่นอยู่ที่ไหน
Nursery / Hong Naang Laen Yoo Thee Nai

Where can I warm the baby's bottle?
ผม / ฉันจะอุ่นขวดนมเด็กทารกได้ที่ไหน
Phom / Chan Ja Oon Kuad Nom Dek Tharok Dai Thee Nai

Customs and Passports

Passports, please!
ขอพาสปอร์ตคืนด้วยครับ / ค่ะ
Kor Passport Kuen Duai Krub / Ka

I have nothing / wine / spirits (alcohol) / tobacco to declare
ผม / ฉันไม่มีรายการใด / ไวน์ / เหล้า (สุรา) /
ยาสูบที่ต้องแสดงหรือไม่
Phom / Chan Mai Mee Rai Kaan Dai / Winr / Lao (Sura) / Yasoob Thee Tong Sadaeng Rue Mai

I will be staying for ... days / weeks / months
ผม / ฉันจะพักอยู่เป็นเวลา ... วัน / สัปดาห์ / เดือน
Phom / Chan Ja Pak Yoo Pen Vela ... Wan / Sarpda / Duean

SIGHTSEEING

Asking the Way

Excuse me, do you speak English?
ขอโทษครับ / ค่ะ คุณพูดภาษาอังกฤษได้ไหม
Kor Thod Krub / Ka Khun Phood Phasa Angrid Dai Mai

T H A I

Excuse me, can you help me please?
ขอโทษครับ / ค่ะ คุณจะช่วยผม / ฉันได้ไหม
Kor Thod Krub / Ka Khun Ja Chuai Phom / Chan Dai Mai

Where is the Tourist Information Office?
ศูนย์บริการข้อมูลนักท่องเที่ยวตั้งอยู่ที่ไหน
Soon Borigarn Khormoon Nak Tong Thiao Tung Yoo Thee Nai

Excuse me, is this the right way to ...?
ขอโทษครับ / ค่ะ นี่เป็นทางที่จะไปยัง ... ใช่ไหม
Kor Thod Krub / Ka Nee Pen Tang Thee Ja Pai Yung ... Chai Mai

... the cathedral / the tourist information office / the castle / the old town
...โบสถ์ / ศูนย์บริการข้อมูลนักท่องเที่ยว / ปราสาท / เมืองเก่า
...Bood / Soon Borigarn Kormoon Nak Tong Thiao / Prasard / Muang Gao

Can you tell me the way to the railway (railroad) station / bus station / taxi rank (stand) / city centre (downtown) / beach?
คุณจะช่วยบอกทางไปยังสถานีรถไฟ (รางรถไฟ) / สถานีรถประจำทาง / ศูนย์บริการแท็กซี่ / ศูนย์กลางเมือง (ดาวน์ทาวน์) / ชายหาดได้ไหม
Khun Ja Chuai Bok Tharng Pai Yung Sathanee Rhodfai (Rang Rhodfai) / Sathanee Rhod Prajam Tharng / Soon Borigarn Taxi / Soon Glang Muang (Downtown) / Chai Haard Dai Mai

First / second / left / right / straight ahead
ที่แรก / ที่สอง / ทางซ้าย / ทางขวา / ตรงไปข้างหน้า
Thee Raek / Thee Sorng / Tharng Sai / Tharng Kwa / Trong Pai Kang Na

At the corner / at the traffic lights
ที่มุม / ที่สัญญาณไฟจราจร
Thee Moom / Thee Sanyarn Fai Jarajorn

Where is the nearest police station / post office?
สถานีตำรวจ / สำนักงานไปรษณีย์ตั้งอยู่ที่ไหน
Sathanee Tamruaj / Samnak Ngan Praisanee Tung Yoo Thee Nai

Is it near / far?
อยู่ใกล้ / ไกลไหม
Yoo Glai / Glai Mai

Do I need to take a taxi / catch a bus?
ผม / ฉันต้องโดยสารรถแท็กซี่ / รถโดยสารหรือไม่
Phom / Chan Tong Doai Saan Rhod Taxi / Rhod Doai Saan Rue Mai

Do you have a map?
คุณมีแผนที่ไหม
Khun Mee Paan Thee Mai

Can you point to it on my map?
คุณจะชี้ให้ผม / ฉันดูบนแผนที่ได้ไหม
Khun Ja Chee Hai Pom / Chan Doo Bon Pan Thee Dai Mai

Thank you for your help
ขอบคุณสำหรับความช่วยเหลือ
Khob Khun Samrap Kwam Chuai Lua

How do I reach the motorway / main road?
ผม / ฉันจะไปยังมอเตอร์เวย์ / ถนนใหญ่ได้อย่างไร
Phom / Chan Ja Pai Yung Motorway / Tanonyai Dai Yang Rai

I think I have taken the wrong turning
ผม / ฉันคิดว่าผม / ฉันเลี้ยวผิด
Phom / Chan Kid Wa Phom / Chan Liao Phid

THAI

I am looking for this address
ผม / ฉันกำลังหาที่อยู่นี้
Phom / Chan Gumlung Kon Haa Thee Yoo Nee

I am looking for the ... hotel
ผม / ฉันกำลังคนหาโรงแรม...
Phom / Chan Gumlung Kon Haa Rongram ...

How far is it to ... from here?
จากตรงนี้อยู่ห่างจาก ... ไกลแค่ไหน
Jak Trong Nee Yoo Harng Jaak ... Glai Kae Nai

Carry straight on for ... kilometres
เดินทางต่อไปอีก ... กิโลเมตร
Dern Tharng Tor Pai Ik ... Kilomaed

Take the next turning on the right / left
เลี้ยวซ้าย / ขวาข้างหน้านี้
Liao Sai / Kwa Kang Naa Nee

Turn right / left at the next crossroads / traffic lights
เลี้ยวขวา / ซ้ายที่แยก / ไฟจราจรข้างหน้า
Liao Kw / Sai Thee Yaek / Fai Jarajorn Kang Naa

You are going in the wrong direction
คุณกำลังไปผิดทางอยู่
Khun Gumlung Pai Phid Tharng Yoo

Where is the cathedral / church / museum / pharmacy?
โบสถ์ฝรั่ง / โบสถ์ / พิพิธภัณฑ์ / ร้านขายยาตั้งอยู่ที่ไหน
Bod Farang / Bod / Pipittaphan / Raan Kai Ya Tung Yoo Thee Nai

How much is the admission / entrance charge?
ค่าธรรมเนียม / ค่าผ่านประตูเท่าไหร่
Ka Thamniam / Ka Paan Pratoo Thao Rai

Is there a discount for children / students / senior citizens?
มีส่วนลดให้กับเด็ก / นักศึกษา / พลเมืองอาวุโสหรือไม่
Mee Suan Lod Hai Gub Dek / Nak Sueksa / Pholamuang Arvuso Rue Mai

What time does the next guided tour (in English) start?
โปรแกรมทัวร์พาเที่ยว (ภาษาอังกฤษ) จะเริ่มกี่โมง
Program Tour Pa Thiao (Pasa Angrid) Ja Rerm Gee Mong

One / two adults / children, please
มีผู้ใหญ่ / เด็กหนึ่ง / สองคนครับ / ค่ะ
Mee Poo Yai / Dek Nueng / Song Kon Krub / Ka

May I take photographs here?
ผม / ฉันขอถ่ายภาพที่นี่ได้ไหมครับ / ค่ะ
Phom / Chan Kor Thai Parb Theenee Dai Mai Krub / Ka

Do you have a map of the town / area?
คุณมีแผนที่เมือง / เขตหรือไม่
Khun Mee Paen Thee Muang / Kaed Rue Mai

Do you have a list of accommodation?
คุณมีรายชื่อที่พักอาศัยหรือไม่
Khun Mee Rai Chue Thee Pak Arsai Rue Mai

Can I reserve accommodation?
ผม / ฉันจะจองที่พักได้ไหม
Phom / Chan Ja Jong Thee Pak Dai Mai

ACCOMMODATION

Hotels

I have a reservation in the name of ...
ผม / ฉันได้จองที่พักในชื่อ ...
Phom / Chan Jong Thee Pak Nai Chue ...

I wrote to / faxed / telephoned you last month / last week
ผม / ฉันได้เขียนถึง / แฟกซ์ /
โทรศัพท์ไปหาคุณเดือน / สัปดาห์ที่แล้ว
Phom / Chan Dai Kian Thueng / Fax / Thorasarb Pai Haa Khun Duan / Sarpda Thee Laew

Do you have any rooms free?
คุณมีห้องพักว่างที่บางไหม
Khun Mee Hong Pak Thee Wang Barng Mai

I would like to reserve a single / double room with / without bath / shower
ผม / ฉันต้องการจองห้องพักเดี่ยว / คู่ที่มี /
ไม่มีห้องน้ำ / ฝักบัวอาบน้ำ
Phom / Chan Tong Garn Jong Hong Paak Diao / Kue Thee Mee / Mai Mee Hong Naam / Fak Bua Arb Nam

I would like bed and breakfast/ (room and) full board
ผม / ฉันอยากได้ที่พักพร้อมเสิร์ฟอาหารเช้า /
(มีห้องพักและ) เต็มอัตรา
Phom / Chan Yaak Dai Thee Pak Phrom Serp Arhaan Chao / (Mee Hong Paak Lae) Tem Artra

How much is it per night?
ราคาต่อคืนเท่าไหร่
Raka Tor Kuen Thao Rai

Is breakfast included?
ราคานี้รวมอาหารเช้าหรือไม
Raka Nee Ruam Arhaan Chao Rue Mai

Do you have any cheaper rooms?
คุณมีห้องพักราคาถูกกว่านี้ไหม
Khun Mee Hong Paak Raka Thook Gwa Nee Mai

I would like to see / take the room
ผม / ฉันอยากขอดู / พักห้องนี้
Phom / Chan Yaak Kor Doo / Paak Hong Nee

I would like to stay for ... nights
ผม / ฉันต้องการขอพัก ... คืน
Phom / Chan Tong Garn Kor Paak ... Kuen

The shower / light / tap / hot water doesn't work
ฝักบัวอาบน้ำ / ไฟ / ก๊อกน้ำ / น้ำร้อนใช้ทำงาน
Fak Bua Arb Nam / Fai / Kok Nam / Nam Ron Mai Tham Ngan

At what time / where is breakfast served?
อาหารเช้าเสิร์ฟตอนกี่โมง / ที่ไหน
Arhaan Chao Serp Ton Gee Mong / Thee Nai

What time do I have to check out?
ผม / ฉันต้องเช็คเอาต์ตอนกี่โมง
Phom / Chan Tong Check-Out Ton Gee Mong

Can I have the key to room number ... ?
ผม / ฉันขอกุญแจและหมายเลขห้องพักเลขที่ ... ได้ไหม
Phom / Chan Kor Goonjae Lae Mai Laek Hongpak Laek Thee ... Dai Mai

My room number is ...
ผม / ฉันพักที่ห้องพักเลขที่ ...
Phom / Chan Paak Thee Hong Paak Laek Thee ...

THAI

ACCOMMODATION

THAI

My room is not satisfactory / not clean enough / too noisy

ห้องพักของผม / ฉันไม่เป็นที่น่าพอใจ / ไมสะอาดพอ / เสียงดังเกินไป

Hong Paak Khong Phom / Chan Mai Pen Thee Naa Por Jai / Mai Sa Ard Phor / Siang Dung Gern Pai

Please can I change rooms?

ผม / ฉันขอเปลี่ยนห้องพักได้ไหมครับ / คะ

Phom / Chan Kor Plian Hong Paak Dai Mai Krub / Ka

Where is the bathroom?

ห้องน้ำอยู่ที่ไหน

Hong Naam Yoo Thee Nai

Do you have a safe for valuables?

คุณมีตู้นิรภัยสำหรับเก็บของมีค่าไหม

Khun Mee Too Neeraphai Samrap Geb Khong Mee Ka Mai

Is there a laundry / do you wash clothes?

มีห้องซักรีดไหม / คุณซักเสื้อผ้าไหม

Mee Hong Saak Reed Mai / Khun Saak Sua Paa Mai

I would like an air-conditioned room

ผม / ฉันอยากได้ห้องพักปรับอากาศ

Phom / Chan Yaak Dai Hong Paak Prab Ar Gard

Do you accept traveller's cheques / credit cards?

คุณรับเช็คนักเดินทาง / บัตรเครดิตหรือไม

Khun Rab Check Nak Dern Tharng / Bard Credit Rue Mai

May I have the bill please?

ขอเช็คบิลได้ไหมครับ / คะ

Kor Check Bill Dai Mai Krub / Ka

Excuse me, I think there may be a mistake in this bill

ขอโทษครับ / คะ ผม / ฉันคิดวาอาจมีความผิดพลาดในบิลนี้

Kor Thod Krub / Ka Phom / Chan Kid Wa Ard Mee Kwam Phid Plard Nai Bill Nee

Youth Hostels

How much is a dormitory bed per night?

ห้องนอนที่มีเตียงนอนราคาเท่าไหร่

Hong Non Thee Mee Tiang Non Raka Thao Rai

I am / am not an HI member

ผม / ฉันเป็น / ไม่ได้เป็นสมาชิกของ HI

Phom / Chan Pen / Mai Dai Pen Samachic Khong HI

May I use my own sleeping bag?

ผม / ฉันขอใช้ถุงนอนที่เอามาเองได้ไหม

Phom / Chan Kor Chai Tung Non Thee Aow Ma Aeng Dai Mai

What time do you lock the doors at night?

คุณล็อคประตูกี่โมงในตอนกลางคืน

Khun Lock Pratoo Gee Mong Nai Ton Glang Kuen

Camping

May I camp for the night / two nights?

ผม / ฉันขอตั้งแคมพ์หนึ่งคืน / สองคืนได้ไหม

Phom / Chan Kor Tung Camp Nueng Kuen / Song Kuen Dai Mai

Where can I pitch my tent?

ผม / ฉันจะตั้งเต็นท์ได้ที่ไหน

Phom / Chan Ja Tung Tent Dai Thee Nai

How much does it cost for one night / week?
คาพักแรมหนึ่งคืน / สองคืนราคาเท่าไหร
Ka Paak Raem Nueng Kuen / Song Kuen Raka Thao Rai

Where are the washing facilities?
อุปกรณ์ทำความสะอาดอยู่ที่ไหน
Oopakorn Tham Kwam Sa Ard Yoo Thee Nai

Is there a restaurant / supermarket / swimming pool on site / nearby?
มีภัตตาคาร / ซุปเปอร์มาร์เก็ต / สระว่ายน้ำที่นี่ / ที่ใกล้เคียงหรือไม
Mee Puttakarn / Super Market / Sra Wai Nam Thee Nee / Thee Glai Kiang Rue Mai

Do you have a safety deposit box?
คุณมีกล่องเก็บของนิรภัยหรือไม่
Khun Mee Glong Geb Khong Niraphai Rue Mai

EATING AND DRINKING

Cafés and Bars

I would like a cup of / two cups of / another coffee / tea
ผม / ฉันอยากได้ชา / กาแฟหนึ่ง / สองถ้วย / อีกถ้วยครับ / คะ
Phom / Chan Yaak Dai Cha / Gafae Nueng / Song Tuai / Ik Tuai Krub / Ka

With / without milk / sugar
ใส่ / ไม่ใส่นม / น้ำตาล
Sai / Mai Sai Nom / Nam Taan

I would like a bottle / glass / two glasses of mineral water / red wine / white wine, please
ผม / ฉันอยากได้น้ำแร่ / ไวน์แดง / ไวน์ขาวหนึ่ง / สองขวด / แก้วได้ไหมครับ / คะ
Phom / Chan Yaak Dai Nam Rae / Wine Daeng / Wing Kao Nueng / Song Kuad / Gaew Dai Mai Krub / Ka

I would like a beer / two beers, please
ผม / ฉันอยากได้เบียร์หนึ่ง / สองขวดครับ / คะ
Phom / Chan Yaak Dai Beer Nueng / Song Kuad Krub / Ka

Please may I have some ice?
ขอน้ำแข็งได้ไหมครับ / คะ
Kor Namkaeng Dai Mai Krub / Ka

Do you have any matches / cigarettes / cigars?
คุณมีไม้ขีดไฟ / บุหรี่ / ซีการ์บางไหม
Khun Mee Mai Keed / Boori / Cigar Barng Mai

Restaurants

Can you recommend a good / cheap restaurant in this area?
คุณจะแนะนำภัตตาคารที่ดี / ถูกในพื้นที่ได้ไหม
Khun Ja Nae Nam Pattakarn Thee Dee / Thook Nai Puen Thee Dai Mai

I would like a table for ...people
ผม / ฉันอยากได้โต๊ะรับประทานอาหารสำหรับ ... คน
Phom / Chan Yaak Dai Toe Rub Prathan Arhaan Samrap ... Kon

Do you have a non-smoking area?
คุณมีเขตปลอดบุหรี่ไหมครับ / คะ
Khun Mee Ked Plord Boori Mai Krub / Ka

Waiter / Waitress!
พนักงานเสิร์ฟ / พนักงานเสิร์ฟหญิง
Phanak Ngan Serp / Phanak Ngan Serp Ying

253

THAI

Excuse me, please may we order?
ขอโทษครับ / ค่ะ เราขอสั่งอาหารได้ไหม
Kor Thod Krub / Ka
Rao Kor Sung Arhaan Dai Mai

Do you have a set menu / children's menu / wine list?
คุณมีอาหารชุด / เมนูสำหรับเด็ก / รายการไวน์ไหม
Khun Mee Arhaan Chood / Menu
Sumrap Dek / Rai Garn Wine Mai

Do you have any vegetarian dishes?
คุณมีอาหารมังสวิรัติไหม
Khun Mee Arhaan Mungsavirath Mai

Do you have any local specialities?
คุณมีอาหารพื้นเมืองจานพิเศษไหม
Khun Mee Arhaan Puen Muang Jarn
Pised Mai

Are vegetables included?
รายการนี้รวมผักหรือไม่
Rai Garn Nee Ruam Phak Rue Mai

Could I have it well-cooked / medium / rare please?
ผม / ฉันขออาหารแบบสุกพอดี / สุกปานกลาง / ดิบได้ไหมครับ / ค่ะ
Phom / Chan Kor Arhaan Baab Sook
Phordee / Sook Plan Klang / Dib Dai
Mai Krub / Ka

What does this dish consist of?
อาหารจานนี้ประกอบด้วยอะไรบ้าง
Arhaan Jhan Nee Prakorb Duai Aria
Barng

I am a vegetarian. Does this contain meat?
ผม / ฉันรับประทานมังสวิรัติ อาหารจานนี้มีเนื้อปนหรือไม่
Phom / Chan Rab Prathan Mangsavirath
Arhaan Jhan Nee Mee Nuea Phon Rue
Mai

I do not eat nuts / dairy products / meat / fish
ผม / ฉันไม่ทานถั่ว / ผลิตภัณฑ์ที่ทำจากนม / เนื้อ / ปลา
Phom / Chan Mai Tharn Tua /
Paritaphan Thee Thum Jaak Nom /
Nua / Pla

Not (very) spicy, please
ขอแบบไม่เผ็ด (มาก) ครับ / ค่ะ
Kor Bab Mai Phed (Mak) Krub / Ka

I would like the set menu, please
ผม / ฉันอยากได้อาหารชุดครับ / ค่ะ
Phom / Chan Yaak Dai Arhaan Chood
Krub / Ka

We are still waiting to be served
เรากำลังรออาหารมาเสิร์ฟอยู่
Rao Gumlung Ror Arhaan Ma Serb Yoo

Please bring a plate / knife / fork
กรุณาหยิบจาน / มีด / ส้อมให้หนึ่งอันครับ / ค่ะ
Garuna Yib Jaan / Meed / Som Hai
Nueng Aan Krub / Ka

Excuse me, this is not what I ordered
ขอโทษครับ / ค่ะ นี่ไม่ใช่รายการที่ผม / ฉันสั่งไป
Kor Thod Krub / Ka Ni Mai Chai Rai
Garn Thee Phom / Chan Sang Pai

May I have some / some more bread / water / coffee / tea?
ขอขนมปัง / น้ำ / ชา / กาแฟเพิ่มได้ไหมครับ / ค่ะ
Kor Kanompung / Nam / Cha / Gafae
Perm Dai Mai Krub / Ka

May I have the bill, please?
ขอเช็คบิลได้ไหมครับ / ค่ะ
Kor Check Bill Dai Mai Krub / Ka

Does this bill include service?
บิลนี้รวมค่าบริการแล้วใช่ไหม
Bill Nee Ruam Ka Borigarn Laew Chai
Mai

Do you accept traveller's
cheques / MasterCard / US
dollars?

คุณรับเช็คนักเดินทาง / บัตรมาสเตอร์การ์ด /
เงินดอลลาร์สหรัฐหรือไม่ครับ / คะ
*Khun Rub Check Nakderntharng / Baad
MasterCard / Ngern Dollar Saharath
Rue Mai Krub / Ka*

Can I have a receipt, please?

ขอใบเสร็จได้ไหมครับ / คะ
Kor Bai Sed Dai Mai Krub / Ka

Where is the toilet (restroom),
please?

สุขา (ห้องน้ำ) อยู่ที่ไหนครับ / คะ
*Sukha (Hong Narm) Yoo Thee Nai
Krub / Ka*

On the Menu

อาหารมื้อเช้า / กลางวัน / ค่ำ
Arhaan Mue Chao / Glangwan / Kum
Breakfast / Lunch / Dinner

จานแรก
Jarn Raek
First courses

น้ำซุป
Narm Soop
Soups

จานหลัก
Jarn Lark
Main courses

อาหารประเภทปลา
Arhaan Praphed Pla
Fish dishes

อาหารประเภทเนื้อ
Arhaan Praphed Nua
Meat dishes

เนื้อวัว
Nua Woua
Beef

สเต็ก
Sa Taek
Steak

หมู
Moo
Pork

เนื้อลูกวัว
Nua Look Vua
Veal

ไก่
Gai
Chicken

เนื้อลูกแกะ
Nua Look Gae
Lamb

แฮม
Ham
Ham

อาหารประเภทมังสวิรัติ
Arhaan Praphed Mangsavirath
Vegetarian dishes

ผัก
Phak
Vegetables

มันฝรั่งทอด (เฟรนช์ฟรายด์)
Maan Farang Thod (French Fries)
Chips (french fries)

มันต้ม / หมักเกลือ / บด
Maan Thom / Maak Gluea / Bod
**Boiled / sauté /
mached potatoes**

ข้าว
Kao
Rice

ชีส
Cheese
Cheese

ของหวาน
Khong Waan
Desserts

ไอศครีม
Ice Cream
Ice cream

เค้ก
Cake
Cakes

ขนมปัง
Kanom Pung
Pastries

T H A I

ผลไม้
Phol Lamai
Fruit

ขนมปัง
Kanom Pung
Bread

โรล
Roll
Rolls

ขนมปังปิ้ง
Kanom Pung Ping
Toast

เนย
Noey
Butter

เกลือ / พริกไทย
Gluea / Prik Thai
Salt / pepper

น้ำตาล
Nam Tarn
Sugar

อาหารจานพิเศษ
Arhaan Jarn Pee Sed
Specialities

อาหารพื้นเมืองจานพิเศษ
Arhaan Puen Muang Jarn Pised
Local specialities

อาหารชุด
Arhaan Chood
Set Menu

รายการไวน์
Rai Garn Wine
Wine list

ไวน์แดง
Wine Daeng
Red wines

ไวน์ขาว
Wine Kao
White wines

ไวน์โรเส่
Wine Rosé
Rosé wines

ไวน์สปาร์คกลิ้ง
Wine Sparkling
Sparkling wines

เบียร์
Beer
Beer

เบียร์บรรจุขวด / เบียร์สด
Beer Banjoo Kuad / Beer Sod
**Bottled beer /
Draught (draft) beer**

เครื่องดื่มไม่ผสมแอลกอฮอล์
Kruang Duem Mai Pasom Alcohol
Non-alcoholic drinks

น้ำแร่
Nam Rae
Mineral water

น้ำผลไม้
Nam Phol Lamai
Fruit juices

น้ำส้มคั้น
Nam Som Kaan
Orange juice

น้ำมะนาว
Nam Manao
Lemonade

น้ำแข็ง
Nam Kaeng
Ice

กาแฟใส่นม / กาแฟดำ / เอ็กเปรสโซ่
*Gafae Sai Nom / Gafae Dum /
Expresso*
**White coffee / black coffee /
espresso coffee**

ชาใส่นม / ใส่มะนาว
Cha Sai Nom / Sai Manao
Tea with milk / with lemon

ช็อกโกเลต (พร้อมดื่ม)
Chocolate (Prom Duem)
Chocolate (drink)

นม
Nom
Milk

ขนม / อาหารว่าง
Kanom / Arhaan Wang
Snacks / Light meals

สลัด
Salad
Salads

แซนวิช
Sand wich
Sandwiches

ไข่
Kai
Eggs

ไส้กรอก
Sai Krok
Sausage

ไข่ต้ม / เจียว / คน
Kai Tom / Jiao / Kon
Boiled / fried / scrambled eggs

Typical Local Dishes

ผัดไทย
Pad Thai
Thai style fried noodles

ต้มยำ
Tom Yum
Spicy and sour Thai soup

แกงเขียวหวาน
Gaeng Kiao Waan
Thai green curry

ผัดกะเพราหมู
Paad Krabrao Moo
Stir-fried pork with basil leaf

ส้มตำไทย
Som Tum Thai
Hot papaya salad

Public Transport

Where is the bus stop / coach stop / nearest metro (subway) station?
ป้ายรถโดยสาร / รถตู้ / สถานีรถไฟ (ใต้ดิน) ที่ใกล้ที่สุดอยู่ที่ไหน
Pai Rhod Doai Sarn / RodToo / Satanee Rhodfai (Tai Din) Thee Glai Thee Sood Yoo Thee Nai

When is the next / last bus to ...?
รถโดยสารคันต่อไป / สุดท้ายที่จะไปยัง ... ออกคอนกี่โมง
Rhod Doai Sarn Kan Tor Pai / Sood Thai Thee Ja PaiYung ... Ok Torn Gee Mong

How much is the fare to the city centre (downtown) / railway station / airport?
ค่าโดยสารไปยังใจกลางเมือง (ดาวน์ทาวน์) / สถานีรถไฟ / สนามบินราคาเท่าไร
Ka Doai Sarn Pai Yang Jai Glang Muang (Downtown) / Satanee Rhodfai / Sanambin Raka Thao Rai

Will you tell me when to get off?
กรุณาบอกผม / ฉันที่ว่าต้องลงป้ายไหน
Garuna Bok Phom / Chan Thee Wa Tong Long Pai Nai

Does this bus go to ...?
รถโดยสารคันนี้ไปยัง ... ไหม
Rhod Doai Sarn Kan Nee Pai Young ... Mai

Which number bus goes to ...?
รถโดยสารที่จะไปยัง ... หมายเลขเท่าไร
Rhod Doai Sarn Thee Ja Pai Young ... Mai Laek Thao Rai

T H A I

May I have a single (oneway) / return (round-trip) / day ticket / book of tickets?

ผม / ฉันขอซื้อตั๋วโดยสารเที่ยวเดียว / ไป-กลับ / ตั๋ววัน / ตั๋วเล่มหนึ่งได้ไหมครับ / คะ
Phom / Chan Kor Sue Thua Doai Sarn Thiao Diao / Pai Glub / Tua Waan / Tua Lem Nueng Dai Mai Krub / Ka

Taxis and Rickshaws

I would like to go to ...

ผม / ฉันต้องการไปที่ ...
Phom / Chan Tong Garn Pai Thee ...

How much will it cost?

ต้องมีค่าใช้จ่ายจ่ายเท่าไหร่
Tong Mee Ka Chai Jai Thao Rai

Please may I stop here?

ผม / ฉันขอลงตรงนี้ได้ไหมครับ / คะ
Phom / Chan Kor Loeng Trong Nee Dai Mai Krub / Ka

I would like to order a taxi today / tomorrow / at 2pm to go from ... to ...

ผม / ฉันต้องการเรียกแท็กซี่วันนี้ / พรุ่งนี้ / ตอนบ่ายสองเพื่อเดินทางจาก ... ไป ...
Phom / Chan Tong Garn Reak Taxi Wannee / Prueng Nee / Ton Bai Song Puea Dern Tharng Jaak ... Pai ...

Entertainment

Can you recommend a good bar / nightclub?

คุณจะแนะนำบาร์ / ไนท์บาร์ดี ๆ ให้ผม / ฉันได้ไหม
Khun Ja Nae Num Bar / Night Bar Dee Dee Hai Phom / Chan Dai Mai

Do you know what is on at the cinema (playing at the movies) / theatre at the moment?

คุณรู้รายการหนัง (ในโรงภาพยนตร์) / โรงละครในขณะนี้ไหม
Khun Roo Rai Garn Nang (Nai Rong Phappayon) / Rong Lakorn Nai Khana Nee Mai

I would like to book (purchase) ... tickets for the matinee / evening performance on Monday

ผม / ฉันต้องการจอง (ซื้อ) ตั๋ว ... ใบสำหรับรายการ Matinee / การแสดงยามค่ำในวันจันทร์
Phom / Chan Tong Garn Jong (Suea) Tua ... Bai Samrup Rai Garn Matinee / Garn Sadaeng Yam Kum Nai Wan Jaan

What time does the film / performance start?

ภาพยนตร์ / การแสดงจะเริ่มตอนกี่โมง
Phappayon / Garn Sadaeng Ja Rerm Ton Gee Mong

Post

How much will it cost to send a letter / postcard / this package to Britain / Ireland / America / Canada / Australia / New Zealand?

คิดค่าบริการจัดส่งจดหมาย / โปสการ์ด / พัสดุไปยัง ประเทศอังกฤษ / ไอแลนด์ / อเมริกา / แคนนาดา / ออสเตรเลีย / นิวซีแลนด์เท่าไหร่
Kid Ka Borigarn Jad Song Jod Mai / Postcard / Pasadoo Pai Yang Prathed Angrid / I Land / America / Canada / Australia / New Zealand Tang Rai

I would like one stamp / two stamps

ผม / ฉันอยากได้แสตมป์หนึ่ง / สองดวง
Phom / Chan Yaak Dai Stamp Nueng / Song Duang

I'd like ... stamps for postcards to send abroad, please
ผม / ฉันอยากได้แสตมป์...ดวงสำหรับโปสการ์ดเพื่อส่งไปยังต่างประเทศครับ / ค่ะ
Phom / Chan Yaak Dai Stamp... Duang Sumrap Postcard Puea Song Pai Yang Tang Prathed Krub / Ka

Phones

I would like to make a telephone call / reverse the charges to (make a collect call to) ...
ผม / ฉันต้องการโทรศัพท์ / เก็บค่าโทรปลายทาง (ณ ที่หมายที่) ...
Phom / Chan Tong Garn Torasarp / Geb Ka Thoe Plai Tharng (Na Thee Mai Thee) ...

Which coins do I need for the telephone?
ผม / ฉันต้องใช้เหรียญไหนเพื่อโทรศัพท์
Phom / Chan Chai Rean Nai Puea Torasarp

The line is engaged (busy)
สายนี้ไม่ว่าง
Sai Nee Mai Wang

The number is ...
เลขหมายที่โทรคือ...
Laek Mai Thee Thoe Kue...

Hello, this is ...
สวัสดีครับ / ค่ะ ผม / ฉันชื่อ ...
Sawasdee Krub / Ka Phom / Chan Chue...

Please may I speak to ... ?
ผม / ฉันขอคุยสายกับ ... ได้ไหมครับ / ค่ะ
Phom / Chan Kor Kui Sai Gub ... Dai Mai Krub / Ka

He / she is not in at the moment. Can you call back?
เขา / เธอไม่อยู่ในขณะนี้
คุณจะโทรกลับมาได้ไหมครับ / ค่ะ

Kao / Ter Mai Yoo Nai KananeeKhun Ja Thoe Glub Ma Dai Mai Krub / Ka

SHOPPING

Shops

ร้านหนังสือ / เครื่องเขียน
Raan Nangsue / Kruang Kian
Bookshop / Stationery

จิวเวอรี่ / ร้านของขวัญ
Jewverree / Raan Khong Kwan
Jeweller / Gifts

รองเท้า
Rong Thao
Shoes

ฮาร์ดแวร์
Hardware
Hardware

ช่างทำผม
Chang Tham Phom
Hairdresser

(ชาย) / (หญิง)
(Chai) / (Ying)
(men's) / (women's)

ร้านขายขนมปัง
Raan Kai Kanom Pung
Baker

ตู้โทรศัพท์
Too Torasarp
Phones

ซุปเปอร์มาร์เก็ต
Supermarket
Supermarket

THAI

THAI

ร้านอัดรูปถ่าย
Raan Ud Roop Thai
Photo-Shop

เอเยนต์ทัวร์
Ae Yen Tour
Travel agent

ร้านขายยา
Raan Kai Yaa
Pharmacy

In the Shops

What time do the shops open / close?
ร้านค้าเปิด / ปิดตอนกี่โมง
Raan Kaa Perd / Pid Ton Gee Mong

Where is the nearest market?
ตลาดที่ใกล้ที่สุดอยู่ที่ไหน
Talard Thee Glai Thee Sud Yoo Thee Nai

Can you show me the one in the window / this one?
ขอดูสินค้าตรงหน้าต่าง / ชิ้นนี้ได้ไหม
Kor Doo Sin Ka Trong Na Tarng / Chin Nee Dai Mai

Can I try this on?
ขอลองชุดนี้ได้ไหม
Kor Long Chood Nee Dai Mai

What size is this?
นี่ขนาดเท่าไหร่
Nee Kanard Thao Rai

This is too large / too small / too expensive.
นี่ขนาดใหญ่ / เล็ก / แพงเกินไป
Nee Kanard Yai / Lek / Paeng Gern Pai

Do you have any others?
คุณมีตัวอื่นไหม
Khun Mee Tua Uen Mai

My size is ...
ขนาดที่ผม / ฉันใส่คือ ...
Kanard Thee Phom / Chan Sai Kue ...

Where is the changing room / children's / cosmetic / ladieswear / menswear / food department?
ห้องเปลี่ยนเสื้อ / แผนกเสื้อผ้าเด็ก / เครื่องสำอาง / ชุดชั้นในชาย / หญิง / แผนกอาหารอยู่ที่ไหน
Hong Plean Sua / Phanaek Sua Paa Dek / Kruang Sam Arng / Chud Chan Nai Chai / Ying / Panak Arhaan Yoo Thee Nai

I would like ... a quarter of a kilo / half a kilo / a kilo of bread / butter / cheese / ham / this fruit
ผม / ฉันอยากได้ ... เศษหนึ่งส่วนสี่กิโลกรัม / ครึ่งกิโลกรัม / หนึ่งกิโลกรัมสำหรับขนมปัง / เนย / ชีส / แฮม / ผลไม้ชนิดนี้
Phom / Chan Yaak Dai ... sed Nueng Suan See Kilogram / Krueng Kilogram / Nueng Kilogram Sumrap Kanom Pung / Noey / Cheese / Ham / Phol Lamai Chanid Nee

How much is this?
นี่ราคาเท่าไหร่
Nee Raka Thao Rai

I'll take this one, thank you
ผม / ฉันขอซื้ออันนี้ ขอบคุณครับ / ค่ะ
Phom / Chan Kor Sue Aan Nee Kob Khun Krub / Ka

Do you have a carrier (shopping) bag?
คุณมีถุงใส่ของ (ชอปปิ้ง) ไหม
Khun Mee Toong Sai Khong (Shopping) Mai

Do you have anything cheaper / larger / smaller / of better quality?

คุณมีสินค้าที่ถูกกว่า / ใหญ่กว่า / เล็กกว่า / คุณภาพดีกว่านี้ไหม
Khun Mee Sin Kha Thee Thook Gwa / Yai Gwa / Lek Gwa / Kunaparb Dee Gwa Nee Mai

I would like a film / to develop this film for this camera

ผม / ฉันอยากได้ฟิล์ม / ล้างรูปในกล้องนี้
Phom / Chan Yaak Dai Film / Lang Roop Nai Glong Nee

I would like some batteries, the same size as this old one

ผม / ฉันอยากได้แบตเตอรี่ขนาดเดียวกันกับอันเก่านี้
Phom / Chan Yaak Dai Battery Kanard Diao Gaan Gub Un Gao Nee

Would you mind wrapping this for me, please?

คุณจะห่อสินค้าชิ้นนี้ให้ได้ไหมครับ / คะ
Khun Ja Hor Sin Ka Chin Nee Hai Dai Mai Krub / Ka

Sorry, but you seem to have given me the wrong change

ขอโทษครับ / คะ แต่รู้สึกว่าคุณจะให้เงินทอนผม / ฉันผิด
Kor Thod Krub / Ka Tae Roo Suek Wa Khun Ja Hai Ngorn Thon Phom / Chan Phid

MOTORING

Car Hire (Rental)

I have ordered (rented) a car in the name of ...

ผม / ฉันได้สั่ง (เช่า) รถยนต์โดยใช้ชื่อ ...
Phom / Chan Dai Sung (Chao) Rhod Yhon Doai Chai Chue ...

How much does it cost to hire (rent) a car for one day / two days / a week?

คิดค่าบริการเช่ารถยนต์เป็นเวลาหนึ่งวัน / สองวัน / หนึ่งสัปดาห์เท่าไหร่
Kid Ka Borigarn Chao Rhod Yhon Pen Vela Nueng Wan / Song Wan / Nueng Sarpda Thao Rai

Is the tank already full of petrol (gas)?

เติมน้ำมันเชื้อเพลิง (แก๊ส) เต็มถังแล้วใช่ไหม
Term Nam Mun Chuea Plerng (Gas) Tem Thung Laew Chai Mai

Is insurance and tax included? How much is the deposit?

ราคานี้รวมค่าประกันและภาษีแล้วหรือไม่ ค่ามัดจำคิดเท่าไหร่
Raka Nee Ruam Ka Pragun Lae Phasee Laew Rue Mai. Ka Mud Jum Kid Thao Rai

By what time must I return the car?

ผม / ฉันต้องนำรถไปคืนตอนกี่โมง
Phom / Chan Tong Num Rhod Pai Kuen Ton Gee Mong

I would like a small / large / family / sports car with a radio / cassette player

ผม / ฉันต้องการรถขนาดเล็ก / ใหญ่ / ครอบครัว / สปอร์ตพร้อมวิทยุ / เครื่องเล่นเทป
Phom / Chan Tong Garn Rhod Kanard Lek / Yai / Krob Krua / Sport Prom Vittayoo / Kruang Len Tape

Do you have a road map?

คุณมีแผนที่เส้นทางไหม
Khun Mee Phaen Thee Sen Tarng Mai

T H A I

Parking

How long can I park here?
ผม / ฉันจะจอดรถที่นี่ได้นานแค่ไหน
Phom / Chan Ja Jod Rhod Thee Nee Dai Naan Kae Nai

Is there a car park near here?
มีที่จอดรถที่อยู่ใกล้ๆ กับที่นี่ไหม
Mee Thee Jod Rhod Thee Yoo Glai Glai Gub Thee Nee Mai

At what time does this car park close?
ที่จอดรถแห่งนี้ปิดตอนกี่โมง
Thee Jod Rhod Haeng Nee Phid Ton Gee Mong

Signs and Notices

ทางเดียว
Tharng Diao
One way

ห้ามเข้า
Haam Kao
No entry

ห้ามจอด
Haam Jord
No parking

ทางเลี่ยง (เบี่ยง)
Tharng Liang (Biang)
Detour (diversion)

หยุดรถ
Yood Rhod
Stop

ให้ทาง (ขอทาง)
Hai Tharng (Kor Tharng)
Give way (yield)

ถนนลื่น
Thanon Luean
Slippery Road

ห้ามแซง
Haam Saeng
No overtaking

อันตราย!
Un Tarai
Danger!

At the Filling Station

Unleaded (lead-free) / standard / premium / diesel
เบนซินไร้สาร (ไม่มีตะกั่วผสม) / มาตรฐาน / พรีเมี่ยม / ดีเซล
Benzine Rai Sarn (Mai Mee Tha Gua Phasom) / Matrathan / Premium / Dee Sel

Fill the tank please
ช่วยเติมน้ำมันให้เต็มถังได้ไหมครับ / คะ
Chuai Term Nam Mun Hai Tem Thung Dai Mai Krub / Ka

Do you have a road map?
คุณมีแผนที่เส้นทางไหม
Khun Mee Pan Thee Sen Tharng Mai

How much is the car wash?
คิดค่าบริการล้างรถเท่าไหร่
Kid Ka Borigarn Larng Rhod Thao Rai

Breakdowns

I've had a breakdown at ...
รถของผม / ฉันเสียที่ ...
Rhod Khong Phom / Chan Sia Thee ...

I am a member of the [motoring organisation]
ผม / ฉันเป็นสมาชิกของ [องค์กรยานยนต์]
Phom / Chan Pen Samachick Khong [Ong Gorn Rhod Yhon]

I am on the road from ... to ...
ผม / ฉันอยู่บนเส้นทางจาก ... ไปยัง ...
Phom / Chan Yoo Bon Sen Tharng Jaak ... Pai Yung ...

I can't move the car. Can you send a tow-truck?
ผม / ฉันเลื่อนรถไม่ได้
คุณจะช่วยส่งรถลากมาได้ไหมครับ / คะ
Phom / Chan Luean Rhod Mai Dai. Khun Ja Chuai Song Rhod Lark Ma DaiMai Krub / Ka

I have a flat tyre
ยางรถของผม / ฉันแบน
Yarng Rhod Khong Phom / Chan Baen

The windscreen (windshield) has smashed / cracked
กระจกหน้ารถยนต์แตก / เกิดรอยร้าว
Krajok Na Rhod Yon Taek / Gerd Roi Rao

There is something wrong with the engine / brakes / lights / steering / gearbox / clutch / exhaust
มีความผิดปกติบางอย่างกับเครื่องยนต์ / ระบบเบรก / ไฟ / การควบคุม / ชุดเกียร์ / คลัตช์ / ไอเสีย
Mee Kwam Phid Prokathi Bang Yarng Gub Kruang Yhon / Rabob Brake / Fai / Garn Kuab Koom / Chud Gear / Clutch / Ai Sia

It's overheating
ความร้อนขึ้นสูงเกินไป
Kwam Ron Kuen Soong Gern Pai

It won't start
รถไม่ยอมสตาร์ทติด

Rhod Mai Yhom Start Tid

Where can I get it repaired?
จะทำซ่อมรถได้ที่ไหน
Ja Haa Oo Som Rhod Dai Thee Nai

Can you take me there?
คุณจะช่วยพาผม / ฉันไปที่นั่นได้ไหม
Khun Ja Chuai Paa Phom / Chan Pai Thee Naan Dai Mai

Will it take long to fix?
จะใช้เวลาซ่อมนานไหม
Ja Chai Vela Sorm Naan Mai

How much will it cost?
คิดค่าบริการซ่อมเท่าไหร่
Kid Ka Borigarn Som Thao Rai

Please can you pick me up / give me a lift?
คุณจะช่วยรับผม / ฉันไป /
ขับรถไปส่งได้ไหมครับ / คะ
Khun Ja Chuai Rub Phom / Chan Pai / Khub Rhod Pai Song Dai Mai Krub / Ka

Accidents and Traffic Offences

Can you help me? There has been an accident
คุณจะช่วยผม / ฉันได้ไหม ขณะนี้ได้เกิดอุบัติเหตุขึ้น
Khun Ja Chuai Phom / Chan Dai Mai Kananee Dai Gerd Oobad Tihead Kuen

Please call the police / an ambulance
คุณช่วยโทรเรียกตำรวจ /
รถพยาบาลให้ที่ได้ไหมครับ / คะ
Khun Ja Chuai Thoe Reak Tumruad / Rhod Phayabaan Hai Thee Dai Mai Krub / Ka

Is anyone hurt?
มีใครได้รับบาดเจ็บไหม
Mee Krai Dai Rub Bard Jeb Mai

I'm sorry, I didn't see the sign
ผม / ฉันขอโทษครับ / คะ ผม / ฉันมองไม่เห็นป้าย
*Phom / Chan Kor Thod Krub / Ka
Phom / Chan Mong Mai Hen Phai*

Must I pay a fine? How much?
ผม / ฉันต้องชำระค่าปรับไหม คิดเป็นเงินจำนวนเทาใหร
*Phom / Chan Tong Chamra Kaa Prub
Mai. Kid Pen Jum Nuan Ngern Thao Rai*

Show me your documents
ขอผม / ฉันดูเอกสารของคุณได้ไหม
*Kor Hom / Chan Doo Ekasan Khong
Khun Dai Mai*

Pharmacy

Do you have anything for a stomach ache / headache / sore throat / toothache?
คุณมียาแก้อาการปวดท้อง / ปวดหัว /
เจ็บคอ / ปวดฟันบ้างไหม
*Khun Mee Yaa Gae Argarn Puad
Thong / Puad Hua / Jeb Kor /
Puad Fun Barng Mai*

I need something for diarrhoea / constipation / a cold / a cough / insect bites / sunburn / travel (motion) sickness (car) (plane) (boat)
ผม / ฉันอยากได้ยาแก้อาการท้องร่วง / ท้องผูก /
หวัด / ไอ / แมลงกัดตอย / ผิวหนังถูกแดดเผาไหม้ /
คลื่นไส้อาเจียน (จากการเดินทาง) (โดยรถยนต์)
(โดยเครื่องบิน) (โดยเรือ)

*Phom / Chan Yark Dai Ya Gae Argaan
Thong Ruang / Thong Pook / Waad /
Ai / Malaeng Gud Toi / Phew Nung Took
Daad Mai / Kluen Sai Arjian (Jak Garn
Dern Thang) (Doai Rhod Yoan) (Doai
Kruang Bin) (Doai Rua)*

How much / how many do I take?
ผม / ฉันต้องรับประทานในปริมาณเท่าไหร่ / กี่เม็ด
*Phom / Chan Tong Rub Prathan Nai
Porimarn Thao Rai / Gee Med*

How often do I take it / them?
ผม / ฉันต้องรับประทานบ่อยแค่ไหน
*Phom / Chan Tong Rub Pratharn Bouy
Kae Nai*

I am / he is / she is taking this medication
ผม / ฉัน / เขา / เธอกำลังรับประทานยานี้อยู่
*Phom / Chan / Kao / Ther Gumlung
Rub Pratharn Yaa Nee Yoo*

How much does it cost?
คิดคายาเป็นเงินเท่าไหร
Kid Ka Yaa Pen Ngern Thao Rai

Can you recommend a good doctor / dentist?
คุณจะช่วยแนะนำหมอ / ทันตแพทย์ที่เก่งให้ได้ไหม
*Khun Ja Chuai Nae Num Mor / Thanta
Paed Thee Geng Hai Dai Mai*

Is it suitable for children?
ยานี้เหมาะสำหรับเด็กไหม
Yaa Nee Mor Sumrab Dek Mai

Doctor

I have a pain here / in my arm / leg / chest / stomach
ผม / ฉันรู้สึกปวดตรงจุดนี้ / ในแขน / ขา /
หนาอก / กระเพาะ

Phom / Chan Roo Suek Puad Trong Jud
Nee / Nai Kaen / Kha / Na Ok / Gra
Phror

Please call a doctor, this is an emergency
กรุณาโทรตามหมอให้ที มีเหตุฉุกเฉิน
Garuna Thoe Tam Mor Hai Thee Mee
Haed Chook Chern

I would like to make an appointment to see the doctor
ผม / ฉันต้องการนัดหมอเพื่อเข้ารับการตรวจเช็ค
Phom / Chan Tong Garn Nard Mor
Puea Kao Rub Garn Truad Check

I am diabetic / pregnant
ผม / ฉันเป็นโรคเบาหวาน / ตั้งครรภ์
Phom / Chan Pen Rok Bao Wan /
Tung Kaan

I need a prescription for ...
ผม / ฉันอยากได้ยาสำหรับ...
Phom / Chan Yaak Dai Ya Sumrab ...

Can you give me something to ease the pain?
คุณจะให้ยาเพื่อบรรเทาอาการปวดได้ไหม
Khun Ja Hai Ya Puea Bunthao Argarn
Puad Dai Mai

I am / he is / she is allergic to penicillin
ผม / ฉัน / เขา / เธอแพ้ยาเพนนิซิลิน
Phom / Chan / Kao / Ther Pae Yaa
Penicillin

Does this hurt?
นี่เจ็บไหม
Nee Jeb Mai

You must / he must / she must go to hospital
คุณ / เขา / เธอต้องไปโรงพยาบาล
Khun / Kao / Ther Tong Pai Rhong
Phayabarn

Take these once / twice / three times a day
รับประทานยานี้หนึ่ง / สอง / สามครั้งต่อวัน
Rub Pratharn Yaa Nee Nueng / Song /
Sam Krung Tor Wan

I am / he is / she is taking this medication
ผม / ฉัน / เขา / เธอกำลังรับประทานยานี้อยู่
Phom / Chan / Kao / Ther Gumlung
Rub Pratharn Yaa Nee Yoo

I have medical insurance
ผม / ฉันมีใบประกันทางการแพทย์
Phom / Chan Mee Bai Rub Pragun
Tharng Garn Paed

I have toothache
ผม / ฉันปวดฟัน
Phom / Chan Puad Fun

My filling has come out
ผลการตรวจของผม / ฉันเสร็จแล้ว
Phon Garn Truad Khong Phom / Chan
Sed Laew

I do / do not want to have an injection first
ผม / ฉันไม่ต้องการให้ฉีดยาก่อน
Phom / Chan Mai Tong Garn Hai Cheed
Yaa Gorn

Help!
ช่วยด้วย!
Chuai Duai

Fire!
ไฟไหม้!
Fai Mui

T
H
A
I

265

T
H
A
I

Stop!
หยุดนะ!
Yood Na

Call an ambulance / a doctor / the police / the fire brigade!
ช่วยโทรเรียกรถพยาบาล / หมอ / ตำรวจ / พนักงานดับเพลิงให้ที!
Chuai Thoe Reak Rod Phayabarn / Mor / Tumruad / Phanak Ngan Dub Plerng Hai Thee

Please may I use a telephone?
ผม / ฉันขอใช้โทรศัพท์ได้ไหมครับ / คะ
Phom / Chan Kor Chai Thorasarb Dai Mai Krub / Ka

I have had my traveller's cheques / credit cards / handbag / rucksack / (knapsack) / luggage / wallet / passport / mobile phone stolen.
เช็คนักเดินทาง / บัตรเครดิต / กระเป๋าสะพาย / กระเป๋าป้ / กระเป๋าเดินทาง / กระเป๋าสตางค์ / พาสปอร์ต / โทรศัพท์มือถือของผม / ฉันถูกขโมยไป
Check Nak Dern Thamg / Baad Credit / Krapao Saphai / Krapao Pae / Krapao Dern Tharng / Krapao Satarng / Passport / Thorasarb Mue Tue Khong Phom / Chan Thook Kamoey Pai

May I please have a copy of the report for my insurance claim?
ผม / ฉันขอสำเนาของรายงานที่ส่งไปเคลมประกัน ได้ไหมครับ / คะ
Phom / Chan Kor Sumnao Khong Rai Garn Ngarn Thee Song Pai Claim Pragun Dai Mai Krub / Ka

Can you help me? I have lost my daughter / my son / my companion(s)
คุณจะช่วยผม / ฉันได้ไหมคะ / ฉันพลัดหลงกับบุตรสาว / บุตรชาย / เพื่อนร่วมเดินทางของผม / ฉัน

Khun Ja Chuai Phom / Chan Dai Mai. Phom / Chan Plad Long Gub Bood Sao / Bood Chai / Puean Ruam Dern Tharng KongPhom / Chan

Please go away / leave me alone
กรุณาไปให้พ้น / ให้ผม / ฉันอยู่คนเดียว
Garuna Pai Hai Phon / Hai Phom / Chan Yoo Kon Diao

I'm sorry
ผม / ฉันขอโทษ
Phom / Chan Kor Thoad

I want to contact the British / American / Canadian / Irish / Australian / New Zealand / South African consulate
ผม / ฉันต้องการติดต่อกับสถานกงสุลของประเทศอังกฤษ / สหรัฐอเมริกา / แคนนาดา / ไอร์แลนด์ / ออสเตรเลีย / นิวซีแลนด์ / แอฟริกาใต้
Phom / Chan Tong Garn Tid Tor Gub Sathan Ghongsoon Khong Prathed Angrid / Saharad America / Canada / I Land / Australia / New Zealand / Africa Tai

I'm / we're / he is / she is ill / lost / injured
ผม / เรา / เขา / เธอไม่สบาย / หลงทาง / ได้รับบาดเจ็บ
Phom / Rao / Kao / Ther Mai Sabai / Long Tharng / Dai Rub Bard Jeb

They are ill / lost / injured
พวกเขาไม่สบาย / หลงทาง / ได้รับบาดเจ็บ
Puak Kao Mai Sabai / Long Tharng / Dai Rub Bard Jeb

VIETNAMESE
TIẾNG VIỆT

VIETNAMESE

INTRODUCTION

Vietnamese is the official language of Vietnam, and is a member of the Austro-Asiatic language family; French, Chinese, English, Khmer and tribal dialects, particularly in the more remote mountainous areas, are also spoken. Vietnamese was originally written in Chinese characters until, estimates say, the fourteenth century, when it was written using a script known as Chu Nom. That didn't last either: a romanised script, quoc ngu (meaning national language) took over and this is the form that remains today. There are only three main dialects found in the north, south and central regions and they are quite similar in sound.

Addresses for Travel and Tourist Information

Australia: Embassy of the Socialist Republic of Vietnam, 6 Timbarra Crescent, O'Malley, Canberra ACT 2606. Tel: 02 628 66059; Fax: 02 628 64534; Email: vembassy@webone.com.au; Web: www.vietnamembassy.org.au

Canada: Embassy of Vietnam, 470 Wilbrod Street, Ottawa, Ontario K1N 6MB. Tel: 613 236 1398; Fax: 613 236 0819; Email: vietem@istar.ca

UK: Embassy of Vietnam, 12 Victoria Road, London W8 5RD. Tel: 020 7937 1912; Fax: 020 7937 6108; Email: consular@vietnamembassy.org.uk

USA: Embassy of the Socialist Republic of Vietnam, 1233 20th St NW, Suite 400, Washington DC 20036. Tel: 202 861 0737; Fax: 202 861 0917; Email: info@vietnamembassy.us; Web: www.vietnamembassy-usa.org

Vietnam Facts

CAPITAL: Hanoi

CURRENCY: Dong (d)

OPENING HOURS: Banks: Mon-Fri: 0730-1130 and 1330-1530,
Sat 0730-1130. Shops: Most open 7 days a week, many opening until 2000
in the evening. Museums: 0800-1100 and 1400-1600, most closed Mon.

TELEPHONES: Tel: International Access Code + 84 + Area Code minus
first 0. Outgoing, Tel: 00 + Country Code.

EMERGENCY NUMBERS: Police, Tel: 113. Fire; Tel: 114.
Ambulance; Tel: 115.

PUBLIC HOLIDAYS: Jan 1 (New Year), late Jan / mid – Feb (dates vary each
year) – Tet, three days to a week celebrating the Vietnamese New Year;
Apr 30 – Liberation of Saigon (1975); May 1 (International Labour Day)
and Sept 2 (National Day).

Technical Language Hints

- In Vietnamese the phrase will vary according to the relative age and
  gender of the person to whom you are speaking. In order to ensure that
  no offence is caused, the polite forms of address have been given here.

Notes for addressing in compliance with Vietnamese customs:

- When interacting with the older generation

  Male: Anh [An] (the same generation as your older brother)
  Chú, Bác [Choo, Bach] (the same generation as your uncle]
  Ông [Ong] (the same generation as your grandfather)

  Female: chị [chee] (the same generation as your older sister)
  Cô, Bác [Koh, Bach] (the same generation as your aunt)
  Bà [bah] (the same generation as your grandmother)

- When interacting with the younger generation
  Em [ehm] (the same generation as your younger brother or sister)
  Cháu [chau] (the same generation as your nephew or niece)

VIETNAMESE

Alphabet

A	Ă
Ah	*Áh*
Â	B
Éh	*Ber*
C	D
Ker	*Zer*
Đ	E
Der	*Erh*
Ê	G
Eh	*Ger*
H	I
Her	*E*
K	L
Cah	*Ler*
M	N
Mer	*Ner*
O	Ô
Or	*Oh*
Ơ	P
Er	*Per*
Q	R
Kuh	*Rer*
S	T
Sher	*Ter*
U	Ư
Uh	*Uuh*
V	X
Ver	*Ser*
Y	
E	

Basic Words and Phrases

Yes	**No**
Có	Không
Koh	*Kong*
Please	**Thank you**
Xin	Cảm ơn
Sin	*Kahm Earn*
Hello	**Goodbye**
Xin chào	Tạm biệt
Sin Chow	*Tahm Bee-Et*
Excuse me	**Sorry**
Xin lỗi	Xin lỗi
Sin Loy	*Sin Loy*
How	**When**
Làm thế nào	Bao giờ
Lahm Theh Now	*Bow Zor*
Why	**What**
Tại sao	Gì
Tay-Ee Show	*Zee*
Who	
Ai	
Ay	
That's O.K.	**Perhaps**
OK	Có lẽ
OK	*Koh Leh*
To	**From**
Đến	Từ
Dain	*Tuh*
Here	**There**
Đây	Đó
Day	*Doh*
I don't understand	
Tôi không hiểu	
Toy Kong Hee-You	

I don't speak Vietnamese
Tôi không nói tiếng Việt
Toy Kong Noy Tee-Eng Vee-Et

Do you speak English?
Bạn có nói tiếng Anh không?
Bahn Koh Noy Tee-Eng An Kong

Can you please write it down?
Bạn viết ra được không?
Bahn Vee-Et Rah Dook Kong

Please can you speak more slowly?
Bạn nói chậm lại được không?
Bahn Noy Chum Lie Dook Kong

Greetings

**Good morning /
Good afternoon /
Good evening / Goodnight**
Xin chào / xin chào / xin chào /
chúc ngủ ngon
*Sin Chow / Sin Chow / Sin Chow /
Chook Noo Nohn*

Pleased to meet you
Hân hạnh gặp bạn
Hun Han Gup Bahn

How are you?
Bạn khỏe không?
Bahn Ko-Eh Kong

Well, thank you. And you?
Khỏe, cảm ơn. Còn bạn?
Ko-Eh, Kahm Earn. Kohn Bahn

My name is ...
Tên tôi là...
Tain Toy Lah...

**This is my friend / boyfriend /
girlfriend / husband / wife /
brother / sister**
Đây là - bạn tôi / bạn trai tôi /
bạn gái tôi / chồng tôi / vợ tôi /
anh tôi / chị tôi
*Day Lah – Bahn Toy / Bahn Chy Toy /
Bahn Gy Toy / Chong Toy / Voh Toy /
An Toy / Chee Toy*

Where are you travelling to?
Bạn đi đâu?
Bahn Dee Dow

I am / we are going to ...
Tôi / chúng tôi - đi đến...
Toy / Choong Toy – Dee Dain...

How long are you travelling for?
Bạn đi du lịch bao lâu?
Bahn Dee Zoo Leek Bow Low

Where do you come from?
Bạn từ đâu đến?
Bahn Tuh Dow Dain

**I am / we are from Australia /
Britain / Canada / America**
Tôi từ / chúng tôi từ Úc / Anh /
Canada / Mỹ
*Toy Tuh / Choong Toy Tuh Ook / An /
Cah-Nah-Dah / Mee*

We are on holiday
Chúng tôi đang đi nghỉ
Choong Toy Dang Dee Nee

This is our first visit here
Đây là lần đầu tiên chúng tôi đến
đây
*Day Lah Lun Dow Tee-En Choong Toy
Dain Day*

How old are you?
Bạn bao nhiêu tuổi?
Bahn Bow New Too-Ey

VIETNAMESE

I am ... years old
Tôi ... tuổi
Toy ... Too-Ey

I am a businessman / business woman / doctor / journalist / manual worker / administrator / scientist / student / teacher
Tôi là - thương gia / thương gia / bác sỹ / nhà báo / công nhân / quản trị viên / nhà khoa học / sinh viên / giáo viên
Toy Lah Thoo-Ong Zah / Thoo-Ong Zah / Bak Shee / Nah Bow / Kong Nun / Kwan Chee Vee-En / Nah Ko-Ah Hok / Sin Vee-En/ Zow Vee-En

Would you like / may I have a cigarette?
Bạn có thích / tôi có thể xin - một diếu thuốc lá không?
Bahn Koh Theek / Toy Koh Theeh Sin – Mote Dee-Ew Thoo-Ok Lah Kong

Do you mind if I smoke?
Tôi hút thuốc được không?
Toy Hoot Thoo-Ok Dook Kong

Do you have a light?
Bạn có bật lửa không?
Bahn Koh But Lu-Ah Kong

I am waiting for my husband / wife / boyfriend / girlfriend
Tôi đang đợi - chồng tôi / vợ tôi / bạn trai tôi / bạn gái tôi
Toy Dang Do-Ee – Chong Toy / Voh Toy / Bahn Chy Toy / Bahn Gy Toy

Days	
Monday	**Tuesday**
Thứ hai	Thứ ba
Thuh Hi	*Thuh Bah*

Wednesday	**Thursday**
Thứ tư	Thứ năm
Thuh Tuh	*Thuh Num*

Friday	**Saturday**
Thứ sáu	Thứ bảy
Thuh Show	*Thuh Bay*

Sunday
Chủ nhật
Choo Nut

Morning	**Afternoon**
Chiều	Sáng
Chee-Ew	*Shang*

Evening	**Night**
Tối	Đêm
Toy	*Dehm*

Yesterday / Today / Tomorrow
Hôm qua / hôm nay / ngày mai
Hom Kwa / Hom Nay / Nay My

Numbers	
Zero	**One**
Không	Một
Kong	*Mote*

Two	**Three**
Hai	Ba
Hi	*Bah*

Four	**Five**
Bốn	Năm
Bone	*Num*

Six	**Seven**
Sáu	Bảy
Show	*Bay*

Eight	**Nine**
Tám	Chín
Tahm	*Chin*

Ten
Mười
Moo-Ee

Eleven
Mười một
Moo-Ee Mote

Twelve
Mười hai
Moo-Ee Hi

Thirteen
Mười ba
Moo-Ee Bah

Fourteen
Mười bốn
Moo-Ee Bone

Fifteen
Mười lăm
Moo-Ee Lum

Sixteen
Mười sáu
Moo-Ee Show

Seventeen
Mười bảy
Moo-Ee Bay

Eighteen
Mười tám
Moo-Ee Tahm

Nineteen
Mười chín
Moo-Ee Chin

Twenty
Hai mươi
Hi Moo-Ee

Twenty-one
Hai mốt
Hi Mote

Twenty-two
Hai hai
Hi Hi

Thirty
Ba mươi
Bah Moo-Ee

Forty
Bốn mươi
Bone Moo-Ee

Fifty
Năm mươi
Num Moo-Ee

Sixty
Sáu mươi
Show Moo-Ee

Seventy
Bảy mươi
Bay Moo-Ee

Eighty
Tám mươi
Tahm Moo-Ee

Ninety
Chín mươi
Chin Moo-Ee

One hundred
Một trăm
Mote Chum

Five hundred
Năm trăm
Num Chum

One thousand
Một ngàn
Mote Nahn

One million
Một triệu
Mote Chee-You

Time

What time is it?
Mấy giờ rồi?
May Zor Roy

It is ...
Bây giờ là...
Bay Zor Lah...

9.00
Chín giờ
Chin Zor

9.05
Chín giờ năm
Chin Zor Num

9.15
Chín giờ mười lăm
Chin Zor Moo-Ee Lum

9.20
Chín giờ hai mươi
Chin Zor Hi Moo-Ee

9.30
Chín giờ ba mươi
Chin Zor Bah Moo-Ee

9.35
Chín giờ ba lăm
Chin Zor Bah Lum

9.40
Chín giờ bốn mươi
Chin Zor Bone Moo-Ee

9.45
Chín giờ bốn lăm
Chin Zor Bone Lum

V
I
E
T
N
A
M
E
S
E

V
I
E
T
N
A
M
E
S
E

9.50
Chín giờ năm mươi
Chin Zor Num Moo-Ee

9.55
Chín giờ năm lăm
Chin Zor Num Lum

12.00 / Midday / Midnight
Mười hai giờ / trưa / đêm
Moo-Ee Hì Zor / Chu-Ah / Dehm

Money

I would like to change these traveller's cheques / this currency
Tôi muốn đổi - những séc du lịch này / tiền này
Toy Moo-On Doy – Noong Cheque Zoo Leek Nay / Tee-En Nay

How much commission do you charge? (What is the service charge?)
Phí dịch vụ là bao nhiêu?
Fee Zeek Voo Lah Bow New

Can I obtain money with my MasterCard?
Tôi có thể lấy tiền với thẻ Mastercard không?
Toy Koh Theh Lay Tee-En Vo-Ee Theh Mastercard Kong

Where is the nearest ATM?
Máy rút tiền ATM gần đây nhất ở đâu?
May Root Tee-En ATM Gun Day Nut Er Dow

My name is ... Some money has been wired to here for me to collect
Tên tôi là…. Có một khoản tiền đã được chuyển đến đây cho tôi
Tain Toy Lah… Koh Mote Kwoan Tee-En Dah Dook Chu-Yuan Dain Day Choh Toy

ARRIVING AND DEPARTING

Airport

Excuse me, where is the check-in desk for ... airline?
Xin lỗi, quầy thủ tục check-in của hãng hàng không…. ở đâu?
Sin Loy, Kway Thoo Took Check-In Cu-Ah Hang Hang Kong… Er Dow

What is the boarding gate / time for my flight?
Chuyến bay của tôi lên cửa nào? / chuyến bay của tôi lúc mấy giờ?
Chu-Yuan Bay Ku-Ah Toy Lain Ku-Ah Now / Chu-Yuan Bay Ku-Ah Toy Look May Zor

How long is the delay likely to be?
Chuyến bay bị trễ bao lâu?
Chu-Yuan Bay Bee Cheh Bow Low

Where is the duty-free shop?
Cửa hàng miễn thuế ở đâu?
Ku-Ah Hang Mee-En Thu-Eh Er Dow

Which way is the baggage reclaim?
Lấy hành lý ở đâu?
Lay Hanh Lee Er Dow

I have lost my luggage. Please can you help?
Tôi bị mất hành lý. Bạn giúp tôi được không?
Toy Bee Mut Hanh Lee. Bahn Zoop Toy Dook Kong

I am flying to …
Tôi bay đến…
Toy Bay Dain…

Where can I get the bus to the city centre?
Tôi có thể đón xe buýt vào trung tâm thành phố ở đâu?
Toy Koh Theh Don S-Eh Bu-Eet Vow Choong Tum Thanh Foh Er Dow

Trains and Boats

Where is the ticket office / information desk?
Phòng vé / Quầy thông tin - ở đâu?
Fong Veh / Kway Thong Teen – Er Dow

Which platform does the train / speedboat / ferry to … depart from?
Tàu / tàu nhanh / phà tới… khởi hành ở bến nào?
Tow / Tow Nanh / Fah – To-Ee…
Ku-Le Hanh Er Bain Now

Where is platform …?
Bến … ở đâu?
Bain … Er Dow

When is the next train / boat to …?
Bao giờ có chuyến tàu / tàu - tới…?
Bow Zor Koh Chu-Yuan Tow / Tow – Tei…

Is there a later train / boat to …?
Có tàu / tàu - nữa đi… không?
Koh Tow / Tow – Nu-Ah Dee… Kong

Notices and Signs

Khoang ăn
Ko-Ang Un
Buffet (Dining) car

Xe buýt
Se-H Bu-Eet
Bus

Nước - uống / không uống
Nook – Oo-Ong / Kong Oo-Ong
Drinking / Non-drinking water

Lối vào
Loy Vow
Entrance

Lối ra
Loy Rah
Exit

Bệnh viện
Beng Vec-En
Hospital

Thông tin
Thong Teen
Information

Hành lý bỏ quên
Hanh Lee Boh Kwen
Left luggage (Baggage claim)

Tủ hành lý
Too Hanh Lee
Luggage lockers

VIETNAMESE

275

VIETNAMESE

Bưu điện
Bew Dee-En
Post office

Đường ray
Doo-Ong Ray
Platform

Ga tàu
Gah Tow
Railway (Railroad) station

Sân bay
Shun Bay
Airport

Đồn công an
Don Kong Ahn
Police station

Cảng
Kang
Port

Nhà hàng
Nah Hang
Restaurant

Hút thuốc / không hút thuốc
Hoot Thoo-Ok / Kong Hoot Thoo-Ok
Smoking / Non-smoking

Điện thoại
Dee-En Thoa-Ee
Telephone

Phòng vé
Fong Veh
Ticket office

Quầy thủ tục check-in
Kway Thoo Took Check-In
Check-in desk

Lịch bay
Leek bay
Timetables (Schedules)

Toilet
Toilet
Toilets (Restrooms)

Quý bà / quý ông
Kwee Bah / Kwee Ong
Ladies / Gentlemen

Đường ngầm
Doo-Ong Num
Underground (Subway)

Phòng đợi
Fong Do-Ee
Waiting room

Buying a Ticket

I would like a first-class / second-class single (oneway) / return (round-trip) ticket to ...
Tôi muốn mua một vé - hạng nhất / hạng nhì - một chiều / khứ hồi - tới...
Toy Moo-On Moo-Ah Mote Veh Hang Nut / Hang Nee – Mote Chee-Ew / Kuh Hoy – To-Ee...

Is it an express (fast) train / bus?
Đây là tàu / xe buýt nhanh - phải không?
Day Lah Tow / S-Eh Bu-Eet Nah – Fy Khong

Is my rail pass valid on this train / ferry / bus?
Vé của tôi có đi được tàu / phà / xe buýt - này không?

276

*Veh Cu-Ah Toy Koh Dee Dook Tow /
Fah / S-Eh Bu-Eet - Nay Kong*

**I would like an aisle /
window seat**
Tôi muốn chỗ ngồi cạnh -
lối đi / cửa sổ
*Toy Moo-On Choh Noy Cahn –
Loy Dee / Ku-Ah Shoh*

No smoking / smoking, please
Xin không hút thuốc / hút thuốc
*Sin Kong Hoot Thoo-Ok /
Hoot Thoo-Ok*

We would like to sit together
Chúng tôi muốn ngồi cùng nhau
Choong Toy Moo-On Noy Koong Now

**I would like to make a seat
reservation**
Tôi muốn đặt chỗ
Toy Moo-On Dat Choh

**I would like to reserve a
couchette / sleeper for one
person / two people / my family**
Tôi muốn đặt giường / chỗ
ngủ - cho một người / hai người /
gia đình tôi
*Toy Moo-On Dat Zoo-Ong /
Choh Ngoo – Choh Mot Noo-Oe /
Hi Noo-Oe / Zah Ding Toy*

I would like to reserve a cabin
Tôi muốn đặt một khoang
Toy Moo-On Dat Mote Ko-Ang

Timetables (Schedules)

Đến
Dain
Arrive

Dừng ở…
Zoong Er…
Calls (Stops) at …

Dịch vụ đặt đồ ăn
Zeek Voo Dat Doh An
Catering service

Chuyển ở…
Chu-Yuan Er…
Change at …

Nối / qua
Noy / kwa
Connection / Via

Hàng ngày
Hang Nay
Daily

Bốn mươi phút một lần
Bone Moo-Ee Foot Mote Lun
Every 40 minutes

Hạng nhất
Hang Nut
First class

Hàng giờ
Hang Zoh
Hourly

Nên đặt chỗ trước
Nain Dat Choh Trook
**Seat reservations are
recommended**

Hạng nhì
Hang Nee
Second class

Phụ phí phải trả
Foo Fee Fi Chah
Supplement payable

V
I
E
T
N
A
M
E
S
E

277

**V
I
E
T
N
A
M
E
S
E**

Luggage

How much will it cost to send (ship) my luggage in advance?
Gửi hành lý của tôi đi trước tốn bao nhiêu tiền?
Goo-Ee Hanh Lee Ku-Ah Toy Dee Troo-Ok Tohn Bow New Tee-En

Where is the left luggage (baggage claim) office?
Văn phòng lấy hành lý bỏ quên ở đâu?
Van Fong Lay Hanh Lee Boh Kwen Er Dow

What time do you open / close?
Mấy giờ – mở / đóng cửa?
May Zor – Moh / Dong Ku-Ah

Where are the luggage trolleys (carts)?
Xe đẩy hành lý ở đâu?
S-Eh Day Hanh Lee Er Dow

Where are the lockers?
Tủ để hành lý ở đâu?
Too Deh Hanh Lee Er Dow

I have lost my locker key
Tôi mất chìa khóa tủ để hành lý
Toy Mut Chee-Ah Ko-Ah Too Deh Hanh Lee

On Board

Is this seat free?
Chỗ này có người ngồi chưa?
Choh Nay Koh Noo-Ee Noy Chu-Ah

Excuse me, you are sitting in my reserved seat
Xin lỗi, chỗ này tôi đã đặt trước
Sin Loy, Choh Nay Toy Dah Dat Chook

Which station is this?
Ga nào đây?
Gah Now Day

What time is this train / bus / ferry / flight due to arrive / depart?
Tàu này / xe buýt này / phà này / chuyến bay này - đến / khởi hành - lúc mấy giờ?
Tow Nay / S-Eh Bu-Eet Nay / Fah Nay / Chu-Yuan Bay Nay – Dain / Kei Hanh – Look May Zor

Travelling with Children

Do you have a high chair / babysitting service / cot?
Bạn có - ghế cho em bé / dịch vụ trông trẻ / nôi - không?
Bahn Koh Geh Choh Ehm Beh / Deek Vuh Chong Cheh / Noy – Kong

Where is the nursery / playroom?
Phòng thay tã / phòng chơi cho em bé - ở đâu?
Fong Thay Tah / Fong Chei Choh Ehm Beh – Er Dow

Where can I warm the baby's bottle?
Tôi có thể hâm nóng bình sữa cho em bé ở đâu?
Toy Koh Theh Hum Nong Bing Shu-Ah Choh Ehm Beh Er Dow

Customs and Passports

Passports, please!
Xin cho xem hộ chiếu!
Sin Choh Sehm Hoh Chee-Ew

I have nothing / wine / spirits (alcohol) / tobacco to declare
Tôi không có - gì / rượu vang / rượu (rượu cồn) / thuốc lá - phải khai báo
Toy Kong Koh – Zee / Ree-Ew Van / Ree-Ew (Ree-Ew Kohn) / Thoo-Ok Lah – Fi Kite Bow

I will be staying for ... days / weeks / months
Tôi sẽ ở … ngày / tuần / tháng
Toy S-Eh Er … Nay / Tuan / Tang

SIGHTSEEING

Asking the Way

Excuse me, do you speak English?
Xin lỗi, bạn có nói tiếng anh không?
Sin Loy, Bahn Koh Noy Tee-Eng An Kong

Excuse me, can you help me please?
Xin lỗi, bạn có thể giúp tôi không?
Sin Loy, Bahn Koh Theh Zoop Toy Kong

Where is the Tourist Information Office?
Văn phòng Thông tin Du lịch ở đâu?
Van Fong Thong Teen Zoo Leek Er Dow

Excuse me, is this the right way to ...?
Xin lỗi, đây có phải là đường đến…?
Sin Loy, Day Koh Fi Lah Doo-Ong Dain…

... the cathedral / the tourist information office / the castle / the old town
…nhà thờ / văn phòng thông tin du lịch / lâu đài / phố cổ

…Nah Thoh / Van Fong Thong Teen Zoo Leek / Low Day / Foh Coh

Can you tell me the way to the railway (railroad) station / bus station / taxi rank (stand) / city centre (downtown) / beach?
Bạn chỉ đường cho tôi đến - ga tàu / ga xe buýt / nơi chờ taxi / trung tâm thành phố / bãi biển - được không?
Bahn Chee Doo-Ong Choh Toy Dain – Gah Tow / Gah S-Eh Bu-Eet / Nei Choh Taxi / Choong Tam Thanh Foo / Bye Bee-En – Dook Kong

First / second / left / right / straight ahead
Thứ nhất / thứ hai / trái / phải / thẳng phía trước
Tuh Nut / Tuh Hi / Chi / Fi / Tang Fee-Ah Chook

At the corner / at the traffic lights
Ở góc đường / ở cột đèn giao thông
Er Gok Doo-Ong / Er Kote Dehn Zow Tong

Where is the nearest police station / post office?
Đồn công an / bưu điện gần nhất ở đâu?
Dohn Kong Ahn / Bew Dee-En – Gun Nut Er Dow

Is it near / far?
Có gần / xa không?
Koh Gun / Sah Kong

Do I need to take a taxi / catch a bus?
Tôi có cần đi taxi / xe buýt không?
Toy Koh Cun Dee Taxi / S-Eh Bu-Eet Kong

279

VIETNAMESE

Do you have a map?
Bạn có bản đồ không?
Bahn Koh Bahn Doh Kong

Can you point to it on my map?
Bạn chỉ trên bản đồ cho tôi được không?
Bahn Chee Chain Bahn Doh Choh Toy Dook Kong

Thank you for your help
Cảm ơn rất nhiều
Kahm Earn Rut New

How do I reach the motorway / main road?
Làm thế nào tôi đến được - đường cao tốc / đường cái?
Lahm T-Eh Now Toy Dain Dook – Doo-Ong Kow Tok / Doo-Ong Kite

I think I have taken the wrong turning
Tôi nghĩ tôi đã rẽ sai đường
Toy Nee Toy Dah Reh Shy Doo-Ong

I am looking for this address
Tôi tìm địa chỉ này
Toy Teem Dee-Ah Chee Nay

I am looking for the ... hotel
Tôi tìm khách sạn ...
Toy Teem Kak Shahn ...

How far is it to ... from here?
Từ đây đến ... bao xa?
Tuh Day Dain ... Bow Sah

Carry straight on for ... kilometres
Tiếp tục đi thẳng ...kilomet
Tee-Ep Took Dee Tang ... Kilomet

Take the next turning on the right / left
Chỗ rẽ tới rẽ phải / trái
Choh Reh To-Ee Reh Fy / Chy

Turn right / left at the next crossroads / traffic lights
Rẽ phải / trái ở ngã rẽ / cột đèn giao thông - tới
Reh Fy / Chy Er Nah Reh / Kote Dehn Zow Tong – To-Ee

You are going in the wrong direction
Bạn đang đi sai hướng
Bahn Dang Dee Shy Hoo-Ong

Where is the cathedral / church / museum / pharmacy?
Thánh đường / nhà thờ / bảo tàng / hiệu thuốc này ở đâu?
Than Doo-Ong / Nah Thoh / Bow Tang / Hee-Ew Thook Nay Er Dow

How much is the admission / entrance charge?
Vé vào cửa bao nhiêu?
Veh Vow Ku-Ah Bow New

Is there a discount for children / students / senior citizens?
Có giảm giá cho trẻ em / sinh viên / người cao tuổi không?
Koh Zahm Zah Choh Cheh Ehm / Sheeng Vee-En / Noo-Ee Kow Too-Ey Kong

What time does the next guided tour (in English) start?
Tour có hướng dẫn (tiếng Anh) tới bắt đầu lúc mấy giờ?
Tour Koh Hoo-Ong Zun (Tee-Eng An) Tei But Dow Look May Zor

**V
I
E
T
N
A
M
E
S
E**

One / two adults / children, please
Một / hai - người lớn / trẻ em
Mote / Hi – Noo-Ee Learn / Cheh Ehm

May I take photographs here?
Tôi có thể chụp ảnh ở đây không?
Toy Koh T-Eh Choop An Er Day Kong

At the Tourist Office

Do you have a map of the town / area?
Bạn có bản đồ của khu / vùng này không?
Bahn Koh Bahn Doh Ku-Ah Koo / Voong Nay Kong

Do you have a list of accommodation?
Bạn có danh sách chỗ ở không?
Bahn Koh Zahn Shach Choh Er Kong

Can I reserve accommodation?
Tôi đặt chỗ ở được không?
Toy Dut Choh Er Dook Kong

ACCOMMODATION

Hotels

I have a reservation in the name of ...
Tôi đã đặt trước dưới tên...
Toy Dah Dut Trook Zoo-Ee Tain...

I wrote to / faxed / telephoned you last month / last week
Tôi viết / fax / gọi điện cho bạn - tháng trước / tuần trước
Toy Vee-Et / Fax / Goy Dee-En Choh Bahn – Thang Chook / Tuan Chook

Do you have any rooms free?
Bạn có phòng trống không?
Bahn Koh Fong Chong Kong?

I would like to reserve a single / double room with / without bath / shower
Tôi muốn đặt một phòng - đơn / đôi - có / không có - bồn tắm / vòi hoa sen
Toy Moo-On Dut Mote Fong – Dearn / Doy Koh / Kong Koh – Bohn Tum / Voy Ho-Ah Shehn

I would like bed and breakfast / (room and) full board
Tôi muốn giường và bữa sáng / (phòng và) các bữa ăn
Toy Moo-On Zoo-Ong Vah Bu-Ah Shang / (Fong Vah) Kak Bu-Ah An

How much is it per night?
Bao nhiêu tiền một đêm?
Bow New Tee-En Mote Dehm

Is breakfast included?
Có gồm bữa sáng không?
Koh Gohm Bu-Ah Shang Kong

Do you have any cheaper rooms?
Bạn có phòng rẻ hơn không?
Bahn Koh Fong Reh H-Earn Kong

I would like to see / take the room
Tôi muốn - xem / lấy - phòng này
Toy Moo-On – Sehm / Lay – Fong Nay

I would like to stay for ... nights
Tôi muốn ở... đêm
Toy Moo-On Er...Dehm

V I E T N A M E S E

The shower / light / tap / hot water doesn't work
Vòi hoa sen / đèn / vòi nước / nước nóng - hỏng
Voy Hu-Ah Shehn / Dehn / Voy Nook / Nook Nong – Hong

At what time / where is breakfast served?
Ăn sáng lúc mấy giờ / ở đâu?
An Shang Look May Zor / Er Dow

What time do I have to check out?
Mấy giờ tôi phải trả phòng?
May Zor Toy Fy Chah Fong

Can I have the key to room number ... ?
Tôi lấy chìa khóa phòng số…được không?
Toy Lay Chee-Ah Kua Fong Shoh … Dook Kong

My room number is ...
Phòng tôi số …
Fong Toy Shoh …

My room is not satisfactory / not clean enough / too noisy
Phòng tôi - chưa được / không sạch lắm / quá ồn
Fong Toy – Chu-Ah Dook / Kong Shach Lum / Kwa Ohn

Please can I change rooms?
Tôi có thể đổi phòng được không?
Toy Coh Theh Doy Fong Dook Kong

Where is the bathroom?
Phòng tắm ở đâu?
Fong Tum Er Dow

Do you have a safe for valuables?
Bạn có két để đồ quý không?
Bahn Coh Ket Deh Doh Kwee Kong

Is there a laundry / do you wash clothes?
Có chỗ giặt đồ không? / bạn có dịch vụ giặt đồ không?
Koh Choh Zut Doh Kong / Bahn Koh Zeek Voo Zut Doh Kong

I would like an air-conditioned room
Tôi muốn phòng có máy lạnh
Toy Moo-On Fong Koh May Lahn

Do you accept traveller's cheques / credit cards?
Bạn có chấp nhận - séc du lịch / thẻ tín dụng - không?
Bahn Koh Chup Nun Cheque Zoo Leek / Theh Teen Zoong – Kong

May I have the bill please?
Tôi muốn thanh toán?
Toy Moo-On Thanh To-An

Excuse me, I think there may be a mistake in this bill
Xin lỗi, tôi nghĩ là hóa đơn này chưa đúng
Sin Loy, Toy Nee Lah Hua Dearn Nay Chu-Ah Doong

Youth Hostels

How much is a dormitory bed per night?
Giường ký túc xá bao nhiêu tiền một đêm?
Zoo-Ong Kee Took Sah Bow New Tee-En Mote Dehm

I am / am not an HI member
Tôi không phải là thành viên HI
Toy Kong Fy Lah Thanh Vee-En HI

May I use my own sleeping bag?
Tôi dùng túi ngủ của tôi được
không?
*Toy Zoong Tu-Ee Nu Ku-Ah Toy Dook
Kong*

**What time do you lock the
doors at night?**
Buổi đêm bạn khóa cửa lúc mấy
giờ?
*Boo-Ey Dehm Bahn Ko-Ah Ku-Ah Look
May Zor*

Camping

**May I camp for the night /
two nights?**
Tôi cắm trại - một đêm /
hai đêm - được không?
*Toy Cum Chy Mote Dehm /
Hi Dehm Dook Kong*

Where can I pitch my tent?
Tôi có thể dựng lều ở đâu?
Toy Coh Theh Zoong Le-Uh Er Dow

**How much does it cost for one
night / week?**
Bao nhiêu tiền - một đêm /
một tuần?
*Bow New Tee-En - Mote Dehm /
Mote Tu-Un*

**Where are the washing
facilities?**
Chỗ giặt đồ ở đâu?
Choh Zut Doh Er Dow

**Is there a restaurant /
supermarket / swimming pool
on site / nearby?**
Ở đây / gần đây - có nhà hàng /
siêu thị / bể bơi không?
*Er Day / Gun Day – Koh Nah Hang /
Shee-Ew Thee / Beh Bo-Ee Kong*

**Do you have a safety deposit
box?**
Bạn có két an toàn không?
Bahn Koh Keht Ahn To-An Kong

Cafés and Bars

**I would like a cup of / two cups
of / another coffee / tea**
Tôi muốn - một tách / hai tách /
cà phê / trà - nữa
*Toy Moo-On Mote Tak / Hi Tak /
Kah Feh / Chah Nu Ah*

With / without milk / sugar
Có / không sữa / đường
Koh / Kong Shu-Ah / Doong

**I would like a bottle / glass /
two glasses of mineral water /
red wine / white wine, please**
Tôi muốn một chai / một ly /
hai ly - nước khoáng / vang đỏ /
vang trắng
*Toy Moo-On Mote Chy / Mote Lee / Hi
Lee – Nook Ko-Ang / Vang Doh / Vang
Chung*

**I would like a beer / two beers,
please**
Tôi muốn - một bia / hai bia
Toy Moo-On – Mote Beer / Hi Beer

Please may I have some ice?
Cho tôi xin đá?
Choh Toy Sin Dah

**Do you have any matches /
cigarettes / cigars?**
Bạn có - diêm / thuốc lá /
xì gà - không?
*Bahn Coh – Dee-Em / Thoo-Ok Lah /
See Gah – Kong*

VIETNAMESE

Restaurants

Can you recommend a good / cheap restaurant in this area?
Bạn có thể giới thiệu một nhà hàng ngon / rẻ trong khu này không?
Bahn Koh Theh Zo-Ee Thee-Ew Mote Nah Hang Non / Reh Chong Koo Nay Kong

I would like a table for ... people
Tôi muốn một bàn cho.... người
Toy Moo-On Mote Bahn Choh... Noo-Ee

Do you have a non-smoking area?
Bạn có khu không hút thuốc không?
Bahn Koh Koo Kong Hoot Thoo-Ok Kong

Waiter / Waitress!
Hầu bàn / Hầu bàn!
How Bahn / How Bahn

Excuse me, please may we order?
Xin lỗi, chúng tôi đặt món được không?
Sin Loy, Choong Toy Dut Mohn Dook Kong

Do you have a set menu / children's menu / wine list?
Bạn có - thực đơn bữa / thực đơn trẻ em / danh sách rượu - không?
Bahn Koh - Thook Dearn Bu-Ah / Thu-Ah Dearn Cheh Ehm / Zahn Shach Ree-Ew Kong

Do you have any vegetarian dishes?
Bạn có đồ ăn chay không?
Bahn Koh Doh An Chay Kong

Do you have any local specialities?
Bạn có đặc sản địa phương nào không?
Bahn Koh Duk Shahn Dee-Ah Foo-Ong Now Kong

Are vegetables included?
Có rau không?
Koh Ra-Uh Kong

Could I have it well-cooked / medium / rare please?
Tôi muốn nấu kỹ / hơi tái / tái
Toy Moo-On Now Kee / Hei Ty / Ty

What does this dish consist of?
Món này gồm những gì?
Mohn Nay Gohm Noong Zee

I am a vegetarian. Does this contain meat?
Tôi ăn chay. Món này có thịt không?
Toy An Chay. Mohn Nay Koh Theet Kong

I do not eat nuts / dairy products / meat / fish
Tôi không ăn - lạc / bơ sữa / thịt / cá
Toy Kong Un Lak / Boh Shu-Ah / Theet / Kah

Not (very) spicy, please
Không cay (quá)
Kong Kay (Kwa)

I would like the set menu, please
Xin cho tôi xem thực đơn bữa
Sin Choh Toy Sehm Thook Dearn Bu-Ah

We are still waiting to be served
Chúng tôi vẫn đang đợi
Choong Toy Vun Dang Do-Ee

Please bring a plate / knife / fork
Xin mang cho tôi một đĩa / dao / đĩa
Sin Mang Choh Toy Mote Dee-Ah / Zow / Zee-Ah

Excuse me, this is not what I ordered
Xin lỗi, tôi không đặt món này
Sin Loy, Toy Kong Dut Mohn Nay

May I have some / some more bread / water / coffee / tea?
Tôi có thể có / có thêm - bánh mỳ / nước / cà phê / trà - không?
Toy Koh Theh Koh / Koh Thehm – Bahn Mee / Nook / Kah Feh / Chah – Kong

May I have the bill, please?
Xin cho tôi thanh toán?
Sin Choh Toy Thanh To-An

Does this bill include service?
Hóa đơn này đã có phí dịch vụ chưa?
Ho-Ah Dearn Nay Dah Koh Fee Zeek Voo Chu-Ah

Do you accept traveller's cheques / MasterCard / US dollars?
Bạn có chấp nhận - séc du lịch / Master Card / đôla Mỹ - không?
Bahn Koh Chup Nan – Cheque Zoo Leek / MasterCard / Dollar Mee – Kong

Can I have a receipt, please?
Xin cho tôi hóa đơn?
Sin Choh Toy Ho-Ah Dearn

Where is the toilet (restroom), please?
Toilet ở đâu ạ?
Toilet Er Dow Ah

On the Menu

Bữa sáng / bữa trưa / bữa tối
Bu-Ah Shang / Bu-Ah Chu-Ah / Bu-Ah Toy
Breakfast / Lunch / Dinner

Món khai vị	Xúp
Mohn Kite Vee	*Soup*
First courses	**Soups**
Món chính	Món cá
Mohn Cheeng	*Mohn Kah*
Main courses	**Fish dishes**
Món thịt	Thịt bò
Mohn Theet	*Theet Boh*
Meat dishes	**Beef**
Steak	Thịt lợn
Steak	*Theet Learn*
Steak	**Pork**
Thịt bê	Thịt gà
Theet Beh	*Theet Gah*
Veal	**Chicken**
Thịt cừu	Giăm bông
Theet Kew	*Zum Bong*
Lamb	**Ham**

Món chay
Mohn Chay
Vegetarian dishes

Rau
Ra-Uh
Vegetables

Khoai tây rán
Ko-Ay Tay Rahn
Chips (french fries)

VIETNAMESE

Khoai tây luộc / áp chảo / nghiền
Ko-Ay Tay Look / Áp Chow / Nee-En
**Boiled / sauté /
mashed potatoes**

Cơm
Kirm
Rice

Phomát
Foh Maht
Cheese

Tráng miệng
Chang Mee-Eng
Desserts

Kem
Kehm
Ice cream

Bánh
Bahn
Cakes

Bánh ngọt
Bahn Noht
Pastries

Hoa qua
Ho-Ah Kwa
Fruit

Bánh mỳ
Bahn Mee
Bread

Ổ bánh
Oh Bahn
Rolls

Bánh nướng
Bahn Noo-Ong
Toast

Bơ
Boh
Butter

Muối / tiêu
Moo-Ey / Tee-Ew
Salt / pepper

Đường
Doo-Ong
Sugar

Đặc sản
Dak Shahn
Specialities

Đặc sản địa phương
Dak Sshan Dee-Ah Foo-Ong
Local specialities

Thực đơn bữa
Thook Dearn Bu-Ah
Set Menu

Danh sách rượu
Zahn Shach Ree-Ew
Wine list

Vang đỏ
Vang Doh
Red wines

Vang trắng
Vang Chung
White wines

Rượu rose
Ree-Ew Rose
Rose wine

Rượu có ga
Ree-Ew Koh Gah
Sparkling wines

Bia
Beer
Beer

Bia chai / bia hơi
Beer Chy / Beer Ho-Ee
**Bottled beer / Draught
(draft) beer**

Đồ uống không cồn
Doh Oo-Ong Kong Kohn
Non-alcoholic drinks

Nước khoáng
Nook Ko-Ang
Mineral water

Nước quả
Nook Kwa
Fruit juices

Nước cam
Nook Kahm
Orange juice

Nước chanh
Nook Chanh
Lemonade

Đá
Dah
Ice

Cà phê sữa / cà phê đen /
cà phê espresso
*Kah Feh Shu-Ah / Kah Feh Dehn /
Kah Feh Espresso*
**White coffee / black coffee /
espresso coffee**

Trà với sữa / với chanh
Chah Vo-Ee Shu-Ah / Vo-Ee Chanh
Tea with milk / with lemon

Sôcôla
Shoh-Koh-Lah
Chocolate (drink)

Sữa
Shu-Ah
Milk

Bữa nhẹ
Bu-Ah Neh
Snacks / Light meals

Xalat — Sandwitches
Salad — *Sandwitche*
Salads — **Sandwiches**

Trứng — Xúc xích
Choong — *Sook Seek*
Eggs — **Sausage**

Trứng luộc / rán / bác
Choong Lu-Ok / Rahn / Bac
Boiled / fried / scrambled eggs

Typical Local Dishes

Phở Bò
Foh Boh
Beef Noodle

Mỳ
Mee
Noodle

Thịt nguội
Teet Noo-Ey
Cold cut

Nem
Nehm
Spring roll

Canh chua cá
Kanh Choo-Ah Kah
Fish sour soup

GETTING AROUND

Public Transport

Where is the bus stop / coach stop / nearest metro (subway) station?
Bến xe buýt / bến xe / bến tàu điện ngầm - gần nhất ở đâu?
Behn S-Eh Bu-Eet / Behn S-Eh / Behn Tow Dee-En Num – Gun Nut Er Dow

When is the next / last bus to ...?
Bao giờ có - chuyến buýt tới / cuối cùng – đi…?
Bow Zor Koh – Chu-Yuan Bu-Eet To-Ee / Koo-Ey Cung – Dee…

How much is the fare to the city centre (downtown) / railway station / airport?
Đi đến - trung tâm thành phố / ga tàu / sân bay - hết bao nhiêu tiền?
Dee Dain – Choong Tum Thanh Foh / Gah Tow / Shun Bay – Heht Bow New Tee-En

Will you tell me when to get off?
Bạn bảo tôi khi nào xuống được không?
Bahn Bow Toy Kee Now Soo-Ong Dook Kong

V I E T N A M E S E

Does this bus go to ...?
Xe buýt này có đi đến... không?
S-Eh Bu-Eet Nay Koh Dee Dain... Kong

Which number bus goes to ...?
Xe buýt số mấy đi đến...
S-Eh Bu-Eet Soh May Dee Dain...

May I have a single (oneway) / return (round-trip) / day ticket / book of tickets?
Tôi muốn mua vé một chiều / vé khứ hồi / vé ngày / đặt vé
Toy Moo-On Mu-Ah Veh Mote Chee-Ew / Veh Koo Hoy / Veh Nay / Dat Veh

Taxis and Rickshaws

I would like to go to ...
Tôi muốn đi đến...
Toy Muoo-On Dee Dain...

How much will it cost?
Bao nhiêu tiền?
Bow New Tee-En

Please may I stop here?
Tôi dừng ở đây được không?
Toy Zoong Er Day Dook Kong

I would like to order a taxi today / tomorrow / at 2pm to go from ... to ...
Tôi muốn đặt một taxi - hôm nay / ngày mai / lúc 2 giờ chiều - để đi từ...đến...
Toy Moo-On Dat Mote Taxi – Hohm Nay / Nay My / Look Hi Zor Chee-Ew – Deh Dee Tuh ... Dain....

Entertainment

Can you recommend a good bar / nightclub?
Bạn có thể giới thiệu một - quán bar / club đêm - không?
Bahn Koh Theh Zo-Ee Thee-Ew Mote – Kwan Bar / Club Dehm – Kong

Do you know what is on at the cinema (playing at the movies) / theatre at the moment?
Bạn có biết - rạp / nhà hát - này đang có chương trình gì không?
Bahn Koh Bee-Et Rap / Nah Haht Nay – Dang Koh Choo-Ong Ching Zee Kong

I would like to book (purchase) ... tickets for the matinee / evening performance on Monday
Tôi muốn đặt (mua) ...vé cho buổi diễn - chiều / tối - thứ hai
Toy Moo-On Dat (Mu-Ah)...Veh Choh Boo-Ey Zee-En – Chee-Ew / Toy – Thuh Hi

What time does the film / performance start?
Mấy giờ - phim / chương trình - bắt đầu?
May Zor – Film / Choo-Ong Ching – But Dow

COMMUNICATIONS

Post

How much will it cost to send a letter / postcard / this package to Britain / Ireland / America / Canada / Australia / New Zealand?

Gửi - thư / bưu ảnh / gói hàng
này - đi Anh / Ireland / Mỹ /
Canada / Úc / New Zealand
bao nhiêu tiền?
*Gu-Ee – Thuh / Bew An / Goy Hang
Nay – Dee An / Ire-Lahn / Mee /
Cah-Nah-Dah / Ook / New Zealand
Bow New Tee-En*

I would like one stamp / two stamps
Tôi muốn mua - một tem / hai tem
*Toy Moo-On Mu-Ah – Mote Tehm /
Hi Tehm*

I'd like ... stamps for postcards to send abroad, please
Tôi muốn ...tem cho bưu ảnh gửi
đi nước ngoài
*Toy Moo-On ... Tehm Choh Bew An
Gu-Ee Dee Nook Noa-Ee*

Phones

I would like to make a telephone call / reverse the charges to (make a collect call to) ...
Tôi muốn gọi điện / gọi điện collect
call ...
*Toy Moo-On Goy Dee-En /
Goy Dee-En Collect Call ...*

Which coins do I need for the telephone?
Tôi cần tiền xu nào để gọi điện
thoại?
*Toy Cun Tee-En Suh Now Deh Goy
Dee-En Thoa-Ee*

The line is engaged (busy)
Đường dây bận
Doo-Ong Day Bun

The number is ...
Số điện thoại là ...
Shoh Dee-En Thoa-Ee Lah ...

Hello, this is ...
Xin chào, đây là ...
Sin Chow, Day Lah ...

Please may I speak to ...?
Tôi muốn nói chuyện với...?
Toy Moo-On Noy Chu-Yuan Vo-Ee...

He / she is not in at the moment. Can you call back?
Anh ấy / cô ấy - hiện không có ở
đây. Bạn gọi lại được không?
*An Ay / Koh Ay – Hee-En Kong Koh Er
Day. Bahn Goy Ly Dook Kong*

SHOPPING

Shops

Hiệu sách / hiệu văn phòng phẩm
*Hee-Ew Shach / Hee-Ew Vun Fong
Fum*
Bookshop / Stationery

Trang sức / quà tặng
Chang Shook / Kwa Tang
Jeweller / Gifts

Giầy
Zay
Shoes

Dụng cụ
Zoong Koo
Hardware

Cắt tóc
Kut Tok
Hairdresser

V I E T N A M E S E

(nam) / (nữ)
(Nahm) / (Nuh)
(men's) / (women's)

Hiệu bánh
Hee-Ew Bahn
Baker

Điện thoại
Dee-En Thoa-Ee
Phones

Siêu thị
Shee-Ew Thee
Supermarket

Hiệu ảnh
Hee-Ew An
Photo-Shop

Đại lý du lịch
Dy Lee Zoo Leek
Travel agent

Hiệu thuốc
Hee-Ew Thook
Pharmacy

In the Shops

What time do the shops open / close?
Mấy giờ hiệu mở / đóng?
May Zor Hee-Ew Mor / Dong

Where is the nearest market?
Chợ gần nhất ở đâu?
Choh Gun Nut Er Dow

Can you show me the one in the window / this one?
Cho tôi xem - cái trong cửa sổ / cái này
Choh Toy Sehm – Kite Chong Cu-Ah Shoh / Kite Nay

Can I try this on?
Tôi thử cái này được không?
Toy Thuh Kite Nay Dook Kong

What size is this?
Số mấy đây?
Shoh May Day

This is too large / too small / too expensive
Cái này - quá to / quá nhỏ / quá đắt
Kite Nay – Kwa Toh / Kwa Noh / Kwa Dut

Do you have any others?
Bạn còn cái khác không?
Bahn Kohn Kite Kac Kong

My size is ...
Size của tôi là ...
Size Ku-Ah Toy Lah ...

Where is the changing room / children's / cosmetic / ladieswear / menswear / food department?
Phòng thử / khu trẻ em / khu mỹ phẩm / khu quần áo nữ / khu quần áo nam / khu thực phẩm - ở đâu?
Fong Thuh / Koo Cheh Ehm / Koo Mee Fum / Koo Kwan Ow Nuh / Koo Kwan Ow Nahm / Koo Thuk Fum – Er Dow

I would like ... a quarter of a kilo / half a kilo / a kilo of bread / butter / cheese / ham / this fruit
Tôi muốn ... hai trăm năm mươi gram / nửa kilo / một kilo - bánh mỳ / bơ / phomát / giăm bông / quả này
Toy Moo-On ... Hi Chum Num Moo-Ee Gram / Nu-Ah Kilo / Mote Kilo – Bahn Mee / Boh / Foh-Maht / Zum Bong / Kwa Nay

How much is this?
Cái này bao nhiêu tiền?
Kite Nay Bow New Tee-En

I'll take this one, thank you
Tôi lấy cái này, cảm ơn
Toy Lay Kite Nay, Kahm Earn

Do you have a carrier (shopping) bag?
Bạn có túi đựng không?
Bahn Koh Tu-Ee Doong Kong

Do you have anything cheaper / larger / smaller / of better quality?
Bạn có thứ nào - rẻ hơn / to hơn / nhỏ hơn / tốt hơn - không?
Bahn Koh Too Now – Reh Hohn / Toh Hohn / Noh Hohn / Tote Hohn Kong

I would like a film / to develop this film for this camera
Tôi muốn - mua phim / tráng phim - cho máy ảnh này
Toy Moo-On – Mu-Ah Film / Chang Film – Choh May An Nay

I would like some batteries, the same size as this old one
Tôi muốn mua pin, cùng cỡ với pin cũ này
Toy Moo-On Mu-Ah Peen, Koong Koh Vo-Ee Peen Koo Nay

Would you mind wrapping this for me, please?
Bạn có thể gói lại cho tôi không?
Bahn Koh Theh Goy Lye Choh Toy Kong

Sorry, but you seem to have given me the wrong change
Xin lỗi, có lẽ bạn trả lại tiền sai cho tôi
Sin Loy, Koh Leh Bahn Chah Lye Tee-En Shy Choh Toy

Car Hire (Rental)

I have ordered (rented) a car in the name of ...
Tôi đặt (thuê) một xe hơi với tên…
Toy Dat (Thu-Eh) Mote S-Eh Ho-Ee Vo-Ee Tain…

How much does it cost to hire (rent) a car for one day / two days / a week?
Thuê một xe hơi - một ngày / hai ngày / một tuần - bao nhiêu tiền?
Thu-Eh Mote S-Eh Ho Ec   Mote Nay / Hi Nay / Mote Tu-An – Bow New Tee-En

Is the tank already full of petrol (gas)?
Bình đầy xăng chưa?
Bihn Day Sang Chu-Ah

Is insurance and tax included? How much is the deposit?
Gồm bảo hiểm và thuế chưa? Đặt cọc bao nhiêu?
Gohm Bow Hee-Em Vah Thu-Eh Chu-Ah? Dat Kok Bow New

By what time must I return the car?
Mấy giờ tôi phải trả xe?
May Zor Toy Fy Chah S-Eh

I would like a small / large / family / sports car with a radio / cassette player
Tôi muốn một xe - nhỏ / to / gia đình / thể thao - có dài / cassette
Toy Moo-En Mote S-Eh – Noh / Toh / Zah Ding / Theh Thow – Koh Dye / Cassette

291

**V
I
E
T
N
A
M
E
S
E**

Do you have a road map?
Bạn có bản đồ không?
Bahn Koh Bahn Doh Kong

Parking

How long can I park here?
Tôi có thể đỗ xe ở đây bao lâu?
Toy Koh Theh Doh S-Eh Er Day Bow Low

Is there a car park near here?
Có bãi đỗ xe ở gần đây không?
Koh By Doh S-Eh Er Gun Day Kong

At what time does this car park close?
Mấy giờ bãi đỗ xe này đóng?
May Zor By Doh S-Eh Nay Dong

Signs and Notices

Một chiều
Mote Chee-Ew
One way

Miễn vào
Mee-En Vow
No entry

Không đỗ xe
Kong Doh S-Eh
No parking

Đi vòng
Dee Vong
Detour (diversion)

Dừng
Zoong
Stop

Những đường
Noo-Ong Doo-Ong
Give way (yield)

Đường trơn
Doo-Ong Chern
Slippery road

Không vượt
Kong Voo-Ot
No overtaking

Nguy hiểm!
Nu-Ee Hee-Em
Danger!

At the Filling Station

Unleaded (lead-free) / standard / premium / diesel
Không chì / chuẩn / cao / diesel
Kong Chee / Chuan / Kow / Diesel

Fill the tank please
Xin đổ xăng
Sin Doh Sang

Do you have a road map?
Bạn có bản đồ không?
Bahn Koh Bahn Doh Kong

How much is the car wash?
Rửa xe bao nhiêu tiền?
Ru-Ah S-Eh Bow New Tee-En

Breakdowns

I've had a breakdown at ...
Tôi bị hỏng xe ở...
Toy Bee Hong S-Eh Er...

**I am a member of the
[motoring organisation]**
Tôi là hội viên của [hội xe]
*Toy Lah Hoy Vee-En Ku-Ah
[Hoy S-Eh]*

I am on the road from ... to ...
Tôi đang trên đường từ... đến...
Toy Dang Chain Doo-Ong Tuh ... Duin ...

**I can't move the car. Can you
send a tow-truck?**
Xe không đi được. Bạn gửi xe kéo
đến được không?
*S-Eh Kong Dee Dook. Bahn Gu-Ee
S-Eh Ke-Oh Dain Dook Kong*

I have a flat tyre
Tôi bị xịt lốp
Toy Bee Seet Lop

**The windscreen (windshield)
has smashed / cracked**
Kính chắn gió bị - hỏng / nứt
King Chun Zoh Bee – Hong / Nut

**There is something wrong with
the engine / brakes / lights /
steering / gearbox / clutch /
exhaust**
Động cơ / phanh / đèn / thiết bị
lái / hộp số / côn / ống xả - trục
trặc
*Dong Koh / Fahn / Dehn / Thee-Et Bee
Lye / Hop Shoh / Kohn /
Ong Sah – Chook Chak*

It's overheating
Nó quá nóng
Noh Kwa Nong

It won't start
Nó không khởi động
Noh Kong Ko-Ee Dong

Where can I get it repaired?
Tôi có thể sửa xe ở đâu?
Toy Koh Theh Su-Ah S-Eh Er Dow

Can you take me there?
Bạn có thể mang tôi đến đó không?
*Bahn Koh Theh Mang Toy Dain Doh
Kong*

Will it take long to fix?
Sửa có lâu không?
Suah Koh Low Kong

How much will it cost?
Bao nhiêu tiền?
Bow New Tee-En

**Please can you pick me up / give
me a lift?**
Bạn - đón tôi /
cho tôi đi nhờ - được không?
*Bahn – Dohn Toy /
Choh Toy Dee Noh – Dook Kong*

Accidents and
Traffic Offences

**Can you help me? There has
been an accident**
Bạn giúp tôi được không?
Có tai nạn
*Bahn Zoop Toy Dook Kong?
Koh Tye Nahn*

**Please call the police / an
ambulance**
Xin gọi cảnh sát / xe cấp cứu
Sin Goy Kanh Shaht / S-Eh Kup Kew

Is anyone hurt?
Có ai bị thương không?
Koh Ay Bee Thoo-Ong Kong

I'm sorry, I didn't see the sign
Xin lỗi, tôi không nhìn thấy biển báo
Sin Loy, Toy Kong Neen Thay Bee-En Bow

Must I pay a fine? How much?
Tôi có phải trả tiền phạt không? Bao nhiêu?
Toy Koh Fye Chah Tee-En Faht Kong? Bow New

Show me your documents
Cho tôi xem giấy tờ
Choh Toy Sehm Zay Toh

HEALTH

Pharmacy

Do you have anything for a stomach ache / headache / sore throat / toothache?
Bạn có thuốc - đau bụng / đau đầu / đau họng / đau răng - không?
Bahn Koh Thook – Dow Boong / Dow Dow / Dow Hong / Dow Rang – Kong

I need something for diarrhoea / constipation / a cold / a cough / insect bites / sunburn / travel (motion) sickness (car)(plane) (boat)
Tôi cần thuốc - đi ngoài / táo bón / cảm / ho / côn trùng cắn / cháy nắng / say xe (car) / say máy bay (plane) / say sóng (boat)
Toy Cun Thook – Dee Ngoa-Ee / Tow Bohn / Kahm / Hoh / Kohn Choong Cun / Chay Nang / Shay S-Eh / Shay May Bay / Shay Shong

How much / how many do I take?
Tôi phải uống bao nhiêu?
Toy Fye Oo-Ong Bow New

How often do I take it / them?
Bao lâu uống một lần?
Bow Low Oo-Ong Mote Lun

I am / he is / she is taking this medication
Tôi / anh ấy / cô ấy - đang uống thuốc này
Toy / An Ay / Koh Ay – Dang Oo-Ong Thoo-Ok Nay

How much does it cost?
Bao nhiêu tiền?
Bow New Tee-En

Can you recommend a good doctor / dentist?
Bạn có thể giới thiệu một - bác sỹ / nha sỹ - giỏi không?
Bahn Koh Theh Zo-Ee Thee-Ew Mote – Bak Shee / Nah Shee – Zoy Kong

Is it suitable for children?
Cho trẻ em được không?
Choh Cheh Ehm Dook Kong

Doctor

I have a pain here / in my arm / leg / chest / stomach
Tôi bị đau ở - đây / tay / chân / ngực / bụng
Toy Bee Dow Oh – Day / Tay / Chun / Nuk / Boong

Please call a doctor, this is an emergency
Xin gọi bác sỹ, cấp cứu
Sin Goy Bak Shee, Kup Kew

I would like to make an appointment to see the doctor
Tôi muốn hẹn gặp bác sỹ
Toy Moo-On Hehn Gap Bak Shee

I am diabetic / pregnant
Tôi - bị tiểu đường / có thai
Toy – Bee Tee-Eu Doong / Koh Thy

I need a prescription for ...
Tôi cần đơn thuốc cho…
Toy Cun Dohn Thoo-Ok Choh…

Can you give me something to ease the pain?
Có thể cho tôi thuốc gì giảm đau không?
Koh Theh Choh Toy Thoo-Ok Zee Zahm Dow Kong

I am / he is / she is allergic to penicillin
Tôi / anh ấy / cô ấy - dị ứng với penicillin
Toy / Anh Ay / Koh Ay – Zee Ung Vo-Ee Penicillin

Does this hurt?
Có đau không?
Koh Dow Kong

You must / he must / she must go to hospital
Bạn phải / anh ấy phải / cô ấy phải - đi bệnh viện
Bahn Fye / An Ay Fye / Koh Ay Fye – Dee Benh Vee-En

Take these once / twice / three times a day
Uống thuốc này - một lần / hai lần / ba lần - một ngày
Oo-Ong Thoo-Ok Nay – Mote Lun / Hi Lun / Bah Lun – Mote Nay

I am / he is / she is taking this medication
Tôi / anh ấy / cô ấy - đang uống thuốc này
Toy / An Ay / Koh Ay – Dang Oo-Ong Thoo-Ok Nay

I have medical insurance
Tôi có bảo hiểm y tế
Toy Koh Bow Hee-Em Ee Teeh

Dentist

I have toothache
Tôi bị đau răng
Toy Bee Dow Rang

My filling has come out
Mảnh hàn răng của tôi bị rơi ra
Manh Hahn Rang Ku-Ah Toy Bee Ro-Ee Rah

I do / do not want to have an injection first
Tôi - muốn / không muốn - tiêm trước
Toy - Moo-On / Kong Moo-On – Tee-Em Trook

EMERGENCIES

Help!
Cứu!
Kew

Fire!
Lửa!
Lu-Ah

Stop!
Dừng lại!
Zoong Lye

Call an ambulance / a doctor / the police / the fire brigade!
Gọi - xe cấp cứu / bác sỹ / công an / cứu hỏa!
Goy – S-Eh Cup Kew / Bak Shee / Kong Ahn / Kew Ho-Ah

VIETNAMESE

Please may I use a telephone?
Tôi dùng điện thoại được không?
Toy Zoong Dee-En Thoa-Ee Dook Kong

I have had my traveller's cheques / credit cards / handbag / rucksack / (knapsack) / luggage / wallet / passport / mobile phone stolen
Tôi bị mất cắp - séc du lịch / thẻ tín dụng / túi xách tay / balô / hành lý / ví / hộ chiếu / mobile
Toy Bee Mut Cup – Cheque Zoo Leek / Theh Teen Zoong / Tu-Ee Sach Tay / Bah Loh / Hanh Lee / Vee / Hoh Chee-Ew / Mobile

May I please have a copy of the report for my insurance claim?
Cho tôi xin một bản copy của báo cáo này để đòi tiền bảo hiểm?
Choh Toy Sin Mote Bahn Copy Cu-Ah Bow Kow Nay Deh Doy Tee-En Bow Hee-Em

Can you help me? I have lost my daughter / my son / my companion(s)
Bạn giúp tôi được không? Tôi bị lạc mất - con gái tôi / con trai tôi / bạn tôi
Bahn Zoop Toy Dook Kong? Toy Bee Lak Mut – Kohn Gy Toy / Kohn Chy Toy / Bahn Toy

Please go away / leave me alone
Xin đi đi / để tôi yên
Sin Dee Dee / Deh Toy Yuan

I'm sorry
Tôi xin lỗi
Toy Sin Loy

I want to contact the British / American / Canadian / Irish / Australian / New Zealand / South African consulate
Tôi muốn liên lạc với lãnh sự quán Anh / Mỹ / Canada / Ireland / Úc / New Zealand / Nam Phi
Toy Moo-En Lee-En Lak Vo-Ee Lanh Shuh Kwan An / Mee / Cah-Nah-Dah / Ireland / Ook / New Zealand / Nahm Fee

I'm / we're / he is / she is ill / lost / injured
Tôi bị / chúng tôi bị / anh ấy bị / cô ấy bị - ốm / lạc / thương
Toy Bee / Choong Toy Bee / An Ay Bee / Koh Ay Bee – Ohm / Lak / Thoo-Ong

They are ill / lost / injured
Họ bị ốm / lạc / thương
Hoh Bee Ohm / Lak / Thoo-Ong

If you found this phrasebook useful, or even if you didn't, please help us to improve future editions by taking part in our reader survey. Every returned form will be acknowledged, and to show our appreciation we'll also give you £1 off your next purchase of any Thomas Cook guidebook. Please take a few minutes to complete and return this form to:

The Editor, South-East Asian Phrasebook, Thomas Cook Publishing, PO Box 227, Unit 18, Coningsby Road, Peterborough PE3 8SB, UK.

When and where did you buy this book? (Please give town / country and if possible name of retailer).

When was / is your trip and which countries did you / will you visit?

Did you / do you intend to buy any other guidebooks for your trip? Please specify:

What tempted you to buy this book? Please tick as many as appropriate:

❑ Price   ❑ Cover   ❑ Content   ❑ Size

Other (Please specify)

What do you think of:

The cover design?

The design and layout styles within the book?

The content?

READER SURVEY

Please rate the following features of the South-East Asian Phrasebook
for their value to you:
(Circle the 1 for "little or no use", 2 for "useful", 3 for "very useful").

Language introduction sections	1	2	3
Alphabet and pronunciation guides	1	2	3
Phonetic spellings	1	2	3
Side indexing	1	2	3
Menu sections	1	2	3

Please use this space to indicate any additional phrases you would find
useful.

Please use this space to tell us about any features that in your opinion
could be changed, improved, or added in future editions of the book, or
any other comments you would like to make about the book.

Your age category: ☐ Under 21 ☐ 21-30 ☐ 31-40 ☐ 41-50 ☐ 51 +

Mr/Mrs/Miss/Ms/Other

First name or initials:

Surname:

Your full address (please include postal or zip code):

Your daytime telephone number:

E-mail address: